INTERPRETATION

AN APPROACH
TO THE STUDY
OF LITERATURE

INTERPRETATION

Joanna H. Maclay, University of Illinois, Urbana

Thomas O. Sloan, University of California, Berkeley

Consulting Editor: **Russel Windes,** Queens College

AN APPROACH TO THE STUDY OF LITERATURE

Random House   New York

ACKNOWLEDGMENTS

James Dickey. "A Birth" copyright © 1960 by James Dickey. Reprinted from *Poems 1957–1967,* by James Dickey, by permission of Wesleyan University Press. "A Birth" was first published in *The New Yorker.*

E. M. Forster. "Alexandria: A History and a Guide" from *Alexandria* by E. M. Forster. Copyright © 1961 by Edward Morgan Forster. Reprinted by permission of Doubleday & Company, Inc.

Lawrence Durrell. Letter to Henry Miller from the book *Lawrence Durrell and Henry Miller: A Private Correspondence* by Lawrence Durrell. Edited by George Wickes. Copyright, ©, 1962, 1963 by Lawrence Durrell and Henry Miller. Published by E. P. Dutton & Co., Inc. and reprinted with their permission.

Lawrence Durrell. Excerpt from the book *Justine* by Lawrence Durrell. Copyright, ©, 1957 by Lawrence Durrell. Published by E. P. Dutton & Co., Inc. and reprinted with their permission.

Emily Dickinson. Letter to Austin reprinted by permission of the publishers from *The Letters of Emily Dickinson,* edited by Thomas H. Johnson. The Belknap Press of Harvard University Press. Permission granted for the United States.

Edith Sitwell. "The War in Ireland" from *The Queens and the Hive* by Edith Sitwell, by permission of Atlantic–Little, Brown and Co. Copyright © 1962 by Dame Edith Sitwell.

T. H. White. Excerpt reprinted by permission of G. P. Putnam's Sons from *The Bestiary: A Book of Beasts* by T. H. White. Capricorn edition 1960.

John Dos Passos. "Art and Isadora" from *The Big Money/USA* reprinted by permission of the author's agent, Brandt & Brandt. Copyright © 1933, 1934, 1935, 1936 by John Dos Passos.

D. H. Lawrence. Letter to Willard Johnson from *The Letters of D. H. Lawrence* edited by Aldous Huxley. Copyright 1932 by The Estate of D. H. Lawrence, copyright © renewed 1960 by Angelo Ravagli & C. Montague Weekley, Executors of The Estate of Frieda Lawrence Ravagli. Reprinted by permission of The Viking Press, Inc.

George Bernard Shaw and Mrs. Patrick Campbell. Letters reprinted from *Bernard Shaw and Mrs. Patrick Campbell: Their Correspondence,* edited by Alan Dent, by permission of Bartlett & Gluckstein.

Martin Luther King, Jr. "I Have a Dream" reprinted by permission of Joan Daves. Copyright © 1963 by Martin Luther King, Jr.

Mark Twain. "The Story of a Speech" from *Mark Twain's Speeches* by Mark Twain, edited by Albert Bigelow Paine. Copyright, 1923, 1951 by Mark Twain Company. Reprinted by permission of Harper & Row, Publishers, Inc.

Malcolm X. Excerpt from *Mecca* from *The Autobiography of Malcolm X* reprinted

John Frederick Nims. "The Young Ionia" from *Knowledge of the Evening,* pp. 12–13. Rutgers University Press. Copyright © 1960 by Rutgers, The State University.

Leonard Nathan. "Niagara" from *Chicago Tribune,* by permission of the author.

Anthony Hecht. "The Dover Bitch" from *The Hard Hours* by Anthony Hecht. Copyright © 1960 by Anthony Hecht. Reprinted by permission of Atheneum Publishers. Appeared originally in *Transatlantic Review.*

Anne Sexton. "The Farmer's Wife" from *To Bedlam and Part Way Back.* Copyright © 1960 by Anne Sexton. Reprinted by permission of the publisher, Houghton-Mifflin Company.

Philip Larkin. "Wedding-Wind" reprinted from *The Less Deceived,* © copyright The Marvell Press 1955, 1970, by permission of The Marvell Press, Hessle, Yorkshire, England.

Ezra Pound. "The River-Merchant's Wife: A Letter" from Ezra Pound, *Personae.* Copyright 1926 by Ezra Pound. Reprinted by permission of New Directions Publishing Corporation.

James Dickey. "The Bee" copyright © 1966 by James Dickey. Reprinted from *Poems 1957–1967,* by James Dickey, by permission of Wesleyan University Press.

Richard Wilbur. "My Father Paints the Summer" from *The Beautiful Changes and Other Poems,* copyright, 1947, by Richard Wilbur. Reprinted by permission of Harcourt Brace Jovanovich, Inc.

LeRoi Jones. "Preface to a Twenty Volume Suicide Note" from *Preface to a Twenty Volume Suicide Note* copyright © 1961 by LeRoi Jones. Published by Corinth Books.

T. S. Eliot. "Preludes" from *Collected Poems 1909–1962* by T. S. Eliot, copyright, 1936, by Harcourt Brace Jovanovich, Inc.; copyright, © 1963, 1964, by T. S. Eliot. Reprinted by permission of the publisher.

Richard Wilbur. "Digging for China" from *Things of This World,* © 1956, by Richard Wilbur. Reprinted by permission of Harcourt Brace Jovanovich, Inc.

e. e. cummings. "Chanson Innocente" copyright, 1923, 1951, by E. E. Cummings. Reprinted from his volume *Poems 1923–1954* by permission of Harcourt Brace Jovanovich, Inc.

Dylan Thomas. "In My Craft or Sullen Art" from Dylan Thomas, *Collected Poems.* Copyright 1939, 1946 by New Directions Publishing Corporation. Reprinted by permission of New Directions Publishing Corporation.

Rabindranath Tagore. "Here I send you my poems" from *Poems,* reprinted by permission of Visva-Bharati, Santiniketan, India.

Robinson Jeffers. "The Purse-Seine" copyright 1937 and renewed 1956 by Donnan Jeffers and Garth Jeffers. Reprinted from *Selected Poems of Robinson Jeffers* by permission of Random House, Inc.

Thom Gunn. "Innocence" from *My Sad Captains* (Chicago: University of Chicago Press, 1961). Copyright 1961 by Thom Gunn. Reprinted by permission of the author and the publisher.

Robert Frost. "Mending Wall" from *The Poetry of Robert Frost* edited by Edward Connery Latham. Copyright 1930, 1939, © 1969 by Holt, Rinehart and Winston, Inc. Copyright © 1958 by Robert Frost. Copyright © 1967 by Lesley Frost Ballar tine. Reprinted by permission of Holt, Rinehart and Winston, Inc.

William Stafford. "Fifteen" from *The Rescued Year* by William Stafford. Copyright © 1964 by William E. Stafford. Reprinted by permission of Harper & Row, Publishers, Inc.

W. H. Auden. "Law Like Love" copyright 1940 and renewed 1968 by W. H. Auden. Reprinted from *Collected Shorter Poems 1927–1957,* by W. H. Auden, by permission of Random House, Inc.

John Logan. "The Preparation" from *Saturday Review,* May 5, 1956, p. 24. Copyright 1956 The Saturday Review Associates, Inc. Reprinted by permission of the author and the publisher.

Gwendolyn Brooks. "Bronzeville Woman in a Red Hat" from *Selected Poems* by Gwendolyn Brooks. Copyright © 1960 by Gwendolyn Brooks. Reprinted by permission of Harper & Row, Publishers, Inc.

Howard Nemerov. "Santa Claus" from *The Next Room of the Dream,* copyright by Howard Nemerov, 1962. Reprinted by permission of Margot Johnson Agency.

LeRoi Jones. "The Turncoat" from *Preface to a Twenty Volume Suicide Note* copyright © 1961 by LeRoi Jones. Reprinted by permission of The Sterling Lord Agency.

Richard Wilbur. "Love Calls Us to the Things of This World" from *Things of This World,* © 1956, by Richard Wilbur. Reprinted by permission of Harcourt Brace Jovanovich, Inc.

Lawrence Durrell. "Alexandria" from the book *Collected Poems* by Lawrence Durrell. Copyright © 1956, 1960 by Lawrence Durrell. Published by E. P. Dutton & Co., Inc. and reprinted with their permission.

Robert Beloof. "Visiting Home in Wichita" reprinted by permission of the author.

Allen Ginsberg. "Song" from *Howl and Other Poems* copyright © 1956, 1959 by Allen Ginsberg. Reprinted by permission of City Lights Books.

James Dickey. "The Leap" copyright © 1964 by James Dickey. Reprinted from *Poems 1957–1967,* by James Dickey, by permission of Wesleyan University Press.

Wilfred Owen. "Arms and the Boy" from Wilfred Owen, *Collected Poems.* Copyright Chatto & Windus, Ltd. 1946, © 1963. Reprinted by permission of New Directions Publishing Corporation.

Thom Gunn. "Rites of Passage" reprinted by permission of Faber and Faber Ltd. from *Moly.*

Gregory Corso. "Marriage" from Gregory Corso, *The Happy Birthday of Death.* Copyright © 1960 by New Directions Publishing Corporation. Reprinted by permission of New Directions Publishing Corporation.

Philip Larkin. "Church Going" reprinted from *The Less Deceived,* © copyright The Marvell Press 1955, 1970, by permission of The Marvell Press, Hessle, Yorkshire, England.

Gwendolyn Brooks. "A Bronzeville Mother Loiters in Mississippi. Meanwhile, a Mississippi Mother Burns Bacon" from *Selected Poems* by Gwendolyn Brooks. Copyright © 1960 by Gwendolyn Brooks. Reprinted by permission of Harper & Row, Publishers, Inc.

Agyeya (S. Vatsyayan). "The Unmastered Lute" from *First Person, Second Person,* Occasional Paper Series (Center for South and South East Asia Studies, 1971), by permission of Leonard Nathan.

Sherwood Anderson. "I Want to Know Why" from *The Triumph of the Egg* reprinted by permission of Harold Ober Associates Incorporated. Copyright 1921 by B. W. Huebsch. Renewed 1948 by Eleanor C. Anderson.

Eudora Welty. "Why I Live at the P. O." copyright, 1941, 1969, by Eudora Welty. Reprinted from her volume *A Curtain of Green and Other Stories* by permission of Harcourt Brace Jovanovich, Inc.

William Carlos Williams. "The Use of Force" from William Carlos Williams, *The Farmers' Daughters.* Copyright 1938 by William Carlos Williams. Reprinted by permission of New Directions Publishing Corporation.

Ernest Hemingway. "The Killers" (Copyright 1927 Charles Scribner's Sons; renewal copyright © 1955) is reprinted by permission of Charles Scribner's Sons from *Men Without Women* by Ernest Hemingway.

A. E. Coppard. "The Third Prize" from *The Collected Tales of A. E. Coppard* published by Jonathan Cape Ltd. Reprinted by permission of David Higham Associates.

Irwin Shaw. "The Girls in Their Summer Dresses" copyright 1939 and renewed 1967 by Irwin Shaw. Reprinted from *Selected Stories of Irwin Shaw* by permission of Random House, Inc.

D. H. Lawrence. "The Horse Dealer's Daughter" from *The Complete Short Stories of D. H. Lawrence,* Volume II. Copyright 1922 by Thomas B. Seltzer, Inc., renewed 1950 by Frieda Lawrence. Reprinted by permission of The Viking Press, Inc.

Flannery O'Connor. "Everything That Rises Must Converge" reprinted with the permission of Farrar, Straus, and Giroux, Inc. from *Everything That Rises Must Converge* by Flannery O'Connor, copyright © 1961, 1965 by The Estate of Mary Flannery O'Connor.

Jean Stafford. "A Country Love Story" reprinted with the permission of Farrar, Straus, and Giroux, Inc. from *The Collected Stories* by Jean Stafford. Copyright © 1950, 1969 by Jean Stafford.

Katherine Anne Porter. "Flowering Judas" copyright, 1930, 1958, by Katherine Anne Porter. Reprinted from her volume, *Flowering Judas and Other Stories* by permission of Harcourt Brace Jovanovich, Inc.

John Barth. "Night-Sea Journey" copyright © 1966 by John Barth (first published in *Esquire* magazine) from *Lost in the Funhouse* by John Barth. Reprinted by permission of Doubleday & Company, Inc.

James Purdy. "Eventide" from James Purdy, *Color of Darkness.* Copyright © 1957 by James Purdy. Reprinted by permission of New Directions Publishing Corporation.

William Faulkner. "A Rose for Emily" copyright 1930 and renewed 1958 by William Faulkner. Reprinted from *Selected Short Stories of William Faulkner* by permission of Random House, Inc.

Archibald Marshall. "The Ancient Roman" from *Simple Stories,* by Archibald Marshall. Copyright © 1968 by Elizabeth Lawrence Potts. Reprinted by permission of Pantheon Books, a Division of Random House, Inc.

Langston Hughes. "Rock, Church" from *Something in Common and Other Stories* by Langston Hughes. Copyright © 1963 by Langston Hughes. Reprinted by permission of Hill and Wang, Inc.

PREFACE

This book is based on the premise that interpretation is a viable and valuable means of studying literature—that by speaking a literary work, by assuming the roles of literary speakers, by doing what the work itself does, we can come close to a full realization and understanding of that work. To interpret a literary work means to speak it, to oneself or to others.

For two centuries interpretation has been considered a special kind of performing art with certain prescriptive rules of decorum, regardless of the nature of the literature being performed. However, in recent times a second view has become prominent. Encouraged by such books as Wallace A. Bacon and Robert S. Breen's *Literature as Experience* (New York: McGraw-Hill, 1959) and Don Geiger's *The Sound, Sense, and Performance of Literature* (Chicago: Scott, Foresman, 1963), some teachers have come to believe that the great pedagogical value of interpretation lies in its usefulness as a means for exploring literature. The older view of interpretation as a performing art has become complemented—and, in some cases, replaced—by the view of interpretation as an instrument of understanding in literary study.

This book is based on the newer view and is designed for use in either basic or advanced interpretation classes. It is organized by literary genres: nonfictional prose, poetry, and prose fiction. Chapters 2, 3, and 4 begin with essays that briefly outline some of the basic characteristics and structural principles of the literary genre under consideration. These essays are followed by literary selections and accompanying study questions. Concluding each chapter are some suggestions for materials to assist further study of problems raised in these discussions. Because the introductory essays are purposefully brief, the exercises and bibliography at the end of each chapter may particularly aid the student who wishes to pursue the theoretical foundations of our approach to literature. These sections may even provide the basis for class discussions or short papers. They should at least indicate the kinds of concerns that are integral to the advanced undergraduate and graduate levels in interpretation.

We consider the most important part of this book to be the anthologized literary selections and their accompanying study questions. These series of study questions are intended to help the student and teacher in their mutual study of the literary works. The questions are by no means exhaustive but serve rather as starting points for exploration. The notion of *exploration* is central to our purpose, for the questions are not intended to lead to any predetermined answers, but to open a few doors onto corridors of investigation. We hope—indeed, expect—that students and teachers alike will have many more questions about the individual selections than we have provided.

Conspicuous by its absence in this book is any discussion of drama. We believe that one must study drama in terms of entire plays, that one cannot really study drama by simply studying isolated scenes. Spatial limitations of this book have made the inclusion of complete plays prohibitive. We believe, too, that although much can be learned from one person's enactment or interpretation of a play, drama must finally meet the test of the stage. We would suggest that the teacher who wishes to include the study of drama in his introductory course in interpretation use a supplemental drama anthology. Students interested in pursuing the study of drama through interpretation can perhaps utilize, in connection with the drama anthology, Joanna Maclay's *Readers Theatre: Toward a Grammar of Practice* (New York: Random House, 1971), which explores methods of staging literature in such a way as to "feature the text," one of the basic principles of our book.

Finally we wish to express our appreciation to all those whose help we sought and received in preparing this text. We are particularly grateful to those of our students who helped create this book—through their criticism, their suggestions for selections and study questions, and their moral support. A special thanks is offered to Miss Fran Guthrie for her countless hours of deciphering and typing an often unreadable manuscript.

November 1971   J . H . M .
                                                                 T . O . S .

CONTENTS

INTERPRETATION
AN APPROACH
TO THE STUDY
OF LITERATURE

INTERPRETING LITERATURE: SOME PRELIMINARY REMARKS

Imagine a time when there was no such thing as written language—when everyone was "illiterate," that is, unlettered, because letters had not yet been invented. No one had yet thought that sound could be represented by a mark made in clay or on a stone. No one had yet thought that if a man's speech could be divided into sounds and if each sound could be captured in visual symbols and left behind as a record, then another man upon seeing those symbols hours or even years later could reproduce the first man's speech. Writing and reading did not exist.

Even in that illiterate age, man had something like what we call literature today. This idea is put in such a tentative, roundabout way because when you think about it, the word "literature" refers to something written down, for it comes from the Latin word *literae,* meaning "letters." Sometimes this "illiterate" literature is referred to in scholarly writing as "oral" literature. Sometimes it is referred to as song, or tales, or poetry. Today we keep songs, tales, and poems neatly differentiated—as we do such other verbal arts as fiction, nonfiction, drama, logic, and prayer. But in the days before man learned to differentiate sounds by means of visual representation, he probably had few means of clearly differentiating other processes in his life, such as singing, arguing, or celebrating.

Modern scholars studying poetry in remote illiterate areas of the world have pictured for us what ancient methods of poetic composition may have been like. The poet appeared in person before his audience. Either he accompanied himself in some musical or rhythmical way, or he had an assistant who accompanied him. The poet had in the storehouse of his memory a vast collection of themes, images, plots, characters, and formulas for performance. As he created a new poem or recited one he had heard earlier, he worked these stock ideas into his presentation, using them to refresh his audience's memory or to get their attention or to give him something to say while he invented subsequent lines. Thus, he probably never "literally" recited an earlier poem exactly as he had heard it. It was probably altered each time it was performed, because of the pressures of live performance, transmutations of memory, or the necessity to adapt to the peculiar characteristics of the audience.

In ancient days, poetry was something that was *heard* by someone— usually in public or at least in the presence of another who was either the poet or his interpreter—and the difference between the poet and his interpreter was slight. Poetry did not belong to anyone. It belonged to the moment in which it was being performed. It had a kind of vibrant presence. It was as existential as speech; that is, it existed in the way speech exists, inhabiting an instant in time, though maybe setting off some echoes reverberating into the future. It was something that *happened* and was then carried in the ears and mouths of individuals who might later cause it to happen again.

This kind of hearing, vibrant presence, existential process, or happening is still possible in literature. But we must work to achieve it, for now literature means, in an important way, letters, writing, books, and printed pages. Now we think of literature for the most part as something we read, usually silently and alone. Any literary speaking we do is usually *about* the literature that we have acquired from pages silently and alone. Such speaking about literature we usually call "criticism."

But there is another kind of literary speaking that comes as close as is possible in our age to reasserting and reaffirming the ancient oral values of literature: "interpretation," performing literature aloud for oneself and for others. In this way, literature becomes speech, or speech becomes literature; the interpreter and his audience are brought into the *presence* of literature through the spoken word.

Of course, one cannot get rid of the printed page, nor should one seek to. It is not merely an important medium of literature; it has itself produced certain effects on literature. Perhaps the most important of these is the heightening of "linearity," or seriality. When we read words on the page, we are at first primarily aware of their order, their sequential march through space toward completion of an idea. With some training—such as that offered through interpretation—we may also become aware of some of the oral values of these words. That is, we may become conscious of their tone, of the sound of the voice of the person who is speaking these words, or of their associations through sounds and emotions. Certainly, oral speech has linearity, too. But it has also a certain associativeness, circularity, an echoing quality, even at times an ungrammatical quality, which are devalued by written or printed language.

Our experience of literature may be considered a balancing of several kinds of tensions. Two of these tensions have already been mentioned. One is between the sequential ordering of words and the total structuring of those words into an artistic whole. Another tension, which is related to this, exists between our primitive sense of literature as speech—something which happens, whose presence envelops us—and our sense of literature as black marks on the page.

A third tension is that between the activities of interpretation and criticism. Interpreting literature and criticizing it are simply two different ways of experiencing literature. One distinction between the two is that criticism is *talking about* the literary work and that interpretation is *speaking* the literary work *itself*. However, there are other more important, even more fundamental, differences. Let us consider criticism first.

Usually when we criticize a literary work, we analyze it, divide it into parts and examine the relationship of these parts to each other. We might examine the individual stanzas in a poem or the episodes in a plot. Having looked at these parts and having seen how they relate to each other, we then try to discover a basic principle, or set of principles, that causes the entire work to cohere, that is, that causes an individual part to relate to each other part and to contribute to the total structure of the work. Or we may work in the opposite order. At any rate, we are usually seeking some organizing principle that holds the work together and gives it its coherence. Maybe the ordering principle one can discover is a speaker's distance from an object in space—as in Philip Larkin's poem "Church Going," where the order of what is said depends largely on the order in which the speaker discovers objects in space. Maybe the principle is time—as in Eudora Welty's "Petrified Man," where the order of what is said rests mainly on the order of events in time as encountered by Leota, the major speaker in the story within the story. In any case, the critic looks carefully for these principles, for what he seeks is a means of conceptualizing the entire work, to grasp its breadth and depth so that the work can become the subject of his own discourse. The goal of his work is to write an essay or deliver a speech on the literary work in which he tells others what he understands its principle of coherence to be and whether he thinks the work deserves serious attention by others.

The interpreter, on the other hand, performs all the tasks of the critic but the final one of preparing the essay or the speech, that is, the discourse in his own words. The critic analyzes the literary work only finally to depart from it, to speak in his own character from a point somewhere outside the literary work. The interpreter should acquire all the critic's insights but speak finally from a point *within* the work itself. Yet he must never lose a sense of the critical worth of the literary work, and that necessarily involves some detachment, some feeling of a perspective from the outside. Here, then, is the basic duality of the interpreter's role: He is the speaker in the work, from the inside, as in performing the role of Leota; but at the same time he is also a critical member of Eudora Welty's audience, outside the work, *showing* rather than *telling* other members of the audience how he feels about the work. He is an unusual critic, for he actually tests the attitudes and actions of the work by acting them out, matching words with physical responses. He is something more than a critic. For he not only has an intellectual understanding of the work, a conceptualization of its principles of structure, but he also has an understanding that is partly irrational, that is formed by the necessity, not of writing an articulate reasoned discourse about the work, but of acting out the attitudes and actions within the work, of "becoming" the work. Unlike the critic's, his performance is not the *record* of his previous experience with a particular work but a real *experiencing* of that very work. The interpreter is an experiencer of a literary work—a speaker of it, a doer of it—and each time he experiences the work, whether with only himself as audience or with others, he finds out something about it. This is the task of the interpreter. To call him an oral interpreter, the term most frequently used in this field of study, is redundant. A person might criticize literature silently—but how could he interpret it except orally? Furthermore, the tag "oral" is finally too restrictive, for it suggests that the speakers in literature are disembodied voices whose life force resides somewhere above the neck, divorced from the gestures, actions, and attitudes implicit in utterance and in life.

The interpreter seeks to experience the literary work not simply in the silent, reasoned terms required for writing critical discourse but also in the terms of "dramatic immediacy." This tension in his role, this duality, is also related to the first two tensions discussed earlier. For he gives this dramatic immediacy to the printed page, and the printed page is both a record of something that has been created before and an abstraction, a skeleton, from which the full body of the work may be created anew.

The creation of the poem in utterance, in full dramatic immediacy, should not be confused with what is often called "re-creation." Re-creation usually implies a kind of duplication. One may duplicate the printed page or simply repeat words. But to create anew the experience of which those words are a part is in large measure an existential process, that is, something that is "going on" right now in someone's body and mind. Creation, in short, is four-fifths of interpretation.

The fourth tension to be discussed in this introductory chapter is the most complicated. It can be understood on an abstract level, but it must finally be known in relation to individual selections. It is a tension inherent in the very nature of songs, poems, tales, and every form of literature. Viewed in one way, this could be called the tension between the two kinds of temporal and spatial perspectives involved in literary structure.

As noted earlier, linearity, or seriality, in literature is the effect produced by a sequential order of words, actions, objects, or events. Consider the following example:

John walked into the room, glanced briefly at the large jade Buddha that sat on the table in the center, noticed the massive walnut cases filled with ornately bound books, and passed rapidly through to the next room, bright with sunlight, where Marsha stood by the window smiling at him.

The principle of arrangement here is primarily spatial and secondarily temporal. At first the reader moves with John, seeing what he sees in the order in which he sees them.

But there is still another perspective, one that belongs to the speaker of the sentence, someone who is not John and who knows that the action has already occurred. The speaker knows what will happen to John *after* this action, why it is important that John noticed the jade figure and the books, and what is significant about the appearance of Marsha in a brightly lit room. The speaker is aware of the place of this sentence in the total story. He has a sense of the complete structure of the story and the shape of the entire process with all its characters, actions, and scenes. A tension arises from the juxtaposition of the space-time unit occupied by John and the space-time unit inhabited by the person who speaks *about* John.

One might also think of the difference between the two kinds of space and time in a literary work as the difference between two kinds of perspectives, or voices, or, better still, "persons." One person has a limited perspective. He experiences actions, objects, and events in the order in which they are presented in the work. He is John in our earlier example. The other person, the one who utters the sentence about John, is the one who actually presents those actions, objects, and events. Perhaps he is the narrator; perhaps he is the author. He at least knows how each action, object, and event relates to those that were presented earlier and those that will be presented later. One might think of him as the author's surrogate or deputy—a narrator, a storyteller, or a persona of the author.

John is a speaker for whom the experience has optimum immediacy. For him it is actually happening *now*. The second person, the one who has a different perspective, is a speaker for whom the experience is a relived moment whose significance and shape he well understands. Put the two together, and you have that dramatic immediacy that is the interpreter's major goal. The interpreter makes the action happen now, like an actor in a play, but he is also like the director of a play, or the playwright himself, for he knows fully what the purpose of the action is, its probable impact on the audience, and the relationship of any one single actor to the total drama. For the interpreter, literature has all the immediacy of experiencing drama. It is like an experience in real life, except that it is not randomly encountered, for it is an experience that he chooses to undergo, and it has been structured by an artist. Calling this experience a "virtual" one in no way lessens its impact, because oftentimes people's most meaningful experiences are those derived from literature, whether from the media of print, drama, or interpretation. One could say that the interpreter *realizes* literature by engaging his mind and his body, his voice and his senses in the virtual experience that literature offers. He makes literature dramatically immediate for himself and the other members of his audience—dramatic in the sense of the emphatic or vivid, but above all dramatic in the important twin perspective discussed in this context.

Finally, let us turn to another tension or duality which has been touched on without being named explicitly: The interpreter is not only a speaker but a member of his own audience. To think of communication in terms of speaker (stimulus) separate from audience (response) is to think of it in rather simplistic terms. This is to view the speaker as a source of information, ideas, attitudes that he amplifies and passes on to the audience. Of course, an audience does not usually respond passively. They applaud or grumble, they praise or heckle, they are rapt and silent, or they are inattentive. All these responses act on the speaker and in subtle ways influence his performance. The response becomes a stimulus. This simple view of speaker and audience is sometimes referred to as a "cycle of empathy." However, some contemporary theories of communication go beyond this. According to them, communication is a process of internal and external activities with a multiplicity of speaker-audience relationships. The speaker is viewed as a member of his own audience, and audience members are seen as speakers, too. When the speaker empathizes with his audience, or when the audience empathizes with the speaker, they switch roles in their imaginations. In short, the thread linking speaker and audience has become woven into a larger texture of activity.

The new theories of communication have also affected the traditional idea of the interpreter. He is a speaker of literature—in fact, as already discussed, he is usually *two* speakers of any one sentence—and he is his own audience, too. He is two kinds of audience: an audience of himself as interpreter and a critical member of the author's audience. It is hoped that the two will be the same. As the interpreter works on his selection, he should grow in his capacity as an audience. Keeping constantly in mind the concept of communication as an inter- and intra-active process, the interpreter should be aware that he is continually a part of the "other" who may be in his audience. When he performs in class or in public, he is engaged in a process wherein he joins his audience and shares with them the responsibilities of stimulus and response. Thinking about this idea may allay some of your nervousness about performing literature for others, if you are nervous at all, or if perhaps you are only nervous because that unfortunate term "tension" is used here.

Tension, however, is the best word to describe these effects—speakers in the work, dual perspectives, and interpretation as a communicative process. Insofar as "tension" implies life, activity, or effort, the word is particularly expressive, better than, say, "duality." One understands and creates only through life, activity, and effort—in short, through tension. The passive, completely homeostatic body at rest will neither create nor expend the energy to understand.

Perhaps the following poem will help summarize some of the ideas in this opening chapter.

A Birth/James Dickey

Inventing a story with grass,
I find a young horse deep inside it.
I cannot nail wires around him;
My fence posts fail to be solid,

And he is free, strangely, without me.
With his head still browsing the greenness,
He walks slowly out of the pasture
To enter the sun of his story.

My mind freed of its own creature,
I find myself deep in my life
In a room with my child and my mother,
When I feel the sun climbing my shoulder

Change, to include a new horse.

The first speaker, the speaker of the line, is a storyteller or poet. He tells of an experience with which all creators are probably familiar: The created object itself comes to life; and, though invested with certain principles of life by its creator, once it begins to move, it moves independently of him. The first speaker recounts the experience in the sequence in which the events occurred. While inventing a story that had grass in it, he began, probably, describing the grass only to have the image of a horse appear within his imagination. So discovered, the horse assumed a life of its own and determined the nature of the creation. The grass became "the pasture." The horse browses, then slowly walks toward the center of time in his own story. Perhaps his story is not the "story with grass" that the first speaker is inventing. Perhaps the horse's story is relevant to this first story only for the brief instant that he appears in the grass, turning it into a pasture. Nonetheless, in that brief moment when he appears within the first speaker's invented time, he is vividly realized. In fact, he is so vividly realized that the speaker finds his own "real" time strangely altered. When the speaker is back among his family, in a reality he did not invent (at least, in exactly the same manner), he finds his perceptions changed. The sun of *his* story now shines upon an invented horse, which has become a part of the speaker's total world. He has "given birth" to this creature, as surely as his mother gave birth to him and as surely as he "invented" his own child.

The first speaker moves from invented time to "actual" time, only to find the two merge. He moves from one kind of space within which he creates objects and events into his own life within which he is both creator and creation, only to see the two kinds of space, or two orders of reality, become one.

There is, however, a second speaker for whom the poem is a somewhat different experience. He is aware of the final lines as he utters the first. He is not the person to whom the experience is happening but to whom it has *already* happened. He knows the order of the statements has been carefully arranged in sentences and stanzas so that the final stanza bears a tremendous weight of emphasis. One can go even further and say that he is the one who "speaks" the title and supplies the name of the author.

Note that Dickey's poem depicts creation as if it were a *process* within which the creator is part of the creation. The author created a horse, and this action has strangely altered his life, regardless of how insignificant the creation may have appeared at the time. The poem presents creation as a fusion of two realities. The interpreter performing the poem participates in both kinds of reality. He adopts the function of both speakers within the work. He performs within a total process of action and interaction in which he becomes a member of his own audience and, like the speaker in the poem, a part of his own creation.

A great deal more could be said about this poem. But to say any more might contradict the purpose of interpretation. We find out about a poem by performing it. Never try—at least while you are working with this book—to apprehend a piece of literature by reading it silently. Read it aloud. Put your body to the work of literary understanding. Communicate the poem to yourself through performance—then try it out for others. Be highly suspicious of critical essays, like the few paragraphs offered on the Dickey poem, until you have had a chance to test their insights through performing the work. A healthy contempt for literary criticism is an invaluable aid to the student of literature and an absolutely necessary requirement for interpretation. You should strive to explore literature by means of oral performance; all the study questions following the literary selections in this book are geared to exploration, as indicated in the Preface. They are not to shove you toward answers that literary critics have discovered. More than that, you should try to *interpret* a literary work before you write a critical essay about it. Do the important task first; it should make the secondary one meaningful.

2

INTERPRETING NONFICTIONAL PROSE

poses of either demonstration and expression or persuasion. The speaker may demonstrate an action—that is, he may re-create actions that have occurred in the past or help the audience see events that are occurring now but that only he can see. Or he may do both. If so, the speaker assumes the role of an "actor." An actor, of course, always performs within a scene or an environment that causes and conditions an audience to respond in a certain way. He may control an audience's perception of, or sympathies toward, something or someone; or he may even direct an audience's reaction. If so, the speaker assumes the function of a "rhetor." Again, all these kinds of actions may occur within the course of a single speech. To analyze the actions of a speaker as actor, dramatic analysis is used. His actions as rhetor are analyzed by way of rhetorical analysis.

Before one explores these two types of analysis, one further duality must be discussed. One has to consider that the speaker *in* a literary work may not necessarily be the speaker *of* the work. The author is always the speaker *of* the work. One of his created characters is usually the speaker *in* the work. This is a distinction that is seldom made when speaking informally of a literary work. You might say something like the following: "Emily Dickinson calls despair an 'imperial affliction' that God sends us in the symbol of a wavering, fading slant of light on winter afternoons." In making such a statement you may think you have said something about Dickinson's poem "A Certain Slant of Light." Yet, you have also said something about the speaker: You have indicated her sex, told her name, and allowed the audience to interpret your statement in terms of their conventional images of a poet named Emily Dickinson. On the other hand, if you were to say, as a lecturer did recently, "Shakespeare calls discretion the better part of valor," your mistake would be far more serious. Shakespeare, after all, gives this epigram to his character Falstaff, one whose opinions are necessarily qualified by arrogance, cowardice, wit, and flatulence.

Even though in nonfictional prose and in lyric poetry, the distinctions between speakers of and speakers in the work may not be major, it usually is wise to assume that some distinction exists. (For that matter, it is generally safe to assume that some distinction exists between the author as a person and the author as a writer, a public figure.) To help maintain these distinctions clearly, the terms "persona" and "narrator" shall be used to name the major speakers *in* the work. In Chapter 4, for example, the narrator is a persona who speaks as the storyteller. The speaker *of* the work shall be denoted by the term "implied author"—not only to maintain the distinction between a man as a person and that same man as an author, but also to indicate that the speaker that is of particular importance is the one *implied by the work* under consideration. As shall be seen continually, all of these considerations are complicated by another duality in speakers *of* the work: The implied author is one, and the interpreter is another.

Of course, these distinctions in speaking levels bring about a distinction in audiences. The audience may be *in* the work. When the persona is engaged in meditation, he is, obviously, speaking to an audience in the work. When he is engaged in communication, he may be speaking to another person or to a group of people who exist only within the work itself. This audience shall be called a "fictive audience." But a speaker—either the persona or the implied author—may also be speaking to a real audience, a group of readers, say, who may exist outside the structure of the work. "Ah, gentle reader" is a form of address that begins the remarks of countless narrators in the fiction of the eighteenth and nineteenth centuries—narrators who, regardless of how fictive *they* were, nonetheless consciously addressed a living group of people. Just as every work has a real author, so every work has a real audience. It may or may not be the audience the *persona* is addressing. It *is* the audience that the *implied author* is addressing. Furthermore, this is the audience the interpreter usually seeks to create. This audience shall, therefore, be termed an "implied audience."

To summarize, the speakers in nonfictional prose (or, for that matter, in all literature) may be involved in actions of meditation or communication. The actions may serve the purposes of the actor or of the rhetor. The persona is the speaker *in* the work, and his audience may be either a fictive audience or the implied audience *of* the work. The implied author is one speaker *of* the work, and his audience is always the implied audience.

The interpreter is a second speaker *of* the work. He usually strives to make his audience one with the implied author's implied audience. By centering on the major speaker *in* the literary work the analysis proceeds toward the level on which the implied author is communicating to his implied audience and toward the level beyond that, on which the interpreter is performing the literary work for his own audience. You use the dramatic analysis to analyze the persona in his speaking situation, performing the actions of an actor. You employ the rhetorical analysis to examine the actions of the persona as rhetor. You also use the rhetorical analysis to study closely the communication of the implied author with his implied audience, assuming that he attempts to persuade his audience to perceive an experience in a certain way. The interpreter's work embraces all of these actions. He may be acting or persuading or both. Thus, the dramatic and the rhetorical analyses should provide him with patterns for his own speech behavior.

The three speaking levels in a work may be diagramed as follows:

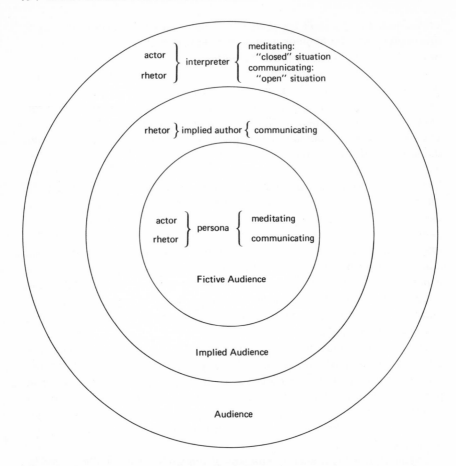

It is important to note that the circles are concentric, with the persona as the center. But it is also necessary to keep in mind something the diagram does not show: The circles *may* be coterminal, with no distinctions in behavior between the persona, the implied author, and the interpreter, or with no distinctions in their audiences. It is important to observe, too, that the large circle does not really contain the two smaller ones. It merely marks a *context* for the perception of the *text* as marked by the two inner circles, and, as suggested earlier, the text of a literary communication potentially transcends its context.

Utilizing the dramatic and the rhetorical analyses allows you to take a closer look at the speech behavior on the three levels.

Through the dramatic analysis, whereby you analyze a work dramatically, you are considering its similarities with plays, literary works designed for presentation on stage. You particularly examine the basic dramatic situation: a character in a clearly defined role moving and speaking within a clearly defined scene.

Nonfictional prose includes such literary types as letters, histories, journals, essays, speeches, travel reports, and biographies. As you begin to explore these types, it would be wise first to forget any preconceived notions you may have concerning what constitutes nonfiction and prose. Trying to find a tangible difference between fiction and nonfiction or between prose and poetry can become as frustrating as trying to put your finger on a bead of mercury. Although these categories are convenient groupings, often the similarities between them are more important than their differences.

You will discover that one of the major characteristics of the selections grouped under the category "nonfictional prose" is their relative simplicity of structure. Most nonfictional prose selections seem to present the responses of *one* speaker. (Thus, as you will discover in the next chapter, the closest ally to nonfictional prose is lyric poetry.) In the first chapter your attention was called to certain dualities that exist in literary structure, such as linearity and circularity or dramatic immediacy and perspective. It was also noted that the primary emphasis in analysis will be on those aspects of the literary experience that are conveyed through the speaker's behavior, because this view is, obviously, most closely akin to the interpreter's work. To begin your analysis you center on the actions of the major speaker of the literary work—the person whose presence unifies the entire structure. In nonfictional prose the task is made somewhat simpler than in fiction or drama because usually only one speaker is present. In analyzing nonfictional prose you look for the ways in which the behavior of that speaker conflicts with or reflects the viewpoint of the author and how that speaker's behavior can serve as a pattern for the interpreter's reaction.

There are certain general principles that concern the behavior of literary speakers. The first set of principles applies to the speaker's relationship to the audience. The audience may either be inside the speaker (in which case the action shall be called "meditation") or it may be outside him (in which case the action shall be called "communication"). Certainly, the actions of meditation and communication overlap; in fact, meditation is ordinarily considered a form of communication, it being oftentimes defined as communication with oneself. In this book the two terms shall, however, be considered as implying two different kinds of relationships between the speaker and the audience. Meditation usually takes the form of soliloquy; communication takes such forms as monologue, dialogue, and oratory. It is important to keep in mind, moreover, that the actions of meditation and communication form another duality, which may occur within the action of any one speaker. He may be speaking *both* to himself *and* to others in the course of a single speech.

There is a second duality in the speaker's actions. In addition to relating to the audience in a certain way, his behavior may serve the pur-

You begin the dramatic analysis by asking these questions as you read along:

1 Who is the speaker?
2 To whom is he speaking?
3 Where is the speaker?
4 When is he speaking?
5 How is he speaking?
6 Why is he speaking?
7 What is he saying?

Obviously, the character in a role does more than merely "speak." He has "nonverbal" as well as "verbal" behavior. But you always begin your analysis by concentrating on the verbal one first.

In some ways the dramatic analysis is like a house of cards: All of the questions lean on and support the others. In attempting to analyze the personality of the character who is speaking (Who?), you need to consider all of the other questions as well. In Hawthorne's essay, which follows, the persona's words are motivated in part (Why?) by his desire for a companion whose presence could dispel the horrible visions that come to him during a sleepless night. That desire indicates both his loneliness and his character. The persona seems to be telling about his nightmare soon after it occurred, perhaps during the following day. But this is not the only answer to the When? question, for as the character is telling of his nightmare, he is also imaginatively reexperiencing it. The action is both present and past, producing a compression of time, which is always possible for the imagination. The persona is apparently speaking to himself (To whom?). However, in exploring the structure of the essay, you will note times at which he seems to visualize an audience external to himself. Obviously, the character's fears are recalled as he reexperiences the vision (How?), an emotional fact that qualifies the urgency of his desire for a companion. Thus, the What? question properly comes last in your consideration. The character's words in the work can be taken at a simple verbal level only at the risk of missing much of the richness. To utter a desire for a companion is surely as universal and ancient as human experience itself. But in the Hawthorne example that desire is expressed by an anxious, tormented, lonely man, whose simple verbal utterance is compounded by the character of the man himself.

The dramatic analysis helps us primarily to understand two literary qualities. The first, which has already been touched on, is the way a character's words are defined by his or her personality. In working with this quality, the interpreter is faced with a task identical to that of an actor in a play. In trying to fit utterance and character together, he is like an actor "working up a part," giving probability to the character by making it seem as if this person could indeed express these thoughts. It is at this point that the interpreter becomes concerned with the non-verbal part of his character's behavior. He asks himself what facial expressions, gestures, movements are appropriate to a character who speaks in this manner. As he begins to work with this problem, his experience with the dramatic analysis should lead him to the exploration of the second quality: the physical, temporal, and emotional relationships between the character and his scene.

From what distance or angles of vision does the character perceive the scene? To answer this question, one must think again about the questions of where, when, and to whom. Is the character immediately within the scene, or is he remote from it? Is he removed from the scene by space or time? If the audience is external, how remote from the audience does he seem to be? As noted earlier, the character in the Hawthorne essay is involved in two scenes: the seemingly calm and isolated one within which he is meditating, and the turbulent scene of nightmarish visions which he is re-creating.

The first quality explored through the dramatic analysis, the meaningful relationships between character and utterance, shall be called "probability." The second quality, the physical, temporal, and emotional relationships between character and scene, shall be called "point of view." Again, these two terms are related. A strong, aggressive individual may be more likely to participate in the scene and serve not as an observer of, but as an agent in, the action he is talking about. A rather more passive individual, such as the one implied in Hawthorne's essay, is more likely to stand on the edge of the scene he is describing, reacting like a secretary taking dictation, or a recording angel, or a philosopher building a monument for contemplation.

These two literary qualities bring up problems that directly relate to the task of the third literary speaker, the interpreter. For the interpreter, such concepts as probability and point of view cannot be considered in isolation from the effects they are likely to produce on his own audience. The interpreter must not only establish the probability of the persona's behavior for himself but must also communicate that probability to his audience. Since point of view also pertains to angle of vision, the interpreter in his role as persona has to determine the angle from which he allows his audience to perceive the literary work. One can put this matter as a general question the interpreter may ask at the end of his dramatic analysis: Given the character of the persona and the necessity to establish probability between him and his actions, from what point of view will my audience perceive the work?

Another duality may be discussed at this point. There are two general angles of vision, or points of view, from which the interpreter's audience may perceive a work of literature: They may be only *overhearing* the persona as he speaks to himself or to some other audience within the work, or they may be *directly addressed* by the persona. The first effect is usually called a "closed" speaking situation, the second an "open" speaking situation. Although both of these effects pertain to possible relationships of the interpreter's audience to the literary work (if, for example, the persona is communicating with any willing listener, his speaking situation is apparently open), and although the interpreter can usually solve questions of openness and closure simply by applying the dramatic analysis to the persona, he should first consider complex distances that may exist between the persona and the implied author. He should concentrate next upon the rhetorical actions of the second speaker, the implied author, through applying the rhetorical analysis first to the persona and then to the implied author.

Actually, the rhetorical analysis involves the same questions as the dramatic analysis. Again, the interpreter is concerned with who the speaker is, to whom he is speaking, where, when, how, why, and what he is saying. The central difference between the two analyses lies in the Why? question. You will recall that when a speaker is performing as an actor, he is either demonstrating or expressing something. When he is performing as a rhetor, he is persuading someone of something. Thus, the real difference between the two analyses lies in the intentions that are assigned to the speaker in terms of the probable effects his actions are producing on the audience.

In the rhetorical analysis one always assumes that the speaker's intentions are to persuade an audience. Persuasion, of course, has many dimensions of meaning. It could simply mean to alter an attitude, to control someone's perception of something, or to direct someone's sympathies toward an action or a person. To summarize, there is a distinction between persuasion on the one hand and demonstration and expression on the other. The Why? question of the *dramatic* analysis assigns demonstrative and expressive intentions to the speaker. The word "assigns" is used here simply because intentions can seldom be known with certainty. The interpreter tries to find intentions by observing the speaker's behavior and by testing that behavior in terms of the dramatic or the rhetorical analysis. As indicated, in Hawthorne's essay, part of the answer to the Why? question in the dramatic analysis is that the persona's utterance is motivated, among other things, by his desire for a companion. To pursue the matter further, one should say that the intentions behind his words are almost solely to express himself. His words do not seem motivated by the desire to persuade another person, to change another person's attitude, or even to persuade himself. However, this possibility should be explored by the interpreter, as will be indicated in the study questions following that essay.

The rhetorical analysis may or may not be relevant to analyzing the actions of the speaker *in* the work. But it is always relevant to analyzing the actions of the speaker *of* the work. One always assumes that the implied author is engaged in persuading his implied audience and that the interpreter is at least partly involved in shaping the attitudes or perceptions of his own audience. Now, many philosophical arguments have been and can be raised against that position. There are those critics who insist that the literary artist is not trying to persuade anybody of anything and who argue that the rhetorical analysis of the implied author drags ethics, morality, and politics into the pure "a-ethical," amoral, and apolitical world of art. Then there are other critics who are content merely to roll on their backs and purr, "A poem should not [even] mean/ But be." But this critical position is bound to seem a little dusty to a student who perhaps could not care less about literary theory but is asked to interpret a literary work, to make it "part of his nervous system," and who later realizes the impact literature can have when interpreted before an audience. Every literary work carefully utilizes certain strategies that make its audience respond in a certain way. Because in interpretation you look at literature as the utterance of a speaker, you see these strategies as if they were the rhetorical actions of the implied author. By these strategies the implied author has shaped an experience and placed controls on the way in which you, as members of his audience, can perceive that experience and on the way in which you, as interpreters, can influence the responses of your own audiences. Rather than insisting that the implied author as rhetor is trying to persuade the reader of a certain thesis or argument (which would indeed arouse the ire of a whole host of critics), it shall at least be maintained that the implied author as rhetor is always attempting to persuade you to look in a certain way and take a special attitude toward the experience that his work structures. Thus, to return to the Hawthorne example, though the rhetorical analysis may not be relevant to the actions of the persona in the essay, it is relevant to the actions of Hawthorne as the implied author. And, it shall also be claimed that the rhetorical analysis is relevant to the actions of the interpreter as he seeks to impose "Hawthorne's" controls on the responses of his own audience.

As noted, in the dramatic analysis your explorations may help you to understand two literary qualities: probability and point of view. In the rhetorical analysis you are pointed toward two other qualities: "ethos" and "viewpoint." Just as probability and point of view are related, so are ethos and viewpoint. Ethos and viewpoint differ from the two dramatic qualities by virtue of audience considerations: When you analyze the implied author or consider that the persona, the speaker *in* the work, is using persuasion, you consider the impact of ethos and viewpoint upon his audience.

Ethos pertains to the impact of a speaker's character on an audience. It represents that oftentimes intangible feature of a speaker's character that causes an audience to like or dislike him and, in turn, to approve or disapprove of his arguments. Since ancient times rhetoricians have well understood that *logic* alone will not move an audience. A speaker may have the best argument possible before a particular audience only to have that audience reject the argument because it rejects the man himself. Like most rhetorical considerations ethos is highly relativistic. What one audience approves may be rejected by another. One need only consider most American political campaigns to test the truth of that statement.

Viewpoint pertains to a speaker's system of values: What does he approve of? What virtues does he praise? What actions does he condemn? In working with the dramatic analysis, the tight interrelationships of probability and point of view were noted. Similarly close interrelationships exist between ethos and viewpoint. If you were to consider the ethos and viewpoint of the implied author in Hawthorne's essay, you would need to state his approval of the quiet, simple, domestic life and his image of the ideal female companion as a serene, purer soul. Yet, at the same time, you would have to point out his realization that within man's haunted mind there exist always the possibilities for contraries and perversions of these ideals. These give us a sense of the implied author's system of values and, at the same time, a fuller realization of his character.

In the simplest terms the interpreter's work as a rhetor consists of shaping his audience's attitudes toward the ethos and viewpoint of the implied author. That might imply that he ought to speak always in an open situation, assuming the role of the implied author speaking to his audience. Yet, in the Hawthorne essay the persona speaks meditatively, and there appears to be no distance in attitudes or beliefs between the persona and the implied author. It is most likely, then, that in interpreting that work you will find you can best convey the ethos and viewpoint of the implied author by presenting it in a closed situation. But the possibilities for openness are always present in a rhetorical view of the actions of the implied author, that is, in a view of the literary work as communication.

After this lengthy and at times complicated introduction to the behavior of speakers in and of literature, it may seem ironical to return to the original statement concerning the relative simplicity of structure in nonfictional prose. Yet, that statement stands. At the beginning of this chapter it was said that the relative simplicity of structure in nonfictional prose arises from the apparent concentration on *one* speaker. But, as discussed, no student of literature can be concerned with only *one* speaker, for behind that speaker, or in that speaker, or above, or even in front of him, is the author. Every literary work—even selections as structurally simple as nonfictional prose—has both a *persona* and an *implied author*. Of course, the interpreter is not just "a student of literature," either. He will also function as another speaker of that work. Thus, so far as the interpreter is concerned, every literary work always has three speakers. They may speak in one voice. They may not.

Unless the interpreter understands the complexities of speech behavior possible in the structurally simple selections of nonfictional prose, he will be truly at sea in attempting to explore the structures of other literary types. Lyric poetry, which will be studied in the following chapter, usually adds only one more speaker or voice to those normally found in nonfictional prose: one who is less a "speaker" than a "singer." Fiction adds a multitude of speakers. So does drama. In fact, in the latter two types the number of speakers possible is infinite.

The following list will conclude this introduction and begin your explorations.

A speaker may be:

1 meditating or communicating;
2 acting (in which case probability and point of view are to be considered) or persuading (in which case ethos and viewpoint also are involved);
3 speaking *in* the work (like a persona to a fictive audience) or serving as speaker *of* the work (an implied author to an implied audience or an interpreter to *his* audience);
4 performing in an open situation or a closed situation (particularly so far as the interpreter and his audience are concerned).

Or:

5 he may be doing all of these things.

The list reiterates the central philosophy of this book: Interpretation as an approach to the study of literature requires that one conceive of literature as a complex of many kinds of speech behavior. In order to get you started, the first two chapters have presented several basic concepts—perhaps you got the feeling you were simply reading one definition after another. But defining these concepts is an important part of the task of the authors of this text, just as utilizing them is an important part of yours. From this point on some of the remaining definitions will be placed in footnotes, for some of the new terms that will be introduced are more specific and limited in scope and, therefore, somewhat ancillary to the more basic concepts. With these basic concepts in mind you should be ready to begin your first interpretive exploration of literature.

E. M. Forster/Alexandria: A History and a Guide

born 1879

The situation of Alexandria is most curious. To understand it we must go back many thousand years.

Ages ago, before there was civilisation in Egypt, or the delta of the Nile had been formed, the whole of the country as far south as Cairo lay under the sea. The shores of this sea were a limestone desert. The coastline was smooth as a rule, but at the north-west corner an extraordinary spur jutted out from the main mass. It was not more than a mile wide, but many miles long. Its base is not far from the modern Bahig. Alexandria is built half-way down it, and its tip is the headland of Aboukir. On each side of it there used to be deep salt water.

Centuries passed, and the Nile, issuing out of his crack above Cairo, kept carrying down the muds of Upper Egypt, and dropping them as soon as his current slackened. In the north-west corner they were arrested by this spur, and began to silt up against it. It was a shelter not only from the outer sea, but from the prevalent wind. Alluvial land appeared; the huge shallow lake of Mariout was formed; and the current of the Nile, unable to escape through the limestone barrier, rounded the headland of Aboukir, and entered the outer sea by what was known in historical times as the "Canopic" Mouth.

This explains one characteristic of Alexandrian scenery—the long narrow ridge edged on the north by the sea and on the south by a lake and flat fields. But it does not explain why Alexandria has a harbour.

To the north of the spur, and more or less parallel to it, runs a second limestone range. It is much shorter than the spur and much lower, being often below the surface of the sea in the form of reefs. It seems unimportant. But without it there would have been no harbour (and consequently no town), because it breaks the force of the waves. Starting at Agame it continues as a series of rocks across the entrance of the modern harbour. Then it re-emerges to form the hammer-headed promontory of Ras-el-Tin, disappears into a second series of rocks that close the entrance of the Eastern Harbour, and makes its final appearance at the promontory of Silsileh, after which it rejoins the big spur.

Such are the main features of the situation; a limestone ridge, with harbours on one side of it, and alluvial country on the other. It is a situation unique in Egypt, and the Alexandrians have never been truly Egyptian.

. . .

Lawrence Durrell/Letter to Henry Miller

born 1912

[Spring, 1944]

Yes, I got the letters. I'm in touch with the embassy, representing them, so they pass them on. Your news sounds marvellous. Of course anything is less than what the world owes you for opening up the world with your own bright eye. Seventeen books sounds an awful lot to me. Let me have any old duplicate proofs that come your way—I haven't read anything of yours since the marvellous Greek book. Here we are sweltering in an atmosphere that demands a toast—great passions, short lives. Everything is worn thin as an eggshell; it's the fifth year now and the nervous breakdown is coming into the open. Old women, ginger dons, nursing sisters begin to behave like bacchantes; they are moving in and out of nursing homes with a steady impetus. Meanwhile we are crippled here by an anemia and an apathy and a censorship which prevents the least trace of the human voice—of any calibre. We exist on a machine-made diet of gun bomb and tank—backed up by the slogan.

The atmosphere in this delta is crackling like a Leyden jar. You see, in normal times all the local inhabitants spend six months in Europe a year, so they are as stale and beaten thin as the poor white collar man. The poetry I exude these days is dark grey and streaky, like bad bacon. But the atmosphere of sex and death is staggering in its intensity. Meanwhile the big shots come and go, seeing nothing, feeling nothing, in a money daydream; there is still butter and whisky and café viennois. A kind of diseased fat spreads over the faces and buttocks of the local populations, who have skimmed the grease off the war effort in contracts and profiteering. No, I don't think you would like it here. First this steaming humid flatness—not a hill or mound anywhere—choked to bursting point with bones and crummy deposits of wiped out cultures. Then this smashed up broken down shabby Neapolitan town, with its Levantine mounds of houses peeling in the sun. A sea flat, dirty brown and waveless rubbing the port. Arabic, Coptic, Greek, Levant French; no music, no art, no real gaiety. A saturated middle European boredom laced with drink and Packards and beach-cabins. NO SUBJECT OF CONVERSATION EXCEPT MONEY. Even love is thought of in money terms. "You are getting on with her? She has ten thousand a year of her own." Six hundred greaseball millionaires sweating in their tarbushes and waiting for the next shot of root-hashish. And the shrieking personal unhappiness and loneliness showing in every face. No, if one could write a single line of anything that had a human smell to it here, one would be a genius. Add to all this a sort of maggot-dance of minor official place-hunting, a

Florentine atmosphere of throat-slitting and distrust, and you will have some idea of what anyone with a voice or tongue is up against. I am hoping the war will be over soon so I can quit; I'm glad of this little death for all the material it's put in my way about people and affairs in general. But I'm worn thin with arse-licking and having my grammar corrected by subeditors from the Bush Times in South America. Here in Alexandria, though, I have my own office and almost no interference; so I can run things in the way I like. . . .

.   .   .

I am in charge of a goodish-sized office of war-propaganda here, trying to usher in the new washboard world which our demented peoples are trying to "forge in blood and iron." It's tiring work. However, it's an office full of beautiful girls, and Alexandria is, after Hollywood, fuller of beautiful women than any place else. Incomparably more beautiful than Athens or Paris; the mixture Coptic, Jewish, Syrian, Egyptian, Moroccan, Spanish, gives you slant dark eyes, olive freckled skin, hawk lips and noses, and a temperament like a bomb. Sexual provender of quality, but the atmosphere is damp, hysterical, sandy, with the wind off the desert fanning everything to mania. Love, hashish and boys is the obvious solution to anyone stuck here for more than a few years. I am sharing a big flat with some nice people, and atop it I have a tower of my own from which the romantics can see Pompey's Pillar, Hadra Prison, and the wet reedy wastes of Lake Mareotis stretching away into the distance and blotting the sky.

This is the world of the desert fathers and the wandering Jews; the country is eaten away like the carious jawbone of a mummy. Alexandria is the only possible point in Egypt to live in because it has a harbour and opens on a flat turpentine sea line—a way of escape.

.   .   .

STUDY QUESTIONS

1. Although the subject matter of these two excerpts is similar, the attitudes of the two writers are not. Does Forster's persona seem more "clinical" in his attitude? More objective? Is this position qualified in any way? What do you make of his remark, "It is a situation unique in Egypt, and the Alexandrians have never been truly Egyptian"? Does Durrell's persona seem more "sensuous"? More subjective? Is this position qualified in any way? Do the terms "objective" and "subjective" really seem functional or valuable in getting at the comparative styles? How do the differing degrees of actual physical involvement in the environment of Alexandria tend to condition the attitudes? How does it condition your performance?

2. How would you describe the diction of Forster's writing? How do such phrases as "most curious" and "as it were," which are characteristic idioms of British diction, relate to your translating your *description* of his verbal diction into your own diction in *delivery?*

3. In attempting to perform these two excerpts, what can you find in your non-verbal behavior that would illustrate the manner or style of the two writers?

4. Although Forster's work is a "written" history and guide and Durrell's letter is "written" to Henry Miller, is there any indication that either selection has elements of "spoken style" present? Is any attention drawn to the fact that either work is in the process of being written? How do these observations function in your presentation of these works?

5. The two excerpts above were written by real-life authors. Now consider the following description of Alexandria, written by a fictional character—the fictional narrator of Lawrence Durrell's novel *Justine* (New York: Dutton, 1958, pp. 2–3).

> Notes for landscape-tones. . . . Long sequences of tempera. Light filtered through the essence of lemons. An air full of brick-dust—sweet-smelling brick-dust and the odour of hot pavements slaked with water. Light damp clouds, earth-bound yet seldom bringing rain. Upon this squirt dust-red, dust-green, chalk-mauve and watered crimson-lake. In summer the sea-damp lightly varnished the air. Everything lay under a coat of gum.
>
> And then in autumn the dry, palpitant air, harsh with static electricity, inflaming the body through its light clothing. The flesh coming alive, trying the bars of its prison. A drunken whore walks in a dark street at night, shedding snatches of song like petals. Was it in this that Anthony heard the heart-numbing strains of the great music which persuaded him to surrender for ever to the city he loved?
>
> The sulking bodies of the young begin to hunt for a fellow nakedness, and in those little cafés where Balthazar went so often with the old poet of the city, the boys stir uneasily at their backgammon under the petrol-lamps: disturbed by this dry desert wind—so unromantic, so unconfiding—stir, and turn to watch every stranger. They struggle for breath and in every summer kiss they can detect the taste of quicklime. . . .

How would you compare and contrast Forster's style and Durrell's style to the style of the narrator of *Justine?* Do your comments about this narrator's style tend to condition any of your previous remarks about Durrell's or Forster's style?

Emily Dickinson/Letter to Austin

born 1830

17 October 1851

We are waiting for breakfast, Austin, the meat and potato and a little pan of your favorite brown bread are keeping warm at the fire, while father goes for shavings.

While we were eating supper Mr Stephen Church rang the door bell very violently and offered to present us with *three barrels of shavings.* We are much overcome by this act of magnanimity and father has gone this morning to claim his proffered due. He wore a palm leaf hat, and his pantaloons tucked in his boots and I couldn't help thinking of *you* as he strode along by the window.

I dont think "neglige" quite becoming to so mighty a man. I had rather a jacket of green and your barndoor apparrel, than all the mock simplicity of a lawyer and a man. The breakfast is so warm and pussy is here a singing and the teakettle sings too as if to see which was loudest and I am so afraid lest kitty should be beaten—yet a *shadow* falls upon my morning picture—where is the youth so bold, the bravest of our fold, a seat is empty here—spectres sit in your chair and now and then nudge father with their long, bony elbows. I wish you were here dear Austin—the dust falls on the bureau in your deserted room and gay, frivolous spiders spin away in the corners. I dont go there after dark whenever I can help it, for the twilight seems to pause there and I am half afraid, and if I ever have to go, I hurry with all my might and never look behind me for I know who I should see.

Before next Tuesday—Oh before the coming stage will I not brighten and brush it, and open the long closed blinds, and with a sweeping broom will I not bring each spider down from its home so high and tell it it may come back again when master has gone—and oh I will bid it to be a tardy spider, to tarry on the way, and I will think my eye is fuller than sometimes, tho' *why* I cannot tell, when it shall rap on the window and come to live again. I am so happy when I know how soon you are coming that I put away my sewing and go out in the yard to think. I have tried to delay the frosts, I have coaxed the fading flowers, I thought I *could* detain a few of the crimson leaves until you had smiled upon them, but their companions call them and they cannot stay away—you will find the blue hills, Austin, with the autumnal shadows silently sleeping on them, and there will be a glory lingering round the day, so you'll know autumn has been here, and the *setting sun* will tell you, if you dont get home till evening. How glad I am you are well—you must try hard to be careful and not get sick again. I hope you will be better than ever you were in your life when you come home *this time,* for it never seemed so long since we have seen you. I thank you for such a long letter, and yet if I might choose, *the next* should be a longer. I think a letter just about *three days* long would make me happier than any other kind of one—if you please, dated at Boston, but thanks be to our Father, you may conclude it *here.* Everything has changed since my other letter—the doors are shut this morning, and all the kitchen wall is covered with chilly flies who are trying to warm themselves—poor things, they do not understand that there are no summer mornings remaining to them and me and they have a bewildered air which is really very droll, didn't one feel *sorry* for them. You would say t'was a gloomy morning if you were sitting here—the frost has been severe and the few lingering leaves seem anxious to be going and wrap their faded cloaks more closely about them as if to shield them from the chilly northeast wind. The earth looks like some poor old lady who by dint of pains has bloomed e'en till *now,* yet in a forgetful moment a few silver hairs from out her cap come stealing, and she tucks them back so hastily and thinks nobody *sees.* The cows are going to pasture and little boys with their hands in their pockets are whistling to try to keep warm. Dont think that the sky will frown so the day when you come home! She will smile and look happy, and be full of sunshine *then*—and even *should* she frown upon her child returning, there is *another* sky ever serene and fair, and there is *another* sunshine, tho' it be darkness there—never mind faded forests, Austin, never mind silent fields—*here* is a little forest whose leaf is ever green, here is a *brighter* garden, where not a frost has been, in its unfading flowers I hear the bright bee hum, prithee, my Brother, into *my* garden come!

STUDY QUESTIONS

1. In this letter, what seems to be the relationship between the letter writer and Austin? The letter writer refers to Austin as "my Brother," but the tone of the letter and the images used to express her feeling toward him suggest something other than a sibling relationship. Can you discover evidence, particularly in her description of the "exterior" environment, of how she reveals her own "interior" environment? (Look, for example, at the passage, "yet a *shadow* falls upon my morning picture—where is the youth so bold, the bravest of our fold, a seat is empty here—spectres sit in your chair and now and then nudge father with their long, bony elbows.")
2. How would you describe the diction in this letter? Does the diction in the first half of the letter seem childlike to you? Where? What does this reveal to you about the character of the speaker? How can you express, in your presentation of this letter, the shifts in diction, exemplified in such passages as the second paragraph, the first sentence in the final paragraph, and the final sentence in the letter?
3. Would you describe this situation as "open" or "closed"? Is the writer making contact with someone specific? Does she ever indicate any immediate response to any specific person?
4. This letter was written by the nineteenth-century poet Emily Dickinson to her older brother Austin, who had left home to attend Harvard. If you are interested enough to pursue this, why not see how further knowledge of Emily Dickinson (as revealed in her poetry and Edward Johnson's biography, for example) would tend to support or qualify some of your findings above.
5. The final sentence in this letter could be described as "more poetry than prose," and indeed the passage can be set up typographically to resemble verse, complete with stress and rhyme patterns:

hére is a líttle fórest	A
whose léaf is éver gréen,	B
heŕe is a *bríghter* gárden,	C
where nót a fróst has béen,	B
in íts unfáding flówers	D
I héar the bríght bee húm,	E
príthee, mý Bróther,	F
into *mý* gárden cóme!	E

Looked at in this way, your phrasing and stresses in this section might be rather different from the rest of the letter. Read the section aloud so that the stress pattern and line lengths are made clear in your reading. How does the reading of this passage compare to the reading of, say, the first paragraph of the letter? Furthermore, the writer seems to have taken her previous metaphorical and literal images of the external world and is using them to describe her inner feelings. How does this relate to the questions raised in number 1? Is there any way in your performance for you to express this tension between the *re*pression and the *ex*pression of her feelings toward Austin?

Nathaniel Hawthorne/The Haunted Mind

born 1804

What a singular moment is the first one, when you have hardly begun to recollect yourself, after starting from midnight slumber! By unclosing your eyes so suddenly, you seem to have surprised the personages of your dream in full convocation round your bed, and catch one broad glance at them before they can flit into obscurity. Or, to vary the metaphor, you find yourself, for a single instant, wide awake in that realm of illusions, whither sleep has been the passport, and behold its ghostly inhabitants and wondrous scenery, with a perception of their strangeness, such as you never attain while the dream is undisturbed. The distant sound of a church clock is borne faintly on the wind. You question with yourself, half seriously, whether it has stolen to your waking ear from some gray tower, that stood within the precincts of your dream. While yet in suspense, another clock flings its heavy clang over the slumbering town, with so full and distinct a sound, and such a long murmur in the neighboring air, that you are certain it must proceed from the steeple at the nearest corner. You count the strokes—one—two, and there they cease, with a booming sound, like the gathering of a third stroke within the bell.

If you could choose an hour of wakefulness out of the whole night, it would be this. Since your sober bedtime, at eleven, you have had rest enough to take off the pressure of yesterday's fatigue; while before you, till the sun comes from 'far Cathay' to brighten your window, there is almost the space of a summer night; one hour to be spent in thought, with the mind's eye half shut, and two in pleasant dreams, and two in that strangest of enjoyments, the forgetfulness alike of joy and woe. The moment of rising belongs to another period of time, and appears so distant, that the plunge out of a warm bed into the frosty air cannot yet be anticipated with dismay. Yesterday has already vanished among the shadows of the past; to-morrow has not yet emerged from the future. You have found an intermediate space, where the business of life does not intrude; where the passing moment lingers, and becomes truly the present; a spot where Father Time, when he thinks nobody is watching him, sits down by the wayside to take breath. Oh, that he would fall asleep, and let mortals live on without growing older!

Hitherto you have lain perfectly still, because the slightest motion would dissipate the fragments of your slumber. Now, being irrevocably awake, you peep through the half drawn window curtain, and observe that the glass is ornamented with fanciful devices in frost-work, and that each pane presents something like a frozen dream. There will be time enough to trace out the analogy, while waiting the summons to breakfast. Seen through the clear portion of the glass, where the silvery mountain peaks of the frost scenery do not ascend, the most conspicuous object is the steeple; the white spire of which directs you to the wintry lustre of the firmament. You may almost distinguish the figures on the clock that has just told the hour. Such a frosty sky, and the snow-covered roofs, and the long vista of the frozen street, all white, and the distant water hardened into rock, might make you shiver, even under four blankets and a woollen comforter. Yet look at that one glorious star! Its beams are distinguishable from all the rest, and actually cast the shadow of the casement on the bed, with a radiance of deeper hue than moonlight, though not so accurate an outline.

You sink down and muffle your head in the clothes, shivering all the while, but less from bodily chill, than the bare idea of a polar atmosphere. It is too cold even for the thoughts to venture abroad. You speculate on the luxury of wearing out a whole existence in bed, like an oyster in its shell, content with the sluggish ecstasy of inaction, and drowsily conscious of nothing but delicious warmth, such as you now feel again. Ah! that idea has brought a hideous one in its train. You think how the dead are living in their cold shrouds and narrow coffins, through the drear winter of the grave, and cannot persuade your fancy that they neither shrink nor shiver, when the snow is drifting over their little hillocks, and the bitter blast howls against the door of the tomb. That gloomy thought will collect a gloomy multitude, and throw its complexion over your wakeful hour.

In the depths of every heart, there is a tomb and a dungeon, though the lights, the music, and revelry above may cause us to forget their existence, and the buried ones, or prisoners whom they hide. But sometimes, and oftenest at midnight, those dark receptacles are flung wide open. In an hour like this, when the mind has a passive sensibility, but no active strength; when the imagination is a mirror, imparting vividness to all ideas, without the power of selecting or controlling them; then pray that your griefs may slumber, and the brotherhood of remorse not break their chain. It is too late! A funeral train comes gliding by your bed, in which Passion and Feeling assume bodily shape, and things of the mind become dim spectres to the eye. There is your earliest Sorrow, a pale young mourner, wearing a sister's likeness to first love, sadly beautiful, with a hallowed sweetness in her melancholy features, and grace in the flow of her sable robe. Next appears a shade of ruined loveliness, with dust among her golden hair, and her bright garments all faded and defaced, stealing from your glance with drooping head, as fearful of reproach; she was your fondest Hope, but a delusive one; so call her Disappointment now. A sterner form succeeds, with a brow of wrinkles, a look and gesture of iron authority; there is no name for him unless it be Fatality, an emblem of the evil influence that rules your fortunes; a demon to whom you subjected yourself by some error at the outset of life, and were bound his slave forever, by once obeying him. See! those fiendish lineaments graven on the darkness, the writhed lip of scorn, the mockery of that living eye, the pointed finger, touching the sore place in your heart! Do you remember any act of enormous folly at which you would blush, even in the remotest cavern of the earth? Then recognise your Shame.

Pass, wretched band! Well for the wakeful one, if, riotously miserable, a fiercer tribe do not surround him, the devils of a guilty heart, that holds its hell within itself. What if Remorse should assume the features of an injured friend? What if the fiend should come in woman's garments, with a pale beauty amid sin and desolation, and lie down by your side? What if he should stand at your bed's foot, in the likeness of a corpse, with a bloody stain upon the shroud? Sufficient without such guilt, is this nightmare of the soul; this heavy, heavy sinking of the spirits; this wintry gloom about the heart; this indistinct horror of the mind, blending itself with the darkness of the chamber.

By a desperate effort, you start upright, breaking from a sort of conscious sleep, and gazing wildly round the bed, as if the fiends were any where but in your haunted mind. At the same moment, the slumbering embers on the hearth send forth a gleam which palely illuminates the whole outer room, and flickers through the door of the bed-chamber, but cannot quite dispel its obscurity. Your eye searches for whatever may remind you of the living world. With eager minuteness, you take note of the table near the fireplace, the book with an ivory knife between its leaves, the unfolded letter, the hat, and the fallen glove. Soon the flame vanishes, and with it the whole scene is gone, though its image remains an instant in your mind's eye, when darkness has swallowed the reality. Throughout the chamber, there is the same obscurity as before, but not the same gloom within your breast. As your head falls back upon the pillow, you think— in a whisper be it spoken—how pleasant in these night solitudes, would be the rise and fall of a softer breathing than your own, the slight pressure of a tenderer bosom, the quiet throb of a purer heart, imparting its peacefulness to your troubled one, as if the fond sleeper were involving you in her dream.

Her influence is over you, though she have no existence but in that momentary image. You sink down in a flowery spot, on the borders of sleep and wakefulness, while your thoughts rise before you in pictures, all disconnected, yet all assimilated by a pervading gladsomeness and beauty. The wheeling of gorgeous squadrons, that glitter in the sun, is succeeded by the merriment of children round the door of a schoolhouse, beneath the glimmering shadow of old trees, at the corner of a rustic lane. You stand in the sunny rain of a summer shower, and wander among the sunny trees of an autumnal wood, and look upward at the brightest of all rainbows, overarching the unbroken sheet of snow, on the American side of Niagara. Your mind struggles pleasantly between the dancing radiance round the hearth of a young man and his recent bride, and the twittering flight of birds in spring, about their new-made nest. You feel the merry bounding of a ship before the breeze; and watch the tuneful feet of rosy girls, as they twine their last and merriest dance in a splendid ball-room; and find yourself in the brilliant circle of a crowded theatre, as the curtain falls over a light and airy scene.

With an involuntary start you seize hold on consciousness, and prove yourself but half awake by running a doubtful parallel between human life and the hour which has now elasped. In both you emerge from mystery, pass through a vicissitude that you can but imperfectly control, and are borne onward to another mystery. Now comes the peal of the distant clock, with fainter and fainter strokes as you plunge farther into the wilderness of sleep. It is the knell of a temporary death. Your spirit has departed, and strays like a free citizen, among the people of a shadowy world, beholding strange sights, yet without wonder or dismay. So calm, perhaps, will be the final change; so undisturbed, as if among familiar things, the entrance of the soul to its Eternal home!

STUDY QUESTIONS

1. As you read this essay aloud, try various "masks" for the speaker. For example, try giving him a melancholy attitude that might arise from feelings of age or of the rapid wearing of time; then read the essay through aloud a second time by giving the speaker a wonder that might arise from a childlike, youthful discovery of some new facets of experience. Which mask seems more appropriate? Why? Might the speaker be wearing these masks—and others—at various times in this discourse? If so, where does he seem to change masks?

2. Whom does the speaker seem to mean by "you"? Is he ever aware of an audience, outside himself, that might be "you" at least part of the time? On the other hand, might "you" refer to certain aspects—masks, perhaps—of the speaker's own sense of himself? What shift in point of view is indicated by the shift from "you" to "him"?

3. This essay was first published in 1842. That fact may be important to an analysis of what Hawthorne calls "control." Reread the second sentence of the final paragraph and note how it summarizes the speaker's view of the shape of his experience. How "imperfectly" does he seem to control the second part of the experience through the structure of his essay? Are there times when control seems to be superimposed upon this part of the experience? Might this superimposed control, if it exists, be related in any way to the speaker's deferring to an audience outside himself (has he put in the discourse certain elements for the sake of an audience) or to placate certain aspects of his own self? Does there appear to be a tension in the essay between the thoughts Hawthorne can only "imperfectly control" and those he has controlled by deferring, say, to a public, puritanical code? Pursuing these questions in depth would be aided by research into modern critical thought on Hawthorne's mind and milieu; an excellent source to open this research, which could lead to writing a long term paper on Hawthorne's essay, is Hyatt H. Waggoner, *Nathaniel Hawthorne* (Minneapolis, Minn.: University of Minnesota Pamphlets on American Writers, No. 23).

4. The structural elements indicated in the first three questions might be approached in yet a fourth way: Imagine the essay as being spoken not by one speaker but by two or more. What are the differences between the speakers? Which seem to address an audience directly? Which appear to be speaking to the other speakers? Which seem to be soliloquizing?

5. Note carefully your rate and your pauses. What aspects of the essay cause you to speed up or slow down? What do these differences in speed tell you about the structure of the essay? Does the punctuation serve as a guide to phrasing? What differences are there between Hawthorne's use of the comma and his use of the semicolon?

Edith Sitwell/The War in Ireland

born 1887

The history of the war in Ireland during the reign of Elizabeth is so long and so complicated, and the behaviour of the English so infamous, that it cannot be gone into in detail in this book.

After an interminable open and guerrilla warfare, during which—to give two instances of the English behaviour—the heads of two young men, Pat Tallon and his brother David, were sent, on the 17th of May 1572, according to the account of the officer in charge, 'like a bag of game to the Lord Keeper' and, within a few days of this, another party of the same family were caught, some killed, and others, to amuse the bored soldiers, 'stripped naked, and put in the bog' [1]—the former Lord Essex, the Lord Deputy,* reported that Ulster was quiet, and prepared to return to Dublin.

But certain of the English army continued their campaign of horror, and turned into Antrim from Tyrone—hunting the Irish as if they were game —this was, indeed, regarded by them as 'sport'; sweeping into Antrim 'not to conquer but to hunt', said Froude [2] 'to chastise, as it was called, Surley boy and the Scots'.†

There is a small island off the coast of Antrim, not far from the Giant's Causeway. Its name is the Island of Raithlin. Accessible only from one spot, it is dangerous to approach it in rough weather.

Here it was that Surley boy and the other Scots hid their wives and children when Essex came to Antrim.

On the 22nd of July 1575, there was no wind. The sea was like glass.

On passing through Carrickfergus, on his return journey to Dublin, Lord Essex learned that the wives and children of Surley boy and his followers were absent. He therefore ordered John Norreys, the second son of Lord Norreys and the Queen's friend, her 'Crow', to take a company of soldiers, cross to the island, rush it, and kill.

There were on the island twenty or more Scots in charge of the women and children, but the gallant Norreys had brought cannon with him. After a rejected offer to surrender, every creature the invaders could find was massacred, with the exception of the chief and his family—reserved, probably, for ransom. But there were others, hidden in the caves on the shore —mothers and their little children. 'These', says Froude, 'were hunted out as if they had been seals or otters, and all destroyed.'

Essex wrote, with pride, that the wives and children of Surley boy and the other chiefs 'were all taken and executed to the extent of six hundred' whilst Surley boy 'stood upon the mainland . . . and saw the tak-

* Father of the young man who became the Queen's favourite.
† Surley boy: meaning Sarley or Charley the yellow-haired.

ing of the island and was like to have run mad for sorrow, tearing and tormenting himself, and saying that he there lost all that he ever had'.[3]

Essex was delighted with this victory, and the Queen, writing to him on the 12th of August,[4] sent a message to John Norreys, 'the executioner of his well-designed enterprise, that she would not be unmindful of his services'.

□ □ □

Edmund Spenser, when in Ireland, was the witness of monstrous and varied horrors.

'At the execution of a notable tratour',* he wrote, 'I saw an old woman which was his foster-mother tooke up his head whilst he was quartered and sucked upp all the blood running there and saying that the earthe was not worthie to drincke yt, and therewith also steeped her face and brest and tare her haire, cryinge and shriking out most terrible. . . .' The Irish 'were brought to such wretchedness, as that any stonie hart would have rewed the same. Out of everie Corner of the woodes and glennes, they came crepinge forth upon theire handes, for theire legges could not beare them, they looked anatomies of death, they spake like ghostes cryinge out of theire graves, they did eate of the dead carryons, happye were they could fynde them, yea and one another soone after in so much as the verie Carcases they spared not to scrape out of theire graves, and if they found a plotte of water cresses or shamrockes, then they flocked as to a feast for the tyme, yet not able longe to contynewe therwithall, that in short space there were none almost left, and a most populous and plentifull countrye suddenlie lefte voyde of man or beast, yet sure in all that warr there perished not manye by the sword, but all by the extremitie of famyne. . . .'

'The common sort of the Rebels', wrote Fynes Morrison, another eyewitness, 'was driven to unspeakable extremities (beyond the record of most Histories that ever I did reade in that kind). . . . Captain Trevor and many honest Gentlemen lying in the Newry can witness, that some old women in these parts, used to make a fier in the fields, and divers little children driving out the cattel in the cold mornings, and coming thither to warme them, were by them surprised, killed and eaten, which at last was discovered by a great girle breaking from them by strength of her body, and Captain Trevor sending out to know the truth, they found the childrens' skulls and bones, and apprehended the old women, who were executed. . . .'

'Sir Arthur Chichester, Sir Richard Moryson, and the other Commanders of the Forces sent against Bryan Mac Air . . . in their returne homeward saw a most horrible spectacle of three children, (whereof the eldest was

* Murrough O'Brien, executed on the 1st of July 1576.

not above ten yeeres old) all eating and gnawing with their teeth the entrails of their dead mother, upon whose flesh they had fed twenty dayes
past, and having eaten all from the feete upward to the bare bones, rosting
it continually by a slow fire, were now coming to the eating of her entrails,
in like sort rosted, not yet divided from the body, being as yet raw. . . .'

Oh, look at the little sparrows flying! Not a sparrow that falleth. . . .

In the churches in England the Bishops thundered. The virtuous
preened themselves.

NOTES TO APPENDIX H

[1] Report of the Officer in Charge, named Agard.
[2] Froude, XI, 184.
[3] Essex to Walsingham, 31st July 1575. Essex to the Queen, 31st July 1575.
[4] Carew Papers.

STUDY QUESTIONS

1. This essay is "Appendix H" to Edith Sitwell's long semidocumentary account of
   the lives of Elizabeth I and Mary of Scotland, *The Queens and the Hive* (Boston:
   Little, Brown, 1962, pp. 528–530). The details of the war in Ireland, according
   to Sitwell, are too complicated to be treated at length in her book. But what
   kind of details has she selected to treat in this essay? What is their effect?
2. Note that each of the first three paragraphs consists of one long sentence,
   compounded of details and complicated by many qualifying phrases. What
   happens to your speech behavior as you proceed in your reading from these
   paragraphs to the short, simple fourth, fifth, and sixth paragraphs? What tonal
   or structural functions do these first six paragraphs serve?
3. What differences in types of commentary are there between "Sitwell's" and
   those of the authorities she quotes? How do the authorities differ from her
   either in attitude or manner? What differences occur in your delivery as you
   distinguish between "Sitwell" and the voices she echoes? Are their voices
   conditioned perhaps by hers?
4. Consider carefully the final two paragraphs.
   a. What or where are the sparrows "Sitwell" seems to see? Of all the many
      answers you can think of, which seem most functional within the structure of
      the essay?
   b. By what association of materials throughout the entire essay are the ideas
      in the final two paragraphs produced? In this respect, note that the first
      eleven paragraphs use no imagery that might suggest birds—aside, perhaps,
      from a reference to the Queen's habit of giving animal names to her close
      advisers (her "Crow") and the reference to the Irish as "game"—yet, other
      animals are suggested. Review carefully the suggestions in Spenser's
      speech and Morrison's.

   c. How many relationships can you find *between* the last two paragraphs?

   d. How do the last two paragraphs serve to conclude the major ideas and attitudes of the entire essay? What aspects of these two paragraphs reiterate
the characteristic speaking style of "Sitwell" in this essay?

5. All of the footnotes are provided by Sitwell. Try reading the essay by inserting
them in the text where their numbers or marks appear. First read the footnotes
"parenthetically," as if they were slightly unnecessary to the argument; then
read them in an "underlining" way by looking directly at your audience. Try
reading the footnotes at the bottom of the pages after the ideas to which they
refer and read the end-of-the-essay footnotes at the end of the essay. What
differences are there in the footnotes? What purposes do the footnotes serve?

From *The Bestiary: A Book of Beasts* translated and edited by **T. H. White**

born 1896

There is an animal called an ELEPHANT, which has no desire to copulate.

People say that it is called an Elephant by the Greeks on account of its
size, for it approaches the form of a mountain: you see, a mountain is
called *'eliphio'* in Greek. In the Indies, however, it is known by the name
of *'barrus'* because of its voice—whence both the voice is called *'bari*tone'
and the tusks are called 'ivory' (*ebur*). Its nose is called a proboscis (for
the bushes), because it carries its leaf-food to its mouth with it, and it
looks like a snake.[1]

Elephants protect themselves with ivory tusks. No larger animals can
be found. The Persians and the Indians, collected into wooden towers
on them, sometimes fight each other with javelins as if from a castle.
They possess vast intelligence and memory. They march about in herds.
And they copulate back-to-back.[2]

Elephants remain pregnant for two years, nor do they have babies more

---

[1] Pro-boscis—for the bushes!
  'Th' unwieldy Elephant
To make them mirth us'd all his might, and wreathd
His Lithe Proboscis.'
               Paradise Lost, IV, 347

[2] The copulation of elephants was a matter for speculation in the dark ages, and
still is, as it is rarely witnessed. Solinus quotes Pliny to the effect that their geni-
tals, like those mentioned by Sir Thomas Browne in his note on hares,
were put on backward. It was supposed that, being modest, they preferred to
look the other way while they were about it. Albertus Magnus held that they
copulated like other quadrupeds, but that, owing to the great weight of the husband, he either had to dig a pit for his wife to stand in or else he had to float
himself over her in a lake, where his gravity would naturally be less. In fact,
they copulate in the ordinary way and, according to Lieut.-Colonel C. H. Williams,
more gracefully than most.

than once, nor do they have several at a time, but only one. They live three hundred years. If one of them wants to have a baby, he goes eastward toward Paradise, and there is a tree there called Mandragora,[3] and he goes with his wife. She first takes of the tree and then gives some to her spouse. When they munch it up, it seduces them, and she immediately conceives in her womb. When the proper time for being delivered arrives, she walks out into a lake, and the water comes up to the mother's udders. Meanwhile the father-elephant guards her while she is in labour, because there is a certain dragon which is inimical to elephants. Moreover, if a serpent happens by, the father kills and tramples on it till dead. He is also formidable to bulls—but he is frightened of mice, for all that.

The Elephant's nature is that if he tumbles down he cannot get up again. Hence it comes that he leans against a tree when he wants to go to sleep, for he has no joints in his knees. This is the reason why a hunter partly saws through a tree, so that the elephant, when he leans against it, may fall down at the same time as the tree.[4] As he falls, he calls out loudly; and immediately a large elephant appears, but it is not able to lift him up. At this they both cry out, and twelve more elephants arrive upon the scene: but even they cannot lift up the one who has fallen down. Then they all shout for help, and at once there comes a very Insignificant Elephant, and he puts his mouth with the proboscis under the big one, and lifts him up. This little elephant has, moreover, the property that nothing evil can come near his hairs and bones when they have been reduced to ashes, not even a Dragon.

Now the Elephant and his wife represent Adam and Eve. For when they were pleasing to God, before their provocation in the flesh, they knew nothing about copulation nor had they knowledge of sin. When, however, the wife ate of the Tree of Knowledge, which is what Mandragora means, and gave one of the fruits to her man, she was immediately made a wanderer and they had to clear out of Paradise on account of it. For, all the time that they were in Paradise, Adam did not know her. But then,

---

[3] Mandrake. There is still a genus of plants called the Mandragora, said to be emetic, narcotic and 'fertilizing'. 'The mandrakes which Reuben found in the field were used by his mother Leah for venereal purposes (Gen. xxx. 14–16), and this precious peculiarity is enlarged upon in rabbinical literature. The Greeks spoke of them as anthropomorphic; and according to popular superstition they spring from human sperm spilled on the ground, and are so full of animal life and consciousness that they shriek when torn out of the earth, so "that living mortals, hearing them, run mad".' E. P. Evans.

[4] Julius Caesar, in his *Gallic War*, relates the same fable about the elks (*alces*). The present translator is informed by Captain A. A. F. Minchin of the Indian Forest Service that elephants do have, as it were, scratching posts at their watering places, and that the hunter is able to forecast the size of his quarry by the height of the mud rubbed off against these trees.

the Scriptures say: 'Adam went in to his wife and she conceived and bore Cain, upon the waters of tribulation'. Of which waters the Psalmist cries: 'Save me, O God, for the waters have entered in even unto my soul'. And immediately the dragon subverted them and made them strangers to God's refuge. That is what comes of not pleasing God.

When the Big Elephant arrives, i.e. the Hebrew Law, and fails to lift up the fallen, it is the same as when the Pharisee failed with the fellow who had fallen among thieves. Nor could the Twelve Elephants, i.e. the Band of the Prophets, lift him up, just as the Levite did not lift the man we mentioned. But it means that Our Lord Jesus Christ, although he was the greatest, was made the most Insignificant of All the Elephants. He humiliated himself, and was made obedient even unto death, in order that he might raise men up.

The little elephant also symbolizes the Samaritan who put the man on his mare. For he himself, wounded, took over our infirmities and carried them from us. Moreover, this heavenly Samaritan is interpreted as the Defender about whom David writes: 'The Lord defending the lowly ones'. Also, with reference to the little elephant's ashes: 'Where the Lord is present, no devil can come nigh'.

It is a fact that Elephants smash whatever they wind their noses round, like the fall of some prodigious ruin, and whatever they squash with their feet they blot out.

They never quarrel about their wives, for adultery is unknown to them. There is a mild gentleness about them, for, if they happen to come across a forwandered man in the deserts, they offer to lead him back into familiar paths. If they are gathered together into crowded herds, they make way for themselves with tender and placid trunks, lest any of their tusks should happen to kill some animal on the road. If by chance they do become involved in battles, they take no little care of the casualties, for they collect the wounded and exhausted into the middle of the herd.

. . .

The VIPER (*vipera*) is called this because it brings forth in violence (*vi*). The reason is that when its belly is yearning for delivery, the young snakes, not waiting for the timely discharge of birth, gnaw through the mother's sides and burst out to her destruction.

It is said, moreover, that the male puts his head into the female's mouth and spits the semen into it. Then she, angered by his lust, bites off his head when he tries to take it out again.

Thus both parents perish, the male when he copulates, and the female when she gives birth.

According to St Ambrose, the viper is the most villainous kind of beast, and particularly because it is the cunningest of all species when it feels the lust for coition. It decides to have a bastard union with the sea eel (Murena) and makes ready for this unnatural copulation. Having gone down to the seashore and made its presence known with a wolf-whistle, it calls the Murena out of the waters for the conjugal embrace. The invited eel does not fail him, but offers the desired uses of her coupling to the venomous reptile.

Now what can anybody make of a sermon like this, unless it is to show up the habits of married couples, and, if you do not get this point, it shall now be explained to you.

Your husband, I admit, may be uncouth, undependable, disorderly, slippery and tipsy—but what is worse than the ill which the murena-mistress does not shun in him, once he has called her? *She* does not fail him. *She* embraces the slipperiness of the serpent with careful zeal. *She* puts up with your troubles and offers the comfort of womanly good cheer. But you, O Woman, like the lady-snake who bites off his head, are not able to support your own man.

Adam was deceived by Eve, not Eve by Adam. Consequently it is only good sense that the man, who was first got into trouble by the woman, should now take the leadership, for fear that he should once again be ruined by feminine whims.

But he is rough and savage, you will say: in short, he has ceased to please.

Well, is a man always to be choosing new wives? Even a horse loves truly and an ox seeks one single mate. And if one ox is changed in a yoke of oxen, the other one cannot drag the yoke but feels uncomfortable. Yet you women put away your husbands and think that you ought to be changing frequently. And if he happens to be away for one day, you give him a rival on mere suspicion, as if his inconstancy were proved. You do an injury to modesty.

A mere viper searches for his absent one, he calls his absent one, he cries out to her with a flattering note. And when he senses his partner approaching, he bashfully sicks up his poison, in reverence to the lady and in nuptial gratitude. You women, on the contrary, reject the coming union from afar, with insults. The viper even looks toward the sea, looks forward to the coming of his lady-friend. You women impede with contumely the approaches of your men.

But there is a catch in this for you too, my dear Man. You do *not* sick up your poisons when you excite the marriage girdle. In its season you ferment the fearful poison of the conjugal embrace, nor do you blush at the nuptials, nor feel respect for marriage.

Lay aside, O Man, the pride of your heart and the harshness of your conduct when that diligent wife does hasten to you.[5] Drive away the

[5] Pepys would have added 'poor wretch'.

sulks when that solicitous wife does excite your affection. You are not her lord, but her husband, nor have you chosen a female slave, but a wife. God wants you to be the director of the weaker sex, but not by brute force. Return sympathy for her misfortunes, kindness for her love. Sometimes, where the viper is able to get rid of his poison, you are not able to get rid of the hard-heartedness of your mind. Well, if you have a natural coldness, you ought to temper it out of respect for the institution of marriage; you ought to lay aside the savagery of your brain out of respect to the union. Thus you may be able to get her to accept you after all!

Man! do not seek a corrupt union. Do not lie in wait for a different connection. Adultery is unpleasant, it is an injury to Nature.[6] God first made two people, Adam and Eve, and they were to be man and wife. She was made from the rib of Adam and both were ordained to be in one body and to live in one spirit. So why separate the body, why divide the mind? It is adultery to Nature.

. . .

STUDY QUESTIONS

1. These selections are modern translations of a twelfth-century bestiary, or book of beasts, a kind of ancient scientific description of the animals. The bestiary might also be considered a kind of primitive biology textbook. It is obvious that there are two speakers in these selections: the twelfth-century bestiarist and the modern translator, the late English writer T. H. White. As you consider the problems in presenting these two personae, you will of course need to look carefully at the style each uses, and for the T. H. White persona this will mean looking at (and presenting to your audience) the style of the footnotes. What does White's attitude seem to be? Is he contemptuous of the bestiarist? Amused by him? Does he share jokes about him with his audience, behind the bestiarist's back? Do these attitudes also reveal themselves in the style whereby White translated the bestiarist?

2. As you study these first two personae, pay particular attention to their individual relationships to their audiences. The bestiarist's audience was, of course, not White's. An interesting project might be to turn these selections into a kind

---

[6] Eels are not the only creatures of the sea who misbehave themselves in another element.

'Th' adulterous *Sargus* [a sea-bream] doth not only change
Wives every day, in the deep streams; but (strange)
As if the honey of Sea-loves delights
Could not suffice his ranging appetites,
Courting the Shee-Goats on the grassie shore,
Would horn their Husbands that had horns before.'
Sylvester's *Du Bartas.*

of readers theater, with one interpreter demonstrating the relationship between White and his audience and another interpreter demonstrating the relationship between the bestiarist and his audience.

3. There is yet a third speaker. Perhaps you have already become aware of his presence. The twelfth-century bestiarist was actually making a Christian interpretation of traditional knowledge about animals. We could perhaps think of this third speaker as the voice, or embodiment, of traditional knowledge. We are most aware of him at the first of the section on elephants, just before the first major break in the text, when the bestiarist presents his interpretation of what this ancient knowledge really means. Consider this third speaker as an observer, collector, and transmitter of "facts," and the second speaker as a cleric in the Church (he was probably a monk), who believes God works in mysterious ways to reveal his truths and teach man lessons. Are there places in the text where these two personae seem to blend and speak at the same time? What are the differences in their audiences?

4. Literally, the three speakers are engaged in these actions: The first speaker, the voice of traditional knowledge, is passing on to his audience the "facts" about animals; the second speaker, the bestiarist, is a twelfth-century Christian interpreter who is putting into manuscript form the "facts" about animals plus his own interpretation of their meaning for the edification and salvation of his audience; the third speaker is a modern translator, who is trying to make the work accessible to a modern audience, one differing vastly from that addressed by the first two speakers. How may these varying attitudes, actions, and relationships be demonstrated?

Anonymous/Witches Apprehended, Examined and Executed, for Notable Villainies by Them Committed both by Land and Water. With a Strange and Most True Trial How to Know Whether a Woman be a Witch or Not. (London, 1613)

The writer, who is not identified, offers this discourse on witchcraft to his readers as evidence of the corruption of the times. At a place called Milton, three miles from Bedford, lived an aged widow called Mother Sutton, her daughter Mary, and Mary's son, Henry (one of Mary's three bastards, according to the writer). Mother Sutton was known merely as a poor hogsherd, or hogkeeper, and though many strange diseases and accidents had befallen the cattle in the country around her place, no one had for the space of twenty-one years suspected Mother Sutton of being a witch. But then some sort of disagreement arose between Mother Sutton and "a Gentleman of worship called Master Enger." She vowed revenge, and the following day his horses were found mysteriously dead and his swine drowned themselves in his mill dam. In two years' time she caused him losses in the amount of two

*hundred pounds. One day Henry Sutton, "the bastard son of
Mary Sutton," was discovered by one of Enger's servants
(an old man) throwing "stones, dirt and filth" into the mill dam.
The old servant admonished the little boy and boxed him on
the ears. Henry reported the incident to his mother and grandmother, who vowed revenge. On the following day the old
servant and another of Master Enger's men took a cartload
of corn to market at Bedford. On their way they noticed a
"goodly fair black Sow" keeping pace with them, until just a
mile outside Bedford when she spun around two or three
times, throwing the horse into a frenzy and causing him to
run away with the cart. The servants overtook the cart,
reloaded the corn, proceeded to Bedford, and passed off the
incident as an amusing happening. On their return from
Bedford, the same sow again threw the horse into a frenzy.
This time the servants followed the black sow and found that
she went into Mother Sutton's house. When they returned to
Master Enger, they told him of these happenings, but he made
slight of it and supposed that they were drunk.*

The same old servant of Master Enger's, within a few days after going to
plough, fell into talk of Mother Sutton and of Mary Sutton, her daughter,
of what pranks he had heard they had plaid thereabouts in the country, as
also what accidents had befallen him and his fellow as they had passed to
and from Bedford. In discoursing of which a Beetle came and stroke the
same fellow on the breast: and he presently fell into a trance as he was
guiding the plough, the extremity whereof was such that his senses were
altogether distract and his body and mind utterly distempered. The be-
holders deemed him clean hopelesse of recovery. Yea, his other fellow
upon this sudden sight was stricken into such amazement that he stood
like a livelesse trunke divided from his vital spirits and was as unable to
help him as the other was needful to be helpt by him. At length being
some what recovered and awaked from that astonishment, the other
servant made haste homeward and carried his master word of what had
happened.

Upon delivery of this news (for he was a man highly esteemed by his
master for his honest and long service) there was much moan made for
him in the house, and Master Enger himself had not the least part of grief
for his old servant's extremity, but with all possible speed hastened into
the field and used help to have him brought home. After which he neglected no means nor spared any cost that might ease his servant, or re-
deeme him from the misery he was in, but all was in vaine: for his extasies
were nothing lessened, but continued a long time in as grievous perplexity
as at first. Yet though they suspected much they had no certain proof or

knowledge of the cause. Their means were therefore the shorter to cure the effect. But as a thief when he entereth into a house to robbe first putteth out the lights—according to that saying, *Qui male agit, odit lucem,* He that doth evil, hateth light—so these Imps that live in the gunshot of devillish assaults, go about to darken and disgrace the light of such as are toward and virtuous, and make the night the instrument to contrive their wicked purposes. For these Witches, having so long and covertly continued to do much mischief by their practises, were so hardened in their lewde and vile proceeding that the custom of their sin had quite taken away the sense and feeling thereof, and they spared not to continue the perplexity of this old servant both in body and mind, in such sort that his friends were as desirous to see death rid him from his extremity, as a woman great with child is ever musing upon the time of her delivery. For where distress is deep, and the conscience clear, *Mors expectatur absque formidine, exoptatur cum dulcedine, excipitur cum devotione,* death is looked for without fear, desired with delight, and accepted with devotion. In the perseverance of this fellow's perplexity, he—being in his distraction both of body and mind, yet in bed and awake—espied Mary Sutton (the daughter) in a Moonshine night come in at the window in her accustomed and personal habit and shape, with her knitting work in her hands, and sitting down at his bed's feet, sometimes working, and knitting with her needles, and sometimes gazing and staring him in the face. His grief was thereby redoubled and increased. Not long after she drew neerer unto him, and sat by his bedside (yet all this while he had neither power to stir or speak) and told him if he would consent she should come to bed to him, he should be restored to his former health and prosperity. Thus the Devil strives to enlarge his Kingdome, and upon the necke of one wickedness to heap another. So that *Periculum probat transeuntium raritas, pereuntium multitudo:* In the dangerous Sea of this world, the rareness of those that pass the same oversafe, and the multitude of others that perish in their passage, sufficiently prove the peril we live in. In the Ocean Sea, of four ships not one miscarries. In the Sea of this world, of many sowers, not one escapes his particular cross and calamity. Yet in our greatest weakness and debility, when the Devil is most busy to tempt us and seduce us from God, then is God strongest in the hearts of his children, and most ready to be auxiliant and helping to save and uphold them from declining and falling. God's liberality appears more than his rigor, for whom he draws out of the Devil's throat by faith, he would have him trample the Devil down by virtue least he should only have fled, not foiled his enemy.

This is made known in His miraculous working with this fellow: for he that before had neither power to move or speak, had then presently by divine assistance free power and liberty to give repulse to her assault and denial to her filthy and detested motion; and to upbraid her of her abominable life and behaviour, having before had three bastards and never married. She upon this (seeing her suite cold, and that God's power was more predominant with him then her devillish practise) vanished and departed the same way she came.

She was no sooner gone, but as well as he could, he called for his master, told him that now he could tell him the cause of this vexation; that Mother Sutton's daughter came in at the window, sat knitting and working by him, and that if he would have consented to her filthinesse, he should have been freed from his misery, and related all that had happened.

His master was glad of this news, for that the means found out, the matter and manner of his grief might be the easier helped and redressed: yet was he distrustful of the truth and rather esteemed it an idleness of his servant's brain, than an accident of verity. Nevertheless, he resolved to make proof thereof.

The next morrow he took company along with him and went into the fields, where he found her working, and tending her hogs. There Master Enger said to her, she was a very good huswife, and that she followed her work night and day. No sir, said she, My huswifery is very slender, neither am I so good a follower of my work as you persuade me. With that, he told her that she was and that she had been working at his house the night before. She would confess nothing, but stood in stiff denial upon her purgation—insomuch that the Gentleman by fair entreaties persuaded her to go home with him, to satisfy his man, and to resolve some doubts that were had of her. She utterly refused and made answer she would not stir a foot, neither had they authority to compel her to go without a Constable. Which Master Enger perceiving, and seeing her obstinacy to be so great, fell into a greater dislike and distrust of her than he did before, and made no more a do, but caused her to be set upon a horseback to be brought to his house. All the company could hardly bring her away, for as fast as they set her up, in despight of them she would swarve downe, first on the one side, then the other, till at last they were fain by main force to join together and hold her violently down to the horseback, and so bring her to the place where this perplexed person lay in his bed. Where being come, and brought by force to his bedside he (as directions had been given unto him) drew blood of her, and presently began to amend, and be well again. But her assiduity and continual exercise in doing mischief did so prevail with her to do this fellow further hurt, that she watched for advantage and opportunity to touch his neck again with her finger. It was no sooner done, and she departed, but he fell into as great or far worse vexation than he had before.

The report of this was carried up and down all Bedfordshire, and this

Mary Sutton's wicked and lewd courses being rumored as well abroad as in Master Enger's house, at last it came into the mouth of Master Enger's sonne (being a little boy of seven years old), who not long after espying old Mother Sutton going to the Mill to grind corn, and remembering what speeches he had heard past of her and her daughter followed the old woman, flinging stones at her, and calling her Witch, which she observing conceited a rancour and deadly hatred to his young child and purposed not to suffer opportunity pass to be revenged. As soon therefore as she had dispatcht at the Mill, she hasted homewards, and could not be quiet till she had grumbled to her daughter what had happened and how the child had served her. Then conferring how Master Enger had used Mary Sutton the daughter, and how his little sonne had used the Mother, they both resolved and vowed revenge. This conference and consultation of villainy was had, and concluded in the presence and hearing of Henry Sutton (the Bastard of Mary Sutton) little thinking that his fortune should be to give in evidence to break the neck of his own Mother and Grandmother.

To effect their devillish purpose to the young child of Master Enger, they called up their two Spirits, whom Mother Sutton called Dick and Jude: and having given them suck at their two teats which they had on their thighs (found out afterwards by inquiry and search of the women) they gave them charge to strike the little boy and to turn him to torment. Which was not long in performing, but the child, being distract, was put to such bitter and insupportable misery that by his life his torments were augmented and by his death they were abridged. For his tender and unripe age was so infeebled and made weak by that devillish infection of extremity that in five days, not able longer to endure them, death gave end of his perplexities.

The Gentleman did not so much grieve for the loss and hindrance he had in his cattle (which was much) nor for the miserable distress that his servant had endured (which was more) as that the hopeful days of his young son were so untimely cut off (which touched his heart most of all). Yet did his discretion temper his passions with such patience that he referred the remembrance of his wrongs to that heavenly power, that permits not such iniquity to pass unrevealed or unrevenged.

As he was thus wrapt in a Sea of woes, there came a Gentleman a friend of his forth from the North, who travelling towards London sojourned with him all night. He, perceiving Master Enger to be full of grief, was desirous to know the cause thereof, and he was as unwilling by the discourse of his misfortunes to renew his many sorrows, till at last his friend's urgent importunacy persuaded him not to pass it over with silence. Upon Master Enger's relation of what had happened, the Gentleman demanded if he had none in suspicion that should do these wrongs unto him. Yes, quoth Master Enger, and therewithall he named this Mary Sutton and her mother, and told him the particulars of his losses and miseries. His friend, understanding this, advised him to take them, or any one of them, to his mill dam, having first shut up the mill gates that the water might be at highest; and then binding their arms cross, stripping them into their Smocks, and leaving their legs at liberty, throw them into the water. Yet least they should not be Witches, and that their lives might not be in danger of drowning, let there be a rope tied about their middles, so long that it may reach from one side of your dam to the other, where on each side let one of your men stand, that if she chance to sink they may draw her up and preserve her. Then if she swim, take her up, and cause some women to search her, upon which, if they find any extraordinary marks about her, let her the second time be bound, and have her right thumb bound to her left toe, and her left thumb to her right toe, and your men with the same rope (if need be) to preserve her, and be thrown into the water, then if she swim, you may build upon it, that she is a Witch. I have seen it often tried in the North country.

The morrow after, Master Enger rode into the fields where Mary Sutton (the daughter) was, having some of his men to accompany him, where after some questions made unto her, they assayed to bind her on horseback, when all his men being presently stricken lame, Master Enger himself began to remember that once rating her about his man, he was on the sudden in the like perplexity; and then taking courage, and desiring God to be his assistance, with a cudgell which he had in his hand, he beat her till she was scarce able to stir. At which his men presently recovered, bound her to their Master's horse, and brought her home to his house, and shut up his mill gates did as before the Gentleman had advised him. When being thrown in the first time, she sunk some two foot into the water with a fall, but rose again and floated upon the water like a plank. Then he commanded her to be taken out, and had women ready that searched her and found under her left thigh a kind of Teat, which after the Bastard sonne confessed her Spirits in severall shapes as Cats, Moles, etc. used to suck her.

Then was she the second time bound cross her thumbs and toes, according to the former direction, and then she sunk not at all, but sitting upon the water, turned round about like a wheel, or as that which commonly we call a whirlpool—withstanding Master Enger's men standing on each side of the dam with a rope tossing her up and down to make her sink, but could not.

And then being taken up, she as boldly as if she had been innocent asked them if they could do any more to her. When Master Enger began to accuse her with the death of his cattle, the languish of his man, who continued in sorrow both of body and mind from Christmas to Shrovetide, as also the death of his son, all which she constantly denied and stood at defiance with him till being carried towards a Justice. Master Enger told her it was bootless to stand so obstinately upon denial of those matters, for her own son Henry had revealed all, both as touching her selfe and her mother, and of the time and manner of their plotting to torment his little boy. When she heard that, her heart misgave her, she confessed all, and acknowledged the Devil had now left her to that shame that is reward to such as follow him. Upon which confession, the mother also was apprehended, and both being committed to Bedford Gaol, many other matters were there produced against them, of long continuance (for they had remained as before, about twenty years) in the prosecution of these lewd and wicked practices. But for this matter of Master Enger at the last Assises, the evidence of the Bastard son, and the confessions severally taken both of old Mother Sutton & her daughter Mary, found them guilty in all former objections. So that arained at Bedford on Monday, the thirtieth of March last past, they had a just conviction, and on Tuesday the next day after they were executed.

STUDY QUESTIONS

1. The study of this piece could be conducted in two manners of approach: the "intrinsic," in which one makes a structural analysis of the work, based strictly on evidence found within the text; and the "extrinsic," in which one turns to materials outside the text to assist his analysis. The piece is, obviously, rhetorical in its action.
2. To do the intrinsic analysis imagine yourself as the persona's audience. Note that you have no way of distinguishing between the persona and the implied author, except by allowing the implied author (who is anonymous) the perspective of the total work and by giving the persona only the perspective of the work as it unfolds sequentially in time.
   a. How does the persona establish his ethos? On what basis does he seek to prove his credibility as a reliable reporter and interpreter of these events?
   b. Note the reporting of dialogue, how dialogue mingles easily with the persona's own words. Is it possible to distinguish the other characters—especially Master Enger, Mary Sutton, the old servant, and Master Enger's friend from the North—from the persona?
      (1) If so, what seem to be the major characteristics of each? Is it possible, for example, to feel a kind of unintended pity for Mary Sutton during her "examination"?
      (2) If not, do the characters seem to be merely stick men being manipulated by the persona? Or do they seem to be merely projections of his own mind?
   c. Consider carefully the "evidence" the persona finds so convincing and note the way in which it has been worked into the structure of the persona's argument. How valid is his case? What gaps are to be found, if any? In what ways might the case be a reflection of the persona's character?

3. An extrinsic analysis might be conducted by asking some additional questions, which should in turn throw light on the questions above.
    a. What was the "temper" of London society in 1613, especially insofar as its attitude toward witches was concerned?
    b. Who or what provided moral and legal sanctions for witch-hunting?
    c. Are these sanctions reflected in the persona's case? Is he catering to certain prominent attitudes of his day?
    d. If possible, find a copy of the original work (STC 25872, available on microfilm) and compare the original with the present version. You will note that much of the original punctuation has been changed and modernized. However, if one can accustom himself to seventeenth-century punctuation and use it as a guide to his voice (as it was so intended), one has found yet another approach to the character of the persona.
4. The intrinsic and extrinsic approaches have special relevance for the interpreter of this work: Shall he perform the work as if he were a seventeenth-century persona speaking before a modern audience? Or shall he give his audience a role to play, too?

John Dos Passos/Art and Isadora

born 1896

In San Francisco, in eighteen seventyeight Mrs. Isadora O'Gorman Duncan, a high-spirited lady with a taste for the piano, set about divorcing her husband, the prominent Mr. Duncan, whose behavior we are led to believe had been grossly indelicate; the whole thing made her so nervous that she declared to her children that she couldn't keep anything on her stomach but a little champagne and oysters; in the middle of the bitterness and recriminations of the family row,

into a world of gaslit boardinghouses kept by ruined southern belles and railroad-magnates and swinging doors and whiskery men nibbling cloves to hide the whiskey on their breaths and brass spittoons and four-wheel cabs and basques and bustles and long ruffled trailing skirts (in which lecturehall and concertroom, under the domination of ladies of culture, were the centers of aspiring life)

she bore a daughter whom she named after herself Isadora.

The break with Mr. Duncan and the discovery of his duplicity turned Mrs. Duncan into a bigoted feminist and an atheist, a passionate follower of Bob Ingersoll's lectures and writings; for God read Nature; for duty beauty, *and only man is vile.*

Mrs. Duncan had a hard struggle to raise her children in the love of beauty and the hatred of corsets and conventions and manmade laws. She gave pianolessons, she did embroidery and knitted scarves and mittens.

The Duncans were always in debt.

The rent was always due.

Isadora's earliest memories were of wheedling grocers and butchers and landlords and selling little things her mother had made from door to door,
helping hand valises out of back windows when they had to jump their bills at one shabbygenteel boardinghouse after another in the outskirts of Oakland and San Francisco.
The little Duncans and their mother were a clan; it was the Duncans against a rude and sordid world. The Duncans weren't Catholics any more or Presbyterians or Quakers or Baptists; they were Artists.

When the children were quite young they managed to stir up interest among their neighbors by giving theatrical performances in a barn; the older girl Elizabeth gave lessons in society dancing; they were westerners, the world was a goldrush; they weren't ashamed of being in the public eye. Isadora had green eyes and reddish hair and a beautiful neck and arms. She couldn't afford lessons in conventional dancing, so she made up dances of her own.

They moved to Chicago. Isadora got a job dancing to *The Washington Post* at the Masonic Temple Roof Garden for fifty a week. She danced at clubs. She went to see Augustin Daly and told him she'd discovered
the Dance
and went on in New York as a fairy in cheesecloth in a production of *Midsummer Night's Dream* with Ada Rehan.

The family followed her to New York. They rented a big room in Carnegie Hall, put mattresses in the corners, hung drapes on the wall and invented the first Greenwich Village studio.
They were never more than one jump ahead of the sheriff, they were always wheedling the tradespeople out of bills, standing the landlady up for the rent, coaxing handouts out of rich philistines.
Isadora arranged recitals with Ethelbert Nevin
danced to readings of Omar Khayyám for society women at Newport. When the Hotel Windsor burned they lost all their trunks and the very long bill they owed and sailed for London on a cattleboat
to escape the materialism of their native America.

In London at the British Museum
they discovered the Greeks;
the Dance was Greek.
Under the smoky chimneypots of London, in the sootcoated squares

they danced in muslin tunics, they copied poses from Greek vases, went
to lectures, artgalleries, concerts, plays, sopped up in a winter fifty years
of Victorian culture.

Back to the Greeks.

Whenever they were put out of their lodgings for nonpayment of rent
Isadora led them to the best hotel and engaged a suite and sent the
waiters scurrying for lobster and champagne and fruits outofseason;
nothing was too good for Artists, Duncans, Greeks;

and the nineties London liked her gall.

In Kensington and even in Mayfair she danced at parties in private
houses,

the Britishers, Prince Edward down,

were carried away by her preraphaelite beauty

her lusty American innocence

her California accent.

After London, Paris during the great exposition of nineteen hundred.
She danced with Loïe Fuller. She was still a virgin too shy to return the
advances of Rodin the great master, completely baffled by the extraordinary behavior of Loïe Fuller's circle of crackbrained invert beauties.
The Duncans were vegetarians, suspicious of vulgarity and men and
materialism. Raymond made them all sandals.

Isadora and her mother and her brother Raymond went about Europe in
sandals and fillets and Greek tunics

staying at the best hotels leading the Greek life of nature in a flutter of
unpaid bills.

Isadora's first solo recital was at a theater in Budapest;

after that she was the diva, had a loveaffair with a leading actor; in
Munich the students took the horses out of her carriage. Everything was
flowers and handclapping and champagne suppers. In Berlin she was
the rage.

With the money she made on her German tour she took the Duncans all
to Greece. They arrived on a fishingboat from Ithaca. They posed in the
Parthenon for photographs and danced in the Theater of Dionysus and
trained a crowd of urchins to sing the ancient chorus from the *Suppliants*
and built a temple to live in on a hill overlooking the ruins of ancient
Athens, but there was no water on the hill and their money ran out before the temple was finished

so they had to stay at the Hôtel d'Angleterre and run up a bill there.
When credit gave out they took their chorus back to Berlin and put on
the *Suppliants* in ancient Greek. Meeting Isadora in her peplum marching

through the Tiergarten at the head of her Greek boys marching in order all in Greek tunics, the kaiserin's horse shied,

and her highness was thrown.

Isadora was the vogue.

She arrived in St. Petersburg in time to see the night funeral of the marchers shot down in front of the Winter Palace in 1905. It hurt her. She was an American like Walt Whitman; the murdering rulers of the world were not her people; artists were not on the side of the machine-guns; she was an American in a Greek tunic; she was for the people.

In St. Petersburg, still under the spell of the eighteenthcentury ballet of the court of the Sunking,

her dancing was considered dangerous by the authorities.

In Germany she founded a school with the help of her sister Elizabeth who did the organizing, and she had a baby by Gordon Craig.

She went to America in triumph as she'd always planned and harried the home philistines with a tour; her followers were all the time getting pinched for wearing Greek tunics; she found no freedom for Art in America.

Back in Paris it was the top of the world; Art meant Isadora. At the funeral of the Prince de Polignac she met the mythical millionaire (sewingmachine king) who was to be her backer and to finance her school. She went off with him in his yacht (whatever Isadora did was Art)

to dance in the Temple at Paestum

only for him,

but it rained and the musicians all got drenched. So they all got drunk instead.

Art was the millionaire life. Art was whatever Isadora did. She was carrying the millionaire's child to the great scandal of the oldlady club-women and spinster artlovers when she danced on her second American tour;

she took to drinking too much and stepping to the footlights and bawling out the boxholders.

Isadora was at the height of glory and scandal and power and wealth, her school going, her millionaire was about to build her a theater in Paris, and the Duncans were the priests of a cult (Art was whatever Isadora did),

when the car that was bringing her two children home from the other side of Paris stalled on a bridge across the Seine. Forgetting that he'd left the car in gear the chauffeur got out to crank the motor. The car started, knocked down the chauffeur, plunged off the bridge into the Seine.

The children and their nurse were drowned.

The rest of her life moved desperately on

in the clatter of scandalized tongues, among the kidding faces of reporters, the threatening of bailiffs, the expostulations of hotelmanagers bringing overdue bills.

Isadora drank too much, she couldn't keep her hands off goodlooking young men, she dyed her hair various shades of bright-red, she never took the trouble to make up her face properly, was careless about her dress, couldn't bother to keep her figure in shape, never could keep track of her money

but a great sense of health

filled the hall

when the pearshaped figure with the beautiful arms tramped forward slowly from the back of the stage.

She was afraid of nothing; she was a great dancer.

In her own city of San Francisco the politicians wouldn't let her dance in the Greek Theater they'd built under her influence. Wherever she went she gave offense to the philistines. When the war broke out she danced the *Marseillaise,* but it didn't seem quite respectable and she gave offense by refusing to give up Wagner or to show the proper respectable feelings

of satisfaction at the butchery.

On her South American tour

she picked up men everywhere,

a Spanish painter, a couple of prizefighters, a stoker on the boat, a Brazilian poet,

brawled in tangohalls, bawled out the Argentines for niggers from the footlights, lushly triumphed in Montevideo and Brazil; but if she had money she couldn't help scandalously spending it on tangodancers, handouts, afterthetheater suppers, the generous gesture, no, all on my bill. The managers gypped her. She was afraid of nothing, never ashamed in the public eye of the clatter of scandalized tongues, the headlines in the afternoon papers.

When October split the husk off the old world she remembered St. Petersburg, the coffins lurching through the silent streets, the white faces, the clenched fists that night in St. Petersburg, and danced the *Marche Slave*

and waved red cheesecloth under the noses of the Boston old ladies in Symphony Hall,

but when she went to Russia full of hope of a school and work and a new life in freedom, it was too enormous, it was too difficult: cold, vodka, lice, no service in the hotels, new and old still piled pellmell together, seedbed and scrapheap, she hadn't the patience, her life had been too easy;

she picked up a yellowhaired poet
and brought him back
to Europe and the grand hotels.

Yessenin smashed up a whole floor of the Adlon in Berlin in one drunken party, he ruined a suite at the Continental in Paris. When he went back to Russia he killed himself. It was too enormous, it was too difficult.

When it was impossible to raise any more money for Art, for the crowds eating and drinking in the hotel suites and the rent of Rolls-Royces and the board of her pupils and disciples,

Isadora went down to the Riviera to write her memoirs to scrape up some cash out of the American public that had awakened after the war to the crassness of materialism and the Greeks and scandal and Art, and still had dollars to spend.

She hired a studio in Nice, but she could never pay the rent. She'd quarreled with her millionaire. Her jewels, the famous emerald, the ermine cloak, the works of art presented by the artists had all gone into the pawnshops or been seized by hotelkeepers. All she had was the old blue drapes that had seen her great triumphs, a red-leather handbag, and an old furcoat that was split down the back.

She couldn't stop drinking or putting her arms round the neck of the nearest young man, if she got any cash she threw a party or gave it away.

She tried to drown herself but an English naval officer pulled her out of the moonlit Mediterranean.

One day at a little restaurant at Golfe Juan she picked up a goodlooking young wop who kept a garage and drove a little Bugatti racer.

Saying that she might want to buy the car, she made him go to her studio to take her out for a ride;

her friends didn't want her to go, said he was nothing but a mechanic, she insisted, she'd had a few drinks (there was nothing left she cared for in the world but a few drinks and a goodlooking young man);

she got in beside him and
she threw her heavilyfringed scarf round her neck with a big sweep she had and
turned back and said,
with the strong California accent her French never lost:
Adieu, mes amis, je vais à la gloire.

The mechanic put his car in gear and started.

The heavy trailing scarf caught in a wheel, wound tight. Her head was wrenched against the side of the car. The car stopped instantly; her neck was broken, her nose crushed, Isadora was dead.

STUDY QUESTIONS

1. It probably goes without saying that a biography frequently reveals as much (if not more) about the biographer as it does about the subject of the biography. How does this apply to Dos Passos' "Art and Isadora"? What is Dos Passos' attitude toward Isadora and her life? How does he use the persona of the biographer to reveal his own attitude toward her?

2. One of the most striking aspects of this biography is its style. What seem to be the major structural principles operating in this work? What is the relationship between the organization of the sentences and paragraphs on the one hand and the organization of the subject matter on the other? Is there any sense in which Dos Passos' style dominates the subject matter to the point of obscuring it? Does there seem to be any functional theatricality operating in both the style and the life of Isadora?

3. This is indeed a brief biography, which is not intended to present a full account of all the facts of Isadora Duncan's life. What principles seem to be governing the choices Dos Passos has made? For instance, why does he exclude certain facts (such as the date of her birth, her age at the time of her death, the fact that she was married to the Russian poet Yessenin, the name of "her millionaire," etc.) that you would expect to find in a conventional biography? Why does he repeat certain other observations? Why does he begin his biography of Isadora with a brief sketch of her mother's life? What are the effects of these techniques?

4. Compare Dos Passos' presentation with the views expressed in the biographies of Isadora Duncan by Sewell Stokes (1928), Mary Desti (1929), and Irma Duncan and A. R. Macdougall (1929).

D. H. Lawrence/Letter to Willard Johnson

born 1885

[August, 1924]

JUST BACK FROM THE SNAKE DANCE.

One wonders what one came for—what all those people went for. The Hopi country is hideous—a clayey pale-grey desert with death-grey *mesas* sticking up like broken pieces of ancient dry grey bread. And the hell of a lumpy trail for forty miles. Yet car after car lurched and bobbed and ducked across the dismalness, on Sunday afternoon.

The Hopi country is some forty miles across, and three stale *mesas* jut up in its desert. The dance was on the last *mesa,* and on the furthest brim of the last *mesa,* in Hotevilla. The various Hopi villages are like broken edges of bread crust, utterly grey and arid, on top of these *mesas:* and so you pass them: first Walpi; then unseen Chimopova: then Oraibi on the last *mesa:* and beyond Oraibi, on the same *mesa,* but on a still higher level of grey rag-rock, and away at the western brim, is Hotevilla.

The *pueblos* of little grey houses are largely in ruin, dry raggy bits of disheartening ruin. One wonders what dire necessity or what Cain-like stubbornness drove the Hopis to these dismal heights and extremities. Anyhow, once they got there, there was evidently no going back. But the *pueblos* are mostly ruin. And even then, very small.

Hotevilla is a scrap of a place with a plaza no bigger than a fair-sized back-yard: and the chief house on the square a ruin. But into this plaza finally three thousand onlookers piled. A mile from the village was improvised the official camping ground, like a corral with hundreds of black motor cars. Across the death-grey desert, bump and lurch, came strings of more black cars, like a funeral *cortège.* Till everybody had come— about three thousand bodies.

And all these bodies piled in the oblong plaza, on the roofs, in the ruined windows, and thick around on the sandy floor, under the old walls: a great crowd. There were Americans of all sorts, wild west and tame west, American women in pants, an extraordinary assortment of female breeches: and at least two women in skirts, relics of the last era. There were Navajo women in full skirts and velvet bodices: there were Hopi women in bright shawls: a negress in a low-cut black blouse and a black sailor hat: various half-breeds: and all the men to match. The ruined house had two wide square window-holes: in the one was forced an apparently naked young lady with a little black hat on. She laid her naked handsome arm like a white anaconda along the sill, and posed as Queen Semiramis seated and waiting. Behind her, the heads of various Americans to match: perhaps movie people. In the next window-hole, a poppy-show of Indian women in coloured shawls and glistening long black fringe above their conventionally demure eyes. Two windows to the west!

And what had they all come to see?—come so far, over so weary a way, to camp uncomfortably? To see a little bit of a snake dance in a plaza no bigger than a back-yard? Light grey-daubed antelope priests (so-called) and a dozen black-daubed snake-priests (so-called). No drums, no pageantry. A hollow muttering. And then one of the snake-priests hopping slowly round with the neck of a pale, bird-like snake nipped between his teeth, while six elder priests dusted the six younger, snake-adorned priests with prayer feathers on the shoulders, hopping behind like a children's game. Like a children's game—Old Roger is dead and is low in his grave! After a few little rounds, the man set his snake on the sand, and away it steered, towards the massed spectators sitting around: and after it came a snake-priest with a snake stick, picked it up with a flourish from the shrinking crowd, and handed it to an antelope priest in the background. The six young men renewed their snake as the eagle his youth—sometimes the youngest, a boy of fourteen or so, had a rattlesnake ornamentally dropping from his teeth, sometimes a racer, a thin whip snake, sometimes a heavier bullsnake, which wrapped its long end round his knee like a garter—till he calmly undid it. More snakes, till the priests at the back had little armfuls, like armfuls of silk stockings that they were going to hang on the line to dry.

When all the snakes had had their little ride in a man's mouth, and had made their little excursion towards the crowd, they were all gathered, like a real lot of wet silk stockings—say forty—or thirty—and left to wriggle all together for a minute in meal, corn-meal, that the women of the *pueblo* had laid down on the sand of the plaza. Then, hey presto!—they were snatched up like fallen washing, and the two priests ran away with them westward, down the *mesa,* to set them free among the rocks, at the snake-shrine (so-called).

And it was over. Navajos began to ride to the sunset, black motor-cars began to scuttle with their backs to the light. It was over.

And what had we come to see, all of us? Men with snakes in their mouths, like a circus? Nice clean snakes, all washed and cold-creamed by the priests (so-called). Like wet pale silk stockings. Snakes with little bird-like heads, that bit nobody, but looked more harmless than doves? And funny men with blackened faces and whitened jaws, like a corpse band?

A show? But it was a tiny little show, for all that distance.

Just a show! The south-west is the great playground of the white American. The desert isn't good for anything else. But it does make a fine national playground. And the Indian, with his long hair and his bits of pottery and blankets and clumsy home-made trinkets, he's a wonderful live toy to play with. More fun than keeping rabbits, and just as harmless. Wonderful, really, hopping round with a snake in his mouth. Lots of fun! Oh, the wild west is lots of fun: the Land of Enchantment. Like being right inside the circus-ring: lots of sand, and painted savages jabbering, and snakes and all that. Come on, boys! Lots of fun! The great south-west, the national circus-ground. Come on boys; we've every bit as much right to it as anybody else. Lots of fun!

. . .

STUDY QUESTIONS

1. Consider the various stances or postures Lawrence assumes in his letter. What several masks does he wear, and what is his apparent purpose in putting on each mask? How does the audience *in* the letter shift as the persona shifts his postures? Consider, for example, why the persona begins the letter with

the highly formal and objective sentence *"One* wonders what *one* came for," shifts to "And what had *they* all come to see," and finally moves to "And what had *we* come to see, all of us?" (italics added). With what degree of clarity does Lawrence seem to understand his own position as a spectator at the Snake Dance? What does this qualified clarity suggest about the persona? Is it possible that Lawrence's tone, or the stances he assumes, could interfere with his apparent rhetorical purpose in the letter?

2. How do the recurrent images of "bread" and "greyness" operate in this letter? Do the functions of these images shift when the persona shifts stances?

3. What seem to be Lawrence's attitudes toward Americans? the Southwest? the Hopi ritual? the snakes? How could you express his emotional responses toward the various groups of persons and activities described in this letter? How does Lawrence seem to project himself and his own values into the significance of the dance, and how much does he allow himself to be affected by the values in the ritual (and the culture out of which it grows) itself?

4. J. Middleton Murry's *Reminiscences of D. H. Lawrence* (London: Jonathan Cape, 1933) gives the following brief account of Lawrence's experience at the Hopi Snake Dance: "In August he went to the Hopi country in Arizona to see the Snake Dance, and sent me an essay on it which he was anxious for me to read, because it 'defined somewhat his position.' I don't know that it did this; but it was an essay full of the delicate and spontaneous imaginative sympathy which Lawrence always insisted on calling 'blood-tenderness,' as opposed to the enforced 'benevolence' which he hated" (p. 116). Lawrence's essay was subsequently published in *Theatre Arts* (December 1924), and he was quite pleased with it. Does this article shed any additional light on the position Lawrence takes in his letter to Willard Johnson? How do his impressions immediately after the Snake Dance (those recorded in the letter) compare with his thoughts reflected in his article in *Theatre Arts*? How much of his initial impression has remained constant? What has been altered through the temporal distance of the experience?

George Bernard Shaw (*born 1856*) **and Mrs. Patrick Campbell** (*born 1865*)/Their Correspondence

33, Kensington Square, W.
14th Nov. 1912

You didn't *really* think that I believed you came to see me because you were interested in *me.* I knew it was Liza and I was delighted that you should be so businesslike in such a bewilderingly charming way—

I see how things are going—and you musn't think of me anywhere but still in bed gazing at the cracked Kensington Square ceiling—and a calm and safe peace too!—

No indeed—not for one minute did I flatter myself!—Cissy Loftus—

Lillah—Dolly Minto—Gertrude Kingston—or Lady Bancroft (she would be the best). I can see them all in "Liza".

My love to you,
Stella.

I hope all is going well tonight and our dear friends not killing themselves.

33, Kensington Square, W.
18th Nov. 1912

No more shams—a real love letter this time—then I can breathe freely, and perhaps who knows begin to sit up and get well—

I haven't said "kiss me" because life is too short for the kiss my heart calls for. . . . All your words are as idle wind—Look into my eyes for two minutes without speaking if you dare! Where would be your 54 years? and my grandmothers heart? and how many hours would you be late for dinner?

—If you give me one kiss and you can only kiss me if I say "kiss me" and I will never say "kiss me" because I am a respectable widow and I wouldn't let any man kiss me unless I was sure of the wedding ring—

Stella (Liza. I mean)

Ayot St. Lawrence, Welwyn.
18th Nov. 1912

. . . If I looked into your eyes without speaking for two minutes (Silent for two minutes with an audience even of one! Impossible, cried the fiend; but I don't care) I might see heaven. And then I should just trot off and do ten years hard work and think it only a moment, leaving you staring.

Do you know, I dont hate you one little bit. I am clearly in my second childhood (56, not 54); for you might be the Virgin Mary and I an Irish peasant, and my feeling for you could not be more innocent; and yet there is no relation into which we could enter which would not be entirely natural and happy for me.

Such concord will make me silly. Let us work together and quarrel and come upon all sorts of incompatibilities. Our music must have discords in it or you will tire of it.

I think you are getting well. I hear a ring, I see a flash in your letter. The able courageous Stella is stirring. And perhaps she will put me away with the arrowroot. No matter: I shall rejoice and glory in her. If I could bring her a thousand of the most wonderful lovers, she should have them; and I would polish their boots—and perhaps occasionally their brains—for her with entire contentment.

Goodnightest G. B. S.

33, Kensington Square, W.
[postmark: 26th Nov. 1912]

That was a most nice letter—of course you have guessed I have had a 'set back' and I have been very ill—or I would have written. Please when you have time come and see me, and tell me what to do to be hale and hearty again.

Stella.

. . .

Ayot St. Lawrence, Welwyn.
27th Nov. 1912

Oh, all they say is true. I have no heart. Here I am, with my brains grinding like millstones, writing a preface for my long belated volume of plays, and stopping only to bring my quick firers into action by hurling a devastating letter into some public controversy. Grind, grind; bang, bang; broken heads and broken wings everywhere within range; "and this word Love which greybeard calls Divine, be resident in men like one another and not in me: *I* am myself alone". (Applause, started by the tragedian himself with his boot heels).

Stella! Who is Stella? Did I ever know anybody named Stella? Cant remember: what does it matter? I have articles to write and the preface to finish. I have to debate with Hilaire Belloc in the Queen's Hall on the 28th January. Not an advertisement has appeared, and the hall is nearly sold out already. (And actresses talk to me of their popularity!). Belloc shall perish. I try to get back to Elysium and Stella; but a tempest of blighting, blasting withering arguments bursts out of me and scorches all the trees of Paradise. I want no Stella: I want my brains, my pen, my platform, my audience, my adversary, my mission. I read Belloc's book (*The Servile State,* ha! ha!) the other day. I will tear it to rags. Collapse of Socialism, says Chesterton in *Everyman.* I have already scattered his collapse to the four thousand winds of hell. Parents and Children: that is the theme of my preface. The tears of countless children have fallen unrevenged. I will turn them into boiling vitriol and force it into the souls of their screaming oppressors.

Stella! Who is Stella? A woman, Well, can she love a human dredger? does she want to clasp brass to her bosom—oh, her bosom! I remember now—the jade!—when she first took my hand she shook it so that it touched her bosom, an infamous abandoned trick: it thrilled through me, through all my brass for hours. That must have been centuries ago: I was young and foolish then and could be thrilled. What did she care for me then? What was my knuckle to her—it caught me just on the knuckle —more than a mutton bone or a door knocker? Bear witness, all ye clouds of Kensington Square, that I did not move a muscle. Had she felt what I felt she would have risen up into the skies and set me there at her right hand. Am I the man to whom that happened? No; the grind-stones are at work; it is to their sparks and their whirring that I thrill. Press the levers of Babbage's Calculating Machine to your bosom Stella; and—oh, I am lying: this unlucky recollection has knocked Belloc out of my head and almost made the grindstones stop. It is well that you are ill; if you were to appear in the front row of the balcony of Queen's Hall on 28th January, I might betray my cause; for women always pity the vanquished and hate the insolent conqueror. Think of me always as the hero of a thousand defeats; it is only on paper and in imagination that I do anything brave.

All the same, it is certain that I am a callous creature; for I have let you write to me twice—no; that cant be. I *did* answer. But would not a man with a grain of heart have written ten times? Oh I have been hard as nails for a fortnight past. I was when I began this letter.—I shall be so again when I post it. But now—just for a moment—only a moment— before the grindstones begin again. Perhaps I shall sleep well tonight; it is hard to put a man of brass to sleep.

And now I must stop myself resolutely for a moment, and think of somebody besides myself. I am being kept down here for the good of my health and to save the grindstones from interruption. On Sunday I must go up to town; for I have to address a meeting in the East End in the after-noon and speak at the William Poel dinner in the evening. And I shall spend next week in London. On Monday I have to lecture for Lena Ash-well at her Three Arts Club—something about whether professional artists can have any self respect—or is it Tuesday? Anyhow, Monday and Tues-day are crammed. Later, I may have an afternoon. Your setback makes me desperate: I had set my heart on your getting well with a rush this time. Oh you must, you must, you shall be torn out of bed and shaken into rude health. Or else I will get into the bed myself and we shall perish together scandalously. Oh, why cant I do anything? What use are grind-stones after all? Goodnight, and forgive my follies.

G. B. S.

. . .

33, Kensington Square, W.
2nd Dec. 1912

Most dear man of brass, full of grindstones and things!—its a sad woman thats writing to you—for the doctors tell me that in 6 weeks I have made no improvement and they cannot let me lie here much longer—and —Oh, but I am not going to tell you—I was such a green sick skeleton those days I didn't write and I am so glad you didn't see me—You are raging against the world—I see bits about it in the paper—a letter in the Westminster. I should like to hear you on January 28th.

—I must see that Rodin article. I hear about someone calling it "subtle humour"—and another raging in anger against it, and I want to know what its all about—

—I think if you don't come and see me rather soon there won't be me to see—I forgive you your follies sure enough—think of mine!

Stella.

STUDY QUESTIONS

1. In his edition of the correspondence between Shaw and Mrs. Patrick Campbell, Alan Dent points to the first two letters reprinted here as good examples of why "Mrs. Campbell's epistolary style . . . does not always translate easily to the printed page":

   The word "really" is underlined five times in strokes of gradually diminishing length, the word "me" in the second line seven times. And the whole letter is dashed off with an impetuosity that has no time for a full stop or even, sometimes, conventional capital letters [p. 56].

   Dent has raised an interesting problem here, for as an editor he is faced with the dilemma of the inadequacy of print. However, Mrs. Patrick Campbell, too, has a problem in trying to translate through pen and paper the sounds of her voice and the emotions informing those sounds. She tries through underlinings and dashes to give something of her living presence to her letters. What other evidence of her personality do you find in her style? How could you reinstate these letters to their original form (that is, Mrs. Campbell's situation as she writes them)? What aspects of her nonverbal manner are suggested by her verbal style? How much of "Mrs. Patrick Campbell the Actress" is apparent in her letters to Shaw?

2. Shaw's style is clearly quite different from Mrs. Campbell's; but his style, too, has much of the quality of direct speech. How do such characteristics as the parenthetical remarks, exclamations, repetitions, and quotations function in revealing his personality as well as his nonverbal behavior? How do the bombast and the romance, the apparent self-effacing and the elaborate proclamations balance within his letters? What do the kinds of thought and image transitions Shaw employs reveal about him? How much of "George Bernard Shaw the Dramatist and Critic" is apparent in his letters to Stella?

3. At this stage in their correspondence Shaw was fifty-six and Mrs. Campbell forty-eight. They had been corresponding for nearly fourteen years, during which time Shaw was gaining increasing prominence as a dramatist and critic. Mrs. Campbell, on the other hand, by 1912 had (with the exception of her

highly acclaimed performance in *Pygmalion*) already reached the heights of success that she was to know as an actress. Their correspondence, which began in 1899 and lasted for nearly forty years, provides a striking portrait of the intimate, touching, witty, and, at times, discordant relationship between these two powerful personalities. From the evidence of these letters, how would you describe their relationship at this stage? Read some of their earlier correspondence as well as the later letters and compare the relationship between Shaw and Stella during the different periods in their lives. How does each person's individual character seem to affect their relationship during the various stages of their correspondence? How does their relationship seem to affect their behavior as individuals?

4. Consider several modes of performance that would help clarify the epistolary situations involved in this correspondence. What does each mode reveal about the attitude of each letter writer toward his addressee? What light does it throw on the attitude of the recipient toward the letter writer? Try some of the following possibilities:

   a. Read Shaw's letters as if you (as Shaw) were composing them to Mrs. Campbell at the moment; read Mrs. Campbell's letters as if you (as Mrs. Campbell) were composing them as you speak.

   b. Speak the letters as if they were direct discourse between Shaw and Mrs. Campbell.

   c. Read the entire correspondence from the points of view of either Shaw or Mrs. Campbell.

   d. Read the letters from the points of view of the recipients.

   e. Have two persons read the correspondence so that the utterance and the nonverbal response can be demonstrated simultaneously.

   Does any one mode seem more successful in clarifying the relationship between Shaw and Stella? Can you discover any other possibilities that would move you closer to the experience of these two persons and their relationship?

John Jay Chapman/The Coatesville Address

born 1862

We are met to commemorate the anniversary of one of the most dreadful crimes in history—not for the purpose of condemning it, but to repent for our share in it. We do not start any agitation with regard to that particular crime. I understand that an attempt to prosecute the chief criminals has been made, and has entirely failed; because the whole community, and in a sense our whole people, are really involved in the guilt. The failure of the prosecution in this case, in all such cases, is only a proof of the magnitude of the guilt and of the awful fact that everyone shares in it.

I will tell you why I am here; I will tell you what happened to me. When I read in the newspapers of August 14, a year ago, about the burning alive of a human being, and of how a few desperate, fiend-minded men had been permitted to torture a man chained to an iron bedstead, burning alive, thrust back by pitchforks when he struggled out of it, while around about stood hundreds of well-dressed American citizens, both from the vicinity and from afar, coming on foot and in wagons, assembling on telephone calls, as if by magic, silent, whether from terror or indifference, fascinated and impotent, hundreds of persons watching this awful sight and making no attempt to stay the wickedness, and no one man among them all who was inspired to risk his life in an attempt to stop it, no one man to name the name of Christ, of humanity, of government! As I read the newspaper accounts of the scene enacted here in Coatesville a year ago, I seemed to get a glimpse into the unconscious soul of this country. I saw a seldom revealed picture of the American heart and of the American nature. I seemed to be looking into the heart of the criminal—a cold thing, an awful thing.

I said to myself, "I shall forget this, we shall all forget it; but it will be there. What I have seen is not an illusion. It is the truth. I have seen death in the heart of this people." For to look at the agony of a fellow-being and remain aloof means death in the heart of the onlooker. Religious fanaticism has sometimes lifted men to the frenzy of such cruelty, political passion has sometimes done it, personal hatred might do it, the excitement of the amphitheater in the degenerate days of Roman luxury could do it. But here an audience chosen by chance in America has stood spellbound through an improvised *auto-da-fé,* irregular, illegal, having no religious significance, not sanctioned by custom, having no immediate provocation, the audience standing by merely in cold dislike.

I saw during one moment something beyond all argument in the depth of its significance. You might call it the paralysis of the nerves about the heart in a people habitually and unconsciously given over to selfish aims, an ignorant people who knew not what spectacle they were providing, or what part they were playing in a judgment-play which history was exhibiting on that day.

No theories about the race problem, no statistics, legislation, or mere educational endeavor, can quite meet the lack which that day revealed in the American people. For what we saw was death. The people stood like blighted things, like ghosts about Acheron, waiting for someone or something to determine their destiny for them.

Whatever life itself is, that thing must be replenished in us. The opposite of hate is love, the opposite of cold is heat; what we need is the love of God and reverence for human nature. For one moment I knew that I had seen our true need; and I was afraid that I should forget it and that I should start schemes of education, when the need was deeper than education. And I became filled with one idea, that I must not forget what I had seen, and that I must do something to remember it. And I am here today chiefly that I may remember that vision. It seems fitting to come to this town where the crime occurred and hold a prayer-meeting, so that our hearts may be turned to God through whom mercy may flow into us.

Let me say something more about the whole matter. The subject we are dealing with is not local. The act, to be sure, took place at Coatesville and everyone looked to Coatesville to follow it up. Some months ago I asked a friend who lives not far from here something about this case, and about the expected prosecutions, and he replied to me: "It wasn't in my county," and that made me wonder whose county it was in. And it seemed to be in my county. I live on the Hudson River; but I knew that this great wickedness that happened in Coatesville is not the wickedness of Coatesville nor of today. It is the wickedness of all America and of three hundred years—the wickedness of the slave trade. All of us are tinctured by it. No special place, no special persons, are to blame. A nation cannot practice a course of inhuman crime for three hundred years and then suddenly throw off the effects of it. Less than fifty years ago domestic slavery was abolished among us; and in one way and another the marks of that vice are in our faces. There is no country in Europe where the Coatesville tragedy or anything remotely like it could have been enacted, probably no country in the world.

On the day of the calamity, those people in the automobiles came by the hundred and watched the torture, and passers-by came in a great multitude and watched it—and did nothing. On the next morning the newspapers spread the news and spread the paralysis until the whole country seemed to be helplessly watching this awful murder, as awful as anything ever done on the earth; and the whole of our people seemed to be looking on helplessly, not able to respond, not knowing what to do next. That spectacle has been in my mind.

The trouble has come down to us out of the past. The only reason slavery is wrong is that it is cruel and makes men cruel and leaves them cruel. Someone may say that you and I cannot repent because we did not do the act. But we are involved in it. We are still looking on. Do you not see that this whole event is merely the last parable, the most vivid, the most terrible illustration that ever was given by man or imagined by a Jewish prophet, of the relation between good and evil in this world, and of the relation of men to one another?

This whole matter has been an historic episode; but it is a part, not only of our national history, but of the personal history of each one of us. With the great disease (slavery) came the climax (the war), and after the climax gradually began the cure, and in the process of cure comes now the knowledge of what the evil was. I say that our need is new life, and that books and resolutions will not save us, but only such disposition in our hearts and souls as will enable the new life, love, force, hope, virtue, which surround us always, to enter into us.

This is the discovery that each man must make for himself—the discovery that what he really stands in need of he cannot get for himself, but must wait till God gives it to him. I have felt the impulse to come here today to testify to this truth.

The occasion is not small; the occasion looks back on three centuries and embraces a hemisphere. Yet the occasion is small compared with the truth it leads us to. For this truth touches all ages and affects every soul in the world.

STUDY QUESTIONS

1. What is the principle of arrangement in this speech; that is, how has it been organized? Can you describe a principle of arrangement that will account for the particular order of paragraphs 4 through 7? Change the order of these four paragraphs and read the speech aloud: Has the overall effect of the speech been changed?

2. What sort of person does the speaker seem to be? What image of the speaker does the speech itself present?

3. What seems to be the purpose of this speech?

4. The speech itself was delivered first on Sunday, August 18, 1912. In *Rhetorical Criticism* (New York: Macmillan, 1965), Edwin Black describes the speech setting in these words:

   On August 14, 1911 Chapman read in New York City newspapers an account of a particularly brutal lynching of a Negro in Coatesville, Pennsylvania. Although he was not personally associated in any way with the persons or place involved in the atrocity, Chapman brooded on the event. As the first anniversary of the lynching approached, Chapman announced to his family that he was going to Coatesville to hold a prayer meeting and to deliver a speech commemorating the terrible occasion. In Coatesville Chapman encountered a population suspicious of his motives and growing increasingly sensitive to the approaching anniversary. After frustrating attempts to find a hall in Coatesville suitable for his meeting, Chapman finally succeeded in renting an empty store. He placed advertisements in the local paper, and held his prayer meeting on Sunday, August 18, 1912. The speech was his sermon. He delivered it to an audience of three persons: a lady friend who had accompanied him to Coatesville, an elderly Negro woman, and an unidentified man, believed to be a local spy [pp. 78–79].

   Can you describe exactly how this knowledge contributes to your interpretation of the speech? (It is hoped that you read the text of the speech before you read these exercises.)

5. One of the conventional ways of distinguishing between a speech and a poem is that it is very difficult, if not impossible, to abstract the text of a speech from its particular setting, the character of the speaker, and the nature of the audience. On the other hand, "The Coatesville Address" does not seem designed solely for the three people who comprised its audience in the empty store. Also, the facts of Chapman's life would tend to indicate that the sort of character we glimpse in this speech was assumed for the occasion. In short, Chapman seems to be speaking to a generalized audience, and he has constructed a

persona for the purposes of his discourse in the way a poet might. Furthermore, another conventional distinction between a speech and a poem is that the former has practical persuasion as its aim and the latter seeks to achieve an aesthetic effect. Yet, how different in aim does this speech seem to be from many of the poems in Chapter Three—say, Langston Hughes' "Dream Deferred"? Black argues that Chapman's purpose is "to shape the appropriate reaction to the event." Could it not be argued that this is a persuasive intent inherent in many speeches and poems? The questions raised here could profitably be explored in a short paper comparing the rhetorical qualities of this speech with those of a poem, perhaps the Langston Hughes poem discussed later. The writer of the paper should begin by reading Black's excellent discussion of this speech in *Rhetorical Criticism*, pp. 78–90.

Martin Luther King, Jr./I Have a Dream

born 1929

Five score years ago, a great American, in whose symbolic shadow we stand, signed the Emancipation Proclamation. This momentous decree came as a great beacon light of hope to millions of Negro slaves who had been seared in the flames of withering injustice. It came as a joyous daybreak to end the long night of captivity.

But one hundred years later, we must face the tragic fact that the Negro is still not free. One hundred years later, the life of the Negro is still sadly crippled by the manacles of segregation and the chains of discrimination. One hundred years later, the Negro lives on a lonely island of poverty in the midst of a vast ocean of material prosperity. One hundred years later, the Negro is still languished in the corners of American society and finds himself an exile in his own land. So we have come here today to dramatize an appalling condition.

In a sense we have come to our Nation's Capital to cash a check. When the architects of our Republic wrote the magnificent words of the Constitution and the Declaration of Independence, they were signing a promissory note to which every American was to fall heir. This note was a promise that all men would be guaranteed the unalienable rights of life, liberty, and the pursuit of happiness.

It is obvious today that America has defaulted on this promissory note insofar as her citizens of color are concerned. Instead of honoring this sacred obligation, America has given the Negro people a bad check; a check which has come back marked "insufficient funds." But we refuse to believe that the bank of justice is bankrupt. We refuse to believe that there are insufficient funds in the great vaults of opportunity of this nation. So we have come to cash this check—a check that will give us upon demand the riches of freedom and the security of justice.

We have also come to this hallowed spot to remind America of the fierce urgency of now. This is no time to engage in the luxury of cooling off or to take the tranquilizing drug of gradualism. Now is the time to make real the promises of Democracy. Now is the time to rise from the dark and desolate valley of segregation to the sunlit path of racial justice. Now is the time to open the doors of opportunity to all of God's children. Now is the time to lift our nation from the quicksands of racial injustice to the solid rock of brotherhood.

It would be fatal for the nation to overlook the urgency of the moment and to underestimate the determination of the Negro. This sweltering summer of the Negro's legitimate discontent will not pass until there is an invigorating autumn of freedom and equality; 1963 is not an end, but a beginning. Those who hope that the Negro needed to blow off steam and will now be content will have a rude awakening if the Nation returns to business as usual. There will be neither rest nor tranquility in America until the Negro is granted his citizenship rights. The whirlwinds of revolt will continue to shake the foundations of our Nation until the bright day of justice emerges.

But there is something that I must say to my people who stand on the warm threshold which leads into the palace of justice. In the process of gaining our rightful place we must not be guilty of wrongful deeds. Let us not seek to satisfy our thirst for freedom by drinking from the cup of bitterness and hatred. We must forever conduct our struggle on the high plane of dignity and discipline. We must not allow our creative protest to degenerate into physical violence. Again and again we must rise to the majestic heights of meeting physical force with soul force. The marvelous new militancy which has engulfed the Negro community must not lead us to a distrust of all white people, for many of our white brothers, as evidenced by their presence here today, have come to realize that their destiny is tied up with our destiny and their freedom is inextricably bound to our freedom. We cannot walk alone.

And as we walk, we must make the pledge that we shall march ahead. We cannot turn back. There are those who are asking the devotees of civil rights, "When will you be satisfied?" We can never be satisfied as long as the Negro is the victim of the unspeakable horrors of police brutality. We can never be satisfied as long as our bodies, heavy with the fatigue of travel, cannot gain lodging in the motels of the highways and the hotels of the cities. We cannot be satisfied as long as the Negro's basic mobility is from a smaller ghetto to a larger one. We can never be satisfied as long as a Negro in Mississippi cannot vote and a Negro in New York believes he has nothing for which to vote. No, no we are not satisfied, and we will not be satisfied until justice rolls down like waters and righteousness like a mighty stream.

I am not unmindful that some of you have come here out of great trials and tribulations. Some of you have come fresh from narrow jail cells. Some of you have come from areas where your quest for freedom left you battered by the storms of persecution and staggered by the winds of police brutality. You have been the veterans of creative suffering. Continue to work with the faith that unearned suffering is redemptive.

Go back to Mississippi, go back to Alabama, go back to South Carolina, go back to Georgia, go back to Louisiana, go back to the slums and ghettos of our northern cities, knowing that somehow this situation can and will be changed. Let us not wallow in the valley of despair.

I say to you today, my friends, that in spite of the difficulties and frustrations of the moment I still have a dream. It is a dream deeply rooted in the American dream.

I have a dream that one day this nation will rise up and live out the true meaning of its creed: "We hold these truths to be self-evident; that all men are created equal."

I have a dream that one day on the red hills of Georgia the sons of former slaves and the sons of former slaveowners will be able to sit down together at the table of brotherhood.

I have a dream that one day even the state of Mississippi, a desert state sweltering with the heat of injustice and oppression, will be transformed into an oasis of freedom and justice.

I have a dream that my four little children will one day live in a nation where they will not be judged by the color of their skin but by the content of their character.

I have a dream today.

I have a dream that one day the state of Alabama, whose governor's lips are presently dripping with the words of interposition and nullification, will be transformed into a situation where little black boys and girls will be able to join hands with little white boys and white girls and walk together as sisters and brothers.

I have a dream today.

I have a dream that one day every valley shall be exalted, every hill and mountain shall be made low, the rough places will be made plains, and the crooked places will be made straight, and the glory of the Lord shall be revealed, and all flesh shall see it together.

This is our hope. This is the faith with which I return to the South. With this faith we will be able to hew out of the mountain of despair a stone of hope. With this faith we will be able to transform the jangling discords of our nation into a beautiful symphony of brotherhood. With this faith we will be able to work together, to pray together, to struggle together, to go to jail together, to stand up for freedom together, knowing that we will be free one day.

This will be the day when all of God's children will be able to sing with new meaning, "My country 'tis of thee, sweet land of liberty, of thee I sing.

Land where my fathers died, land of the pilgrim's pride, from every mountainside, let freedom ring."

And if America is to be a great nation this must become true. So let freedom ring from the prodigious hilltops of New Hampshire. Let freedom ring from the mighty mountains of New York. Let freedom ring from the heightening Alleghenies of Pennsylvania!

Let freedom ring from the snowcapped Rockies of Colorado!

Let freedom ring from the curvacious peaks of California!

But not only that; let freedom ring from Stone Mountain of Georgia!

Let freedom ring from every hill and molehill of Mississippi. From every mountainside, let freedom ring.

When we let freedom ring, when we let it ring from every village and every hamlet, from every state and every city, we will be able to speed up that day when all of God's children, black men and white men, Jews and Gentiles, Protestants and Catholics, will be able to join hands and sing in the words of that old Negro spiritual, "Free at last! Free at last! Thank God almighty, we are free at last!"

STUDY QUESTIONS

1. One of the most highly acclaimed speeches of the civil rights movement, "I Have a Dream," was delivered on August 28, 1963, at the climax of the famous March on Washington. A crowd of over 200,000 blacks and whites had converged on the nation's capital to dramatize black demands for equal rights. At the moment of Dr. King's speech the crowd was gathered before the Lincoln Memorial, in front of which a speaker's stand had been erected. Considering this speaking situation, you as the oral interpreter might feel that the speech should be given with force and vehemence. Try delivering the speech forcefully, as if you were addressing a large crowd. Then render the speech quietly, as if you were speaking to a small gathering or only to yourself. What qualities of speech structure are emphasized in each mode of delivery?

2. How is the speech arranged? In a time sequence? In a logical sequence? A profitable way to analyze the structure of this speech may be in terms of its emotional arrangement—that is, the ways in which one emotion leads to, or relates to, the next. In the experiment suggested above, is one mode of delivery more suggestive of the arrangement of emotions than the other?

3. Note the many allusions in the speech, for example, to the Gettysburg Address, to Shakespeare, to Isaiah 40, to an old spiritual. Note, too, the many shifts in style (especially from a high, rather formal style to the colloquial), for example, "One hundred years later, the Negro is still languished in the corners of American society and finds himself an exile in his own land. So we have come here today to dramatize an appalling condition. In a sense we have come to our Nation's Capital to cash a check"; and "We can never be satisfied as long as our bodies, heavy with the fatigue of travel, cannot gain lodging in the

motels of the highways and the hotels of the cities." What do these allusions and shifts indicate about the speaker's character or emotions or the character and emotions of the audience?

4. Perhaps more than any other structural element the repetitions in the speech underscore the speaker's emotions. Note the echoes that these repetitions create. As used in fundamentalist sermons or other types of impassioned oratory, these repetitions, or echoes, have proved to be an extremely effective way of eliciting the audience's response, even the audience's participation in the speech itself. Once the pattern of repetition is set, the audience can anticipate the fulfillment of the pattern. (That this rhetorical strategy worked can be demonstrated by playing a recording of the actual delivery of the speech.) Try reading the speech with a heavy emphasis on its pattern, particularly in the final, italicized part. What happens to your emotions as you do this? Does this pattern serve to underscore, or to call attention away from, the thoughts being expressed?

Mark Twain/The Story of a Speech

born 1835

> *An address delivered in 1877, and a review of it twenty-nine years later. The original speech was delivered at a dinner given by the publishers of* The Atlantic Monthly *in honor of the seventieth anniversary of the birth of John Greenleaf Whittier, at the Hotel Brunswick, Boston, December 17, 1877.*

THE SPEECH

This is an occasion peculiarly meet for the digging up of pleasant reminiscences concerning literary folk; therefore I will drop lightly into history myself. Standing here on the shore of the Atlantic and contemplating certain of its largest literary billows, I am reminded of a thing which happened to me thirteen years ago, when I had just succeeded in stirring up a little Nevadian literary puddle myself, whose spume-flakes were beginning to blow thinly Californiaward. I started an inspection tramp through the southern mines of California. I was callow and conceited, and I resolved to try the virtue of my *nom de guerre.*

I very soon had an opportunity. I knocked at a miner's lonely log cabin in the foot-hills of the Sierras just at nightfall. It was snowing at the time. A jaded, melancholy man of fifty, barefooted, opened the door to me. When he heard my *nom de guerre* he looked more dejected than before. He let me in—pretty reluctantly, I thought—and after the customary bacon and beans, black coffee and hot whiskey, I took a pipe. This sorrowful man had not said three words up to this time. Now he spoke up and said, in the voice of one who is secretly suffering, "You're the fourth—I'm going to move." "The fourth what?" said I. "The fourth literary man that has been here in twenty-four hours—I'm going to move." "You don't tell me!" said I; "who were the others?" "Mr. Longfellow, Mr. Emerson, and Mr. Oliver Wendell Holmes—consound the lot!"

You can easily believe I was interested. I supplicated—three hot whiskies did the rest—and finally the melancholy miner began. Said he:

"They came here just at dark yesterday evening, and I let them in, of course. Said they were going to the Yosemite. They were a rough lot, but that's nothing; everybody looks rough that travels afoot. Mr. Emerson was a seedy little bit of a chap, redheaded. Mr. Holmes was as fat as a balloon; he weighed as much as three hundred, and had double chins all the way down to his stomach. Mr. Longfellow was built like a prize-fighter. His head was cropped and bristly, like as if he had a wig made of hairbrushes. His nose lay straight down his face, like a finger with the end joint tilted up. They had been drinking, I could see that. And what queer talk they used! Mr. Holmes inspected this cabin, then he took me by the buttonhole, and says he:

" 'Through the deep caves of thought
   I hear a voice that sings,
   Build thee more stately mansions,
   O my soul!'

"Says I, 'I can't afford it, Mr. Holmes, and moreover I don't want to.' Blamed if I liked it pretty well, either, coming from a stranger, that way. However, I started to get out my bacon and beans, when Mr. Emerson came and looked on awhile, and then *he* takes me aside by the buttonhole and says:

" 'Gives me agates for my meat;
   Gives me cantharids to eat;
   From air and ocean bring me foods,
   From all zones and altitudes.'

"Says I, 'Mr. Emerson, if you'll excuse me, this ain't no hotel.' You see it sort of riled me—I warn't used to the ways of littery swells. But I went on a-sweating over my work, and next comes Mr. Longfellow and buttonholes me, and interrupts me. Says he:

" 'Honor be to Mudjekeewis!
   You shall hear how Pau-Puk-Keewis—'

"But I broke in, and says I, 'Beg your pardon, Mr. Longfellow, if you'll be so kind as to hold your yawp for about five minutes and let me get this grub ready, you'll do me proud.' Well, sir, after they'd filled up I set out the jug. Mr. Holmes looks at it, and then he fires up all of sudden and yells:

" 'Flash out a stream of blood-red wine!
For I would drink to other days.'

"By George, I was getting kind of worked up. I don't deny it, I was getting kind of worked up. I turns to Mr. Holmes, and says I, 'Looky here, my fat friend, I'm a-running this shanty, and if the court knows herself, you'll take whisky straight or you'll go dry.' Them's the very words I said to him. Now I don't want to sass such famous littery people, but you see they kind of forced me. There ain't nothing onreasonable 'bout me; I don't mind a passel of guests a-treadin' on my tail three or four times, but when it comes to *standing* on it it's different, 'and if the court knows herself,' I says, 'you'll take whisky straight or you'll go dry.' Well, between drinks they'd swell around the cabin and strike attitudes and spout; and pretty soon they got out a greasy old deck and went to playing euchre at ten cents a corner—on trust. I began to notice some pretty suspicious things. Mr. Emerson dealt, looked at his hand, shook his head, says:

" 'I am the doubter and the doubt—'

and ca'mly bunched the hands and went to shuffling for a new layout. Says he:

" 'They reckon ill who leave me out;
They know not well the subtle ways I keep
I pass and deal *again!*'

Hang'd if he didn't go ahead and do it, too! Oh, he was a cool one! Well, in about a minute things were running pretty tight, but all of a sudden I see by Mr. Emerson's eye he judged he had 'em. He had already corralled two tricks, and each of the others one. So now he kind of lifts a little in his chair and says:

" 'I tire of globes and aces!—
Too long the game is played!'

—and down he fetched a right bower. Mr. Longfellow smiles as sweet as pie and says:

" 'Thanks thanks to thee, my worthy friend,
For the lesson thou hast taught,'

—and blamed if he didn't down with *another* right bower! Emerson claps his hand on his bowie, Longfellow claps his on his revolver, and I went under a bunk. There was going to be trouble; but that monstrous Holmes rose up, wobbling his double chins, and says he, 'Order, gentlemen; the first man that draws, I'll lay down on him and smother him!' All quiet on the Potomac, you bet!

"They were pretty how-come-you-so by now, and they begun to blow. Emerson says, 'The nobbiest thing I ever wrote was "Barbara Frietchie." '

Says Longfellow, 'It don't begin with my "Biglow Papers." ' Says Holmes, 'My "Thanatopsis" lays over 'em both.' They mighty near ended in a fight. Then they wished they had some more company—and Mr. Emerson pointed to me and says:

" 'Is yonder squalid peasant all
    That this proud nursery could breed?'

He was a-whetting his bowie on his boot—so I let it pass. Well, sir, next they took it into their heads that they would like some music; so they made me stand up and sing "When Johnny Comes Marching Home" till I dropped —at thirteen minutes past four this morning. That's what I've been through, my friend. When I woke at seven, they were leaving, thank goodness, and Mr. Longfellow had my only boots on, and his'n under his arm. Says I, 'Hold on, there, Evangeline, what are you going to do with *them*?' He says, 'Going to make tracks with 'em, because:

" 'Lives of great men all remind us
    We can make our lives sublime;
And, departing, leave behind us
    Footprints on the sands of time.'

As I said, Mr. Twain, you are the fourth in twenty-four hours—and I'm going to move; I ain't suited to a littery atmosphere."

I said to the miner, "Why, my dear sir, *these* were not the gracious singers to whom we and the world pay loving reverence and homage; these were imposters."

The miner investigated me with a calm eye for awhile; then said he, "Ah! impostors, were they? Are *you*?"

I did not pursue the subject, and since then I have not traveled on my *nom de guerre* enough to hurt. Such was the reminiscence I was moved to contribute, Mr. Chairman. In my enthusiasm I may have exaggerated the details a little, but you will easily forgive me that fault, since I believe it is the first time I have ever deflected from perpendicular fact on an occasion like this.

THE STORY

January 11, 1906

Answer to a letter received this morning:

Dear Mrs. H.,—I am forever your debtor for reminding me of that curious passage in my life. During the first year or two after it happened, I could not bear to think of it. My pain and shame were so intense, and my sense of having been an imbecile so settled, established and confirmed, that I drove the episode entirely from my mind—and so all these twenty-eight or twenty-nine years I have lived in the conviction that my performance of that time was coarse, vulgar, and destitute of humor. But your suggestion that you and your family found humor in it twenty-eight years ago moved me to look into the matter. So I commissioned a Boston typewriter to delve among the Boston papers of that bygone time and send me a copy of it.

It came this morning, and if there is any vulgarity about it I am not to discover it. If it isn't innocently and ridiculously funny, I am no judge. I will see to it that you get a copy.

What I have said to Mrs. H. is true. I did suffer during a year or two from the deep humiliations of the episode. But at last, in 1888, in Venice, my wife and I came across Mr. and Mrs. A. P. C., of Concord, Massachusetts, and a friendship began then of the sort which nothing but death terminates. The C.'s were very bright people and in every way charming and companionable. We were together a month or two in Venice and several months in Rome, afterward, and one day that lamented break of mine was mentioned. And when I was on the point of lathering those people for bringing it to my mind when I had gotten the memory of it almost squelched, I perceived with joy that the C.'s were indignant about the way that my performance had been received in Boston. They poured out their opinions most freely and frankly about the frosty attitude of the people who were present at that performance, and about the Boston newspapers for the position they had taken in regard to the matter. That position was that I had been irreverent beyond belief, beyond imagination. Very well; I had accepted that as a fact for a year or two, and had been thoroughly miserable about it whenever I thought of it—which was not frequently, if I could help it. Whenever I thought of it I wondered how I ever could have been inspired to do so unholy a thing. Well, the C.'s comforted me, but they did not persuade me to continue to think about the unhappy episode. I resisted that. I tried to get it out of my mind, and let it die, and I succeeded. Until Mrs. H.'s letter came, it had been a good twenty-five years since I had thought of that matter; and when she said that the thing was funny I wondered if possibly she might be right. At any rate, my curiosity was aroused, and I wrote to Boston and got the whole thing copied, as above set forth.

I vaguely remembered some of the details of that gathering—dimly I can see a hundred people—no, perhaps fifty—shadowy figures sitting at tables feeding, ghosts now to me, and nameless forevermore. I don't know who they were, but I can very distinctly see, seated at the grand table and facing the rest of us, Mr. Emerson, supernaturally grave, unsmiling; Mr. Whittier, grave, lovely, his beautiful spirit shining out of his face; Mr. Longfellow, with his silken white hair and his benignant face; Dr. Oliver Wendell Holmes, flashing smiles and affection and all good-fellowship everywhere like a rose-diamond whose facets are being turned toward the light first one way and then another—a charming man, and always fascinating, whether he was talking or whether he was sitting still (what *he* would call still, but what would be more or less motion to other people). I can see those figures with entire distinctness across this abyss of time.

One other feature is clear—Willie Winter (for these past thousand years dramatic editor of the *New York Tribune,* and still occupying that high post in his old age) was there. He was much younger then than he is now, and he showed it. It was always a pleasure to me to see Willie Winter at a banquet. During a matter of twenty years I was seldom at a banquet where Willie Winter was not also present, and where he did not read a charming poem written for the occasion. He did it this time, and it was up to standard: dainty, happy, choicely phrased, and as good to listen to as music, and sounding exactly as if it was pouring unprepared out of heart and brain.

Now at that point ends all that was pleasurable about that notable celebration of Mr. Whittier's seventieth birthday—because *I* got up at that point and followed Winter, with what I have no doubt I supposed would be the gem of the evening—the gay oration above quoted from the Boston paper. I had written it all out the day before and had perfectly memorized it, and I stood up there at my genial and happy and self-satisfied ease, and began to deliver it. Those majestic guests, that row of venerable and still active volcanoes, listened, as did everybody else in the house, with attentive interest. Well, I delivered myself of—we'll say the first two hundred words of my speech. I was expecting no returns from that part of the speech, but this was not the case as regarded the rest of it. I arrived now at the dialogue: "The old miner said, 'You are the fourth, I'm going to move.' 'The fourth what?' said I. He answered, 'The fourth littery man that has been here in twenty-four hours. I am going to move.' 'Why, you don't tell me,' said I. 'Who were the others?' 'Mr. Longfellow, Mr. Emerson, Mr. Oliver Wendell Holmes, consound the lot—' "

Now, then, the house's *attention* continued, but the expression of interest in the faces turned to a sort of black frost. I wondered what the trouble was. I didn't know. I went on, but with difficulty—I struggled along, and entered upon that miner's fearful description of the bogus Emerson, the bogus Holmes, the bogus Longfellow, always hoping—but with a gradually perishing hope—that somebody would laugh, or that somebody would at least smile, but nobody did. I didn't know enough to give it up and sit down, I was too new to public speaking, and so I went on with this awful performance, and carried it clear through to the end, in front of a body of people who seemed turned to stone with horror. It was the sort of expression their faces would have worn if I had been making these remarks about the Deity and the rest of the Trinity; there is no milder way in which to describe the petrified condition and the ghastly expression of these people.

When I sat down it was with a heart which had long ceased to beat. I shall never be as dead again as I was then. I shall never be as miserable again as I was then. I speak now as one who doesn't know what the conditions of things may be in the next world, but in this one I shall never be as wretched again as I was then. Howells, who was near me, tried to say a comforting word, but couldn't get beyond a gasp. There was no use—he understood the whole size of the disaster. He had good intentions, but the words froze before they could get out. It was an atmosphere that would freeze anything. If Benvenuto Cellini's salamander had been in that place he would not have survived to be put into Cellini's autobiography. There was a frightful pause. There was an awful silence, a desolating silence. Then the next man on the list had to get up—there was no help for it. That was Bishop—Bishop had just burst handsomely upon the world with a most acceptable novel, which had appeared in The *Atlantic Monthly,* a place which would make any novel respectable and any author noteworthy. In this case the novel itself was recognized as being, without extraneous help, respectable. Bishop was away up in the public favor, and he was an object of high interest, consequently there was a sort of national expectancy in the air; we may say our American millions were standing, from Maine to Texas and from Alaska to Florida, holding their breath, their lips parted, their hands ready to applaud, when Bishop should get up on that occasion, and for the first time in his life speak in public. It was under these damaging conditions that he got up to "make good," as the vulgar say. I had spoken several times before, and that is the reason why I was able to go on without dying in my tracks, as I ought to have done—but Bishop had had no experience. He was up facing those awful deities—facing those other people, those strangers—facing human beings for the first time in his life, with a speech to utter. No doubt it was well packed away in his memory, no doubt it was fresh and usable, until I had been heard from. I suppose that after that, and under the smothering pall of that dreary silence, it began to waste away and disappear out of his head like the rags breaking from the edge of a fog, and presently there wasn't any fog left. He didn't go on—he didn't last long. It was not many sentences after his first before he began to hesitate, and break, and lost his grip, and totter, and wobble, and at last he slumped down in a limp and mushy pile.

Well, the programme for the occasion was probably not more than one-third finished, but it ended there. Nobody rose. The next man hadn't strength enough to get up, and everybody looked so dazed, so stupefied, paralyzed, it was impossible for anybody to do anything, or even try. Nothing could go on in that strange atmosphere. Howells mournfully, and without words, hitched himself to Bishop and me and supported us out of the room. It was very kind—he was most generous. He towed us tottering away into some room in that building, and we sat down there. I don't know what my remark was now, but I know the nature of it. It was the kind of remark you make when you know that nothing in the world can help your case. But Howells was honest—he had to say the heartbreaking things he did say: that there was no help for this calamity, this shipwreck, this cataclysm; that this was the most disastrous thing that had ever happened in anybody's history—and then he added, "That is, for *you*—and consider what you have done for Bishop. It is bad enough in your case, you deserve to suffer. You have committed this crime, and you deserve to have all you are going to get. But here is an innocent man. Bishop had never done you any harm, and see what you have done to him. He can never hold his head up again. The world can never look upon Bishop as being a live person. He is a corpse."

That is the history of that episode of twenty-eight years ago, which pretty nearly killed me with shame during the first year or two whenever it forced its way into my mind.

Now then, I take that speech up and examine it. As I said, it arrived this morning, from Boston. I have read it twice, and unless I am an idiot, it hasn't a single defect in it from the first word to the last. It is just as good as good can be. It is smart; it is saturated with humor. There isn't a suggestion of coarseness or vulgarity in it anywhere. What could have been the matter with that house? It is amazing, it is incredible, that they didn't shout with laughter, and those deities the loudest of them all. Could the fault have been with me? Did I lose courage when I saw those great men up there whom I was going to describe in such a strange fashion? If that happened, if I showed doubt, that can account for it, for you can't be successfully funny if you show that you are afraid of it. Well, I can't account for it, but if I had those beloved and revered old literary immortals back here now on the platform at Carnegie Hall I would take that same old speech, deliver it, word for word, and melt them till they'd run all over that stage. Oh, the fault must have been with *me*, it is not in the speech at all.

STUDY QUESTIONS

1. There are, obviously, three persona-audience situations in this selection: (1) Twain the speaker, (2) Twain the letter writer, and (3) Twain the composer of "The Story of a Speech." What picture (or ethos) does the persona present of himself in each situation? The question is actually a complicated one, and its answer must be sought by doing the remainder of the exercises.
2. Note that the first persona, Twain the speaker, has at least two aspects: the present-time speaker and the first-person narrator of a story. What differences are there between the two? Do the other personae (Twain the letter writer and Twain the composer of this selection) have more than one aspect?

3. Try performing the speech in at least two ways: as the flop it was when it was presented in 1877 and as the successful composition Twain "now" (in 1906) thinks it is. In rendering the first action, follow the cues Twain gives you in "The Story." The speech was a failure as a speech—that is, an immediate failure at the time of its delivery. On what basis does Twain now argue that it is a success? Do you agree with his present evaluation?

4. The project recommended here could become the basis for a longer research project, one involving the bases upon which modern rhetorical critics evaluate speeches. How might a modern rhetorical critic evaluate this speech? What differences are there between the bases on which a speech is evaluated and those on which a literary composition is evaluated? Can you find other speeches that were flops—or, at best, qualified successes—at the time of their delivery and have later been reevaluated? Have they been reevaluated as speeches or as literary compositions?

Malcolm X/Excerpt from *Mecca* from *The Autobiography of Malcolm X*

born 1925

. . .

I had just said my Sunset Prayer, *El Maghrib;* I was lying on my cot in the fourth-tier compartment, feeling blue and alone, when out of the darkness came a sudden light!

It was actually a sudden thought. On one of my venturings in the yard full of activity below, I had noticed four men, officials, seated at a table with a telephone. Now, I thought about seeing them there, and with *telephone,* my mind flashed to the connection that Dr. Shawarbi in New York had given me, the telephone number of the son of the author of the book which had been given to me. Omar Azzam lived right there in Jedda!

In a matter of a few minutes, I was downstairs and rushing to where I had seen the four officials. One of them spoke functional English. I excitedly showed him the letter from Dr. Shawarbi. He read it. Then he read it aloud to the other three officials. "A Muslim from America!" I could almost see it capture their imaginations and curiosity. They were very impressed. I asked the English-speaking one if he would please do me the favor of telephoning Dr. Omar Azzam at the number I had. He was glad to do it. He got someone on the phone and conversed in Arabic.

Dr. Omar Azzam came straight to the airport. With the four officials beaming, he wrung my hand in welcome, a young, tall, powerfully built man. I'd say he was six foot three. He had an extremely polished manner. In America, he would have been called a white man, but—it struck me, hard and instantly—from the way he acted, I had no *feeling* of him being a white man. "Why didn't you call before?" he demanded of me. He showed some identification to the four officials, and he used their phone. Speaking in Arabic, he was talking with some airport officials. "Come!" he said.

In something less than half an hour, he had gotten me released, my suitcase and passport had been retrieved from Customs, and we were in Dr. Azzam's car, driving through the city of Jedda, with me dressed in the *Ihram* two towels and sandals. I was speechless at the man's attitude, and at my own physical feeling of no difference between us as human beings. I had heard for years of Muslim hospitality, but one couldn't quite imagine such warmth. I asked questions. Dr. Azzam was a Swiss-trained engineer. His field was city planning. The Saudi Arabian government had borrowed him from the United Nations to direct all of the reconstruction work being done on Arabian holy places. And Dr. Azzam's sister was the wife of Prince Faisal's son. I was in a car with the brother-in-law of the son of the ruler of Arabia. Nor was that all that Allah had done. "My father will be so happy to meet you," said Dr. Azzam. The author who had sent me the book!

I asked questions about his father. Abd ir-Rahman Azzam was known as Azzam Pasha, or Lord Azzam, until the Egyptian revolution, when President Nasser eliminated all "Lord" and "Noble" titles. "He should be at my home when we get there," Dr. Azzam said. "He spends much time in New York with his United Nations work, and he has followed you with great interest."

I was speechless.

It was early in the morning when we reached Dr. Azzam's home. His father was there, his father's brother, a chemist, and another friend—all up that early, waiting. Each of them embraced me as though I were a long-lost child. I had never seen these men before in my life, and they treated me so good! I am going to tell you that I had never been so honored in my life, nor had I ever received such true hospitality.

A servant brought tea and coffee, and disappeared. I was urged to make myself comfortable. No women were anywhere in view. In Arabia, you could easily think there were no females.

Dr. Abd ir-Rahman Azzam dominated the conversation. Why hadn't I called before? They couldn't understand why I hadn't. Was I comfortable? They seemed embarrassed that I had spent the time at the airport; that I had been delayed in getting to Mecca. No matter how I protested that I felt no inconvenience, that I was fine, they would not hear it. "You must rest," Dr. Azzam said. He went to use the telephone.

I didn't know what this distinguished man was doing. I had no dream. When I was told that I would be brought back for dinner that evening, and that, meanwhile, I should get back in the car, how could I have realized that I was about to see the epitome of Muslim hospitality?

Abd ir-Rahman Azzam, when at home, lived in a suite at the Jedda Palace Hotel. Because I had come to them with a letter from a friend, he was going to stay at his son's home, and let me use his suite, until I could get on to Mecca.

When I found out, there was no use protesting: I was in the suite; young Dr. Azzam was gone; there was no one to protest to. The three-room suite had a bathroom that was as big as a double at the New York Hilton. It was suite number 214. There was even a porch outside, affording a beautiful view of the ancient Red Sea city.

There had never before been in my emotions such an impulse to pray— and I did, prostrating myself on the living-room rug.

Nothing in either of my two careers as a black man in America had served to give me any idealistic tendencies. My instincts automatically examined the reasons, the motives, of anyone who did anything they didn't have to do for me. Always in my life, if it was any white person, I could see a selfish motive.

But there in that hotel that morning, a telephone call and a few hours away from the cot on the fourth-floor tier of the dormitory, was one of the few times I had been so awed that I was totally without resistance. That white man—at least he would have been considered "white" in America— related to Arabia's ruler, to whom he was a close advisor, truly an international man, with nothing in the world to gain, had given up his suite to me, for my transient comfort. He had *nothing* to gain. He didn't need me. He had everything. In fact, he had more to lose than gain. He had followed the American press about me. If he did that, he knew there was only stigma attached to me. I was supposed to have horns. I was a "racist." I was "anti-white"—and he from all appearances was white. I was supposed to be a criminal; not only that, but everyone was even accusing me of using his religion of Islam as a cloak for my criminal practices and philosophies. Even if he had had some motive to use me, he knew that I was separated from Elijah Muhammad and the Nation of Islam, my "power base," according to the press in America. The only organization that I had was just a few weeks old. I had no job. I had no money. Just to get over there, I had had to borrow money from my sister.

That morning was when I first began to reappraise the "white man." It was when I first began to perceive that "white man," as commonly used, means complexion only secondarily; primarily it described attitudes and actions. In America, "white man" meant specific attitudes and actions toward the black man, and toward all other non-white men. But in the Muslim world, I had seen that men with white complexions were more genuinely brotherly than anyone else had ever been.

That morning was the start of a radical alteration in my whole outlook about "white" men.

I should quote from my notebook here. I wrote this about noon, in the hotel: "My excitement, sitting here, waiting to go before the Hajj Committee, is indescribable. My window faces to the sea westward. The streets are filled with the incoming pilgrims from all over the world. The prayers are to Allah and verses from the Quran are on the lips of everyone. Never have I seen such a beautiful sight, nor witnessed such a scene, nor felt such an atmosphere. Although I am excited, I feel safe and secure, thousands of miles from the totally different life that I have known. Imagine that twenty-four hours ago, I was in the fourth-floor room over the airport, surrounded by people with whom I could not communicate, feeling uncertain about the future, and very lonely, and then *one* phone call, following Dr. Shawarbi's instructions. I have met one of the most powerful men in the Muslim world. I will soon sleep in his bed at the Jedda Palace. I know that I am surrounded by friends whose sincerity and religious zeal I can feel. I must pray again to thank Allah for this blessing, and I must pray again that my wife and children back in America will always be blessed for their sacrifices, too."

I did pray, two more prayers, as I had told my notebook. Then I slept for about four hours, until the telephone rang. It was young Dr. Azzam. In another hour, he would pick me up to return me there for dinner. I tumbled words over one another, trying to express some of the thanks I felt for all of their actions. He cut me off. "Ma sha'a-llah"—which means, "It is as Allah has pleased."

I seized the opportunity to run down into the lobby, to see it again before Dr. Azzam arrived. When I opened my door, just across the hall from me a man in some ceremonial dress, who obviously lived there, was also headed downstairs, surrounded by attendants. I followed them down, then through the lobby. Outside, a small caravan of automobiles was waiting. My neighbor appeared through the Jedda Palace Hotel's front entrance and people rushed and crowded him, kissing his hand. I found out who he was: the Grand Mufti of Jerusalem. Later, in the hotel, I would have the opportunity to talk with him for about a half-hour. He was a cordial man of great dignity. He was well up on world affairs, and even the latest events in America.

I will never forget the dinner at the Azzam home. I quote my notebook again: "I couldn't say in my mind that these were 'white' men. Why, the men acted as if they were brothers of mine, the elder Dr. Azzam as if he were my father. His fatherly, scholarly speech. I *felt* like he was my father. He was, you could tell, a highly skilled diplomat, with a broad range of mind. His knowledge was so worldly. He was as current on world affairs as some people are to what's going on in their living room.

"The more we talked, the more his vast reservoir of knowledge and its variety seemed unlimited. He spoke of the racial lineage of the descendants of Muhammad the Prophet, and he showed how they were both black and white. He also pointed out how color, the complexities of color, and the problems of color which exist in the Muslim world, exist only where, and to the extent that, that area of the Muslim world has been influenced by the West. He said that if one encountered any differences based on attitude toward color, this directly reflected the degree of Western influence."

I learned during dinner that while I was at the hotel, the Hajj Committee Court had been notified about my case, and that in the morning I should be there. And I was.

The Judge was Sheikh Muhammad Harkon. The Court was empty except for me and a sister from India, formerly a Protestant, who had converted to Islam, and was, like me, trying to make the Hajj. She was brown-skinned, with a small face that was mostly covered. Judge Harkon was a kind, impressive man. We talked. He asked me some questions, having to do with my sincerity. I answered him as truly as I could. He not only recognized me as a true Muslim, but he gave me two books, one in English, the other in Arabic. He recorded my name in the Holy Register of true Muslims, and we were ready to part. He told me, "I hope you will become a great preacher of Islam in America." I said that I shared that hope, and I would try to fulfill it.

The Azzam family were very elated that I was qualified and accepted to go to Mecca. I had lunch at the Jedda Palace. Then I slept again for several hours, until the telephone awakened me.

It was Muhammad Abdul Azziz Maged, the Deputy Chief of Protocol for Prince Faisal. "A special car will be waiting to take you to Mecca, right after your dinner," he told me. He advised me to eat heartily, as the Hajj rituals require plenty of strength.

I was beyond astonishment by then.

Two young Arabs accompanied me to Mecca. A well-lighted, modern turnpike highway made the trip easy. Guards at intervals along the way took one look at the car, and the driver made a sign, and we were passed through, never even having to slow down. I was, all at once, thrilled, important, humble, and thankful.

Mecca, when we entered, seemed as ancient as time itself. Our car slowed through the winding streets, lined by shops on both sides and with buses, cars, and trucks, and tens of thousands of pilgrims from all over the earth were everywhere.

The car halted briefly at a place where a *Mutawaf* was waiting for me. He wore the white skullcap and long nightshirt garb that I had seen at the airport. He was a short, dark-skinned Arab, named Muhammad. He spoke no English whatever.

We parked near the Great Mosque. We performed our ablution and entered. Pilgrims seemed to be on top of each other, there were so many, lying, sitting, sleeping, praying, walking.

My vocabulary cannot describe the new mosque that was being built around the Ka'ba. I was thrilled to realize that it was only one of the tremendous rebuilding tasks under the direction of young Dr. Azzam, who had just been my host. The Great Mosque of Mecca, when it is finished, will surpass the architectural beauty of India's Taj Mahal.

Carrying my sandals, I followed the *Mutawaf.* Then I saw the Ka'ba, a huge black stone house in the middle of the Great Mosque. It was being circumambulated by thousands upon thousands of praying pilgrims, both sexes, and every size, shape, color, and race in the world. I knew the prayer to be uttered when the pilgrim's eyes first perceive the Ka'ba. Translated, it is "O God, You are peace, and peace derives from You. So greet us, O Lord, with peace." Upon entering the Mosque, the pilgrim should try to kiss the Ka'ba if possible, but if the crowds prevent him getting that close, he touches it, and if the crowds prevent that, he raises his hand and cries out "Takbir!" ("God is great!") I could not get within yards. "Takbir!"

My feeling there in the House of God was a numbness. My *Mutawaf* led me in the crowd of praying, chanting pilgrims, moving seven times around the Ka'ba. Some were bent and wizened with age; it was a sight that stamped itself on the brain. I saw incapacitated pilgrims being carried by others. Faces were enraptured in their faith. The seventh time around, I prayed two *Rak'a,* prostrating myself, my head on the floor. The first prostration, I prayed the Quran verse "Say He is God, the one and only"; the second prostration: "Say O you who are unbelievers, I worship not that which you worship. . . ."

As I prostrated, the *Mutawaf* fended pilgrims off to keep me from being trampled.

The *Mutawaf* and I next drank water from the well of Zem Zem. Then we ran between the two hills, Safa and Marwa, where Hajar wandered over the same earth searching for water for her child Ishmael.

Three separate times, after that, I visited the Great Mosque and circumambulated the Ka'ba. The next day we set out after sunrise toward Mount Arafat, thousands of us, crying in unison: "Labbayka! Labbayka!" and "Allah Akbar!" Mecca is surrounded by the crudest-looking mountains I have ever seen; they seem to be made of the slag from a blast furnace. No vegetation is on them at all. Arriving about noon, we prayed and chanted from noon until sunset, and the *asr* (afternoon) and *Maghrib* (sunset) special prayers were performed.

Finally, we lifted our hands in prayer and thanksgiving, repeating Allah's words: "There is no God but Allah. He has no partner. His are authority and praise. Good emanates from Him, and He has power over all things."

Standing on Mount Arafat had concluded the essential rites of being a pilgrim to Mecca. No one who missed it could consider himself a pilgrim. The *Ihram* had ended. We cast the traditional seven stones at the devil. Some had their hair and beards cut. I decided that I was going to let my beard remain. I wondered what my wife Betty, and our little daughters, were going to say when they saw me with a beard, when I got back to New York. New York seemed a million miles away. I hadn't seen a newspaper that I could read since I left New York. I had no idea what was happening there. A Negro rifle club that had been in existence for over twelve years in Harlem had been "discovered" by the police; it was being trumpeted that I was "behind it." Elijah Muhammad's Nation of Islam had a lawsuit going against me, to force me and my family to vacate the house in which we lived on Long Island.

The major press, radio, and television media in America had representatives in Cairo hunting all over, trying to locate me, to interview me about the furor in New York that I had allegedly caused—when I knew nothing about any of it.

I only knew what I had left in America, and how it contrasted with what I had found in the Muslim world. About twenty of us Muslims who had finished the Hajj were sitting in a huge tent on Mount Arafat. As a Muslim from America, I was the center of attention. They asked me what about the Hajj had impressed me the most. One of the several who spoke English asked; they translated my answers for the others. My answer to that question was not the one they expected, but it drove home my point.

I said, "The *brotherhood!* The people of all races, colors, from all over the world coming together as *one!* It has proved to me the power of the One God."

It may have been out of taste, but that gave me an opportunity, and I used it, to preach them a quick little sermon on America's racism, and its evils.

I could tell the impact of this upon them. They had been aware that the plight of the black man in America was "bad," but they had not been aware that it was inhuman, that it was a psychological castration. These people from elsewhere around the world were shocked. As Muslims, they had a very tender heart for all unfortunates, and very sensitive feelings for truth and justice. And in everything I said to them, as long as we talked, they were aware of the yardstick that I was using to measure everything—that to me the earth's most explosive and pernicious evil is racism, the inability of God's creatures to live as One, especially in the Western world.

· · ·

STUDY QUESTIONS

1. Malcolm X surely does not need to be identified for the modern reader. However, a good way to check your understanding of the man's identity is to ask these questions: Why does he use X for his last name? What does he mean by his "two careers as a black man in America"? Exactly what is the "Nation of Islam"?

2. The scene is Jedda, where Malcolm X in one of the last years of his life (he was assassinated on February 21, 1965, at the age of 39) finally completes the end of his pilgrimage to Mecca—Hajj, the religious obligation that every orthodox Muslim must fulfill at least once in his lifetime, if humanly possible. For Malcolm, moreover, the pilgrimage had deep spiritual implications for his thinking as a leader of the Black Revolution. In composing this section of his autobiography, Malcolm was aware of this pilgrimage as marking a climax, or turning point, in his life. Has the section been structured in such a way that it dramatizes the fact that the pilgrimage was a spiritual journey of specific import?

3. What differences are there in the speeches that Malcolm X reports in his own words and those he quotes directly? What are the differences in content or in importance to Malcolm?

4. Obviously, Malcolm X is aware of an audience outside himself to whom he is telling this story. Are there sections in this total passage where he seems to be meditating—or perhaps recollecting for his audience the thoughts he weighed in his mind?

5. Note also that Malcolm X seems not only to be speaking to an audience, in virtually spontaneous fashion, but that at times he appears to be reading to that audience from his notebook. Then, too, not only does he speak of *past* events, but he makes an effort to re-create those events in the present—as, for example, in the process of meditation mentioned earlier and in his shout "Takbir!" The effect may be one of varying the distance between himself and his audience and between the present and the past. In performance, do these effects create a rhythmical pattern that illuminates the structure of the passage? Do these effects help us understand Malcolm's journey to Mecca as a spiritual journey of very great significance for him?

Eldridge Cleaver/Initial Reactions on the Assassination of Malcolm X

born 1934

Folsom Prison,
June 19, 1965

Sunday is Movie Day at Folsom Prison and I was sitting in the darkened hulk of Mess Hall No. 1—which convicts call "The Folsom Theatre"— watching Victor Buono in a movie called *The Strangler,* when a convict known as Silly Willie came over to where I was sitting and whispered into my ear:

"Brother J sent me in to tell you it just came over the TV that Malcolm X was shot as he addressed a rally in New York."

For a moment the earth seemed to reel in orbit. The skin all over my body tightened up. "How bad?" I asked.

"The TV didn't say," answered Silly Willie. The distress was obvious in his voice. "We was around back in Pipe Alley checking TV when a special bulletin came on. All they said was Malcolm X was shot and they were rushing him to the hospital."

"Thanks," I said to Silly Willie. I felt his reassuring hand on my shoulder as he faded away in the darkness. For a moment I pondered whether to go outside and get more information, but something made me hang back. I remember distinctly thinking that I would know soon enough. On the screen before me, Victor Buono had a woman by the throat and was frantically choking the last gasping twitches of life out of her slumping body. I was thinking that if Malcolm's wounds were not too serious, that if he recovered, the shooting might prove to be a blessing in disguise: it would focus more intensified attention on him and create a windfall of sympathy and support for him throughout America's black ghettos, and so put more power into his hands. The possibility that the wounds may have been fatal, that as I sat there Malcolm was lying already dead, was excluded from my mind.

After the movie ended, as I filed outside in the long line of convicts and saw the shocked, wild expression on Brother J's face, I still could not believe that Malcolm X was dead. We mingled in the crowd of convicts milling around in the yard and were immediately surrounded by a group of Muslims, all of whom, like myself, were firm supporters of Malcolm X. He's dead, their faces said, although not one of them spoke a word. As we stood there in silence, two Negro inmates walked by and one of them said to us, "That's a goddam shame how they killed that man! Of all people, why'd they kill Malcolm? Why'nt' they kill some of them Uncle-Tomming m.f.'s? I wish I could get my hands on whoever did it." And he walked away, talking and cursing to his buddy.

What does one say to his comrades at the moment when The Leader falls? All comment seems irrelevant. If the source of death is so-called natural causes, or an accident, the reaction is predictable, a feeling of impotence, humbleness, helplessness before the forces of the universe. But when the cause of death is an assassin's bullet, the overpowering desire is for vengeance. One wants to strike out, to kill, crush, destroy, to deliver a telling counterblow, to inflict upon the enemy a reciprocal, equivalent loss. But whom does one strike down at such a time if one happens to be in an anonymous, amorphous crowd of convicts in Folsom Prison and The Leader lies dead thousands of miles away across the continent?

"I'm going to my cell," I told the tight little knot of Muslims. "Allah is the Best Knower. Everything will be made manifest in time. Give it a little time. *As-Salaam Aliakum."*

"Wa-Aliakum Salaam," the Brothers returned the salutation and we shook hands all around, the double handshake which is very popular among Muslims in California prisons. (It is so popular that one sometimes grows weary of shaking hands. If a Muslim leaves a group for a minute to go get a drink of water, he is not unlikely to shake hands all around before he leaves and again when he returns. But no one complains and the convention is respected as a gesture of unity, brotherly love, and solidarity—so meaningful in a situation where Muslims are persecuted and denied recognition and the right to function as a legitimate religion.) I headed for my cell. I lived in No. 5 Building, which is Folsom's Honor Unit, reserved for those who have maintained a clean record for a least six months. Advantages: a larger cell, TV every Wednesday, Saturday, and Sunday night, less custodial supervision, easier ingress and egress. If while living in the Honor Unit you get into a "beef" which results in action against you by the disciplinary committee, one of the certain penalties is that you are immediately kicked out of No. 5 Building.

As I walked along the first tier toward my cell, I ran into Red, who lived near me on the tier.

"I guess you heard about Malcolm?"

"Yeah," I said. "They say he got wasted."

Red, who is white, knew from our many discussions that I was extremely partial to Malcolm, and he himself, being thoroughly alienated from the *status quo,* recognized the assassination for what it was: a negative blow against a positive force. Red's questions were the obvious ones: Who? Why? The questions were advanced tentatively, cautiously, because of the treacherous ground he was on: a redheaded, blue-eyed white man concerned by an event which so many others greeted with smiles and sighs. I went into my cell.

Although I heard it blared over the radio constantly and read about it in all the newspapers, days passed during which my mind continued to reject the fact of Malcolm's death. I existed in a dazed state, wandering in a trance around Folsom, drifting through the working hours in the prison bakery; and yet I was keen to observe the effect of the assassination on my fellow inmates. From most of the whites there was a leer and a hint of a smile in the eyes. They seemed anxious to see a war break out between the followers of Elijah and the followers of Malcolm.

There are only a few whites in Folsom with whom I would ever discuss the death of Malcolm or anything else besides baseball or the weather. Many of the Mexican-Americans were sympathetic, although some of them made a point, when being observed by whites, of letting drop sly remarks indicating they were glad Malcolm was gone. Among the Negroes there

was mass mourning for Malcolm X.   Nobody talked much for a few days.
The only Negroes who were not indignant were a few of the Muslims who
remained loyal to Elijah Muhammad.   They interpreted Malcolm's assassination as the will of Allah descending upon his head for having gone
astray.   To them, it was Divine chastisement and a warning to those whom
Malcolm had tempted.   It was not so much Malcolm's death that made
them glad; but in their eyes it now seemed possible to heal the schism in
the movement and restore the monolithic unity of the Nation of Islam, a
unity they looked back on with some nostalgia.

Many Negro convicts saw Malcolm's assassination as a historic turning point in black America.   Whereas Negroes often talk heatedly about
wiping out all the so-called Negro leaders whom they do not happen to
like or agree with, this was the first significant case of Negro leader-killing
that anyone could remember.   What struck me is that the Negro convicts
welcomed the new era.   If a man as valuable to us as Malcolm could go
down, then as far as I was concerned so could any other man—myself
included.   Coming a week after the alleged exposé of the alleged plot to
dynamite the Statue of Liberty, Washington Monument, and the Liberty
Bell, a plot supposedly hatched by discontented blacks, the assassination
of Malcolm X had put new ideas in the wind with implications for the
future of black struggle in America.

I suppose that like many of the brothers and sisters in the Nation of
Islam movement, I also had clung to the hope that, somehow, the rift
between Malcolm X and Elijah Muhammad would be mended.   As long
as Brother Malcolm was alive, many Muslims could maintain this hope,
neatly overlooking the increasing bitterness of their rivalry.   But death
made the split final and sealed it for history.   These events caused a
profound personal crisis in my life and beliefs, as it did for other Muslims.
During the bitter time of his suspension and prior to his break with Elijah
Muhammad, we had watched Malcolm X as he sought frantically to re-
orient himself and establish a new platform.   It was like watching a
master do a dance with death on a highstrung tightrope.   He pirouetted,
twirled, turned somersaults in the air—but he landed firmly on his feet
and was off and running.   We watched it all, seeking a cause to condemn
Malcolm X and cast him out of our hearts.   We read all the charges and
countercharges.   I found Malcolm X blameless.

It had been my experience that the quickest way to become hated by
the Muslims was to criticize Elijah Muhammad or disagree with something
he wrote or said.   If Elijah wrote, as he has done, that the swine is a
poison creature composed of ⅓ rat, ⅓ cat, and ⅓ dog and you attempted
to cite scientific facts to challenge this, you had sinned against the light,
that was all there was to it.   How much more unlikely was it, therefore,
that Muslims would stand up and denounce Elijah himself, repudiate his
authority and his theology, deny his revelation, and take sides against

him, the Messenger of Almighty God Allah? I never dreamed that some-
day I would be cast in that hapless role.

After Malcolm made his pilgrimage to Mecca, completing a triumphal
tour of Africa and the Near East, during which he received the high honors
of a visiting dignitary, he returned to the U.S.A. and set about building
his newly founded Organization of Afro-American Unity. He also established the Muslim Mosque, Inc., to receive the Muslims he thought would
pull away from Elijah. The Muslim Mosque would teach Orthodox Islam,
under the direction of Sheikh Ahmed Hassoun from the Holy City of
Mecca. Grand Sheik Muhammad Sarur Al-Sabban, secretary-general of
the Muslim World League, had offered the services of Sheikh Ahmed,
according to the Los Angeles *Herald-Dispatch,* to "help Malcolm X in
his efforts to correct the distorted image that the religion of Islam has
been given by hate groups in this country."

I began defending Malcolm X. At a secret meeting of the Muslims in
Folsom, I announced that I was no longer a follower of Elijah Muhammad,
that I was throwing my support behind Brother Malcolm. I urged everyone there to think the matter over and make a choice, because it was no
longer possible to ride two horses at the same time. On the wall of my
cell I had a large, framed picture of Elijah Muhammad which I had had
for years. I took it down, destroyed it, and in its place put up, in the
same frame, a beautiful picture of Malcolm X kneeling down in the
Mohammed Ali Mosque in Cairo, which I clipped from the *Saturday Evening Post.* At first the other Muslims in Folsom denounced me; some I'd
known intimately for years stopped speaking to me or even looking at
me. When we met, they averted their eyes. To them the choice was
simple: Elijah Muhammad is the hand-picked Messenger of Allah, the
instrument of Allah's Will. All who oppose him are aiding Allah's enemies,
the White Devils. Whom do you choose, God or the Devil? Malcolm X,
in the eyes of Elijah's followers, had committed the unforgivable heresy
when, changing his views and abandoning the racist position, he admitted the possibility of brotherhood between blacks and whites. In a
letter sent back to the U.S. from the Holy Land, Malcolm X had stated:

You may be shocked by these words coming from me, but I have always been a
man who tries to face facts and to accept the reality of life as new experiences
and knowledge unfold it. The experiences of this pilgrimage have taught me
much and each hour in the Holy Land opens my eyes even more. . . . I have
eaten from the same plate with people whose eyes were the bluest of blue, whose
hair was the blondest of blond and whose skin was the whitest of white . . . and I
felt the sincerity in the words and deeds of these "white" Muslims that I felt among
the African Muslims of Nigeria, Sudan and Ghana.

Many of us were shocked and outraged by these words from Malcolm X,
who had been a major influence upon us all and the main factor in many

of our conversions to the Black Muslims. But there were those of us who were glad to be liberated from a doctrine of hate and racial supremacy. The onus of teaching of racial supremacy and hate, which is the white man's burden, is pretty hard to bear. Asked if he would accept whites as members of his Organization of Afro-American Unity, Malcolm said he would accept John Brown if he were around today—which certainly is setting the standard high.

At the moment I declared myself for Malcolm X, I had some prestige among the Muslims in the prisons of California, because of my active role in proselytizing new converts and campaigning for religious freedom for Muslim convicts. We sent a barrage of letters and petitions to the courts, governmental officials, even the United Nations.

After the death of Brother Booker T. X, who was shot dead by a San Quentin prison guard, and who at the time had been my cell partner and the inmate Minister of the Muslims of San Quentin, my leadership of the Muslims of San Quentin had been publicly endorsed by Elijah Muhammad's west coast representative, Minister John Shabazz of Muhammad's Los Angeles Mosque. This was done because of the explosive conditions in San Quentin at the time. Muslim officials wanted to avert any Muslim-initiated violence, which had become a distinct possibility in the aftermath of Brother Booker's death. I was instructed to impose an iron discipline upon the San Quentin Mosque, which had continued to exist despite the unending efforts of prison authorities to stamp it out. Most of the Muslims who were in prison during those days have since been released. I was one of the few remaining, and I was therefore looked upon by the other Muslims as one who had sacrificed and invested much in the struggle to advance the teachings of Elijah Muhammad. For that reason, my defection to Malcolm X caused a great deal of consternation among the Muslims of Folsom. But slowly, Malcolm was getting his machine together and it was obvious to me that his influence was growing. Negro inmates who had had reservations about Malcolm while he was under Elijah's authority now embraced him, and it was clear that they accepted Malcolm's leadership. Negroes whom we had tried in vain for years to convert to Elijah's fold now lined up with enthusiasm behind Malcolm.

I ran a regular public relations campaign for Malcolm in Folsom. I saw to it that copies of his speeches were made and circulated among Negro inmates. I never missed a chance to speak favorably about Malcolm, to quote him, to explain and justify what he was trying to do. Soon I had the ear of the Muslims, and it was not long before Malcolm had other ardent defenders in Folsom. In a very short time Malcolm became the hero of the vast majority of Negro inmates. Elijah Muhammad was quickly becoming irrelevant, passé.

Malcolm X had a special meaning for black convicts. A former prisoner himself, he had risen from the lowest depths to great heights. For this reason he was a symbol of hope, a model for thousands of black convicts who found themselves trapped in the vicious PPP cycle: prison-parole-prison. One thing that the judges, policemen, and administrators of prisons seem never to have understood, and for which they certainly do not make any allowances, is that Negro convicts, basically, rather than see themselves as criminals and perpetrators of misdeeds, look upon themselves as prisoners of war, the victims of a vicious, dog-eat-dog social system that is so heinous as to cancel out their own malefactions: in the jungle there is no right or wrong.

Rather than owing and paying a debt to society, Negro prisoners feel that they are being abused, that their imprisonment is simply another form of the oppression which they have known all their lives. Negro inmates feel that they are being robbed, that it is "society" that owes them, that should be paying them, a debt.

America's penology does not take this into account. Malcolm X did, and black convicts know that the ascension to power of Malcolm X or a man like him would eventually have revolutionized penology in America. Malcolm delivered a merciless and damning indictment of prevailing penology. It is only a matter of time until the question of the prisoner's debt to society versus society's debt to the prisoner is injected forcefully into national and state politics, into the civil and human rights struggle, and into the consciousness of the body politic. It is an explosive issue which goes to the very root of America's system of justice, the structure of criminal law, the prevailing beliefs and attitudes toward the convicted felon. While it is easier to make out a case for black convicts, the same principles apply to white and Mexican-American convicts as well. They too are victimized, albeit a little more subtly, by "society." When black convicts start demanding a new dispensation and definition of justice, naturally the white and Mexican-American convicts will demand equality of treatment. Malcolm X was a focus for these aspirations.

The Black Muslim movement was destroyed the moment Elijah cracked the whip over Malcolm's head, because it was not the Black Muslim movement itself that was so irresistibly appealing to the true believers. It was the awakening into self-consciousness of twenty million Negroes which was so compelling. Malcolm X articulated their aspirations better than any other man of our time. When he spoke under the banner of Elijah Muhammad he was irresistible. When he spoke under his own banner he was still irresistible. If he had become a Quaker, a Catholic, or a Seventh-Day Adventist, or a Sammy Davis-style Jew, and if he had continued to give voice to the mute ambitions in the black man's soul, his message would still have been triumphant: because what was great was not Malcolm X but the truth he uttered.

The truth which Malcolm uttered had vanquished the whole passle of so-called Negro leaders and spokesmen who trifle and compromise with the truth in order to curry favor with the white power structure. He was stopped in the only way such a man can be stopped, in the same way that the enemies of the Congolese people had to stop Lumumba, by the same method that exploiters, tyrants, and parasitical oppressors have always crushed the legitimate strivings of people for freedom, justice, and equality —by murder, assassination, and mad-dog butchery.

What provoked the assassins to murder? Did it bother them that Malcolm was elevating our struggle into the international arena through his campaign to carry it before the United Nations? Well, by murdering him they only hastened the process, because we certainly are going to take our cause before a sympathetic world. Did it bother the assassins that Malcolm denounced the racist strait-jacket demonology of Elijah Muhammad? Well, we certainly do denounce it and will continue to do so. Did it bother the assassins that Malcolm taught us to defend ourselves? We shall not remain a defenseless prey to the murderer, to the sniper and the bomber. Insofar as Malcolm spoke the truth, the truth will triumph and prevail and his name shall live; and insofar as those who opposed him lied, to that extent will their names become curses. Because "truth crushed to earth shall rise again."

So now Malcolm is no more. The bootlickers, Uncle Toms, lackeys, and stooges of the white power structure have done their best to denigrate Malcolm, to root him out of his people's heart, to tarnish his memory. But their million-worded lies fall on deaf ears. As Ossie Davis so eloquently expressed it in his immortal eulogy of Malcolm:

If you knew him you would know why we must honor him: Malcolm was our man-hood, our living, black manhood! This was his meaning to his people. And, in honoring him, we honor the best in ourselves. . . . However much we may have differed with him—or with each other about him and his value as a man, let his going from us serve only to bring us together, now. Consigning these mortal remains to earth, the common mother of all, secure in the knowledge that what we place in the ground is no more now a man—but a seed—which, after the winter of our discontent will come forth again to meet us. And we will know him then for what he was and is—a Prince—our own black shining Prince!—who didn't hesi-tate to die, because he loved us so.

We shall have our manhood. We shall have it or the earth will be leveled by our attempts to gain it.

STUDY QUESTIONS

1. Consider the persona's diction as it relates to his speaking situation and his audience. These "reactions" were written at Folsom Prison, with the speaker addressing an unidentified audience. Does this specific identification of the persona's writing situation give any clues for the demonstration of this text? Are there perhaps other less specific situations that you could create in the demonstration that would help clarify the persona's particular stance in this essay? How does his diction help you understand not only his stance but also the identity of his audience? Compare, for example, the persona's manner of speaking with that of the two inmates. Notice, also, the shift in tone as he begins to speak of injustices and aspirations. In the paragraph beginning "What does one say . . ." and the two paragraphs beginning "Rather than owing and paying a debt to society . . . ," how do the shifts in verb tense signal a shift in tone as well as in the persona's involvement in what he is saying? One could write a substantial paper analyzing the language in this essay as a key to the understanding of the entire structure as well as the particular structural elements of the speaker-audience situation.

2. The title of this essay would indicate that these reactions of the persona are temporally very close to the event of Malcolm X's assassination. Yet, how is the persona's distance from the event qualified in the text? In this context, how do the following aspects of the text function:
   a. the inclusion of details and parenthetical asides that *apparently* have little connection with the persona's major concern (for example, the details of the movie he was watching, the parenthetical remarks about the Muslim handshake in California prisons, and the advantages of No. 5 Building);
   b. the inclusion of Malcolm X's letter and the eulogy by Ossie Davis.
   In addition to indicating something about the persona's distance from the events, what do these elements show about the persona's motivation for writing this essay? In attempting to discover the persona's motivations, take into account not only the explicit motivations stated in the text (for example, "We shall have our manhood") but also the motivations implicit in the structure and argument of the essay.

3. How carefully has the reader been prepared for the polemic at the end of the essay? Notice the shift in sentence and paragraph structure in the final paragraphs of the essay. How has the way been prepared earlier in the essay for such an apparent change? What are the major structural principles operating in this essay? Are there any structural similarities between this essay and a sermon? And, with this in mind, does the essay seem to have any characteristics of spoken rather than written utterance?

4. This essay is taken from the book *Soul on Ice.* Read some of the other essays and letters in this collection and compare their personae. Does the persona in "Initial Reactions . . ." bear any similarities to the personae in other essays in the book? Do you notice any significant differences? What would a study of all the personae assumed in the book reveal about the persona in this particular essay? What would it reveal about Eldridge Cleaver himself?

Gertrude Stein/My Arrival in Paris from *The Autobiography of Alice B. Toklas*

born 1874

> *As this passage begins, Miss Toklas has recently arrived in Paris and has been invited to a dinner party at Gertrude Stein's home on the rue de Fleurus. The year is 1907.*

. . .

Before I tell about the guests I must tell what I saw. As I said being invited to dinner I rang the bell of the little pavillon and was taken into the tiny hall and then into the small dining room lined with books. On the only free space, the doors, were tacked up a few drawings by Picasso and Matisse. As the other guests had not yet come Miss Stein took me into the atelier. It often rained in Paris and it was always difficult to go from the little pavillon to the atelier door in the rain in evening clothes, but you were not to mind such things as the hosts and most of the guests did not. We went into the atelier which opened with a yale key the only yale key in the quarter at that time, and this was not so much for safety, because in those days the pictures had no value, but because the key was small and could go into a purse instead of being enormous as french keys were. Against the walls were several pieces of large italian renaissance furniture and in the middle of the room was a big renaissance table, on it a lovely inkstand, and at one end of it note-books neatly arranged, the kind of note-books french children use, with pictures of earthquakes and explorations on the outside of them. And on all the walls right up to the ceiling were pictures. At one end of the room was a big cast iron stove that Hélène came in and filled with a rattle, and in one corner of the room was a large table on which were horseshoe nails and pebbles and little pipe cigarette holders which one looked at curiously but did not touch, but which turned out later to be accumulations from the pockets of Picasso and Gertrude Stein. But to return to the pictures. The pictures were so strange that one quite instinctively looked at anything rather than at them just at first. I have refreshed my memory by looking at some snap shots taken inside the atelier at that time. The chairs in the room were also all italian renaissance, not very comfortable for short-legged people and one got the habit of sitting on one's legs. Miss Stein sat near the stove in a lovely high-backed one and she peacefully let her legs hang, which was a matter of habit, and when any one of the many visitors came to ask her a question she lifted herself up out of this chair and usually replied in french, not just now. This usually referred to something they wished to see, drawings which were put away, some german had once spilled ink on one, or some other not to be fulfilled desire. But to return to the pictures. As I say they completely covered the white-washed walls right up to the top of the very high ceiling. The room was lit at this time by high gas fixtures. This was the second stage. They had just been put in. Before that there had only been lamps, and a stalwart guest held up the lamp while the others looked. But gas had just been put in and an ingenious american painter named Sayen, to divert his mind from the birth of his first child, was arranging some mechanical contrivance that would light the high fixtures by themselves. The old landlady extremely conservative did not allow electricity in her houses and electricity was not put in until 1914, the old landlady by that time too old to know the difference, her house agent gave permission. But this time I am really going to tell about the pictures.

It is very difficult now that everybody is accustomed to everything to give some idea of the kind of uneasiness one felt when one first looked at all these pictures on these walls. In those days there were pictures of all kinds there, the time had not yet come when there were only Cézannes, Renoirs, Matisses and Picassos, nor as it was even later only Cézannes and Picassos. At that time there was a great deal of Matisse, Picasso, Renoir, Cézanne but there were also a great many other things. There were two Gauguins, there were Manguins, there was a big nude by Valloton that felt like only it was not like the Odalisque of Manet, there was a Toulouse-Lautrec. Once about this time Picasso looking at this and greatly daring said, but all the same I do paint better than he did. Toulouse-Lautrec had been the most important of his early influences. I later bought a little tiny picture by Picasso of that epoch. There was a portrait of Gertrude Stein by Valloton that might have been a David but was not, there was a Maurice Denis, a little Daumier, many Cézanne water colours, there was in short everything, there was even a little Delacroix and a moderate sized Greco. There were enormous Picassos of the Harlequin period, there were two rows of Matisses, there was a big portrait of a woman by Cézanne and some little Cézannes, all these pictures had a history and I will soon tell them. Now I was confused and I looked and I looked and I was confused. Gertrude Stein and her brother were so accustomed to this state of mind in a guest that they paid no attention to it. Then there was a sharp tap at the atelier door. Gertrude Stein opened it and a little dark dapper man came in with hair, eyes, face, hands and feet all very much alive. Hullo Alfy, she said, this is Miss Toklas. How do you do Miss Toklas, he said very solemnly. This was Alfy Maurer an old habitué of the house. He had been there before there were these pictures, when there were only japanese prints, and he was among those who used to light matches to light up a little piece of the Cézanne portrait. Of course you can tell it is a finished picture, he used to explain to the other american painters who came and looked dubiously, you can tell because it has a frame, now whoever heard of anybody framing a canvas if the picture isn't finished. He had followed, followed, followed always humbly always sincerely, it was he who selected the first lot of pictures for the famous Barnes collection some years later faithfully and enthusiastically. It was he who when later Barnes came to the house and waved his cheque-book said, so help me God, I didn't bring him. Gertrude Stein who has an explosive temper, came in another evening and there were her brother, Alfy and a stranger. She did not like the stranger's looks. Who is that, said she to Alfy. I didn't bring him, said Alfy. He looks like a Jew, said Gertrude Stein, he is worse than that, says Alfy. But to return to that first evening. A few minutes after Alfy came in there was a violent knock at the door and, dinner is ready, from Hélène. It's funny the Picassos have not come, said they all, however we won't wait at least Hélène won't wait. So we went into the court and into the pavillon and dining room and began dinner. It's funny, said Miss Stein, Pablo is always promptness itself, he is never early and he is never late, it is his pride that punctuality is the politeness of kings, he even makes Fernande punctual. Of course he often says yes when he has no intention of doing what he says yes to, he can't say no, no is not in his vocabulary and you have to know whether his yes means yes or means no, but when he says a yes that means yes and he did about tonight he is always punctual. These were the days before automobiles and nobody worried about accidents. We had just finished the first course when there was a quick patter of footsteps in the court and Hélène opened the door before the bell rang. Pablo and Fernande as everybody called them at that time walked in. He, small, quick moving but not restless, his eyes having a strange faculty of opening wide and drinking in what he wished to see. He had the isolation and movement of the head of a bull-fighter at the head of their procession. Fernande was a tall beautiful woman with a wonderful big hat and a very evidently new dress, they were both very fussed. I am very upset, said Pablo, but you know very well Gertrude I am never late but Fernande had ordered a dress for the vernissage tomorrow and it didn't come. Well here you are anyway, said Miss Stein, since it's you Hélène won't mind. And we all sat down. I was next to Picasso who was silent and then gradually became peaceful. Alfy paid compliments to Fernande and she was soon calm and placid. After a little while I murmured to Picasso that I liked his portrait of Gertrude Stein. Yes, he said, everybody says that she does not look like it but that does not make any difference, she will, he said. The conversation soon became lively it was all about the opening day of the salon indépendant which was the great event of the year. Everybody was interested in all the scandals that would or would not break out. Picasso never exhibited but as his followers did and there were a great many stories connected with each follower the hopes and fears were vivacious.

While we were having coffee footsteps were heard in the court quite a number of footsteps and Miss Stein rose and said, don't hurry, I have to let them in. And she left.

When we went into the atelier there were already quite a number of people in the room, scattered groups, single and couples all looking and looking. Gertrude Stein sat by the stove talking and listening and getting up to open the door and go up to various people talking and listening. She usually opened the door to the knock and the usual formula was, de la part de qui venez-vous, who is your introducer. The idea was that anybody could come but for form's sake and in Paris you have to have a formula, everybody was supposed to be able to mention the name of somebody who had told them about it. It was a mere form, really everybody could come in and as at that time these pictures had no value and there was no social privilege attached to knowing any one there, only those came who really were interested. So as I say anybody could come in, however, there was the formula. Miss Stein once in opening the door said as she usually did by whose invitation do you come and we heard an aggrieved voice reply, but by yours, madame. He was a young man Gertrude Stein had met somewhere and with whom she had had a long conversation and to whom she had given a cordial invitation and then had as promptly forgotten.

The room was soon very very full and who were they all. Groups of hungarian painters and writers, it happened that some hungarian had once been brought and the word had spread from him throughout all Hungary, any village where there was a young man who had ambitions heard of 27 rue de Fleurus and then he lived but to get there and a great many did get there. They were always there, all sizes and shapes, all degrees of wealth and poverty, some very charming, some simply rough and every now and then a very beautiful young peasant. Then there were quantities of germans, not too popular because they tended always to want to see anything that was put away and they tended to break things and Gertrude Stein has a weakness for breakable objects, she has a horror of people who collect only the unbreakable. Then there was a fair sprinkling of americans, Mildred Aldrich would bring a group or Sayen, the electrician, or some painter and occasionally an architectural student would accidentally get there and then there were the habitués, among them Miss Mars and Miss Squires whom Gertrude Stein afterwards immortalised in her story of Miss Furr and Miss Skeene. On that first night Miss Mars and I talked of a subject then entirely new, how to make up your face. She was interested in types, she knew that there were femme décorative, femme d'intérieur and femme intrigante; there was no doubt that Fernande Picasso was a femme décorative, but what was Madame Matisse, femme d'intérieur, I said, and she was very pleased. From time to time one heard the high spanish whinnying laugh of Picasso and gay contralto outbreak of Gertrude Stein, people came and went, in and out. Miss Stein told me to sit with Fernande. Fernande was always beautiful but heavy in hand. I sat, it was my first sitting with a wife of a genius.

Before I decided to write this book my twenty-five years with Gertrude Stein, I had often said that I would write, The wives of geniuses I have sat with. I have sat with so many. I have sat with wives who were not wives of geniuses who were real geniuses. I have sat with real wives of geniuses who were not real geniuses. I have sat with wives of geniuses, of near geniuses, of would be geniuses, in short I have sat very often and very long with many wives and wives of many geniuses.

As I was saying Fernande, who was then living with Picasso and had been with him a long time that is to say they were all twenty-four years old at that time but they had been together a long time, Fernande was the first wife of a genius I sat with and she was not the least amusing. We talked hats. Fernande had two subjects hats and perfumes. This first day we talked hats. She liked hats, she had the true french feeling about a hat, if a hat did not provoke some witticism from a man on the street the hat was not a success. Later on once in Montmartre she and I were walking together. She had on a large yellow hat and I had on a much smaller blue one. As we were walking along a workman stopped and called out, there go the sun and the moon shining together. Ah, said Fernande to me with a radiant smile, you see our hats are a success.

Miss Stein called me and said she wanted to have me meet Matisse. She was talking to a medium sized man with a reddish beard and glasses. He had a very alert although slightly heavy presence and Miss Stein and he seemed to be full of hidden meanings. As I came up I heard her say, Oh yes but it would be more difficult now. We were talking, she said, of a lunch party we had in here last year. We had just hung all the pictures and we asked all the painters. You know how painters are, I wanted to make them happy so I placed each one opposite his own picture, and they were happy so happy that we had to send out twice for more bread, when you know France you will know that that means that they were happy, because they cannot eat and drink without bread and we had to send out twice for bread so they were happy. Nobody noticed my little arrangement except Matisse and he did not until just as he left, and now he says it is a proof that I am very wicked. Matisse laughed and said, yes I know Mademoiselle Gertrude, the world is a theatre for you, but there are theatres and theatres, and when you listen so carefully to me and so attentively and do not hear a word I say then I do say that you are very wicked. Then they both began talking about the vernissage of the independent as every one else was doing and of course I did not know what it was all about. But gradually I knew and later on I will tell the story of the pictures, their painters and their followers and what this conversation meant.

Later I was near Picasso, he was standing meditatively. Do you think, he said, that I really do look like your president Lincoln. I had thought a good many things that evening but I had not thought that. You see, he went on, Gertrude, (I wish I could convey something of the simple affection and confidence with which he always pronounced her name and with which she always said, Pablo. In all their long friendship with all its sometimes troubled moments and its complications this has never changed.) Gertrude showed me a photograph of him and I have been trying to arrange my hair to look like his, I think my forehead does. I did not know whether he meant it or not but I was sympathetic. I did not realise then how completely and entirely american was Gertrude Stein. Later I often teased her, calling her a general, a civil war general of either or both sides. She had a series of photographs of the civil war, rather wonderful photographs and she and Picasso used to pore over them. Then he would suddenly remember the spanish war and he became very spanish and very bitter and Spain and America in their persons could say very bitter things about each other's country. But at this my first evening I knew nothing of all this and so I was polite and that was all.

And now the evening was drawing to a close. Everybody was leaving and everybody was still talking about the vernissage of the independent. I too left carrying with me a card of invitation for the vernissage. And so this, one of the most important evenings of my life, came to an end.

.   .   .

STUDY QUESTIONS

1. This "autobiography" presents several problems in speaker identification. As you will notice from the title, the book was written by Gertrude Stein. Indeed, the last several paragraphs of the book read as follows:

   For some time now many people, and publishers, have been asking Gertrude Stein to write her autobiography and she had always replied, not possible.

   She began to tease me and say that I should write my autobiography. Just think, she would say, what a lot of money you would make. She then began to invent titles for my autobiography. My Life With the Great, Wives of Geniuses I Have Sat With, My Twenty-Five Years With Gertrude Stein.

   Then she began to get serious and say, but really seriously you ought to write your autobiography. Finally I promised that if during the summer I could find time I would write my autobiography.

   When Ford Maddox Ford was editing the *Transatlantic Review* he once said to Gertrude Stein, I am a pretty good writer and a pretty good editor and a pretty good business man but I find it very difficult to be all three at once.

   I am a pretty good housekeeper and a pretty good gardener and a pretty good needlewoman and a pretty good secretary and a pretty good editor and a pretty good vet for dogs and I have to do them all at once and I found it difficult to add being a pretty good author.

   About six weeks ago Gertrude Stein said, it does not look to me as if you were ever going to write that autobiography. You know what I am going to do. I am going to write it for you. I am going to write it as simply as Defoe did the autobiography of Robinson Crusoe. And she has and this is it [pp. 251–252].

The speaker *of* the text would clearly seem to be Gertrude Stein and the speaker *in* the text Alice B. Toklas. But there is also a strong sense of Gertrude Stein herself speaking through Miss Toklas, even in the style itself. Consequently, you are not always sure if Miss Toklas is imitating Miss Stein's style, or if Miss Stein is imposing her own style on Miss Toklas. This, in turn, raises the question as to who is the actual subject of this "autobiography"—Miss Toklas or Miss Stein. Does this "confusion" of speakers serve any function in the text? How can you manage to demonstrate these levels of speakers so that the ambiguity of identity is clear?

2. How does the unconventional punctuation (or lack of it) provide clues for the performance? How is the oral quality of speech achieved in this work? Does the written style suggest a breathless or run-on quality that could be clarified in performance? What does this indicate about the quality of the mind that informs this speech?

3. Identify and discuss as fully as possible the particular comic effects in this selection. Describe precisely how these comic effects are achieved. What rhetorical strategies has Gertrude Stein employed in order to elicit the desired response from her audience?

4. Miss Toklas asserts that she wants her listener (or reader) to follow her through the events of her first evening in the home of Gertrude Stein. Yet she is constantly being sidetracked in her narrative. (Notice, for example, how long it takes her to "tell about the pictures.") What do her frequent asides and the voicing of seemingly irrelevant details reveal about her? How "circumstantial" a storyteller is Miss Toklas?

5. How aware does Miss Toklas seem to be of her audience? Who is this audience to whom she speaks? What indirect clues that would help you identify her audience are provided in the text? What seems to be the relationship between Gertrude Stein as implied author and *her* audience? Are Miss Stein's and Miss Toklas' audiences the same?

Thomas Merton/Ishi—A Meditation

born 1915

Genocide is a new word. Perhaps the word is new because technology has now got into the game of destroying whole races at once. The destruction of races is not new—just easier. Nor is it a specialty of totalitarian regimes. We have forgotten that a century ago white America was engaged in the destruction of entire tribes and ethnic groups of Indians. The trauma of California gold. And the vigilantes who, in spite of every plea from Washington for restraint and understanding, repeatedly took matters into their own hands and went out slaughtering Indians. Indiscriminate destruction of the "good" along with the "bad"—just so long as they were Indians. Parties of riffraff from the mining camps and saloons suddenly constituted themselves defenders of civilization. They armed and went out to spill blood and gather scalps. They not only combed the woods and canyons—they even went into the barns and ranch houses, to find and destroy the Indian servants and hired people, in spite of the protests of the ranchers who employed them.

The Yana Indians (including the Yahi or Mill Creeks) lived around the foothills of Mount Lassen, east of the Sacramento River. Their country came within a few miles of Vina where the Trappist monastery in California stands today. These hill tribes were less easy to subdue than their valley neighbors. More courageous and more aloof, they tried to keep clear of the white man altogether. They were not necessarily more ferocious than other Indians, but because they kept to themselves and had a legendary reputation as "fighters," they were more feared. They were understood to be completely "savage." As they were driven further and further back into the hills, and as their traditional hunting grounds gradually narrowed and emptied of game, they had to raid the ranches in order to keep alive. White reprisals were to be expected, and they were ruthless. The Indians defended themselves by guerilla warfare. The whites decided that there could be no peaceful coexistence with such neighbors. The Yahi, or Mill Creek Indians, as they were called, were marked for complete destruction. Hence they were regarded as subhuman. Against them there were no restrictions and no rules. No treaties need be made, for no Indian could be trusted. What was the point of "negotiation"?

Ishi, the last survivor of the Mill Creek Indians, whose story was published by the University of California at Berkeley five years ago [*] was born during the war of extermination against his people. The fact that the last Mill Creeks were able to go into hiding and to survive for another fifty years in their woods and canyons is extraordinary enough. But the courage, the resourcefulness, and the sheer nobility of these few stone-age men struggling to preserve their life, their autonomy and their identity as a people rises to the level of tragic myth. Yet there is nothing mythical about it. The story is told with impeccable objectivity—though also with compassion—by the scholars who finally saved Ishi and learned from him his language, his culture, and his tribal history.

To read this story thoughtfully, to open one's heart to it, is to receive a most significant message: one that not only moves, but disturbs. You begin to feel the inner stirrings of that pity and dread which Aristotle said were the purifying effect of tragedy. "The history of Ishi and his people," says the author, Theodora Kroeber, "is inexorably part of our own history. We have absorbed their lands into our holdings. Just so must we be the responsible custodians of their tragedy, absorbing it into our tradition and morality." Unfortunately, we learned little or nothing about ourselves from the Indian wars!

* Theodora Kroeber, *Ishi* (Berkeley: University of California Press, 1962).—Eds.

"They have separated murder into two parts and fastened the worse on me"—words which William Carlos Williams put on the lips of a Viking exile, Eric the Red. Men are always separating murder into two parts: one which is unholy and unclean: for "the enemy." Another which is a sacred duty: "for our side." He who first makes the separation, in order that he may kill, proves his bad faith. So too in the Indian wars. Why do we always assume the Indian was the aggressor? We were in *his* country, we were taking it over for ourselves, and we likewise refused even to share any of it with him. We were the people of God, always in the right, following a manifest destiny. The Indian could only be a devil. But once we allow ourselves to see all sides of the question, the familiar perspectives of American history undergo a change. The "savages" suddenly become human and the "whites," the "civilized," can seem barbarians.

True, the Indians were often cruel and inhuman (some more than others). True, also, the humanity, the intelligence, the compassion and understanding which Ishi met with in his friends, the scholars, when he came to join our civilization, restore the balance in our favor. But we are left with a deep sense of guilt and shame. The record is there. The Mill Creek Indians, who were once seen as bloodthirsty devils, were peaceful, innocent and deeply wronged human beings. In their use of violence they were, so it seems, generally very fair. It is we who were the wanton murderers, and they who were the innocent victims. The loving kindness lavished on Ishi in the end did nothing to change that fact. His race had been barbarously, pointlessly destroyed.

The impact of the story is all the greater because the events are so deeply charged with a natural symbolism: the structure of these happenings is such that it leaves a haunting imprint on the mind. Out of that imprint come disturbing and potent reflections.

PEACE TREATY

Take for example the scene in 1870 when the Mill Creeks were down to their last twenty or thirty survivors. A group had been captured. A delegation from the tiny remnant of the tribe appeared at a ranch to negotiate. In a symbolic gesture, they handed over five bows (five being a sacred number) and stood, unarmed, waiting for an answer. The gesture was not properly understood, though it was evident that the Indians were trying to recover their captives and promising to abandon all hostilities. In effect, the message was: "Leave us alone, in peace, in our hills, and we will not bother you any more. We are few, you are many, why destroy us? We are no longer any menace to you." No formal answer was given. While the Indians were waiting for some kind of intelligible response, one of the whites slung a rope over the branch of a tree. The Indians quietly withdrew into the woods.

From then on, for the next twelve years, the Yahi disappeared into the hills without a trace. There were perhaps twenty of them left, one of whom was Ishi, together with his mother and sister. In order to preserve their identity as a tribe, they had decided that there was no alternative but to keep completely away from white men, and have nothing whatever to do with them. Since coexistence was impossible, they would try to be as if they did not exist for the white man at all. To be there as if they were not there.

In fact, not a Yahi was seen. No campfire smoke rose over the trees. Not a trace of a fire was found. No village was discovered. No track of an Indian was observed. The Yahi remnant (and that phrase takes on haunting biblical resonances) systematically learned to live as invisible and as unknown.

To anyone who has ever felt in himself the stirrings of a monastic or solitary vocation, the notion has a profound meaning. It has implications that are simply beyond speech. There is nothing one can say in the presence of such a happening and of its connotations for what our spiritual books so glibly call "the hidden life." The "hidden life" is surely not irrelevant to our modern world: nor is it a life of spiritual comfort and tranquility which a chosen minority can happily enjoy, at the price of a funny costume and a few prayers. The "hidden life" is the extremely difficult life that is forced upon a remnant that has to stay completely out of sight in order to escape destruction.

This so-called "long concealment" of the Mill Creek Indians is not romanticized by any means. The account is sober, objective, though it cannot help being an admiring tribute to the extraordinary courage and ingenuity of these lost stone-age people. Let the book speak for itself.

The long concealment failed in its objective to save a people's life but it would seem to have been brilliantly successful in its psychology and techniques of living . . . Ishi's group was a master of the difficult art of communal and peaceful coexistence in the presence of alarm and in a tragic and deteriorating prospect. . . .

It is a curious circumstance that some of the questions which arise about the concealment are those for which in a different context psychologists and neurologists are trying to find answers for the submarine and outer space services today. Some of these are: what makes for morale under confining and limiting life-conditions? What are the presumable limits of claustrophobic endurance? . . . It seems that the Yahi might have qualified for outer space had they lasted into this century.

There is something challenging and awe-inspiring about this thoughtful passage by a scientifically trained mind. And that phrase about "qualifying for outer space" has an eerie ring about it. Does someone pick up the half-heard suggestion that the man who wants to live a normal life span during the next two hundred years of our history must be the kind of person who is "qualified for outer space"? Let us return to Ishi! The following sentences are significant:

In contrast to the Forty-niners . . . whose morality and morale had crumbled, Ishi and his band remained incorrupt, humane, compassionate, and with their faith intact even unto starvation, pain and death. The questions then are: what makes for stability? For psychic strength? For endurance, courage and faith?

The answers given by the author to these questions are mere suggestions. The Yahi were on their own home ground. This idea is not developed. The reader should reflect a little on the relation of the Indian to the land on which he lived. In this sense, most modern men never know what it means to have a "home ground." Then there is a casual reference to the "American Indian mystique," which could also be developed. William Faulkner's hunting stories, particularly "The Bear," give us some idea of what this "mystique" might involve. The word *mystique* has unfortunate connotations: it suggests an emotional icing on an ideological cake. Actually the Indian lived by a deeply religious wisdom which can be called in a broad sense mystical, and that is certainly much more than "a mystique." The book does not go into religious questions very deeply, but it shows us Ishi as a man sustained by a deep and unassailable spiritual strength which he never discussed.

Later, when he was living "in civilization" and was something of a celebrity as well as an object of charitable concern, Ishi was questioned about religion by a well-meaning lady. Ishi's English was liable to be unpredictable, and the language of his reply was not without its own ironic depths of absurdity:

"Do you believe in God?" the lady inquired.

"Sure, Mike!" he retorted briskly.

There is something dreadfully eloquent about this innocent short-circuit in communications.

One other very important remark is made by the author. The Yahi found strength in the incontrovertible fact that they were in the right. *"Of very great importance to their psychic health was the circumstance that their suffering and curtailments arose from wrongs done to them by others. They were not guilt ridden."*

Contrast this with the spectacle of our own country with its incomparable technological power, its unequalled material strength, and its psychic turmoil, its moral confusion and its profound heritage of guilt which neither the righteous declarations of Cardinals nor the moral indifference of "realists" can do anything to change! Every bomb we drop on a defenseless Asian village, every Asian child we disfigure or destroy with fire, only adds to the moral strength of those we wish to destroy for our own profit. It does not make the Viet Cong cause just; but by an accumulation of injustice done against innocent people we drive them into the arms of our enemies and make our own ideals look like the most pitiful sham.

THE HIDDEN REMNANT

Gradually the last members of the Yahi tribe died out. The situation of the survivors became more and more desperate. They could not continue to keep up their perfect invisibility: they had to steal food. Finally the hidden camp where Ishi lived with his sister and sick mother was discovered by surveyors, who callously walked off with the few objects they found as souvenirs. The mother and sister died, and finally on August 29, 1911, Ishi surrendered to the white race, expecting to be destroyed.

Actually, the news of this "last wild Indian" reached the anthropology department at Berkeley and a professor quickly took charge of things. He came and got the "wild man" out of jail. Ishi spent the rest of his life in San Francisco, patiently teaching his hitherto completely unknown (and quite sophisticated) language to experts like Edward Sapir. Curiously enough Ishi lived in an anthropological museum, where he earned his living as a kind of caretaker and also functioned, on occasions, as a live exhibit. He was well treated, and in fact the affection and charm of his relations with his white friends are not the least moving part of his story. He adapted to life in the city without too much trouble and returned once, with his friends, to live several months in his old territory, under his natural conditions, showing them how the Yahi had carried out the fantastic operation of their invisible survival. But he finally succumbed to one of the diseases of civilization. He died of tuberculosis in 1916, after four and a half years among white men.

For the reflective reader who is—as everyone must be today—deeply concerned about man and his fate, this is a moving and significant book, one of those unusually suggestive works that *must* be read, and perhaps more than once. It is a book to think deeply about and take notes on, not only because of its extraordinary factual interest but because of its special quality as a kind of parable.

One cannot help thinking today of the Vietnam war in terms of the Indian wars of a hundred years ago. Here again, one meets the same myths and misunderstandings, the same obsession with "completely wiping out" an enemy regarded as diabolical. The language of the vigilantes had overtones of puritanism in it. The backwoods had to be "completely cleaned out," or "purified" of Indians—as if they were vermin. I have read accounts of American GI's taking the same attitude toward the Viet Cong. The jungles are thought to be "infested" with communists, and hence one goes after them as one would go after ants in the kitchen back home. And in this process of "cleaning up" (the language of "cleansing" appeases and pacifies the conscience) one becomes without realizing it a murderer of women and children. But this is an unfortunate accident, what the moralists call "double effect." Something that is just too bad, but which must be accepted in view of something more important that has to be done. And so there is more and more killing of civilians and less and less of the "something more important" which is what we are trying to achieve. In the end, it is the civilians that are killed in the ordinary course of events, and combatants only get killed by accident. No one worries any more about double effect. War is waged against the innocent to "break enemy morale."

What is most significant is that Vietnam seems to have become an extension of our old western frontier, that enables us to continue the cowboys-and-Indians game which seems to be part and parcel of our national identity. What a pity that so many innocent people have to pay with their lives for our obsessive fantasies!

One last thing: Ishi never told anyone his real name. The California Indians apparently never uttered their own names, and were very careful about how they spoke the names of others. Ishi would never refer to the dead by name either. "He never revealed his own private Yahi name," says the author. "It was as though it had been consumed in the funeral pyre of the last of his loved ones."

In the end, no one ever found out a single name of the vanished community. Not even Ishi's. For Ishi means simply *man*.

STUDY QUESTIONS

1. The most important matter to study in this essay, the one that will constitute the major problem for the interpreter, is the structure. To study structure it is not enough simply to consider organization. One must also consider the character of the man who is speaking, the nature of his mind, the motives that lead him from one part of his discourse to another, and his relationship to his audience. All of the following questions are directed toward this type of structural analysis. Yet, the interpreter should not only try to answer these questions but should also seek to understand the structure of the essay by "trying out" varying modes of performance: He should, for example, perform the persona as if he were sermonizing before an audience, then as if he were ruminating and speaking softly to himself.
2. Does the word "meditation" in the title of this essay serve as an important clue to the nature of the structure? "Meditation" in this book is used to signify a certain kind of relationship between speaker and audience: In effect, the speaker is talking to himself. Does Merton seem aware of an audience outside himself? At all times? Look up definitions of meditation in a large

dictionary. Are there other aspects of its meaning that might serve to clarify the speaker's thought—how he manages to proceed from discussing a book to criticizing certain contemporary events?

3. What seems to be the speaker's attitude? Is he cynical, bitter, or hopeful? Does he write to express his bafflement or to formulate—perhaps mainly for himself—the meaning and significance of this book for modern man?

4. Review carefully all the transitions in the essay, the progressions from one subject to another. What seems to motivate the arrangement of material? Consider carefully the last two paragraphs: Why does Merton introduce his final idea with "one last thing," and why does he choose to end his discourse with these paragraphs?

5. This essay first appeared in *The Catholic Worker*. Look through that newspaper and judge its character; particularly look for some indications of its audience. In a biographical dictionary, look up the life of Thomas Merton. Do the "facts" about the newspaper or about Merton assist you with the performance of the essay or with solving the structural problems? Or do these facts raise other matters that the interpreter must probe?

Lafcadio Hearn/Fuji-No-Yama

born 1850

Kité miréba,
Sahodo madé nashi,
Fuji no Yama!

*Seen on close approach, the mountain of Fuji
does not come up to expectation.*

JAPANESE PROVERBIAL PHILOSOPHY

The most beautiful sight in Japan, and certainly one of the most beautiful in the world, is the distant apparition of Fuji on cloudless days—more especially days of spring and autumn, when the greater part of the peak is covered with late or with early snows. You can seldom distinguish the snowless base, which remains the same color as the sky: you perceive only the white cone seeming to hang in heaven; and the Japanese comparison of its shape to an inverted half-open fan is made wonderfully exact by the fine streaks that spread downward from the notched top, like shadows of fan-ribs. Even lighter than a fan the vision appears—rather the ghost or dream of a fan;—yet the material reality a hundred miles away is grandiose among the mountains of the globe. Rising to a height of nearly 12,500 feet, Fuji is visible from thirteen provinces of the Empire. Nevertheless it is one of the easiest of lofty mountains to climb; and for a thousand years it has been scaled every summer by multitudes of pilgrims. For it is not only a sacred mountain, but the most sacred mountain of Japan—the holiest eminence of the land that is called Divine— the Supreme Altar of the Sun;—and to ascend it at least once in a lifetime is the duty of all who reverence the ancient gods. So from every district of the Empire pilgrims annually wend their way to Fuji; and in nearly all the provinces there are pilgrim-societies—Fuji-Kō—organized for the purpose of aiding those desiring to visit the sacred peak. If this act of faith cannot be performed by everybody in person, it can at least be performed by proxy. Any hamlet, however remote, can occasionally send one representative to pray before the shrine of the divinity of Fuji, and to salute the rising sun from that sublime eminence. Thus a single company of Fuji-pilgrims may be composed of men from a hundred different settlements.

By both of the national religions Fuji is held in reverence. The Shintō deity of Fuji is the beautiful goddess Ko-no-hana-saku-ya-himé—she who brought forth her children in fire without pain, and whose name signifies "Radiant-blooming-as-the-flowers-of-the-trees," or, according to some commentators, "Causing-the-flowers-to-blossom-brightly." On the summit is her temple; and in ancient books it is recorded that mortal eyes have beheld her hovering, like a luminous cloud, above the verge of the crater. Her viewless servants watch and wait by the precipices to hurl down whosoever presumes to approach her shrine with unpurified heart. . . . Buddhism loves the grand peak because its form is like the white bud of the Sacred Flower—and because the eight cusps of its top, like the eight petals of the Lotus, symbolize the Eight Intelligences of Perception, Purpose, Speech, Conduct, Living, Effort, Mindfulness, and Contemplation.

But the legends and traditions about Fuji, the stories of its rising out of the earth in a single night—of the shower of pierced jewels once flung down from it—of the first temple built upon its summit eleven hundred years ago—of the Luminous Maiden that lured to the crater an Emperor who was never seen afterward, but is still worshiped at a little shrine erected on the place of his vanishing—of the sand that daily rolled down by pilgrim feet nightly reascends to its former position—have not all these things been written in books? There is really very little left for me to tell about Fuji except my own experience of climbing it.

I made the ascent by way of Gotemba—the least picturesque, but perhaps also the least difficult of the six or seven routes open to choice. Gotemba is a little village chiefly consisting of pilgrim-inns. You reach it from Tōkyō in about three hours by the Tōkaidō railway, which rises for miles as it approaches the neighborhood of the mighty volcano. Gotemba is considerably more than two thousand feet above the sea, and therefore comparatively cool in the hottest season. The open country about it slopes to Fuji; but the slope is so gradual that the table-land seems almost level to the eye. From Gotemba in perfectly clear weather the mountain looks uncomfortably near—formidable by proximity—though actually miles away. During the rainy season it may appear and disappear alternately many times in one day—like an enormous spectre. But on the gray August morning when I entered Gotemba as a pilgrim, the landscape was muffled in vapors; and Fuji was totally invisible. I arrived too late to attempt the ascent on the same day; but I made my preparations at once for the day following, and engaged a couple of *gōriki* (strongpull men), or experienced guides. I felt quite secure on seeing their broad honest faces and sturdy bearing. They supplied me with a pilgrimstaff, heavy blue *tabi* (that is to say, cleft-stockings, to be used with sandals), a straw hat shaped like Fuji, and the rest of a pilgrim's outfit;— telling me to be ready to start with them at four o'clock in the morning.

What is hereafter set down consists of notes taken on the journey, but afterwards amended and expanded—for notes made while climbing are necessarily hurried and imperfect.

1

August 24th, 1897

From strings stretched above the balcony upon which my inn-room opens, hundreds of towels are hung like flags—blue towels and white, having printed upon them in Chinese characters the names of pilgrimcompanies and of the divinity of Fuji. These are gifts to the house, and serve as advertisements. . . . Raining from a uniformly gray sky. Fuji always invisible.

August 25th

3:30 A.M.—No sleep;—tumult all night of parties returning late from the mountain, or arriving for the pilgrimage;—constant clapping of hands to summon servants;—banqueting and singing in the adjoining chambers, with alarming bursts of laughter every few minutes. . . . Breakfast of soup, fish, and rice. Gōriki arrive in professional costume, and find me ready. Nevertheless they insist that I shall undress again and put on heavy underclothing;—warning me that even when it is Doyō (the period of greatest summer heat) at the foot of the mountain, it is Daikan (the period of greatest winter cold) at the top. Then they start in advance, carrying provisions and bundles of heavy clothing. . . . A kuruma waits for me, with three runners—two to pull, and one to push, as the work will be hard uphill. By kuruma I can go to the height of five thousand feet.

Morning black and slightly chill, with fine rain; but I shall soon be above the rain-clouds. . . . The lights of the town vanish behind us;—the kuruma is rolling along a country-road. Outside of the swinging penumbra made by the paper-lantern of the foremost runner, nothing is clearly visible; but

I can vaguely distinguish silhouettes of trees and, from time to time, of houses—peasants' houses with steep roofs.

Gray wan light slowly suffuses the moist air;—day is dawning through drizzle. . . . Gradually the landscape defines with its colors. The way lies through thin woods. Occasionally we pass houses with high thatched roofs that look like farmhouses; but cultivated land is nowhere visible. . . .

Open country with scattered clumps of trees—larch and pine. Nothing in the horizon but scraggy tree-tops above what seems to be the rim of a vast down. No sign whatever of Fuji. . . . For the first time I notice that the road is black—black sand and cinders apparently, volcanic cinders: the wheels of the kuruma and the feet of the runners sink into it with a crunching sound.

The rain has stopped, and the sky becomes a clearer gray. . . . The trees decrease in size and number as we advance.

What I have been taking for the horizon, in front of us, suddenly breaks open, and begins to roll smokily away to left and right. In the great rift part of a dark-blue mass appears—a portion of Fuji. Almost at the same moment the sun pierces the clouds behind us; but the road now enters a copse covering the base of a low ridge, and the view is cut off. . . . Halt at a little house among the trees—a pilgrims' resting-place—and there find the gōriki, who have advanced much more rapidly than my runners, waiting for us. Buy eggs, which a gōriki rolls up in a narrow strip of straw matting;—tying the matting tightly with straw cord between the eggs—so that the string of eggs has somewhat the appearance of a string of sausages. . . . Hire a horse.

Sky clears as we proceed;—white sunlight floods everything. Road reascends; and we emerge again on the moorland. And, right in front, Fuji appears—naked to the summit—stupendous—startling as if newly risen from the earth. Nothing could be more beautiful. A vast blue cone—warm-blue, almost violet through the vapors not yet lifted by the sun—with two white streaklets near the top which are great gullies full of snow, though they look from here scarcely an inch long. But the charm of the apparition is much less the charm of color than of symmetry—a symmetry of beautiful bending lines with a curve like the curve of a cable stretched over a space too wide to allow of pulling taut. (This comparison did not at once suggest itself: the first impression given me by the grace of those lines was an impression of femininity;—I found myself thinking of some exquisite sloping of shoulders toward the neck.) I can imagine nothing more difficult to draw at sight. But the Japanese artist, through

his marvelous skill with the writing-brush—the skill inherited from generations of calligraphists—easily faces the riddle: he outlines the silhouette
with two flowing strokes made in the fraction of a second, and manages to
hit the exact truth of the curves—much as a professional archer might hit
a mark, without consciously taking aim, through long exact habit of hand
and eye.

2

I see the gōriki hurrying forward far away—one of them carrying the
eggs round his neck! . . . Now there are no more trees worthy of the
name—only scattered stunted growths resembling shrubs. The black
road curves across a vast grassy down; and here and there I see large
black patches in the green surface—bare spaces of ashes and scoriae;
showing that this thin green skin covers some enormous volcanic deposit
of recent date. . . . As a matter of history, all this district was buried two
yards deep in 1707 by an eruption from the side of Fuji. Even in the far-
off Tōkyō the rain of ashes covered roofs to a depth of sixteen centimetres.
There are no farms in this region, because there is little true soil; and
there is no water. But volcanic destruction is not eternal destruction;
eruptions at last prove fertilizing; and the divine "Princess-who-causes-
the-flowers-to-blossom-brightly" will make this waste to smile again in
future hundreds of years.

. . . The black openings in the green surface become more numerous
and larger. A few dwarf-shrubs still mingle with the coarse grass. . . .
The vapors are lifting; and Fuji is changing color. It is no longer a glowing blue, but a dead sombre blue. Irregularities previously hidden by rising ground appear in the lower part of the grand curves. One of these
to the left—shaped like a camel's hump—represents the focus of the last
great eruption.

The land is not now green with black patches, but black with green
patches; and the green patches dwindle visibly in the direction of the
peak. The shrubby growths have disappeared. The wheels of the
kuruma, and the feet of the runners sink deeper into the volcanic sand.
. . . The horse is now attached to the kuruma with ropes, and I am able
to advance more rapidly. Still the mountain seems far away; but we are
really running up its flank at a height of more than five thousand feet.

Fuji has ceased to be blue of any shade. It is black—charcoal-black—
a frightful extinct heap of visible ashes and cinders and slaggy lava. . . .
Most of the green has disappeared. Likewise all of the illusion. The

tremendous naked black reality—always becoming more sharply, more grimly, more atrociously defined—is a stupefaction, a nightmare. . . . Above—miles above—the snow patches glare and gleam against that blackness—hideously. I think of a gleam of white teeth I once saw in a skull—a woman's skull—otherwise burnt to a sooty crisp.

So one of the fairest, if not the fairest of earthly visions, resolves itself into a spectacle of horror and death. . . . But have not all human ideals of beauty, like the beauty of Fuji seen from afar, been created by forces of death and pain?—are not all, in their kind, but composites of death, beheld in retrospective through the magical haze of inherited memory?

3

The green has utterly vanished;—all is black. There is no road—only the broad waste of black sand sloping and narrowing up to those dazzling, grinning patches of snow. But there is a track—a yellowish track made by thousands and thousands of cast-off sandals of straw (*waraji*), flung aside by pilgrims. Straw sandals quickly wear out upon this black grit; and every pilgrim carries several pairs for the journey. Had I to make the ascent alone, I could find the path by following that wake of broken sandals—a yellow streak zigzagging up out of sight across the blackness.

6:40 A.M.—We reach Tarōbō, first of the ten stations on the ascent: height, six thousand feet. The station is a large wooden house, of which two rooms have been fitted up as a shop for the sale of staves, hats, raincoats, sandals—everything pilgrims need. I find there a peripatetic photographer offering for sale photographs of the mountain which are really very good as well as very cheap. . . . Here the gōriki take their first meal; and I rest. The kuruma can go no farther; and I dismiss my three runners, but keep the horse—a docile and surefooted creature; for I can venture to ride him up to Ni-gō-goséki, or Station No. 2½.

Start for No. 2½ up the slant of black sand, keeping the horse at a walk. No. 2½ is shut up for the season. . . . Slope now becomes steep as a stairway, and further riding would be dangerous. Alight and make ready for the climb. Cold wind blowing so strongly that I have to tie on my hat tightly. One of the gōriki unwinds from about his waist a long stout cotton girdle, and giving me one end to hold, passes the other over his shoulder for the pull. Then he proceeds over the sand at an angle, with a steady short step, and I follow; the other guide keeping closely behind me to provide against my slip.

There is nothing very difficult about his climbing, except the weariness of walking through sand and cinders: it is like walking over dunes. . . . We mount by zigzags. The sand moves with the wind; and I have a slightly nervous sense—the feeling only, not the perception; for I keep my eyes on the sand—of height growing above depth. . . . Have to watch my steps carefully, and to use my staff constantly, as the slant is now very steep. . . . We are in a white fog—passing through clouds! Even if I wished to look back, I could see nothing through this vapor; but I have not the least wish to look back. The wind has suddenly ceased—cut off, perhaps, by a ridge; and there is a silence that I remember from West Indian days: the Peace of High Places. It is broken only by the crunching of the ashes beneath our feet. I can distinctly hear my heart beat. . . . The guide tells me that I stoop too much—orders me to walk upright, and always in stepping to put down the heel first. I do this, and find it relieving. But climbing through this tiresome mixture of ashes and sand begins to be trying. I am perspiring and panting. The guide bids me keep my honorable mouth closed, and breathe only through my honorable nose.

We are out of the fog again. . . . All at once I perceive above us, at a little distance, something like a square hole in the face of the mountain— a door! It is the door of the third station—a wooden hut half-buried in black drift. . . . How delightful to squat again—even in a blue cloud of wood-smoke and under smoke-blackened rafters! Time, 8:30 A.M. Height, 7085 feet.

In spite of the wood-smoke the station is comfortable enough inside; there are clean mattings and even kneeling-cushions. No windows, of course, nor any other opening than the door; for the building is half-buried in the flank of the mountain. We lunch. . . . The station-keeper tells us that recently a student walked from Gotemba to the top of the mountain and back again—in *geta!* Geta are heavy wooden sandals, or clogs, held to the foot only by a thong passing between the great and the second toe. The feet of that student must have been made of steel!

Having rested, I go out to look around. Far below white clouds are rolling over the landscape in huge fluffy wreaths. Above the hut, and actually trickling down over it, the stable cone soars to the sky. But the amazing sight is the line of the monstrous slope to the left—a line that now shows no curve whatever, but shoots down below the clouds, and up to the gods only know where (for I cannot see the end of it), straight as a tightened bowstring. The right flank is rocky and broken. But as for the left—I never dreamed it possible that a line so absolutely straight and smooth, and extending for so enormous a distance at such an amazing angle, could exist even in a volcano. That stupendous pitch gives me a sense of dizziness, and a totally unfamiliar feeling of wonder. Such regularity appears unnatural, frightful; seems even artificial—but artificial upon a superhuman and demoniac scale. I imagine that to fall thence from above would be to fall for leagues. Absolutely nothing to take hold of. But the gōriki assure me that there is no danger on that slope: it is all soft sand.

4

Though drenched with perspiration by the exertion of the first climb, I am already dry, and cold. . . . Up again. . . . The ascent is at first through ashes and sand as before; but presently large stones begin to mingle with the sand; and the way is always growing steeper. . . . I constantly slip. There is nothing firm, nothing resisting to stand upon: loose stones and cinders roll down at every step. . . . If a big lava-block were to detach itself from above! . . . In spite of my helpers and of the staff, I continually slip, and am all in perspiration again. Almost every stone that I tread upon turns under me. How is it that no stone ever turns under the feet of the gōriki? *They* never slip—never make a false step—never seem less at ease than they would be in walking over a matted floor. Their small brown broad feet always poise upon the shingle at exactly the right angle. They are heavier men than I; but they move lightly as birds. . . . Now I have to stop for rest every half-a-dozen steps. . . . The line of broken straw sandals follows the zigzags we take. . . . At last—at last another door in the face of the mountain. Enter the fourth station, and fling myself down upon the mats. Time, 10:30 A.M. Height, only 7937 feet;—yet it seemed such a distance!

Off again. . . . Way worse and worse. . . . Feel a new distress due to the rarefaction of the air. Heart beating as in a high fever. . . . Slope has become very rough. It is no longer soft ashes and sand mixed with stones, but stones only—fragments of lava, lumps of pumice, scoriae of every sort, all angled as if freshly broken with a hammer. All would likewise seem to have been expressly shaped so as to turn upside-down when trodden upon. Yet I must confess that they never turn under the feet of the gōriki. . . . The cast-off sandals strew the slope in ever-increasing numbers. . . . But for the gōriki I should have had ever so many bad tumbles: they cannot prevent me from slipping; but they never allow me to fall. Evidently I am not fitted to climb mountains. . . . Height, 8659 feet —but the fifth station is shut up! Must keep zigzagging on to the next. Wonder how I shall ever be able to reach it! . . . And there are people still alive who have climbed Fuji three and four times, *for pleasure!* . . . Dare not look back. See nothing but the black stone always turning under me, and the bronzed feet of those marvelous gōriki who never slip, never pant, and never perspire. . . . Staff begins to hurt my hand. . . . Gōriki push and pull: it is shameful of me, I know, to give them so much trouble. . . . Ah! sixth station!—may all the myriads of the gods bless my gōriki! Time, 2:07 P.M. Height, 9317 feet.

Resting, I gaze through the doorway at the abyss below. The land is now dimly visible only through rents in a prodigious wilderness of white clouds; and within these rents everything looks almost black. . . . The horizon has risen frightfully—has expanded monstrously. . . . My gōriki warn me that the summit is still miles away. I have been too slow. We must hasten upward.

Certainly the zigzag is steeper than before. . . . With the stones now mingle angular rocks; and we sometimes have to flank queer black bulks that look like basalt. . . . On the right rises, out of sight, a jagged black hideous ridge—an ancient lava-stream. The line of the left slope still shoots up, straight as a bow-string. . . . Wonder if the way will become any steeper;—doubt whether it can possibly become any rougher. Rocks dislodged by my feet roll down soundlessly;—I am afraid to look after them. Their noiseless vanishing gives me a sensation like the sensation of falling in dreams. . . .

There is a white gleam overhead—the lowermost verge of an immense stretch of snow. . . . Now we are skirting a snow-filled gully—the lowermost of those white patches which, at first sight of the summit this morning, seemed scarcely an inch long. It will take an hour to pass it. . . . A guide runs forward, while I rest upon my staff, and returns with a large ball of snow. What curious snow! Not flaky, soft, white snow, but a mass of transparent globules—exactly like glass beads. I eat some, and find it deliciously refreshing. . . . The seventh station is closed. How shall I get to the eighth? . . . Happily, breathing has become less difficult. . . . The wind is upon us again, and black dust with it. The gōriki keep close to me, and advance with caution. . . . I have to stop for rest at every turn on the path;—cannot talk for weariness. . . . I do not feel;—I am much too tired to feel. . . . How I managed it, I do not know;—but I have actually got to the eighth station! Not for a thousand millions of dollars will I go one step farther to-day. Time, 4:40 P.M. Height, 10,693 feet.

5

It is much too cold here for rest without winter clothing; and now I learn the worth of the heavy robes provided by the guides. The robes are blue, with big white Chinese characters on the back, and are padded thickly as bed-quilts; but they feel light; for the air is really like the frosty breath of February. . . . A meal is preparing;—I notice that charcoal at this elevation acts in a refractory manner, and that a fire can be maintained only by constant attention. . . . Cold and fatigue sharpen appetite: we consume a surprising quantity of Zō-sui—rice boiled with eggs and a little meat.

By reason of my fatigue and of the hour, it has been decided to remain here for the night.

Tired as I am, I cannot but limp to the doorway to contemplate the amazing prospect. From within a few feet of the threshold, the ghastly slope of rocks and cinders drops down into a prodigious disk of clouds miles beneath us—clouds of countless forms, but mostly wreathings and fluffy pilings;—and the whole huddling mass, reaching almost to the horizon, is blinding white under the sun. (By the Japanese, this tremendous cloud-expanse is well named Wata-no-Umi, "the Sea of Cotton.") The horizon itself—enormously risen, phantasmally expanded—seems halfway up above the world: a wide luminous belt ringing the hollow vision. Hollow, I call it, because extreme distances below the skyline are sky-colored and vague—so that the impression you receive is not of being on a point under a vault, but of being upon a point rising into a stupendous blue sphere, of which this huge horizon would represent the equatorial zone. To turn away from such a spectacle is not possible. I watch and watch until the dropping sun changes the colors—turning the Sea of Cotton into a Fleece of Gold. Half-round the horizon a yellow glory grows and burns. Here and there beneath it, through cloud-rifts, colored vaguenesses define: I now see golden water, with long purple headlands reaching into it, with ranges of violet peaks thronging behind it;—these glimpses curiously resembling portions of a tinted topographical map. Yet most of the landscape is pure delusion. Even my guides, with their long experience and their eagle-sight, can scarcely distinguish the real from the unreal;—for the blue and purple and violet clouds moving under the Golden Fleece, exactly mock the outlines and the tones of distant peaks and capes: you can detect what is vapor only by its slowly shifting shape. . . . Brighter and brighter glows the gold. Shadows come from the west—shadows flung by cloud-pile over cloud-pile; and these, like evening shadows upon snow, are violaceous blue. . . . Then orange-tones appear in the horizon; then smouldering crimson. And now the greater part of the Fleece of Gold has changed to cotton again—white cotton mixed with pink. . . . Stars thrill out. The cloud-waste uniformly whitens; —thickening and packing to the horizon. The west glooms. Night rises; and all things darken except that wondrous unbroken world-round of white—the Sea of Cotton.

The station-keeper lights his lamps, kindles a fire of twigs, prepares our beds. Outside it is bitterly cold, and, with the fall of night, becoming colder. Still I cannot turn away from that astounding vision. . . . Countless stars now flicker and shiver in the blue-black sky. Nothing whatever of the material world remains visible, except the black slope of the peak before my feet. The enormous cloud-disk below continues white; but to all appearance it has become a liquidly level white, without forms—a white flood. It is no longer the Sea of Cotton. It is a Sea of Milk, the Cosmic Sea of ancient Indian legend—and always self-luminous, as with ghostly quickenings.

. . .

7

6:40 A.M.—Start for the top. . . . hardest and roughest stage of the journey, through a wilderness of lava-blocks. The path zigzags between ugly masses that project from the slope like black teeth. The trail of castaway sandals is wider then ever. . . . Have to rest every few minutes. . . . Reach another long patch of the snow that looks like glass beads, and eat some. The next station—a half-station—is closed; and the ninth has ceased to exist. . . . A sudden fear comes to me, not of the ascent, but of the prospective descent by a route which is too steep even to permit of comfortably sitting down. But the guides assure me that there will be no difficulty, and that most of the return journey will be by another way— over the interminable level which I wondered at yesterday—nearly all soft sand, with very few stones. It is called the *hashiri* (glissade) and we are to descend at a run! . . .

All at once a family of field-mice scatter out from under my feet in panic; and the gōriki behind me catches one, and gives it to me. I hold the tiny shivering life for a moment to examine it, and set it free again. These little creatures have very long pale noses. How do they live in this waterless desolation—and at such an altitude—especially in the season of snow? For we are now at a height of more than eleven thousand feet! The gōriki say that the mice find roots growing under the stones. . . .

Wilder and steeper;—for me, at least, the climbing is sometimes on all fours. There are barriers which we surmount with the help of ladders. There are fearful places with Buddhist names, such as the Sai-no-Kawara, or Dry Bed of the River of Souls—a black waste strewn with heaps of rock, like those stone-piles which, in Buddhist pictures of the under-world, the ghosts of children build. . . .

Twelve thousand feet, and something—the top! Time, 8:20 A.M. . . . Stone huts! Shintō shrine with torii; icy well, called the Spring of Gold; stone tablet bearing a Chinese poem and the design of a tiger; rough walls of lava-blocks round these things—possibly for protection against the wind. Then the huge dead crater—probably between a quarter of a mile and half-a-mile wide, but shallowed up to within three or four hundred feet of the verge by volcanic detritus—a cavity horrible even in the tones of its yellow crumbling walls, streaked and stained with every hue of scorching. I perceive that the trail of straw sandals ends *in* the crater. Some hideous overhanging cusps of black lava—like the broken edges of monstrous cicatrix—project on two sides several hundred feet above the opening; but I certainly shall not take the trouble to climb them. Yet these—seen through the haze of a hundred miles—through the soft illusion of blue spring weather—appear as the opening snowy petals of the bud of the Sacred Lotus! . . . No spot in this world can be more horrible, more atrociously dismal, than the cindered tip of the Lotus as you stand upon it.

But the view—the view for a hundred leagues—and the light of the far faint dreamy world—and the fairy vapors of morning—and the marvelous wreathings of cloud: all this, and only this, consoles me for the labor and the pain. . . . Other pilgrims, earlier climbers—poised upon the highest crag, with faces turned to the tremendous East—are clapping their hands in Shintō prayer, saluting the mighty Day. . . . The immense poetry of the moment enters into me with a thrill. I know that the colossal vision before me has already become a memory ineffaceable—a memory of which no luminous detail can fade till the hour when thought itself must fade, and the dust of these eyes be mingled with the dust of the myriad million eyes that also have looked in ages forgotten before my birth, from the summit supreme of Fuji to the Rising of the Sun.

STUDY QUESTIONS

1. A striking feature of this work is its unusual, apparently idiomatic, punctuation —for example, "How I managed it, I do not know;—but I have actually got to the eighth station!" Hearn, who battled his editors on this score, insisted that his punctuation was for the *ear,* not for the *eye.* As an oral interpreter, do you find the punctuation a helpful source of clues for your performance? If you can allow the marks of punctuation to guide your performance, does the performance so guided lead you to an understanding of either the structure of the work or the writer?

2. Obviously, the structure of the work is meant to convey to the reader a sense of the hazards and hard work of the climb. The peak of the mountain represents, in a very real sense, the climax and culmination of the work; thus, the work ends as it does. But during the course of the work there are certain tensions that you are bound to become aware of. One kind is purely rhetorical: the tensions between the immediate impressions jotted down during the climb and the meditative reworking and reshaping of those impressions for a reading, or perhaps listening, audience. Can you locate parts where this kind of tension seems particularly active?

3. Another kind of tension exists within the character of the writer himself. Lafcadio Hearn is much too complicated a person to be analyzed briefly in these notes. Here no more than the general nature of his character can be

suggested. It is hoped that the following passages from Malcolm Cowley's excellent introduction to *The Selected Writings of Lafcadio Hearn* (New York: Citadel Press, 1949, pp. 2–7) will encourage you to look further into Hearn's life for some possible illumination on the complicated workings of the persona's mind:

No American author of the nineteenth century had a stranger life. He was born in 1850 on the Ionian island of Santa Maura—the ancient Leucadia, which explains his given name—and in 1904 his ashes were buried after a Buddhist ceremony in Tokyo. His ancestry was Maltese on his mother's side and hence may be taken as a mixture of Phoenician, Arab, Norman, Spanish, and Italian; on his father's side it was Anglo-Irish with—Lafcadio liked to think—a touch of Romany. He learned to say his first prayers in Italian and demotic Greek. Adopted by a wealthy great-aunt, Sarah Brenane, he was educated by private tutors in Dublin and at Catholic schools in England and France. He was a British subject until he became a naturalized Japanese at the age of forty-six; but he always thought of himself as an American writer. . . . All his life until then [his taking up residence in Japan, where he married into a Japanese family] Hearn had felt himself to be marked off from the rest of mankind by his small stature, his strange appearance and especially by his uneven eyes, one blind, marbled and sunken in his skull, the other myopic and protruding, so that it looked like the single eye of an octopus. . . . On the night when the child was expected, he had knelt at his wife's bedside and prayed in broken Japanese. "Come into the world with good eyes," he had murmured again and again. . . .

Just this small bit of biographical information may aid you to place dramatic importance upon the continual references to eyes throughout this piece (note the prominent reference at the conclusion). Perhaps these references may also serve to dramatize (that is, indicate the connection between utterance and character) the strange, almost dreamlike quality of the visual images. Look, for example, at the sentence "What I have been taking for the horizon, in front of us, suddenly breaks open, and begins to roll smokily away to left and right. In the great rift part of a dark-blue mass appears—a portion of Fuji."

4. Considering Hearn's character as the probable model for the character of the persona in this work may also help to "dramatize" (in the sense in which that word is used in the preceding question) the emphasis he places throughout the work on a kind of loving, yet remote and distant comparison of natural objects to women. Note the two comparisons that come to his mind upon seeing Fuji ("But the charm of the apparition is much less the charm of color than of symmetry . . ."). He may have "corrected" the image as a result of that "rhetorical tension" mentioned earlier. On the other hand, both images are present and the "impression of femininity" seems still to engage the persona's mind. The other image, moreover, speaks of a kind of visual skill and just as inevitably leads us back to the character of the man who is speaking. Nonetheless, an interesting way to explore the tensions in images, particularly the comparisons of natural objects to women throughout this work, may be to explore Hearn's ideas as set forth in his essay "Of the Eternal Feminine." In it he argues that one of the many dividing lines between Western mind and the Japanese is that Western writers steadfastly refuse to see nature as it actually exists, preferring instead to anthropomorphize nature in terms of feminine beauty.

5. Obviously, the direction of all the questions concerning this work is Hearn's character, since it infuses the personality of the persona. But biographical criticism of writers may leave an important question unanswered: Is it the character of the man that ultimately gives value to the work? Or is this particular work valuable because it gives us a view of Mount Fuji as seen by Lafcadio Hearn in 1897? Your experience in attempting to perform every word of this work and your close contact with its attitudes and images should equip you to answer this question.

Fanny Burney/from *Early Diary*

born 1752

[1778]

Friday was a very full day. In the morning we began talking of *Irene,* and Mrs. Thrale made Dr. Johnson read some passages which I had been remarking as uncommonly applicable, and told us he had not ever read so much of it before since it was first printed.

"Why, there is no making you read a play," said Mrs. Thrale, "either of your own, or any other person. What trouble had I to make you hear Murphy's *Know your own Mind!* 'Read rapidly, read rapidly,' you cried, and then took out your watch to see how long I was about it! Well, we won't serve Miss Burney so, sir; when we have her comedy we will do it all justice.". . .

The day was passed most agreeably. In the evening we had, as usual, a literary conversation. I say we, only because Mrs. Thrale will make me take some share, by perpetually applying to me; and, indeed, there can be no better house for rubbing up the memory, as I hardly ever read, saw, or heard of any book that by some means or other has not been mentioned here.

Mr. Lort produced several curious MSS. of the famous Bristol Chatterton; among others, his will, and divers verses written against Dr. Johnson as a placeman and pensioner; all which he read aloud, with a steady voice and unmoved countenance.

I was astonished at him; Mrs. Thrale not much pleased; Mr. Thrale silent and attentive; and Mr. Seward was slily laughing. Dr. Johnson himself, listened profoundly and laughed openly. Indeed, I believe he wishes his abusers no other than a good dinner, like Pope.

Just as we had got our biscuits and toast-and-water, which make the Streatham supper, and which, indeed, is all there is any chance of eating after our late and great dinners, Mr. Lort suddenly said,

"Pray, ma'am, have you heard anything of a novel that runs about a good deal, called *Evelina?*"

What a ferment did this question, before such a set, put me in!

I did not know whether he spoke to me, or Mrs. Thrale; and Mrs. Thrale was in the same doubt, and as she owned, felt herself in a little palpitation for me, not knowing what might come next. Between us both, therefore, he had no answer.

"It has been recommended to me," continued he; "but I have no desire to see it, because it has such a foolish name. Yet I have heard a great deal of it, too."

He then repeated *Evelina*—in a very languishing and ridiculous tone.

My heart beat so quick against my stays that I almost panted with extreme agitation, from the dread either of hearing some horrible criticism, or of being betrayed; and I munched my biscuit as if I had not eaten for a fortnight.

I believe the whole party were in some little consternation; Dr. Johnson began see-sawing; Mr. Thrale awoke; Mr. E——— who I fear has picked up some notion of the affair from being so much in the house, grinned amazingly; and Mr. Seward, biting his nails and flinging himself back in his chair, I am sure had wickedness enough to enjoy the whole scene.

Mrs. Thrale was really a little fluttered, but without looking at me, said, "And pray what, Mr. Lort, what have you heard of it?"

Now, had Mrs. Thrale not been flurried, this was the last question she should have ventured to ask before me. Only suppose what I must feel when I heard it.

"Why, they say," answered he, "that it's an account of a young lady's first entrance into company, and of the scrapes she gets into; and they say there's a great deal of character in it, but I have not cared to look in it, because the name is so foolish—*Evelina!*"

"Why foolish, sir?" cried Dr. Johnson. "Where's the folly of it?"

"Why, I won't say much for the name myself," said Mrs. Thrale, "to those who don't know the reason of it, which I found out, but which nobody else seems to know."

She then explained the name from Evelyn, according to my own meaning.

"Well," said Dr. Johnson, "if that was the reason, it is a very good one."

"Why, have you had the book here?" cried Mr. Lort, staring.

"Ay, indeed, have we," said Mrs. Thrale; "I read it when I was last confined, and I laughed over it, and I cried over it!"

"Oh, ho!" said Mr. Lort, "this is another thing! If you have had it here, I will certainly read it."

"Had it? ay," returned she; "and Dr. Johnson, who would not look at it at first, was so caught by it when I put it in the coach with him that he has sung its praises ever since,—and he says Richardson would have been proud to have written it."

"Oh, ho! this is a good hearing!" cried Mr. Lort; "if Dr. Johnson can read it, I shall get it with all speed."

"You need not go far for it," said Mrs. Thrale, "for it's now upon yonder table."

I could sit still no longer; there was something so awkward, so uncommon, so strange in my then situation, that I wished myself a hundred miles off; and, indeed, I had almost choked myself with the biscuit, for I could not for my life swallow it; and so I got up, and, as Mr. Lort went to the table to look at *Evelina,* I left the room, and was forced to call for water to wash down the biscuit, which literally stuck in my throat. . . .

Dr. Johnson was later than usual this morning, and did not come down till our breakfast was over, and Mrs. Thrale had risen to give some orders, I believe: I, too, rose, and took a book at another end of the room. Some time after, before he had yet appeared, Mr. Thrale called out to me,

"So, Miss Burney, you have a mind to feel your legs before the doctor comes?"

"Why so?" cried Mr. Lort.

"Why, because when he comes she will be confined."

"Ay?—how is that?"

"Why, he never lets her leave him, but keeps her prisoner till he goes to his own room."

"Oh, ho!" cried Mr. Lort, "she is in great favour with him."

"Yes," said Mr. Seward, "and I think he shows his taste."

"I did not know," said Mr. Lort, "but he might keep her to help him in his *Lives of the Poets,* if she's so clever."

"And yet," said Mrs. Thrale, "Miss Burney never flatters him, though she is such a favourite with him;—but the tables are turned, for he sits and flatters her all day long."

"I don't flatter him," said I, "because nothing I could say would flatter him."

Mrs. Thrale then told a story of Hannah Moore, which I think exceeds, in its severity, all the severe things I have yet heard of Dr. Johnson's saying.

When she was introduced to him, not long ago, she began singing his praise in the warmest manner, and talking of the pleasure and the instruction she had received from his writings, with the highest encomiums. For some time he heard her with that quietness which a long use of praise has given him: she then redoubled her strokes, and, as Mr. Seward calls it, peppered still more highly: till, at length, he turned suddenly to her, with a stern and angry countenance, and said, "Madam, before you flatter a man so grossly to his face, you should consider whether or not your flattery is worth his having."

Mr. Seward then told another instance of his determination not to mince the matter, when he thought reproof at all deserved. During a visit of Miss Brown's to Streatham, he was inquiring of her several things that she could not answer; and as he held her so cheap in regard to books, he began to question her concerning domestic affairs—puddings, pies, plain work, and so forth. Miss Brown, not at all more able to give a good account of herself in these articles than in the others, began all her answers with, "Why, sir, one need not be obliged to do so,—or so," whatever was the thing in question. When he had finished his interrogatories, and she had finished her "need nots" he ended the discourse with saying, "As to your needs, my dear, they are so very many, that you would be frightened yourself if you knew half of them."

After breakfast on Friday, or yesterday, a curious trait occurred of Dr. Johnson's jocosity. It was while the talk ran so copiously upon their urgency that I should produce a comedy. While Mrs. Thrale was in the midst of her flattering persuasions, the doctor, see-sawing in his chair, began laughing to himself so heartily as to almost shake his seat as well as his sides. We stopped our confabulation, in which he had ceased to join, hoping he would reveal the subject of his mirth; but he enjoyed it inwardly, without heeding our curiosity,—till at last he said he had been struck with a notion that "Miss Burney would begin her dramatic career by writing a piece called *Streatham*."

He paused, and laughed yet more cordially, and then suddenly commanded a pomposity to his countenance and his voice, and added, "Yes! *Streatham—a Farce.*"

How little did I expect from this Lexiphanes, this great and dreaded lord of English literature, a turn for burlesque humour!

STUDY QUESTIONS

1. One of the central topics of discussion in this diary entry is the novel *Evelina*. Why does Mr. Lort's question about the novel put Fanny Burney in "a ferment"? Is there any difference between the Miss Burney who is distraught by the conversation and the Miss Burney who *writes about* this "ferment"?

2. Why is the discussion of *Evelina* surrounded by Dr. Johnson's reading from *Irene* and later anecdotes about his wit? (Note particularly the function of the Hannah Moore story.) How do these sections interrelate?

3. Who is the "you" implied in the statement "Only imagine what I must feel when I heard of it"?

4. This selection contains a number of allusions to persons and literary works with which you may not be familiar. One excellent source for the further study of Miss Burney's diary is Chauncey Brewster Tinker's *Dr. Johnson and Fanny Burney* (New York: Moffat, Yard & Co., 1911), which is a compilation of those passages from the diary that deal with Dr. Johnson. Furthermore,

Tinker's introductory essay provides a generally sound understanding of the Johnson-Burney relationship; also, his notes are especially helpful in clarifying some of the more obscure allusions.

5. This selection is from a diary usually considered to be in the lyric mode. Yet, the structure of this passage has a highly dramatic quality. What seems to be the function of the dramatic elements in this passage? Why does Miss Burney "show" most of her story through direct discourse and "stage directions"? What stylistic devices does she use to characterize the individual persons in the story? How fully developed is the picture of each person in her story?

6. Accounts of the life of Samuel Johnson were written by several others of his contemporaries. One could make an interesting study comparing Fanny Burney's treatment of Johnson with that of one of the following persons: James Boswell, Mrs. Piozzi, Sir John Hawkins.

Dylan Thomas/How to Be a Poet or The Ascent of Parnassus Made Easy

born 1914

Let me, at once, make it clear that I am not considering, in these supposedly informative jottings, Poetry as an Art or a Craft, as the rhythmic verbal expression of a spiritual necessity or urge, but solely as the means to a social end; that end being the achievement of a status in society solid enough to warrant the poet discarding and expunging those affectations, so essential in the early stages, of speech, dress, and behaviour; an income large enough to satisfy his physical demands, unless he has already fallen victim to the Poet's Evil, or Great Wen; and a permanent security from the fear of having to write any more. I do not intend to ask, let alone to answer, the question, "Is Poetry a Good Thing?" but only, "Can Poetry Be Made Good Business?"

I shall, to begin with, introduce to you a few of the main types of poets who have made the social and financial grade.

First, though not in order of importance, is the poet who has emerged docketed "lyrical," from the Civil Service. He can be divided, so far as his physical appearance goes, into two types. He is either thin, not to say of a shagged-out appearance, with lips as fulsome, sensual, and inviting as a hen's ovipositor, bald from all too maculate birth, his eyes made small and reddened by reading books in French, a language he cannot understand, in an attic in the provinces while young and repellent, his voice like the noise of a mouse's nail on tinfoil, his nostrils transparent, his breath grey; or else he is jowled and bushy, with curved pipe and his nose full of dottle, the look of all Sussex in his stingo'd eyes, his burry tweeds smelling of the dogs he loathes, with a voice like a literate airedale's that has learned its vowels by correspondence course, and an intimate friend of Chesterton's, whom he never met.

Let us see in what manner our man has arrived at his present and enviable position as the Poet who has made Poetry Pay.

Dropped into the Civil Service at an age when many of our young poets now are running away to Broadcasting House, today's equivalent of the Sea, he is at first lost to sight in the mountains of red tape which, in future years, he is so mordantly, though with a wry and puckered smile, to dismiss in a paragraph in his "Around and About My Shelves." After a few years, he begins to peer out from the forms and files in which he leads his ordered, nibbling life, and picks up a cheese crumb here, a dropping there, in his ink-stained thumbs. His ears are uncannily sensitive: he can hear an opening being opened a block of offices away.

And soon he learns that a poem in a Civil Service magazine is, if not a step up the ladder, at least a lick in the right direction. And he writes a poem. It is, of course, about Nature; it confesses a wish to escape from humdrum routine and embrace the unsophisticated life of the farm laborer; he desires, though without scandal, to wake up with the birds; he expresses the opinion that a plowshare, not a pen, best fits his little strength; a decorous pantheist, he is one with the rill, the rhyming mill, the rosy-bottomed milkmaid, the russet-cheeked rat-catcher, swains, swine, pipits, pippins. You can smell the country in his poems, the fields, the flowers, the armpits of Triptolemus, the barns, the byres, the hay, and, most of all, the corn. The poem is published. A single lyrical extract from the beginning must suffice:—

The roaring street is hushed!
Hushed, do I say?
The wing of a bird has brushed
Time's cobwebs away.
Still, still as death, the air
Over the grey stones!
And over the grey thoroughfare
I hear—sweet tones!—
A blackbird open its bill,
—A blackbird, aye!—
And sing its liquid fill
From the London sky.

A little time after the publication of the poem, he is nodded to in the corridor by Hotchkiss of Inland Revenue, himself a weekending poet with two slim volumes to his credit, half an inch in the Poets' Who's Who or the Newbolt Calendar, an ambitious wife with a vee-neck and a fringe who lost the battle of the Slade, a small car that always drives, as though by itself, to Sussex—as a parson's horse would once unthinkingly trot to the public house—and an unfinished monograph on the influence of Blunden on the hedgerow.

Hotchkiss, lunching with Sowerby of Customs, himself a literary figure of importance with a weekly column in Will o' Lincoln's Weekly and his name on the editorial list of the Masterpiece of the Fortnight Club (volumes at reduced rates to all writers, and a complete set of the works of Mary Webb quarter-price at Christmas), says casually, "You've rather a promising fellow in your department, Sowerby. Young Cribbe. I've been reading a little thing of his, 'I Desire the Curlew.'" And Cribbe's name goes the small, foetid rounds.

He is next asked to contribute a *group* of poems to Hotchkiss's anthology, "New Pipes," which Sowerby praises—"a rare gift for the haunting phrase"—in Will o' Lincoln's. Cribbe sends copies of the anthology, each laboriously signed, "To the greatest living English poet, in homage," to twenty of the dullest poets still on their hind legs. Some of his inscribed gifts are acknowledged. Sir Tom Knight spares a few generous, though bemused, moments to scribble a message on a sheet of crested writing paper removed, during a never-to-be-repeated weekend visit, from a shortsighted but not all that shortsighted peer. "Dear Mr. Crabbe," Sir Tom writes, "I appreciate your little tribute. Your poem, 'Nocturne with Lilies,' is worthy of Shanks. Go on. Go on. There is room on the mount." The fact that Cribbe's poem is not "Nocturne with Lilies" at all, but "On Hearing Delius by a Lych-Gate," does not perturb Cribbe, who carefully files the letter, after blowing away the dandruff, and soon is in the throes of collecting his poems together to make, *misericordia,* a book, "Linnet and Spindle," dedicated "To Clem Sowerby, that green-fingered gardener in the Gardens of the Hesperides."

The book appears. Some favourable notice is taken, particularly in Middlesex. And Sowerby, too modest to review it himself after such a gratifying dedication, reviews it under a different name. "This young poet," he writes, "is not, thanks be it, too 'modernistic' to pay reverence to the shining source of his inspiration. Cribbe will go far."

And Cribbe goes to his publishers. A contract is drawn up, Messrs. Stitch and Time undertaking to publish his next book of verse on condition that they have the first option on his next nine novels. He contrives also to be engaged as a casual reader of manuscripts to Messrs. Stitch and Time, and returns home clutching a parcel which contains a book on the Development of the Oxford Movement in Finland by a Cotswold Major, three blank-verse tragedies about Mary Queen of Scots, and a novel entitled "Tomorrow, Jennifer."

Now Cribbe, until his contract, has never thought of writing a novel. But, undaunted by the fact that he cannot tell one person from another—people, to him, are all one dull, grey mass, except celebrities and departmental superiors—that he has no interest whatsoever in anything they do or say, except in so far as it concerns his career, and that his inventive resources are as limited as those of a chipmunk on a treadmill, he sits down in his shirt-sleeves, loosens his collar, thumbs in the shag, and begins to study in earnest how best, with no qualifications, to make a success of commercial fiction. He soon comes to the conclusion that only quick sales and ephemeral reputations are made by tough novels with such titles as "I've Got It Coming" or "Ten Cents a Dice," by proletarian novels about the conversion to dialectical materialism of Palais-de wide boys, entitled, maybe, "Red Rain on You, Alf," by novels, called, maybe, "Melody in Clover," about dark men with slight limps, called Dirk Conway and their love for two women, lascivious Ursula Mountclare and little, shy Fay Waters. And he soon sees that only the smallest sales, and notices only in the loftiest monthlies of the most limited circulation, will ever result from his writing such a novel as "The Inner Zodiac," by G. H. Q. Bidet, a ruthless analysis of the ideological conflicts arising from the relationship between Philip Armour, an international impotent physicist, Tristram Wolf, a bisexual sculptor in teak, and Philip's virginal but dynamic Creole wife, Titania, a lecturer in Balkan Economics, and how these highly sensitised characters—so redolent, as they are, of the post-Sartre Age—react a profound synthesis while working together, for the sake of One-ness, in a Unesco Clinic.

No fool, Cribbe realises, even in the early stages of his exploration, with theodolite and respirator through darkest Foyle, that the novel to write is that which commands a steady, unsensational, provincial and suburban sale and concerns, for choice, the birth, education, financial ups-and-downs, marriages, separations, and deaths of five generations of a family of Lancashire cotton-brokers. This novel, he grasps at once, should be in the form of a trilogy, and each volume should bear some such solid, uneventful title as "The Warp," "The Woof," and "The Way." And he sets to work.

From the reviews of Cribbe's first novel, one may select: "Here is sound craftsmanship allied to sterling characterisation." "Incidents a-plenty." "You become as familiar with George Steadiman, his wife Muriel, old Tobias Matlock (a delightful vignette) and all the inhabitants of Loom House, as you do with your own family." "These dour Northcotes grow on you." "English as Manchester rain." "Mr. Cribbe is a bullterrier." "A story in the Phyllis Bottome class."

On the success of the novel, Cribbe joins the N.I.B. Club, delivers a paper on the Early Brett Young Country, and becomes a regular reviewer, praising every other novel he receives—("The prose shimmers")—and inviting every third novelist to dine at the Servile Club, to which he has recently been elected.

When the whole of the trilogy has appeared, Cribbe rises, like scum, to the N.I.B. committee, attends all the memorial services for men of letters who are really dead for the first time in fifty years, tears up his old contract and signs another, brings out a new novel, which becomes a Book

Society choice, is offered, by Messrs. Stitch and Time, a position in an "advisory capacity," which he accepts, leaves the Civil Service, buys a cottage in Bucks ("You wouldn't think it was only thirty miles from London, would you. Look, old man, see that crested grebe." À starling flies by), a new desk and a secretary whom he later marries for her touch-typing. Poetry? Perhaps a sonnet in the *Sunday Times* every now and then; a little collection of verse once in a while ("My first love, you know"). But it doesn't really bother him any more, though it got him where he is. *He has made the grade!*

2

And now we must move to see, for a moment, a very different kind of poet, whom we shall call Cedric. To follow in Cedric's footsteps—(he'd love you to, and would never call a policeman unless it was that frightfully sinister sergeant you see sometimes in Mecklenburgh Square, just like an El Greco)—you must be born twilightly into the middle classes, go to one of the correct schools—(which, of course, you must loathe, for it is essential, from the first, to be misunderstood)—and arrive at the University with your reputation already established as a coming poet and looking, if possible, something between a Guards officer and a fashionable photographer's doxy.

You may say, But how is one to arrive with one's reputation already established as "a poet to watch"? (Poet-watching may in the future become as popular as bird-watching. And it is quite reasonable to imagine the editorial offices of "The Poetaster" being bought up by the nation as a sanctuary.) But that is a question outside the scope of these all-too-rough notes, as it must be assumed that anyone wishing to take up Poetry as a career has always known how to turn the stuff out when required. And also Cedric's college tutor was his housemaster's best friend. So here is Cedric, known already to the discerning few for his sensitive poems about golden limbs, sun-jeweled fronds, the ambrosia of the first shy kiss in the delicate-traceried caverns of the moon (really the school boot-cupboard), at the threshold of fame and the world laid out before him like a row of balletomanes.

If this were the twenties, Cedric's first book of poems, published while he was still an undergraduate, might be called "Asps and Lutes." It would be nostalgic for a life that never was. It would be world-weary. (He once saw the world, out of a train carriage window: it looked unreal.) It would be a carefully garish mixture, a cunningly evocative pudding full of plums pulled from the Sitwells and others, a mildly cacophonous hot-house of exotic horticultural and comic-erotic bric-a-brac, from which I extract these typical lines:—

A cornucopia of phalluses
Cascade on the vermilion palaces
In arabesques and syrup rigadoons;
Quince-breasted Circes of the zenanas
Do catch this rain of cherry-wigged bananas
And saraband beneath the raspberry moons.

After a tiff with the University authorities he vanishes into the Key of Blue—a made man.

If it were in the thirties, the title of his book might well be "Pharos, I Warn," and would consist of one of two kinds of verse. Either it would be made of long, lax, lackadaisical rhythms, dying falls, and images of social awareness:—

After the incessant means-test of the
    conspiratorial winter
Scrutinizing the tragic history of each
    robbed branch,
Look! the triumphant bourgeoning! spring
    gay as a workers' procession
To the newly-opened gymnasium!
Look! the full employment of the blossoms!

Or it would be daringly full of slang and street phrases, snippets of song hits, Kipling jingles, kippered blues:—

We're sitting pretty
In the appalling city—
I know where we're going but I don't know
    where from—

Take it from me, boy,
You're my cup-of-tea-boy,
We're sitting on a big black bomb.

Social awareness! That was the motto. He would talk over coffee— ("Adrian makes the best coffee in the whole of this uncivilized island." "Tell me, Rodney, where *do* you get these delicious little pink cakes?" "It's a secret!" "Oh, *do* tell. And I'll give you that special receipt that Basil's Colonel brought back from Ceylon, it takes three pounds of butter and a mango pod")—of spending the long vacation in "somewhere *really* alive. I mean, but really. Like the Rhondda Valley or something. I mean, I know I'll feel really *orientated* there. I mean, one's so stagnant here. Books, books. It's people that count. I mean, one's got to know the miners." And he spends the long vacation with Reggie, in Bonn. A volume of politico-travel chat follows, the promise of which is amply fulfilled when, years later, he turns up as Literary Secretary of I.A.C.T.— (International Arts Council Tomorrow).

If Cedric were writing in the forties, he would, perhaps, be engulfed, so that he could not see the wool for the Treece, in a kind of "apocalyptic" batter, and his first volume might be entitled "Plangent Macrocosm," or "Heliogabalus in Pentecost." Cedric can mix his metaphor, bog his cliché, and soak his stolen symbols in stale ass's milk as glibly and glueily as the best of them.

Next, London and reviewing. Reviewing, obviously, the work of other poets. This, to do badly, is simple and, though not at once, financially rewarding. The vocabulary that a conscientiously dishonest reviewer of contemporary verse must learn is limited. Trend, of course, and impact, sphere of influence, Audenesque, the later Yeats, constructivism, schematic, ingeniously sprinkled, will help along, no end, the short and sweeping dismissal of the lifework of any adult and responsible poet.

The principal rules are few to remember: When reviewing, say, two entirely dissimilar books of verse, pit one against the other as though they were originally written in strict competition. "After Mr. A's subtle, taut, and integrated poetical comments or near-epigrams, Mr. B's long and sonorous heroic narrative, for all its textural richness and vibrative orchestration, rings curiously hollow" is an example of this most worth-while and labor-saving device. Decide, quite carefully, to be a staunch admirer of one particular poet, whether you like his poetry or not; cash in on him; make him your own; patent him; carve a niche with him. Bring his name, gratuitously, into your reviews: "Mr. E is, unfortunately, a poet much given to rhodomontade (unlike Hector Whistle)." "Reading Mr. D's admirably scholarly though, in places, pedestrian translations, we find ourselves longing for the cool ardor and consummate craftsmanship of Hector Whistle." Be careful, when you choose your poet, not to poach. Ask yourself first, "Is Hector Whistle anyone else's pigeon?"

Read all other reviews of the books you are about to review before you say a word yourself. Quote from the poems only when pressed for time: a review should be about the reviewer, not the poet. Be careful not to slate a bad rich poet unless he is notoriously mean, dead, or in America, for it is not such a long step from reviewing verse to editing a magazine, and the rich bad poet may well put up the money.

Returning to Cedric, let us suppose that he has, as a result of comparing a rich young man's verse with Auden's, to the detriment of Auden's, been given the editorship of a new literary periodical. (He may also be given a flat. If not, he should insist that the new periodical must have commodious offices. He then lives in them.) Cedric's first problem is what to call the thing. This is not easy, as most of the names that mean nothing at all—essential to the success of a new project—have all been used: *Horizon, Polemic, Harvest, Caravel, Seed, Transition, Arena, Circus,*

Cronos, Signposts, Wind and Rain—they've all been had. Can you hear Cedric's mind churning away? "Vacuum," "Volcano," "Limbo," "Mile-stone," "Need," "Eruption," "Schism," "Data," "Arson." Yes, he's got it: "Chiaroscuro." The rest is easy: just the editing.

But let us look, very quickly, at some other methods of making poetry a going concern.

The Provincial Rush, or the Up-Rimbaud-and-At-Em approach. This is not wholeheartedly to be recommended as certain qualifications are es-sential. Before you swoop and burst upon the center of literary activity —which means, when you are very young, the right pubs, and, later, the right flats, and, later still, the right clubs—you must have behind you a body (it need have no head) of ferocious and un-understandable verse. (It is not, as I said before, my function to describe how these gauche and verbose ecstasies are achieved. Hart Crane found that, while listening, drunk, to Sibelius, he could turn out the stuff like billyho. A friend of mine, who has been suffering from a violent headache since he was eight, finds it so easy to write anyway he has to tie knots in his unpleasant handker-chief to remind him to stop. There are many methods, and always, when there's a will and slight delirium, there's a way.) Again, this poet must possess a thirst and constitution like that of a salt-eating pony, a hippo's hide, boundless energy, prodigious conceit, no scruples, and—most im-portant of all, this can never be overestimated—a home to go *back* to in the provinces whenever he breaks down.

Of the poet who merely writes because he wants to write, who does not deeply mind if he is published or not, and who can put up with poverty and total lack of recognition in his lifetime, nothing of any pertinent value can be said. He is no businessman. Posterity Does Not Pay.

Also, and highly *un*recommended, are the following:—

The writing of limericks. Vast market, little or no pay.
Poems in crackers. Too seasonal.
Poems for children. This will kill you, and the children.
Obituaries in verse. Only established favorites used.
Poetry as a method of blackmail (by boring). Dangerous. The one you blackmail might retaliate by reading you aloud his unfinished tragedy about St. Bernard: "The Flask."
And lastly: *Poems on lavatory walls.* The reward is purely psychological.

(1950)

STUDY QUESTIONS

1. Consider the particular pose or poses that Thomas takes in the course of this essay. What kind of mask has he adopted, and how does the mask suit his purpose? When he occasionally drops the mask, how is the tone affected? How does the dropping of the mask implement his argument? How does it function in achieving a comic effect?

2. Compare Thomas' bravado descriptions of his poets with the relative dullness of the poets being described. What sort of effect is created by this juxtaposition?

3. In this essay Thomas makes quite clear the kinds of poetry he does not like. What poets or groups of poets does he seem to be parodying? Can you discover particular poets or poems by Thomas' contemporaries that might serve as models for his parodies?

4. Thomas also implies what kind of poetry he *does* like. How would you characterize such poetry? How would you describe Thomas' apparent evaluation and description of a poet whom he would like?

5. How much of Thomas' own poetry is evident in this essay? Where? Compare this essay with the poem by Thomas in the following chapter. Are there any similarities in style? tone? diction?

6. While the persona in this essay is obviously speaking (for Thomas' ironic purpose) of "how to be a poet," of how to make poetry "Good Business," Thomas is having a great deal of fun speaking of how *not* to write poetry. Perhaps it would not be unwise to keep this essay in mind as you turn to the next chapter, considering how Thomas (or this persona) would evaluate the poets included there.

EXERCISES AND BIBLIOGRAPHY

1. The literary genre studied in this chapter, nonfictional prose, has for centuries been considered the particular kind of discourse that most clearly belongs to the art of "rhetoric." Thus, many of the study questions are rhetorical in nature: Some concern the relationship between the speaker of or in the selection and his audience. One of the best recent attempts to describe the characteristics of nonfictional prose as a literary genre is Edwin Black's *Rhetorical Criticism* (New York: Macmillan, 1965). In reading this book, pay particular attention to the last two chapters, in which Professor Black proposes a "continuum" along which types of prose discourse may be ranged; he also discusses the characteristics of "exhortative discourse," which may be placed at one end of the continuum, and the "genre of argumentation," which comes near the center of the continuum. In what ways do Black's ideas complement or contradict the characteristics of nonfictional prose offered in this chapter's introductory essay? How might the selections in this chapter be ranged on his hypothetical continuum?

2. A book edited by Edward P. J. Corbett, *Rhetorical Analyses of Literary Works* (New York: Oxford University Press, 1969), gives two examples of analyses of nonfictional prose: Newman's *Apologia* and Chapter 15 of Gibbon's *Decline and Fall of the Roman Empire.* How do the analytical methods employed in those analyses differ from or resemble the ones proposed in this book? Professor Corbett's introductory essay is an excellent attempt to describe the general characteristics of the rhetorical analysis. Having read that introduction, ask yourself, "How does the rhetorical analysis of poetry or of fiction differ from the rhetorical analysis of nonfictional prose?"

3. The various sources cited throughout Professor Corbett's book offer a good preliminary bibliography for the advanced student interested in pursuing problems relating not only to the rhetorical analysis but also to such matters as "extrinsic," or "contextual," analysis. Another good source of aid is Joseph Schwartz and John A. Rycenga (eds.), *The Province of Rhetoric* (New York: Ronald, 1965). The editors provide (pp. 539–557) study questions for further exploration of matters examined in each of the essays included in their book as well as an extensive bibliography for further reading on the subject of rhetoric. After reading Corbett's book and the book by Schwartz and Rycenga, the student might attempt to answer this question: "Of what relevance is the study of rhetoric for the oral interpreter?" Of course, any one of the sets of study questions provided by Schwartz and Rycenga—particularly those for the chapters in which nonfictional prose is analyzed—could be a good basis for a short paper.

4. For centuries the study of style has been primarily devoted to one of two major schools of criticism: (1) one whose studies of style are heavily impressionistic and consequently relatively meaningless as analytical models and (2) another whose studies of style are severely quantitative (for example, studies of word frequencies) and consequently relatively meaningless as paradigms for meaningful interpretation. In the past decade linguists (and literary critics with some knowledge of linguistics) have held out some hope for stylistic models for analysis. They insist that the structure of any text must be understood in relationship to the structure of the language in general. With this idea in mind read the two articles by Richard Ohmann listed below. Do Ohmann's attempts to relate the rules and methods of transformational grammar to the study of literary style provide a reliable method of engaging in meaningful discourse about stylistic characteristics?

   a. "Generative Grammars and the Concept of Literary Style," *Word,* 20 (December 1964), 423–439. Notice particularly in this article Ohmann's discussion of the transformational rules and operations characteristic of the work of certain writers, and the relationship between these rules and operations and a writer's style.

   b. "Literature as Sentences," *College English,* 27 (January 1966), 261–267. In this article pay particular attention to how Ohmann, still attempting to discover a way to deal with the problems of style, suggests a possible parallel between form and surface structure on the one hand and content and deep structure on the other.

5. In the study questions following many of the selections in this chapter, there are a number of references to a writer's diction, or word choice. In pursuing

the question of word choice and its implications in a literary work, read the following works:

a. Richard Ohmann, "Prologomena to the Analysis of Prose Style," in Harold C. Martin (ed.), *Style in Prose Fiction: English Institute Essays, 1958* (New York: Columbia University Press, 1959), pp. 1–24. Ohmann argues in this essay that "stylistic preferences reflect cognitive preference," that the way in which a writer perceives and shapes his life experiences can be discerned and discovered in his prose style. One order reflects the other. Does Ohmann's argument suggest anything special for the interpreter's approach to the study of literary speakers and their behavior?

b. William O. Hendricks, "Three Models for the Description of Poetry," *Journal of Linguistics,* 5 (April 1969), 1–22. Hendricks is dealing largely with poems as examples of his argument, but the article has clear implications for the study and description of any form of imaginative literature. Note particularly the suggestion that the emphasis in stylistic description "be shifted from considerations of poetic LANGUAGE to considerations of poetic TEXTS." How does this relate to the distinction made in the essay between "language structure" and "text structure"? What does Hendricks mean by "text"? What relevance do you find in the notion that structures are characterized by "relationships" rather than by "things"?

6. Thomas A. Sebeok (ed.), *Style in Language* (Cambridge: M.I.T. Press, 1960), is a large collection of essays dealing with style from many points of view. Read some of the essays in this book to see if you can find any other useful models for studying the style of the nonfictional works in this chapter. Do any of the essays seem to provide particular tools for the study of other literary forms, such as poetry?

INTERPRETING POETRY

In the preceding chapter the statement was made that lyric poetry is the closest ally to nonfictional prose. The reason for this is that both tend to center on the responses of *one* speaker. Furthermore, in both kinds of literature the differences between the persona and the implied author, or poet, tend not to be noticeably distinct. With these two characteristics in mind look at a lyric poem—first by examining only what the persona says (thereby leaving out the title and the name of the poet):

What happens to a dream deferred?

> Does it dry up
> like a raisin in the sun?
> Or fester like a sore—
> And then run?
> Does it stink like rotten meat?
> Or crust and sugar over—
> like a syrupy sweet?
>
> Maybe it just sags
> like a heavy load.
>
> *Or does it explode?*

The major clue to the speaker's identity is the kind of images, or comparisons, he uses to express his emotions. The images belong to neither a man's nor a woman's world solely. One can only say that the speaker, whoever "he" may be, is familiar with a world of raisins drying up in the sun, festering sores, rotten meat, syrupy sweets, sagging loads, even explosions. His world is a world of ugliness and violence—at least that is the only world that defines the possibilities of a "dream deferred" so far as the persona is concerned.

In fact, in this world of possibilities the word "deferred" at first seems curiously out of place. It sounds like a word that belongs to another world, transplanted and applied to the dream in the persona's world. It sounds like "officialese," the language of authority.

The persona seems to be meditating, speaking to himself. He asks a philosophical question, then poses several possible answers in question form. Yet the arrangement of the answers might indicate a clear building up to a climax. The increasingly shorter stanzas set the final line off by itself. The location of the only statement, or nonquestion, in the poem just before the final line serves to give that final line added emphasis, in addition to the italics. The dream deferred has not exploded yet, but that is the most important possibility. Perhaps the persona discovers this during his utterance.

The speaking level of the implied author, as noted in the preceding chapter, is also part of the "text" of any literary selection. When information that comes only from the implied author's speaking level is added—notably the title and the author's name—several of the problems touched on in this brief glance at the persona's speaking level become resolved. The author is Langston Hughes, a distinguished, contemporary black poet.

This example should help you see the functional relationship of two roles available in a lyric poem: the role of the poet and the role of the persona. In this case, these two are almost inseparable. The poet supplies the title and his name. The persona speaks the poem. In speaking this poem, the persona is confronted with a host of possible answers to his opening question, answers that are questions and that become arranged in a certain order in the course of his utterance. It is the poet who has supplied that order, which he calls a "dream deferred." The persona, with his point of view confined to the syntactical boundaries of the poem, discovers the climactical arrangement of his utterance at almost the same time as those hearing, or overhearing, him do. The poet, naturally, sees the beginning, the middle, and the end, for he fashioned them. When we have a sense of the structure of the poem—of how the poem was put together—we are sharing the poet's perspective. As has been said repeatedly in this book, the real action of the poem lies in the tension between the persona's and the poet's perspectives.

There is another important difference between the poet and the persona in this poem—their identity. One can easily identify the poet. He is Langston Hughes. If you are familiar with his work, a certain image—called the "implied author," or "implied poet" in this book—comes to mind. Earlier it was indicated that the image that comes to mind is "distinguished, contemporary black poet." But one cannot so easily identify the persona. He may be male or female, old or young; in fact, any specific characteristics he may have belong less to a certain individual than to an entire environment, the environment specified by the title of the poem.

Every poem, however, regardless of how specific its environment, seems to have a universality of application. In this poem, the persona's frustration is potentially *everybody's* frustration—everybody's question—the feeling of anyone who is perplexed, bewildered, and apparently unable to do anything about a process that is destroying people, perhaps even himself. The *poet,* however, has applied that feeling to a specific locale—the locale named in his title. The poem itself comes alive in the tension between the poet and the persona—between the dramatic and the rhetorical—or, for that matter, between our own private feelings and the feelings the poem itself gives voice to and makes public.

It is this kind of tension in the very existence of literature itself that oral interpretation explores.

As demonstrated by this poem, there appear to be three differences between the poet and the persona: perspective, identity, and universality. One could summarize these differences by stating that in this poem they indicate that the persona has been generalized. This generalizing of the persona is one of the most important characteristics of *lyric* poetry. In fact, this generalized persona is usually what is meant by the "lyric voice." In the course of this study you will be examining other kinds of personae—personae that will be called "dramatic," because they have specific characteristics, and/or "narrative," because they tell a story. You will take a closer look at lyrical, dramatic, and narrative personae. Then this book will lead you to examine a few principles of "prosody"—traditional and modern rhythmical structures.

According to some critics, one of the most important characteristics of modern poetry is its "dramatic impulse," its tendency to invest even a lyrical speaker with individuating characteristics that separate him from the poet. Of course, there are always *some* distinctions between the role of the poet and the role of the persona in a lyric poem. Perhaps modern poetry has carried that distinction to a greater degree than had early poetry. Perhaps there is some value in creating a literary category to be known as "dramatic lyric"—following Robert Browning's lead. One can simply state that *lyric* and *dramatic* stand at opposite ends of a continuum along which any one individual poem may be ranged. You can continue to use your "dramatic analysis"—with, it is hoped, a minimum of confusion—asking first, "Who is the speaker?" If the speaker is *generalized,* he will be called a "lyrical" persona in this book. The dramatic analysis always seeks to find the specific, the concrete, the individuating in any one speaker and in his speaking situation. Where it fails to do so are the boundaries of lyric poetry.

Another distinction is sometimes introduced into the study of poetry: Poems are occasionally called "lyric," "dramatic," or "narrative." However, in an important sense this third distinction does not really belong with the other two, for "narrative" names the action in which the speaker may be engaged rather than his specific characteristics or their absence. A narrative is a piece of literature that contains a narrator, who is engaged in telling a story—and he may be more lyrical than dramatic, or vice versa. Perhaps it is best, then, to think of the narrator as a kind of persona. A narrator is a persona who functions as a storyteller. A narrative is a literary work in which the persona is a narrator.

The two general actions that you should always be concerned with as you analyze the persona—even when he is serving as the narrator—are his actions as an actor and those as a rhetor. For the first you use the dramatic analysis, for the second the rhetorical analysis. In the Langston Hughes poem it was suggested that the persona is performing as an actor and the poet (as always) as a rhetor. There are other ways of viewing the poem, of course. In this book the persona is seen as presenting a series of apparently random responses to a specific situation. He does not simply see the life of the people on Lenox Avenue, a life that has become what it is because of the "deferring" of a people's dream of democratic ideals; he *becomes* these people. His response is immediate but only apparently random; for with his perspective the poet can see the function and meaning of the way in which the responses have been arranged. What happens to a dream deferred? The persona posits several answers. For the poet the answers the persona offers are all within the realm of possibility, but the most important of all the answers is the final one: The dream will explode—not ending with a whimper or even merely a bang but violently destroying more than simply itself. This is the poet's message to his audience, and his major strategy is arrangement.

In addition to personae who are lyric or dramatic or who are narrators, another literary quality to be found in all kinds of literature is rhythm. In fact, so easily do we associate this latter quality with poetry that it is sometimes assumed that anything—even a TV commercial—written rhythmically is a poem. Simply put, rhythm means any recurrence of identical or similar elements: a word, a sound, a beat, a character, an action, a sentence, a syntax. All of these create a rhythm when their recurrence is felt. It is best to keep rhythm generally defined, though the rhythm easily associated with poetry is the recurrence of a beat: ta-DUM, ta-DUM, ta-DUM: "It TAKES a HEAP o'LIVin to MAKE a HOUSE a HOME." But in the voice of a competent poet rhythm becomes a highly complex organization of elements—so much so that a description of rhythm is rarely attempted even by graduate students, though rhythm can be intuited by any sensitive reader in junior high school. Here only a most cursory introduction to the matter will be attempted, saving anything like a detailed examination for the study questions later. Note, however, the qualifying phrase "in the voice of a competent *poet*": Rhythmical patterning in a poem is the work of the poet rather than the persona. And, as noted time and time again, when we respond to the structure of a poem— to the way in which the poem has been put together—we are responding to the "poet in the poem."

Prosody—the discipline that studies rhythmical effects in poetry—has traditionally concentrated its efforts on the study of the organization of sounds in "lines" and "stanzas." "Meter" is the name prosodists give to the rhythmical organization of sounds in a line. Traditionally, prosodists have differentiated three kinds of meter: "accentual," in which lines have a corresponding number of beats or stresses; "syllabic," in which lines have a corresponding number of syllables; and "accentual-syllabic" or "foot" meter, in which lines have a corresponding number of accents *and* syllables.

Accentual meter is evident in "The Seafarer" by Ezra Pound, in which the major accents per line are emphasized by alliteration:

May I for my own self song's truth reckon,
Journey's jargon, how I in harsh days
Hardship endured oft.
Bitter breast-cares have I abided,
Known on my keel many a care's hold,
And dire sea-surge, and there I oft spent
Narrow nightwatch nigh the ship's head
While she tossed close to cliffs. Coldly afflicted,
My feet were by frost benumbed. . . .

In the poem "What if this Present" by John Donne, both syllabic and accentual-syllabic meter are evident:

	Syllables	Accents	Rhyme
Whát íf thís présent were the wórld's lást níght?	10	7	A
Márk in my héart, Ó Sóul, where thóu dost dwéll,	10	6	B
The pícture of Chríst crúcified, and téll	10	4	B
Whéther that coúntenance can thée affríght:	10	4	A
Téars in his éyes quénch the amázing líght,	10	5	A
Blóod fílls his frówns, which fróm his píerc'd héad féll.	10	7	B
And cán thát tóngue adjúdge thee únto héll,	10	6	B
Which práy'd forgíveness for his fóes' fíerce spíte?	10	5	A
Nó, nó; but ás in my idólatry	10	4	C
I sáid to áll my profáne místresses,	10	4	D
Béauty, of píty, fóulness ónly is	10	4	D
Ă sígn ŏf rígouř: só Ĭ sáy ťo thée,	10	5	C
Ťo wíckeď spírits̆ aře hórriď shápes ašsígn'd,	11	5	E
Thĭs béauteoŭs fórm ašsúres ă píteoŭs mínd.	10(12)	5	E

Here the change from the syllabic meter to the noticeable regularity and evenness of the accentual-syllabic imitates or echoes the persona's progression through questioning to assurance. The last two lines of this poem may be "scanned" [1] in such a way that the meter could be called

---

[1] *Scansion:* the process of marking the stressed and unstressed syllables in a line. For a further exploration of all of the prosodic matters mentioned in this chapter see the Fussell book in the bibliography at the conclusion of this chapter.

"iambic pentameter"; [2] thus, the accentual-syllabic meter is frequently referred to as "foot" [3] meter.

So far as stanzas are concerned, traditional organization is "strophic" in nature. That is, stanzas are organized by a rhyme scheme or after some more or less standard pattern or both. In any case, form (including both meter and stanza) in poetry should be an imitation or echo of the sense, argument, or experience. The Donne poem is structured in the strophic organization known as the "sonnet," [4] which in this case consists of three "quatrains" [5] and a "couplet," [6] all marked out by the rhyme. The progression from quatrain to quatrain symbolizes also a progression from one stage of the persona's experience to another in his linear journey to an answer marked by the final couplet.

Modern prosody has received its impetus from a number of forces—such as the general spirit of revolt against traditional or received ideas, the new electronic media, and the popularity of professional and amateur performances of poetry. These forces, and others, have produced the suspicion that traditional prosody is really "visualist" in nature, that many of the old metrical and rhyming schemes are really designed for the eye rather than the ear. Or, if they *are* heard, they tend oftentimes not to blend perfectly with the argument, experience, or sense of the poem, as if in some poems "form" and "content" were actually two separate things. Furthermore, modern prosodists argue, traditional forms cannot contain or dramatize modern experience. Poetry, they contend, in our new "oral" age is really "heightened speech" in which form must never be more than an extension of content.

In modern prosody the "line" is a unit of utterance formed by the breathing of the speaker. Thus, in many modern poems the lines tend to be "end-stopped" [7] rather than "run-on." [8] Curiously enough, rhymes are seldom used in modern rhythms. The fact is curious because ryhmes

---

[2] *Iambic pentameter:* a line whose scansion shows ten syllables arranged in a pattern of unstressed, stressed, unstressed, stressed, and so on.

[3] *Foot:* one of the syllabic patterns inherited from classical poetry, such as iamb (unstressed, stressed), trochee (stressed, unstressed), and so on. All accentual-syllabic meter in English can be scanned in a way that reflects the classical foot.

[4] *Sonnet:* literally, a little song; traditionally a fourteen-line poem presenting an argument on love. Donne was one of the first English poets to make "little songs" bear the weight of philosophical argument.

[5] *Quatrain:* a four-line stanza or any unit of four lines marked out by rhyme within a poem.

[6] *Couplet:* a two-line stanza or any unit of two lines marked out by rhyme within a poem.

[7] *End-stopped:* a line that ends with a pause, usually indicated by punctuation.

[8] *Run-on* or *enjambed:* a line that does not end with a pause. In the Donne poem, the third line is enjambed, the fourth end-stopped. In performing the poem, though, note that some pause seems to occur at the end of every line.

would seem to be the most oral of all effects, even in traditional poems. Yet, to the modern poet rhyme schemes are potentially ancillary to the content, superimposed by the weight and force of tradition. In fact, because the word "line" tends to be visual in nature, perhaps the lines in modern rhythms should even be called "breathers."

Traditional poetry tended to be "strophic" in its stanzaic structures because it conceived of a poem in terms of traditional stanza patterns—such as three quatrains and a couplet make a sonnet. Modern poetry is usually "stichic" in its organization. A "stich" is a line, and a "stichic" organization is one in which the attention is called to individual lines—or, to put the matter in less visualist terms, in which pauses are indicated in such a way that a certain part of the persona's utterance is made emphatic.

The Langston Hughes poem is a good example of modern prosodical effects. Note that each line tends to be a unit. Observe that the arrangement of the lines tends to be a visual record of the persona's speech—and, in turn, to provide clues to the way in which the persona's behavior may be performed by the interpreter. This poem inhabits time, not space. The space on its printed page is a clue to the pauses in performance between lines and between groups of lines. The poet e. e. cummings was the most flamboyant experimenter in the use of space for vocal clues.

Finally, there is a third kind of rhythmic organization that is midway between the stichic and the strophic. Here the grammatical structure of the sentences causes lines to correspond or to group themselves. This kind of organization or rhythm may be called "syntactical." For example, in the Langston Hughes poem all the sentences except one are interrogatory. Furthermore, they tend to be grouped in pairs joined by "or." A better example is "A Hub for the Universe" by Walt Whitman, in which recurrent syntax provides not only the major organizing principle of the poem but also the primary rhythm. In the following printing of the poem the syntactical patterns have been italicized:

I have said that the soul *is not more than* the body,
And I have said that the body *is not more than* the soul,
And nothing, not God, is greater to one than one's self is,
And whoever walks a furlong without sympathy walks to his own funeral
    drest in his shroud,
And I or you pocketless of a dime may purchase the pick of the earth,
And to glance with an eye or show a bean in its pod confounds the learn-
    ing of all times,
And there is no trade or employment *but* the young man following it may
    become a hero,
And there is no object so soft *but* it makes a hub for the wheeled universe.

To summarize, in addition to all those general qualities that were noted concerning speakers in nonfictional prose, the speaker or persona *in* a *poem* may be:

lyrical (that is, generalized) or
dramatic (that is, particularized), telling a story (the persona is a narrator).

The structure of his utterance (as far as that aspect of rhythm usually studied in prosody is concerned) may be:

traditional (in which case we shall find accentual, syllabic, or accentual-syllabic meter and strophic organization) or
modern (in which case the lines are "breathers" and the organization is stichic) or
somewhere between the two (as in syntactic rhythms).

It is in the structure of the persona's utterance that the speaker *of* the poem, the poet, is most tangibly present, in addition, of course, to providing the title and his name. Obviously, sound and action are the most important qualities of a poem, as they are of all literature. When we think of a poem and experience no more than a visual image of lines arranged in a certain way on the page, we are missing something. The most important qualities of a poem, any poem, are being left out. The appearance of a poem on a page is important *only* insofar as that visual form gives the interpreter cues for sound and action. The first poem offered for your study was passed down from generation to generation orally for hundreds of years; only recently was it translated and written down. It was a poem, though, before it ever looked like one.

Hamza El Din/Water

Water.
Water made the desert bloom.
The water lay in the midst of the homeland, the water of the Nile.
Girls walking, single file,
Down to the water carrying earthenware jugs.
"Kumban-kash," "kumban-kash"
The sound of the big empty jugs.
The girls fill the jugs and return
The jugs on their heads.
What is heard now?   10

Only the tiny sound of their ankle bracelets:
"King-killing . . . king-killing."
To love one of these girls is to remember,
"Kumban-kash" and "king-killing."

STUDY QUESTIONS

1. Read this poem aloud several times until you get a sense of its stichic organization. Note particularly the way in which the arrangement on the page indicates different degrees of pauses at the line endings.
2. Note the way in which echoing sounds serve to unify the poem (KUM-ban-KASH and KING-kilLING particularly).
3. How are the *images* in the poem related? Once you can answer that question, you have discovered something important about poetic structure, not only in this poem but in many others. Frequently in a poem the world created through the images so tightly coheres that any one image can substitute for or signify any other image or even the entire world of the poem. For example, note this haiku by Issa:

High noon:
   save for reed-sparrows, the river
   makes no sound.

High noon *is* the silent river. The reed-sparrows are part of the river, so much so that their noise is considered the only sound the *river* makes. In the poem "Water" the persona tells us that the sounds of the earthenware jugs and the ankle bracelets is part of his love for these girls: the sounds and the girls are so much a part of each other that one immediately signifies the other. In what way do the sounds, girls, "water," "desert," "desert bloom," "homeland," and "Nile" also belong together in the world of the poem?
4. This poem has its origins in the ancient history of Nubia and is part of the great oral tradition that has been the storehouse of most poetry throughout man's existence. It was interpreted by Hamza El Din, then translated, then written down for the CBS-TV *Camera Three* program "Singing of Gold: Memories of a Nubian Homeland." Only this sort of information can help the reader achieve anything like a "poet's perspective" in this poem, which otherwise would be almost purely the utterance of a lyric persona. Review the ancient and modern history of Nubia. What important—and on the modern scene, poignantly ironical—notes are struck by the water theme?

William Butler Yeats/Lapis Lazuli

born 1865

(For Harry Clifton)

I have heard that hysterical women say
They are sick of the palette and fiddle-bow,
Of poets that are always gay,
For everybody knows or else should know
That if nothing drastic is done
Aeroplane and Zeppelin will come out,
Pitch like King Billy bomb-balls in
Until the town lie beaten flat.

All perform their tragic play,
There struts Hamlet, there is Lear,   10
That's Ophelia, that Cordelia;
Yet they, should the last scene be there,
The great stage curtain about to drop,
If worthy their prominent part in the play,
Do not break up their lines to weep.
They know that Hamlet and Lear are gay;
Gaiety transfiguring all that dread.
All men have aimed at, found and lost;
Black out; Heaven blazing into the head:
Tragedy wrought to its uttermost.   20
Though Hamlet rambles and Lear rages,
And all the drop-scenes drop at once
Upon a hundred thousand stages,
It cannot grow by an inch or an ounce.

On their own feet they came, or on shipboard,
Camel-back, horse-back, ass-back, mule-back,
Old civilisations put to the sword.
Then they and their wisdom went to rack:
No handiwork of Callimachus,
Who handled marble as if it were bronze,   30
Made draperies that seemed to rise
When sea-wind swept the corner, stands;
His long lamp-chimney shaped like the stem
Of a slender palm, stood but a day;
All things fall and are built again,
And those that build them again are gay.

Two Chinamen, behind them a third,
Are carved in lapis lazuli,
Over them flies a long-legged bird,
A symbol of longevity;   40
The third, doubtless a serving-man,
Carries a musical instrument.

Every discoloration of the stone,
Every accidental crack or dent,
Seems a water-course or an avalanche,
Or lofty slope where it still snows
Though doubtless plum or cherry-branch
Sweetens the little half-way house
Those Chinamen climb towards, and I
Delight to imagine them seated there;   50
There, on the mountain and the sky,
On all the tragic scene they stare.
One asks for mournful melodies;
Accomplished fingers begin to play.
Their eyes mid many wrinkles, their eyes,
Their ancient, glittering eyes, are gay.

STUDY QUESTIONS

1. In this poem the persona makes many references to objects and events in the
   poet's world. The lapis lazuli celebrated in the poem was a carving given
   to Yeats by Harry Clifton; King Billy is Kaiser Wilhelm II, whose "aeroplanes"
   and "Zeppelins" bombed London in World War I, just twenty years before the
   poem was probably composed. Most scholars date the composition of the
   poem in the late thirties, the time when Europe was preparing for another
   world war. (Any other references or allusions that are unfamiliar to you should
   be looked up—especially look up Callimachus in a good classical dictionary;
   information about him should clarify the reference to "his long lamp-chimney.")
   What role does the persona play? Is he simply the poet meditating? Consider
   this possibility as you perform the poem: Perhaps the persona himself
   dramatizes what the poem is all about by imaginatively leaving the dreary,
   fearful, everyday world and entering the world of the lapis lazuli carving, the
   world of art—so to say—that contains the essential truths behind the dreari-
   ness, fears, and everydayness of that other world.
2. How is the poem organized? Literally, what seems to be the subject of each
   stanza, and how—silently or verbally—does the persona "get from" one

stanza to the next? Could the strange order of "Pitch like King Billy bomb-balls in" in stanza 1 be a mocking echo of the speech of "hysterical women"? What does "it" refer to in the last line of stanza 2? What is the function of the curious mixture of "art" and "history" in the second and third stanzas? Between the first and the second time the persona refers to himself ("I have heard . . ." and "I/ Delight to imagine them . . ."), what has happened to his relationship to his audience? What differences are there in the kinds of action in which he is engaged in these two references?

3. Are there clear indications in the poem that the persona is communicating to an audience? Are there aspects of the poem that deny a meditative stance—at least at times?

Lawrence Ferlinghetti/"Constantly risking absurdity"

born 1919

Constantly risking absurdity
              and death
     whenever he performs
          above the heads
              of his audience
   the poet like an acrobat
       climbs on rime
          to a high wire of his own making
  and balancing on eyebeams
        above a sea of faces
     paces his way
      to the other side of day
    performing entrechats
       and slight-of-foot tricks
  and other high theatrics
       and all without mistaking
    any thing
      for what it may not be
  For he's the super realist
       who must perforce perceive
    taut truth
      before the taking of each stance or step
  in his supposed advance
      toward that still higher perch
 where Beauty stands and waits
     with gravity
        to start her death-defying leap

And he
>a little charleychaplin man
>>who may or may not catch
>her fair eternal form
>>spreadeagled in the empty air
>of existence

STUDY QUESTIONS

1. How would you describe the rhythm of this poem? (*Note:* Never attempt to answer a question like this until you have read the poem aloud several times.)
2. So far as speaking levels are concerned, the poem is like mirrors in a barber shop: image reflecting image ad infinitum. In this poem about poetry the persona is talking about the poet—*all* poets, as well as the poet who created this poem. Note that the persona—himself a mask, a created "artificial" thing—talks of the poet as a theatrical performer. The artist's creation re-creates the artist in his (the persona's) own image. What *is* that image? What sort of person is the persona? Does he seem to be aware that he is a created, artificial thing? Note the number of *puns* in the poem. Do they add to the theatrical atmosphere within which the persona speaks?
3. Although the speaking levels are like mirrors placed opposite each other, are there any sure clues to the possible separation of images? What does the theatrical, artificial world of the persona tell us of, or show us about, the world of the "super realist" that the poet is? To go further, are there specific points in the poem where you seem to become aware of the poet's voice?
4. One could discuss at great length the philosophical implications of "absurdity" and "death" so far as the poet's work is concerned and perhaps end with a particularly significant insight into the nature of some modern poetry. The interpreter's contribution to that discussion lies in the knowledge he has gained about how the poem performs its ideas—that is, if he has understood how the nature of the persona and of his speech behavior demonstrate what the poem is all about.

Wallace Stevens/The Idea of Order at Key West

born 1879

She sang beyond the genius of the sea.
The water never formed to mind or voice,
Like a body wholly body, fluttering
Its empty sleeves; and yet its mimic motion
Made constant cry, caused constantly a cry,
That was not ours although we understood,
Inhuman, of the veritable ocean.

The sea was not a mask. No more was she.
The song and water were not medleyed sound
Even if what she sang was what she heard,   10
Since what she sang was uttered word by word.
It may be that in all her phrases stirred
The grinding water and the gasping wind;
But it was she and not the sea we heard.

For she was the maker of the song she sang.
The ever-hooded, tragic-gestured sea
Was merely a place by which she walked to sing.
Whose spirit is this? we said, because we knew
It was the spirit that we sought and knew
That we should ask this often as she sang.   20

If it was only the dark voice of the sea
That rose, or even colored by many waves;
If it was only the outer voice of sky
And cloud, of the sunken coral water-walled,
However clear, it would have been deep air,
The heaving speech of air, a summer sound
Repeated in a summer without end
And sound alone. But it was more than that,
More even than her voice, and ours, among
The meaningless plungings of water and the wind,   30
Theatrical distances, bronze shadows heaped
On high horizons, mountainous atmospheres
Of sky and sea.
                        It was her voice that made
The sky acutest at its vanishing.
She measured to the hour its solitude.
She was the single artificer of the world
In which she sang. And when she sang, the sea,
Whatever self it had, became the self
That was her song, for she was the maker. Then we,
As we beheld her striding there alone,   40
Knew that there never was a world for her
Except the one she sang and, singing, made.

Ramon Fernandez, tell me, if you know,
Why, when the singing ended and we turned
Toward the town, tell why the glassy lights,
The lights in the fishing boats at anchor there,
As the night descended, tilting in the air,

Mastered the night and portioned out the sea,
Fixing emblazoned zones and fiery poles,
Arranging, deepening, enchanting night.   50

Oh! Blessed rage for order, pale Ramon,
The maker's rage to order words of the sea,
Words of the fragrant portals, dimly-starred,
And of ourselves and of our origins,
In ghostlier demarcations, keener sounds.

STUDY QUESTIONS

1. Examine carefully the setting of the action described in the poem. Who is "we"? In what direction were "we" facing when "we" observed the singing woman "striding there alone"? What are the natural features of the setting? the man-made ones? How are they arranged in the poem in relation to each other?

2. What exactly does the persona say the woman's song "did to" natural features of the setting? Why is this something only an "artificer" can do? Why can the natural world not have order? In the last stanza, do the lights create "order" or is it "our" perception of the lights that creates order? If the former, what additional insight is being offered by the persona concerning "artifice"? If the latter, what insight does the persona offer concerning the power of "artifice" on human behavior?

3. Ramon Fernandez (1894–1944) was a French critic, whose work *Messages* (1926) could shed light on the ideas in this poem. Fernandez argues that man achieves meaning in life by imposing order on chaos. Order does not exist in the external world but can come about only through man's creative efforts—whether in creating an object of art or in shaping his own perceptions. The importance, urgency, even risk of the action highlights the dimensions of the phrase "rage for order." Moreover, Wallace Stevens denied that he was referring specifically to Fernandez and claimed instead that "Ramon Fernandez" was simply a fictive name. Perhaps, then, all you need to know of Fernandez is what the poem tells you.

4. This poem, like "Constantly risking absurdity" by Ferlinghetti, can help you understand the speaking roles of poets, personae, and interpreters. Note that the persona is most caught up in his experience with a *creator*. Perhaps the woman did not actually compose the song; certainly she assumed a role, or a mask, in singing it; but the ultimate effect on the persona is the way in which the woman—and everyone and everything around her—*became* the song. The interpreter does not become either the persona or the poet but becomes the poem itself—that is, the life within the created object, the order born of the maker's "rage." To reach this understanding the reader must understand (1) the nature of the persona's experience of the woman's song, (2) the order imposed on that experience by the poet, and (3) ultimately the way in which

the entire poem and its interpreter are counterparts of the song and the woman singer. The ultimate question in your study of the poem is this: How, according to this poem, may the *interpreter* be considered a *creator*?

5. In examining the poem's rhythm, pay careful attention to the rhyme scheme. Note the echoes in sound, particularly in the second stanza. What is their function?

Langston Hughes/*Dream Variations*

born 1902

To fling my arms wide
In some place of the sun,
To whirl and to dance
Till the white day is done.
Then rest at cool evening
Beneath a tall tree
While night comes on gently,
    Dark like me—
That is my dream!

To fling my arms wide   10
In the face of the sun,
Dance! Whirl! Whirl!
Till the quick day is done.
Rest at pale evening . . .
A tall, slim tree . . .
Night coming tenderly
    Black like me.

STUDY QUESTIONS

1. How might this poem be considered "variations" on a "dream"? Note *all* the differences between the two stanzas, regardless of how subtle. Then note particularly the different kinds of physical responses each stanza calls from the interpreter. Finally, attempt to answer the question above.

2. Consider the *persona's* speech as variations on the *poet's* vision. The title of the poem is, after all, "Dream Variations," not "Dream and Variations." How might the persona's speech be considered variations on the poet's dream? In exploring this question, consider what you learned from your study of poets and personae in the two preceding poems.

Richard Eberhart/Attitudes

born 1904

Irish Catholic

After the long wake, when many were drunk,
Pat struggled out to the tracks, seething
Blinded, was struck by a train,
Died too. The funeral was for the mother and son.

The Catholic music soared to the high stones,
Hundreds swayed to the long, compulsive ritual.
As the mourners followed the caskets out
Wave followed wave of misery, of pure release.

New England Protestant

When Aunt Emily died, her husband would not look at her.
Uncle Peter, inarticulate in his cold intelligence,   10
Conceded few flowers, arranged the simplest service.
Only the intimate members of the family came.

Then the small procession went to the family grave.
No word was spoken but the parson's solemn few.
Silence, order, a prim dryness, not a tear.
We left the old man standing alone there.

STUDY QUESTIONS

1. In this poem, as in the preceding, the halves of the poem call forth different physical responses from the interpreter. Examine carefully your physical responses as you perform the poem. How do they help you understand the poem?
2. What differences are there in the two personae in the poem? Begin this part of your exploration by noting that the persona in the stanzas "New England Protestant" is easily identifiable.
3. Having considered differences in the physical responses and in the personae, consider now the *similarities* between the two parts, particularly the distance between the speaker and what he is talking about. To what degree is the speaker involved in either action?
4. Does the speaker seem to prefer one attitude over the other? Or does the matter of distance—regardless of how much *empathy* may be shown by the speaker—serve as a check on his approval? That is, he may *imitate* the

expression of "misery"—of "pure release"—in "Irish Catholic," but his implied distance enforces a kind of objectivity, an attitude that is in turn dramatized in "New England Protestant."

5. With this poem as your example, discuss the nature and meaning of the word *attitudes*.

Dylan Thomas/The Force That Through the Green Fuse Drives the Flower

born 1914

The force that through the green fuse drives the flower
Drives my green age; that blasts the roots of trees
Is my destroyer.
And I am dumb to tell the crooked rose
My youth is bent by the same wintry fever.

The force that drives the water through the rocks
Drives my red blood; that dries the mouthing streams
Turns mine to wax.
And I am dumb to mouth unto my veins
How at the mountain spring the same mouth sucks.   10

The hand that whirls the water in the pool
Stirs the quicksand; that ropes the blowing wind
Hauls my shroud sail.
And I am dumb to tell the hanging man
How of my clay is made the hangman's lime.

The lips of time leech to the fountain head;
Love drips and gathers, but the fallen blood
Shall calm her sores.
And I am dumb to tell a weather's wind
How time has ticked a heaven round the stars.   20

And I am dumb to tell the lover's tomb
How at my sheet goes the same crooked worm.

STUDY QUESTIONS

1. In exploring the characteristic of the persona, consider his *age* particularly. Perform the poem as if an old man were speaking, then a young man. Which is more illuminating or probable? Or is the age of the persona insignificant?

2. What sex is the persona? Of course, the tendency is always to assume that a male persona speaks poems by a male poet, unless a female speaker is clearly identified. Yet, we have also seen (as in "Lenox Avenue Mural") the sex of the persona can be unimportant in some poems. *Must* this poem have a male persona?
3. Syntactical rhythm is most prominent in the poem, but note carefully the subtle variations in syntax. Note, too, the echoes of sounds, particularly at line endings. Is the effect of the poem's sound songlike or orationlike?
4. Is the poem climactically arranged or does it have a circular effect? If the former, where is the climax and how is it reached? If the latter, how does the final couplet echo ideas at the opening of the poem and why does it echo the syntax of the final lines in each stanza?
5. After these preliminary considerations, return to the problem of characterizing the persona. What is his motivation for his repeated observation "I am dumb to tell (to mouth)"? What sort of person would be most deeply aware of an inability to communicate with these insensate objects?

John Frederick Nims/The Young Ionia

born 1913

If you could come on the late train for
    The same walk
Or a hushed talk by the fireplace
    When the ash flares
As a heart could (if a heart would) to
    Recall you,
To recall all in a long
    Look, to enwrap you
As it once had when the rain streamed on the
    Fall air,   10
And we knew, then, it was all wrong,
    It was love lost
And a year lost of the few years we
    Account most—
But the bough blew and the cloud
    Blew and the sky fell
From its rose ledge on the wood's rim to
    The wan brook,
And the clock read to the half-dead
    A profound page   20
As the cloud broke and the moon spoke and the
    Door shook—

If you could come, and it meant come at the
    Steep price
We regret yet as the debt swells
    In the nighttime
And the *could come, if you could* hum in
    The skull's drum
And the limbs writhe till the bed
    Cries like a hurt thing—   30
If you could—ah but the moon's dead and the
    Clock's dead.
For we know now: we can give all
    But it won't do,
Not the day's length nor the black strength nor
    The blood's flush.
What we took once for a sure thing,
    For delight's right,
For the clear eve with its wild star in
    The sunset,   40
We would have back at the old
    Cost, at the old grief
And we beg love for the same pain—for a
    Last chance!
Then the god turns with a low
    Laugh (as the leaves hush)
But the eyes ice and there's no twice: the
    Benign gaze
Upon some woe but on ours no.
    And the leaves rush.   50

STUDY QUESTIONS

1. Is the persona male or female? Is the persona's sex important in understanding the poem? Note carefully that though "his" speech is a meditation, "he"
is strongly aware of at least the imaginary presence of his listener, "you." Who
is Ionia? The speaker or the imaginary listener? And why is it significant
that Ionia is "young"?

2. There are at least two settings in this poem: the setting of the experience
described by the persona ("Fall"), and the setting within which the persona
is speaking. If it is possible to think of a setting playing a role (as indeed it
is always possible to think in poetry), what part does the first setting play in
the drama? What is the second setting? If it can be identified, what is *its*
role? If it cannot be identified, what is the significance of its vagueness?

3. Is there a climax in this poem? If so, does the climax mark a resolution of

the conflict within the speaker? or a deepening of his awareness of the conflict? If there is no climax, is there no conflict within the speaker—but only,
say, a realization that his desire, though real and sharp, can never be fulfilled?

4. The accentual-syllabic rhythm of the poem is unavoidable in performance.
Does the striking regularity of the rhythm serve to answer the questions posed
in question 3? For example, perhaps the regularity of the rhythm serves like
a drumbeat emphasizing half of the persona's conflict—the torment of time
from which he wishes to escape. Perhaps, on the other hand, the regularity of
the rhythm serves to emphasize the steady, continuing realization by the speaker
that his desire is hopeless. And, of course, perhaps it does both or neither.

5. The basic foot of the rhythm is composed of the two unaccented syllables followed by two accented ones (xx ̋). The usual name of the foot is "minor ionic"
or "ionia a minore." Thus, the "young Ionia" referred to in the title is not
simply the persona or "his" listener (see question 1) but also the basic prosodic
structure. Consider the possibility that the poem may be a *tour de force*—a
display of the poet's craftsmanship, a demonstration of what he can achieve
through ingenious application of a seldom-used prosodic foot. In this case,
all the earlier questions are idle.

Leonard Nathan/*Niagara*

born 1924

Looking into the Falls, I heard it sing:
Marriage, marriage, one life always,
Beginning to end in simple water music.
And I thought, by you, this isn't music for men,
Who are always bespoken in two places at once,
Who partially stand in the middle of great music
Distracted by distance. I put myself in this poem
With you and with marrying waters, and look at me—still
A little apart, wishing for one whole life
But singing this far-off solo right   10
In the face of the music, as though it could solve me.

STUDY QUESTIONS

1. Note that in this poem the persona is consciously aware that he is speaking a
poem. On the basis of what you have discovered about poets and their personae in lyric poetry (in the introduction to this chapter and in the exercises
up to this point), explain lines 7 and 8.

2. The poem has a clearly defined speaking situation: An "I" is speaking to "you."
Does the poem in performance sound like direct communication? Is the

speaker both communicating and meditating? Is he speaking in a way that
demonstrates or dramatizes what the poem itself is all about?
3. Is the syntactical ambiguity of line 3 functional? Is "bespoken" in line 5 a pun?
What is the antecedent of "it" in the final line?
4. The key to the performance of the poem is in the final two lines. If one can
understand those lines clearly, he can gain a concept of how the poem should
be performed. On the other hand, by attempting to perform the poem one
should gain understanding of what the final lines mean.

Matthew Arnold/Dover Beach

born 1822

The sea is calm to-night.
The tide is full, the moon lies fair
Upon the straits; on the French coast, the light
Gleams and is gone; the cliffs of England stand,
Glimmering and vast, out in the tranquil bay.
Come to the window, sweet is the night-air!
Only, from the long line of spray
Where the sea meets the moon-blanched sand,
Listen! you hear the grating roar
Of pebbles which the waves draw back, and fling,   10
At their return, up the high strand,
Begin and cease, and then again begin,
With tremulous cadence slow, and bring
The eternal note of sadness in.

Sophocles long ago
Heard it on the Aegean, and it brought
Into his mind the turbid ebb and flow
Of human misery: we
Find also in the sound a thought,
Hearing it by this distant northern sea.   20

The sea of faith
Was once, too, at the full, and round earth's shore
Lay like the folds of a bright girdle furled.
But now I only hear
Its melancholy, long, withdrawing roar,
Retreating, to the breath
Of the night-wind, down the vast edges drear
And naked shingles of the world.

Ah, love, let us be true
To one another! for the world, which seems   30
To lie before us like a land of dreams,
So various, so beautiful, so new,
Hath really neither joy, nor love, nor light,
Nor certitude, nor peace, nor help for pain;
And we are here as on a darkling plain
Swept with confused alarms of struggle and flight,
Where ignorant armies clash by night.

STUDY QUESTIONS

1. Is this poem a monologue (is the persona communicating) or a soliloquy (is he meditating)? Or is it a curious mixture of both speaking modes? Try first performing the poem as if it were being addressed primarily to the persona's "love," who is in the room with him. Note the degree to which he seems to be responding to her and to the scene from his window. How *real,* for the speaker, are these two external stimuli? Then try performing the poem as if the persona were primarily wrapped up in his own emotional and intellectual responses to these stimuli—as if he were seeking to interpret, for himself, his responses to the total scene. Does the speaker seem to be projecting upon the total dramatic situation his own doubts, torment, and uncertainty?
2. As you experiment with these two modes, note particularly the organization of the poem. What motivates the opening line? How does the speaker "get" from stanza 1 to 2 to 3 to 4? Does the poem seem to be organized logically or emotionally? If the former, would you say that the poem is an argument? delivered to persuade whom, the woman or the speaker or both? If it does seem to be a logically organized argument, how does the poem differ from "My Last Duchess" by Robert Browning? If it seems to be organized emotionally, what are the persona's emotions? What is the significance of his insistence upon finding a "thought" in the sound of the sea? Is he seeking to tame his emotions?
3. At the conclusion of these experiments you should be ready to tackle the most important question of all: What sort of person is the persona?

Anthony Hecht/The Dover Bitch: A Criticism of Life

born 1923

So there stood Matthew Arnold and this girl
With the cliffs of England crumbling away behind them,
And he said to her, "Try to be true to me,
And I'll do the same for you, for things are bad
All over, etc., etc."

Well now, I knew this girl.   It's true she had read
Sophocles in a fairly good translation
And caught that bitter allusion to the sea,
But all the time he was talking she had in mind
The notion of what his whiskers would feel like   10
On the back of her neck.   She told me later on
That after a while she got to looking out
At the lights across the channel, and really felt sad,
Thinking of all the wine and enormous beds
And blandishments in French and the perfumes.
And then she got really angry.   To have been brought
All the way down from London, and then be addressed
As a sort of mournful cosmic last resort
Is really tough on a girl, and she was pretty.
Anyway, she watched him pace the room   20
And finger his watch-chain and seem to sweat a bit,
And then she said one or two unprintable things.
But you mustn't judge her by that.   What I mean to say is,
She's really all right.   I still see her once in a while
And she always treats me right.   We have a drink
And I give her a good time, and perhaps it's a year
Before I see her again, but there she is,
Running to fat, but dependable as they come.
And sometimes I bring her a bottle of *Nuit d'Amour.*

STUDY QUESTIONS

1. Consider this poem as providing answers to the questions following "Dover
   Beach."   How has Hecht answered each of those questions?
2. Why is this poem called "A Criticism of Life"?   Which or what life is meant?
   Arnold's? the life in Arnold's poem?   Perhaps "Dover Beach" is also a criticism of life.   If so, how do Arnold's and Hecht's criticisms compare?   Is
   Hecht's poem about life or about poetry?
3. How do Arnold's and Hecht's personae compare?

Anne Sexton/The Farmer's Wife

born 1928

From the hodge porridge
of their country lust,
their local life in Illinois,
where all their acres look

like a sprouting broom factory,
they name just ten years now
that she has been his habit;
as again tonight he'll say
honey bunch let's go
and she will not say how there   10
must be more to living
than this brief bright bridge
of the raucous bed or even
the slow braille touch of him
like a heavy god grown light,
that old pantomime of love
that she wants although
it leaves her still alone,
built back again at last,
mind's apart from him, living   20
her own self in her own words
and hating the sweat of the house
they keep when they finally lie
each in separate dreams
and then how she watches him,
still strong in the blowzy bag
of his usual sleep while
her young years bungle past
their same marriage bed
and she wishes him cripple, or poet,   30
or even lonely, or sometimes,
better, my lover, dead.

STUDY QUESTIONS

1. Performance or attempts at performance should illuminate a crucial aspect of
   this poem: What is the relationship between the farmer's wife and the persona?
   What is the nature of the distance, if any, between the two? Is the farmer's
   wife herself the persona? Given the character of the farmer's wife, is it probable that she would speak in this style? Or is another persona serving as a
   kind of "secret sharer" of the wife's thoughts and emotions? Are the final
   three lines indirect discourse—like the earlier, reported speech of the farmer?
   Or do they—particularly the phrase "my lover"—serve to gauge the distance
   between wife and persona?
2. Of course, make certain you have interpreted all expressions and images in
   the poem—such as "hodge porridge," "local life," "brief bright bridge," "raucous bed," "mind's apart," and "blowzy bag." Pay particular attention to the

cataloguing of effects in the final three lines: How do these terms relate to one thought?

3. Perhaps you will find that the most significant question to ask about this poem ultimately pertains not to the persona but to the wife. What sort of person is she who, if she cannot articulate the poem, nonetheless experiences deeply the emotions the poem does articulate? To answer that question one must seek those emotions through performing the poem.

Philip Larkin/Wedding-Wind

born 1922

The wind blew all my wedding-day,
And my wedding-night was the night of the high wind;
And a stable door was banging, again and again,
That he must go and shut it, leaving me
Stupid in candlelight, hearing rain,
Seeing my face in the twisted candlestick,
Yet seeing nothing. When he came back
He said the horses were restless, and I was sad
That any man or beast that night should lack
The happiness I had.

Now in the day   10
All's ravelled under the sun by the wind's blowing.
He has gone to look at the floods, and I
Carry a chipped pail to the chicken-run,
Set it down, and stare. All is the wind
Hunting through clouds and forests, thrashing
My apron and the hanging cloths on the line.
Can it be borne, this bodying-forth by wind
Of joy my actions turn on, like a thread
Carrying beads? Shall I be let to sleep
Now this perpetual morning shares my bed?   20
Can even death dry up
These new delighted lakes, conclude
Our kneeling as cattle by all-generous waters?

STUDY QUESTIONS

1. In performing this poem, one must reach some understanding of the nature of the contrast offered by the two stanzas. What precise change is marked by "Now in the day"? Is the change explained by "day," "ravelled," and "wind"—or perhaps by all of these? Yet, the persona seems to experience

no *reversal* of her emotions, rather a heightening of them. Has the "change" then come about through her discovery that the *world* "bodies forth" her joy?

2. Compare the character of this persona with the wife in "The Farmer's Wife." Note particularly the relationship between each and her locale.

3. As you construct the character of the farmer's wife in Larkin's poem, consider carefully the meaning of all the images. What sort of person would experience these images?

Ezra Pound/*The River-Merchant's Wife: A Letter*

born 1885

While my hair was still cut straight across my forehead
I played about the front gate, pulling flowers.
You came by on bamboo stilts, playing horse,
You walked about my seat, playing with blue plums.
And we went on living in the village of Chokan:
Two small people, without dislike or suspicion.

At fourteen I married My Lord you.
I never laughed, being bashful.
Lowering my head, I looked at the wall.
Called to, a thousand times, I never looked back.   10

At fifteen I stopped scowling,
I desired my dust to be mingled with yours
Forever and forever and forever.
Why should I climb the look out?

At sixteen you departed,
You went into far Ku-to-yen, by the river of swirling eddies,
And you have been gone five months.
The monkeys make sorrowful noise overhead.

You dragged your feet when you went out.
By the gate now, the moss is grown, the different mosses,   20
Too deep to clear them away!
The leaves fall early this autumn, in wind.
The paired butterflies are already yellow with August
Over the grass in the West garden;
They hurt me. I grow older.
If you are coming down through the narrows of the river Kiang,
Please let me know beforehand,
And I will come out to meet you
            As far as Cho-fu-Sa.

STUDY QUESTIONS

1. The utter simplicity of this poem is disarming. The poem expresses in simplest terms a drama of maturation, from a child to a woman. But the images, particularly those located in the present time of the persona, are indirect—as if the persona sought not to present her emotions directly to her husband, but to let them be conveyed by the "monkeys," "moss," and "butterflies." Now test out these observations by attempting to perform the poem. Is line 6 a break in the simplicity? Is line 25 a break in the indirectness? Are "simplicity" and "indirectness" insufficient terms for the qualities of this poem?

2. How is it possible to perform the poem as if it were "a letter"? Shall the persona be seen in the act of composing the letter? or reading the letter after composing it, but before dispatching it? or soliloquizing? Try this experiment: Imagine that you are the merchant who has just received this letter from his wife. How literally must you take the direction that the poem is a letter?

3. Ezra Pound presents this poem as a translation of a poem by the Chinese poet Rihaku. How much Pound or how much Rihaku is in the English version may not be important to the interpreter. However, the interpreter would note that this poem and the one immediately preceding were written by men and that these poems are about very deep emotional experiences from a feminine point of view. Compare these poems with Sexton's: Is not the sex of a *poet* completely insignificant as far as point of view is concerned? Sexton chose not to have her poem spoken by the farmer's wife for reasons that are *in* the poem itself—not because, say, the reader would automatically assume that Sexton herself is the persona talking about a woman she knows. Yet, can you so easily dismiss the sex of the poet from *all* your considerations of these poems? Each poem must make you aware of a choice on the part of its creator: The poet chose *this* point of view, and your major concern is that he make the relationship between the persona and the utterance probable. Perhaps your appreciation for the poet's work is enhanced when you see that he has created a very believable persona highly unlike himself—as is the case in the Larkin and Pound poems. Exploring this idea could be the basis for a long paper on point of view as the poet's major *artifice.*

James Dickey/*The Bee*

born 1923

To the football coaches of Clemson College, 1942

One dot
Grainily shifting   we at roadside and
The smallest wings coming   along the rail fence out
Of the woods   one dot   of all that green. It now
Becomes flesh-crawling   then the quite still
Of stinging. I must live faster for my terrified
Small son   it is on him. Has come. Clings.

Old wingback, come
To life. If your knee action is high
Enough, the fat may fall in time   God damn   10
You, Dickey, *dig*   this is your last time to cut
And run   but you must give it everything you have
Left, for screaming near your screaming child is the sheer
Murder of California traffic: some bee hangs driving

Your child
Blindly onto the highway. Get there however
Is still possible. Long live what I badly did
At Clemson   and all of my clumsiest drives
For the ball   all of my trying to turn
The corner downfield   and my spindling explosions   20
Through the five-hole over tackle. O backfield

Coach Shag Norton,
Tell me as you never yet have told me
To get the lead out   scream whatever will get
The slow-motion of middle age off me   I cannot
Make it this way   I will have to leave
My feet   they are gone   I have him where
He lives   and down we go singing with screams into

The dirt,
Son-screams of fathers   screams of dead coaches turning   30
To approval   and from between us the bee rises screaming
With flight   grainily shifting   riding the rail fence
Back into the woods   traffic blasting past us
Unchanged, nothing heard through the air-
conditioning glass   we lying at roadside full

Of the forearm prints
Of roadrocks   strawberries on our elbows as from
Scrimmage with the varsity   now we can get
Up   stand   turn away from the highway   look straight
Into trees. See, there is nothing coming out   no   40
Smallest wing   no shift of a flight-grain   nothing
Nothing. Let us go in, son, and listen

For some tobacco-
mumbling voice in the branches   to say "That's
a little better,"   to our lives still hanging
By a hair. There is nothing to stop us   we can go

Deep   deeper   into elms, and listen to traffic die
Roaring, like a football crowd from which we have
Vanished.   Dead coaches live in the air, son   live

In the ear   50
Like fathers, and *urge*   and *urge.* They want you better
Than you are. When needed, they rise and curse you   they scream
When something must be saved. Here, under this tree,
We can sit down. You can sleep, and I can try
To give back what I have earned by keeping us
Alive, and safe from bees: the smile of some kind

Of savior—
Of touchdowns, of fumbles, battles,
Lives. Let me sit here with you, son
As on the bench, while the first string takes back   60
Over, far away   and say with my silentest tongue, with the man-
creating bruises of my arms   with a live leaf a quick
Dead hand on my shoulder, "Coach Norton, I am your boy."

STUDY QUESTIONS

1. Note that the persona calls himself "Dickey" and inserts into the poem information that ordinarily one would say belongs to the poet's speaking level.
   That is, one would assume that it is the *poet* who speaks the title and the
   dedication. Yet the persona apparently claims to be James Dickey, too, who
   attended Clemson College twenty years before the incident described in the
   poem, was coached by Shag Norton, and at the time of the present incident
   was living in California. Now consider carefully the character of the persona.
   Even though all you may know about James Dickey the poet is what is provided in this poem, this poem should give you a good opportunity to contrast
   the persona and the poet because here the poem apparently insists upon their
   similarities. Note this important contrast: The *poet* is speaking "after the
   fact," obviously having created the poem after the incident occurred; yet, for
   the *persona* there is only the present time. In contrasting these two roles,
   you can experience the basic tension that is central to the experience of all
   literature: the sense of dramatic immediacy (the voice of the persona) and
   the sense of artistic ordering (the voice of the poet). As suggested in the
   last of the study questions following the preceding poem, the persona is the
   poet's major artifice—even when the differences between poet and persona
   are subtle.
2. As you perform the poem, pay particular attention to your muscular responses.

Note the places in the poem where you feel differences between muscular tension and relaxation. Do those places indicate anything about how the material in the poem is arranged? Why is the poem divided into stanzas of this sort? Why do the lines end where they do?

3. In considering the preceding questions, note also your vocal responses. Follow carefully what may be the poet's directions for phrasing by reading the lines as rhythmical units and by pausing within the lines where the poet has left a space.

4. So far as tone, or the persona's-and-poet's attitude(s), is (are) concerned, the last two stanzas are probably crucial. How does the persona *feel* about this experience? Is the feeling shared by the poet? to the same degree? Do the final stanzas seem only to provide a kind of moralistic tag summing up the meaning of the experience? Or do they spring naturally and probably from the character of the persona? (Note that these questions end with the problem with which they begin: exploring one of the poet's most significant artistic creations, the character of the persona.)

Richard Wilbur/*My Father Paints the Summer*

born 1921

A smoky rain riddles the ocean plains,
Rings on the beaches' stones, stomps in the swales,
Batters the panes
Of the shore hotel, and the hoped-for summer chills and fails.
The summer people sigh,
"Is this July?"

They talk by the lobby fire but no one hears
For the thrum of the rain.   In the dim and sounding halls,
Din at the ears,
Dark at the eyes well in the head, and the ping-pong balls   10
Scatter their hollow knocks
Like crazy clocks.

But up in his room by artificial light
My father paints the summer, and his brush
Tricks into sight
The prosperous sleep, the girdling stir and clear steep hush
Of a summer never seen,
A granted green.

Summer, luxuriant Sahara, the orchard spray
Gales in the Eden trees, the knight again   20

Can cast away
His burning mail, Rome is at Anzio: but the rain
For the ping-pong's optative bop
Will never stop.

Caught Summer is always an imagined time.
Time gave it, yes, but time out of any mind.
There must be prime
In the heart to beget that season, to reach past rain and find
Riding the palest days
Its perfect blaze.   30

STUDY QUESTIONS

1. Where does the persona seem to be as he speaks? Where is his father? What is the physical distance between the two men? To whom is the persona closer—physically, emotionally, even aesthetically—the summer people or his father?
2. If one may assume that the persona is a poet, how do his views of art differ from those of his father? Or if one may assume that the persona is a careful observer of experience, how do his views of the way experience must be observed differ from his father's? Is there no "prime" in the persona's heart?
3. Note that the poem is curiously stichic *and* strophic in organization. Follow these visual clues for performance. Are there sound effects in the poem that do not depend on these visual clues and that may finally be the source of the true rhythmic structure of the poem? In answering this question, listen for effects that are subtler than the sounds of the ping-pong balls.
4. This poem, too, seems to end with a moralistic tag. Is the final stanza only a tag or does it seem to spring naturally and probably from the character of the persona? The answer to that question, of course, depends on the *location* of the persona and his relationship to the persons, objects, and ideas in the poem. To whom is the persona speaking?
5. This time, a final question may pertain not to the persona but to the poet. What difference is there between the two? If there are differences between the ways in which the persona and his father view experience, to which does the poet seem closer? Or is the poet a composite of all points of view arranged in the poem? To answer this last question, compare these views of summer: (1) "the hoped-for summer" of "the summer people," (2) the view of the persona, and (3) the "luxuriant Sahara" of the father's painting. Who is able "to reach past rain"—the persona or the poet? or neither? or both?

LeRoi Jones/*Preface to a Twenty Volume Suicide Note*

born 1934

Lately, I've become accustomed to the way
The ground opens up and envelops me
Each time I go out to walk the dog.
Or the broad edged silly music the wind
Makes when I run for a bus—

Things have come to that.

And now, each night I count the stars,
And each night I get the same number.
And when they will not come to be counted
I count the holes they leave.   10

Nobody sings anymore.

And then last night, I tiptoed up
To my daughter's room and heard her
Talking to someone, and when I opened
The door, there was no one there . . .
Only she on her knees,
Peeking into her own clasped hands.

STUDY QUESTIONS

1. What seems to be the persona's attitude as he says, "Things have come to that"? Is there any difference when he says, "Nobody sings anymore"? Note the stages in time marked by the lines 1, 7, and 12. Do they also mark stages in the persona's emotion?
2. In demonstrating this poem, should the interpreter place the persona in a definite environment? If so, what environment and why, and if not, why not?
3. Do the actions of his daughter have anything to do with what the persona has been experiencing lately? Would the daughter describe her own actions as "Peeking into her own clasped hands"?
4. Does the speaker appear to be speaking to someone? If so, who would be a probable listener to what he says?

T. S. Eliot/Preludes

born 1888

I

The winter evening settles down
With smell of steaks in passageways.
Six o'clock.
The burnt-out ends of smoky days.
And now a gusty shower wraps
The grimy scraps
Of withered leaves about your feet
And newspapers from vacant lots;
The showers beat
On broken blinds and chimney-pots,   10
And at the corner of the street
A lonely cab-horse steams and stamps.
And then the lighting of the lamps.

II

The morning comes to consciousness
Of faint stale smells of beer
From the sawdust-trampled street
With all its muddy feet that press
To early coffee-stands.
With the other masquerades
That time resumes,   20
One thinks of all the hands
That are raising dingy shades
In a thousand furnished rooms.

III

You tossed a blanket from the bed,
You lay upon your back, and waited;
You dozed, and watched the night revealing
The thousand sordid images
Of which your soul was constituted;
They flickered against the ceiling.
And when all the world came back   30
And the light crept up between the shutters
And you heard the sparrows in the gutters,
You had such a vision of the street
As the street hardly understands;

Sitting along the bed's edge, where
You curled the papers from your hair,
Or clasped the yellow soles of feet
In the palms of both soiled hands.

IV

His soul stretched tight across the skies
That fade behind a city block,   40
Or trampled by insistent feet
At four and five and six o'clock;
And short square fingers stuffing pipes,
And evening newspapers, and eyes
Assured of certain certainties,
The conscience of a blackened street
Impatient to assume the world.

I am moved by fancies that are curled
Around these images, and cling:
The notion of some infinitely gentle   50
Infinitely suffering thing.

Wipe your hand across your mouth, and laugh;
The worlds revolve like ancient women
Gathering fuel in vacant lots.

STUDY QUESTIONS

1. In studying the persona's role, consider these effects: No person is mentioned in I, a person (or persons) is referred to by "one" in II, a woman is addressed as "you" in III, a man is referred to in the third-person mode in IV, in the next to the last stanza the persona directly refers to himself as speaker, and in the last stanza the speaker directly addresses his audience. As you study these effects, consider also the structure. Is there a climax? Why is the poem called "Preludes"? Are the four parts, or movements, of the poem "preludes" for the "theme" in the last two stanzas?

2. Having tried to perform the point of view, you should have a good start toward answering these questions: What kinds of actions are grouped within the four divisions of the poem? Why does the persona call these actions "images" in the next to the last stanza? In the same stanza, does "notion" refer to "fancies" or "images"? What kind of action is described in the last stanza? Is the persona directing himself or someone else to perform that action?

3. Consider the first problem raised in question 2 as a way to discuss the rhythm of the poem. That is, perhaps the rhythm of the poem depends not simply on an arrangement of stressed and unstressed syllables, but also on an arrangement of actions and images.

Richard Wilbur/Digging for China

born 1921

"Far enough down is China," somebody said.
"Dig deep enough and you might see the sky
As clear as at the bottom of a well.
Except it would be real—a different sky.
Then you could burrow down until you came
To China! Oh, it's nothing like New Jersey.
There's people, trees, and houses, and all that,
But much, much different. Nothing looks the same."

I went and got the trowel out of the shed
And sweated like a coolie all that morning,   10
Digging a hole beside the lilac-bush,
Down on my hands and knees. It was a sort
Of praying, I suspect. I watched my hand
Dig deep and darker, and I tried and tried
To dream a place where nothing was the same.
The trowel never did break through to blue.

Before the dream could weary of itself
My eyes were tired of looking into darkness,
My sunbaked head of hanging down a hole.
I stood up in a place I had forgotten,   20
Blinking and staggering while the earth went round
And showed me silver barns, the fields dozing
In palls of brightness, patens growing and gone
In the tides of leaves, and the whole sky china blue.
Until I got my balance back again
All that I saw was China, China, China.

STUDY QUESTIONS

1. Why is the first speaker not identified? What sort of person does he seem
   to be?
2. Try performing this poem as if it were being spoken by a grown man telling
   another, or others, of an incident from his childhood. What would be the
   significance of this communication by an adult? Is the story merely one about
   the amusing gullibility of a child? Or does it make a comment on the nature

of imagination and determination, with the childhood setting serving as a background for the persona's comment? Is the final effect of the poem serious, humorous, or both?

3. Try performing the poem as if it were being spoken by the persona to himself alone. Is this meditative view probable?   Does it add another dimension to the questions posed in number 2?

4. Try performing the poem as if it were being spoken by a child. Is this view probable?

e. e. cummings/Chanson Innocente

born 1894

in Just-
spring   when the world is mud-
luscious the little
lame balloonman

whistles   far   and wee

and eddieandbill come
running from marbles and
piracies and it's
spring

when the world is puddle-wonderful   10

the queer
old balloonman whistles
far   and   wee
and bettyandisbel come dancing

from hop-scotch and jump-rope and

it's
spring
and
     the
          goat-footed   20

balloonMan   whistles
far
and
wee

STUDY QUESTIONS

1. Consider carefully the visual clues to the rhythm presented by the poem's appearance on the page and examine the clues to the character of the persona given by this rhythm. Perform the following "prose" version of the poem. How does the performance differ from the one required by the "poetic" version?

    In just-spring when the world is mud-luscious the little lame balloonman whistles far and wee and Eddie and Bill come running from marbles and piracies and it's spring when the world is puddle-wonderful. The queer old balloonman whistles far and wee and Betty and Isbel come dancing from hopscotch and jump-rope and it's spring and the goat-footed balloonman whistles far and wee.

2. In answering the last question in number 1, pay particular attention to differences in sound and in the speaking manner of the persona. To what extent does the rhythm called for by the poetic version clarify the poem? How does the persona in each version differ?

Dylan Thomas/In My Craft or Sullen Art

born 1914

In my craft or sullen art
Exercised in the still night
When only the moon rages
And the lovers lie abed
With all their griefs in their arms,
I labour by singing light
Not for ambition or bread
Or the strut and trade of charms
On the ivory stages
But for the common wages   10
Of their most secret heart.

Not for the proud man apart
From the raging moon I write
On these spindrift pages
Nor for the towering dead
With their nightingales and psalms
But for the lovers, their arms
Round the griefs of the ages,
Who pay no praise or wages
Nor heed my craft or art.   20

STUDY QUESTIONS

1. See the questions for the preceding poem by e. e. cummings. Apply them to this poem, even though this poem is far more conventional in its poetic version than cummings'. The prose version of this poem would be:

> In my craft or sullen art exercised in the still night when only the moon rages and the lovers lie abed with all their griefs in their arms, I labour by singing light not for ambition or bread or the strut and trade of charms on the ivory stages but for the common wages of their most secret heart. Not for the proud man apart from the raging moon I write on these spindrift pages nor for the towering dead with their nightingales and psalms but for the lovers, their arms round the griefs of the ages, who pay no praise or wages nor heed my craft or art.

Rabindranath Tagore/"Here I send you my poems"

born 1861

Here I send you my poems
densely packed in this writing book
like a cage crowded with birds.
The blue space, the infinity around constellations,
through which flocked my verses,
is left outside.
Stars, torn from the heart of night,
and tightly knit into a chain
may fetch a high price
from some jeweller in the suburb of paradise,   10
but the gods would miss from it the ethereal value
of the divinely undefined.
Imagine a song suddenly flashing up like a flying fish,
from the silent depth of time!
Would you care to catch it in your net
and exhibit it in your glass vessel
among a swarm of captives?

In the expansive epoch of lordly leisure,
the poet read his poems day by day
before his bounteous sovereign,   20
when the spirit of the printing press was not there
to smear with black dumbness
the background of a resonant leisure,
alive with the natural accompaniment of the irrelevant;
when the stanzas were not ranged into perfect packets of alphabets,
to be silently swallowed.
Alas, the poems which were for the listening ears

are tied today as chained lines of slaves
before their masters of critical eyes,
and banished into the greyness of tuneless papers,   30
and those that are kissed by eternity
have lost their way in the publishers' market.
For it is a desperate age of hurry and hustle
and the lyric muse has to take her journey
to her tryst of hearts
on trams and buses.

I sigh and wish that I had lived in the golden age of Kalidasa,
that you were,—but what is the use of wild and idle wishing?
I am hopelessly born in the age of the busy printing press,—a belated
    Kalidasa,
and you, my love, are utterly modern.   40

Listlessly you turn the pages of my poems
reclining in your easy chair,
and you never have the chance to listen
with half-shut eyes to the murmur of metre
and at the end to crown your poet with a rose-wreath.
The only payment you make
is the payment of a few silver coins
to the keeper of the bookstall
in the College Square.

STUDY QUESTIONS

1. This poem by the Hindu poet Sir Rabindranath Tagore (1861–1941) was translated into English by the poet himself and was first published in 1932 as the
   introduction to a book of his poems. Of course, to interpret this poem one
   must understand the difference between the persona and his audience. But
   a more important task, one that is directly related to understanding these
   characteristics, is realizing the differences between poems as produced by
   the persona and those same poems as read by his audience.
2. Group the characteristics of poetry as understood by the persona. Note carefully the *metaphors* by which they are described in the first stanza. What is
   "the background of a resonant leisure, alive with natural accompaniment of
   the irrelevant"? How do all these characteristics contrast with those of the
   printed poem?
3. Group the characteristics of printed poetry as read by the persona's audience.
   Note carefully the metaphors in the second stanza. What has the printing
   press to do with the "desperate age of hurry and hustle . . . trams and buses"
   or with the fact that the audience *purchases* the poems?

4. Who was Kalidasa and why does the persona compare himself with him?
5. How is the poem structured? Is the development *linear*—that is, is there a
   development toward a climax or conclusion? (To repeat: Never seek to answer questions like these until you have read the poem aloud several times.)
   On what does the rhythm of the poem depend?
6. In performing the poem, how might the book—with its printed pages—be used
   as part of the persona's gesture, underscore what he means by poetry to an
   "utterly modern" person? How can the persona seem to be speaking to his
   audience when the poem itself complains that the audience is not present and
   cannot hear? In short, how can an *oral* performance of this poem also demonstrate exactly those nonoral features that the persona protests?

Robinson Jeffers/*The Purse-Seine*

born 1887

Our sardine fishermen work at night in the dark of the moon; daylight or
    moonlight
They could not tell where to spread the net, unable to see the phosphores-
    cence of the shoals of fish.
They work northward from Monterey, coasting Santa Cruz; off New Year's
    Point or off Pigeon Point
The look-out man will see some lakes of milk-color light on the sea's night-
    purple; he points, and the helmsman
Turns the dark prow, the motorboat circles the gleaming shoal and drifts
    out her seine-net. They close the circle
And purse the bottom of the net, then with great labor haul it in.

                 I cannot tell you
How beautiful the scene is, and a little terrible, then, when the crowded
    fish
Know they are caught, and wildly beat from one wall to the other of their
    closing destiny the phosphorescent
Water to a pool of flame, each beautiful slender body sheeted with flame,
    like a live rocket   10
A comet's tail wake of clear yellow flame; while outside the narrowing
Floats and cordage of the net great sea-lions come up to watch, sighing in
    the dark; the vast walls of night
Stand erect to the stars.

                 Lately I was looking from a night mountain-top
On a wide city, the colored splendor, galaxies of light: how could I help
    but recall the seine-net
Gathering the luminous fish? I cannot tell you how beautiful the city
    appeared, and a little terrible.

I thought, We have geared the machines and locked all together into
    interdependence; we have built the great cities; now
There is no escape. We have gathered vast populations incapable of free
    survival, insulated
From the strong earth, each person in himself helpless, on all dependent.
    The circle is closed, and the net
Is being hauled in. They hardly feel the cords drawing, yet they shine
    already. The inevitable mass-disasters   20
Will not come in our time nor in our children's, but we and our children
Must watch the net draw narrower, government take all powers—or rev-
    olution, and the new government
Take more than all, add to kept bodies kept souls—or anarchy, the mass-
    disasters.

These things are Progress;
Do you marvel our verse is troubled or frowning, while it keeps its reason?
    Or it lets go, lets the mood flow
In the manner of the recent young men into mere hysteria, splintered
    gleams, cracked laughter. But they are quite wrong.
There is no reason for amazement: surely one always knew that cultures
    decay, and life's end is death.

STUDY QUESTIONS

1. Why does the persona refer to the sardine fishermen as "our"? Could his
audience also call them "our"?

2. Who is the persona's audience? Is it identified explicitly in the last lines of
the poem? Do these lines indicate that the audience is concerned about
poetry? Or do they indicate that the speaker is a poet? or both? or neither?

3. The persona states that he cannot tell his audience "How beautiful the scene
is, and a little terrible" or "how beautiful the city appeared, and a little terrible." Are these lines ironic? Are they indicative of the speaker's character?
If they are literally true, what *can* he tell his audience about the scene and the
city?

4. Having worked out answers to the preceding questions through performance,
try the most difficult question: How do the parts of the poem cohere? Or
what is the work's principle of structure? There are certain obvious visual and
conceptual relationships between the scene and the city—but how do the final
lines about poetry fit in? And what seems to be the basis of rhythm in the
poem?

5. Note that the persona disdains poetry that is "troubled or frowning" or poetry
that is full of "amazement" as appropriate responses to the "inevitable mass-
disasters." What seems to be the tone of the poem in which *he* appears?

Thom Gunn/Innocence

born 1929

to Tony White

He ran the course and as he ran he grew,
And smelt his fragrance in the field. Already,
Running he knew the most he ever knew,
The egotism of a healthy body.

Ran into manhood, ignorant of the past:
Culture of guilt and guilt's vague heritage,
Self-pity and the soul; what he possessed
Was rich, potential, like the bud's tipped rage.

The Corps developed, it was plain to see,
Courage, endurance, loyalty and skill   10
To a morale firm as morality,
Hardening him to an instrument, until

The finitude of virtues that were there
Bodied within the swarthy uniform
A compact innocence, child-like and clear,
No doubt could penetrate, no act could harm.

When he stood near the Russian partisan
Being burned alive, he therefore could behold
The ribs wear gently through the darkening skin
And sicken only at the Northern cold,   20

Could watch the fat burn with a violet flame
And feel disgusted only at the smell,
And judge that all pain finishes the same
As melting quietly by his boots it fell.

STUDY QUESTIONS

1. So far as images are concerned, this poem is in some ways the reverse of the
   preceding one ("The Purse-Seine"). Here the strikingly visual image is placed
   at the end, the central idea (innocence) is located at the center, and the "telling" is placed at the beginning. Note, however, that in the telling first part

there are many images that "show." Carefully examine each comparison in the opening stanzas for the way in which it indicates the persona's attitude.

2. In a sense the poem has two personae: the speaker and the young man whose innocence is the central idea. What differences are there between the two, in attitude and in character? What is the function of the regularity of meter and rhythm? Does this regularity express the attitude and character of the speaker? of the young man?

3. "Innocence" is the "central idea" of the poem. That is, the young man's innocence is the poem's principle of structure; it is what makes the poem cohere. One should not, however, call "innocence" the poem's "message," for that would imply that the poem is simply a medium or a "container" or that after one has received the message he can repeat it by putting it in another container, such as a paraphrase or an essay. After you have performed the poem several times, imagine a paraphrase of, or an essay on, "the message of innocence in a poem by Thom Gunn." Ask yourself what special values or qualities the poet achieves by letting his thoughts about innocence serve as the structural principle of a *poem*.

Robert Frost/Mending Wall

born 1874

Something there is that doesn't love a wall,
That sends the frozen-ground-swell under it
And spills the upper boulders in the sun,
And makes gaps even two can pass abreast.
The work of hunters is another thing:
I have come after them and made repair
Where they have left not one stone on a stone,
But they would have the rabbit out of hiding,
To please the yelping dogs. The gaps I mean,
No one has seen them made or heard them made,   10
But at spring mending-time we find them there.
I let my neighbor know beyond the hill;
And on a day we meet to walk the line
And set the wall between us once again.
We keep the wall between us as we go.
To each the boulders that have fallen to each.
And some are loaves and some so nearly balls
We have to use a spell to make them balance:
"Stay where you are until our backs are turned!"
We wear our fingers rough with handling them.   20
Oh, just another kind of outdoor game,
One on a side. It comes to little more:
There where it is we do not need the wall:

He is all pine and I am apple orchard.
My apple trees will never get across
And eat the cones under his pines, I tell him.
He only says, "Good fences make good neighbors."
Spring is the mischief in me, and I wonder
If I could put a notion in his head:
"Why do they make good neighbors? Isn't it   30
Where there are cows? But here there are no cows.
Before I built a wall I'd ask to know
What I was walling in or walling out,
And to whom I was like to give offense.
Something there is that doesn't love a wall,
That wants it down." I could say "Elves" to him,
But it's not elves exactly, and I'd rather
He said it for himself. I see him there,
Bringing a stone grasped firmly by the top
In each hand, like an old-stone savage armed.   40
He moves in darkness as it seems to me,
Not of woods only and the shade of trees.
He will not go behind his father's saying,
And he likes having thought of it so well
He says again, "Good fences make good neighbors."

STUDY QUESTIONS

1. Does the first persona ever speak to the second? To whom does each speak? How much "dramatic time" (the time indicated by the action described) elapses between the "good fences" statements? how much between the two "something there is" statements?

2. What is the difference in character between the two men? How does each differ in his responses to mending wall? Does the principal speaker of the poem feel only contempt for the effort? If so, why did he notify (line 12) his neighbor of the gaps? Is the neighbor's "darkness" (line 41) merely his unquestioning acceptance of tradition? What sort of hold does he have on the first speaker, who not only talks of his neighbor's darkness but also compares him to "an old-stone savage"?

3. The presentation of the two personae in this poem should be compared to the presentation of the two personae in "Innocence." Are the two personae in Frost's poem farther apart or closer together?

4. Some readers have taken the statement "Good fences make good neighbors" as if it were endorsed by the poet himself. Such a reading, however, lifts the statement out of its dramatic context and confuses point of view with viewpoint. Explain the ways whereby the poet has qualified the "good fences" statement.

5. What is the significance of the title? Why is it not "THE Mending Wall"?

William Stafford/Fifteen

born 1914

South of the bridge on Seventeenth
I found back of the willows one summer
day a motorcycle with engine running
as it lay on its side, ticking over
slowly in the high grass. I was fifteen.

I admired all that pulsing gleam, the
shiny flanks, the demure headlights
fringed where it lay; I led it gently
to the road and stood with that
companion, ready and friendly. I was fifteen.   10

We could find the end of a road, meet
the sky on out Seventeenth. I thought about
hills, and patting the handle got back a
confident opinion. On the bridge we indulged
a forward feeling, a tremble. I was fifteen.

Thinking, back farther in the grass I found
the owner, just coming to, where he had flipped
over the rail. He had blood on his hand, was pale—
I helped him walk to his machine. He ran his hand
over it, called me good man, roared away.   20

I stood there, fifteen.

STUDY QUESTIONS

1. Although there is only one speaker, there are actually four personae in the poem: the speaker, the speaker at age fifteen, the motorcycle, and the owner of the motorcycle. Note carefully how each is characterized. Why is the motorcycle personified?
2. What do the repetitions of "I was fifteen" signify? or the variation in the final line?
3. Although there are four personae in the poem, concentrate your efforts on understanding the first persona through understanding the other three. It is obviously significant that the poet has chosen a grown man, not a boy of fifteen, to speak the poem. What importance or significance is given to the action by having a grown man tell of it?

W. H. Auden/Law Like Love

born 1907

Law, say the gardeners, is the sun,
Law is the one
All gardeners obey
To-morrow, yesterday, to-day.

Law is the wisdom of the old
The impotent grandfathers shrilly scold;
The grandchildren put out a treble tongue,
Law is the senses of the young.

Law, says the priest with a priestly look,
Expounding to an unpriestly people,   10
Law is the words in my priestly book,
Law is my pulpit and my steeple.

Law, says the judge as he looks down his nose,
Speaking clearly and most severely,
Law is as I've told you before,
Law is as you know I suppose,
Law is but let me explain it once more,
Law is The Law.

Yet law-abiding scholars write;
Law is neither wrong nor right,   20
Law is only crimes
Punished by places and by times,
Law is the clothes men wear
Anytime, anywhere,
Law is Good morning and Good night.

Others say, Law is our Fate;
Others say, Law is our State;
Others say, others say
Law is no more
Law has gone away.   30

And always the loud angry crowd
Very angry and very loud
Law is We,
And always the soft idiot softly Me.

If we, dear, know we know no more
Than they about the law,
If I no more than you
Know what we should and should not do
Except that all agree
Gladly or miserably   40
That the law is
And that all know this,
If therefore thinking it absurd
To identify Law with some other word,
Unlike so many men
I cannot say Law is again,
No more than they can we suppress
The universal wish to guess
Or slip out of our own position
Into an unconcerned condition.   50
Although I can at least confine
Your vanity and mine
To stating timidly
A timid similarity,
We shall boast anyway:
Like love I say.

Like love we don't know where or why
Like love we can't compel or fly
Like love we often weep
Like love we seldom keep.   60

STUDY QUESTIONS

1. As the persona speaks this poem, allow him to imitate the various speakers he names. Does the style of the poem's language shift in imitation of these speakers? Does the style provide clues to the personalities of the speakers?
2. What sort of person is the persona? What exactly is his attitude toward his subject and toward his "dear"? May the reader assume the speaker is male and his audience female? How aware is he of "her"? What is the point of his speech? Why does he employ so many shifts in point of view?
3. Exactly how does the argument in the next-to-last stanza prepare us for the argument in the last stanza.
4. What is the rhythm of this poem?

Robert Browning/*My Last Duchess*

born 1812

Ferrara

That's my last Duchess painted on the wall,
Looking as if she were alive. I call
That piece a wonder, now: Frà Pandolf's hands
Worked busily a day, and there she stands.
Will't please you sit and look at her? I said
"Frà Pandolf" by design, for never read
Strangers like you that pictured countenance,
The depth and passion of its earnest glance,
But to myself they turned (since none puts by
The curtain I have drawn for you, but I)   10
And seemed as they would ask me, if they durst,
How such a glance came there; so, not the first
Are you to turn and ask thus. Sir, 'twas not
Her husband's presence only, called that spot
Of joy into the Duchess' cheek: perhaps
Frà Pandolf chanced to say "Her mantle laps
Over my lady's wrist too much," or "Paint
Must never hope to reproduce the faint
Half-flush that dies along her throat:" such stuff
Was courtesy, she thought, and cause enough   20
For calling up that spot of joy. She had
A heart—how shall I say?—too soon made glad,
Too easily impressed; she liked whate'er
She looked on, and her looks went everywhere.
Sir, 'twas all one! My favour at her breast,
The dropping of the daylight in the West,
The bough of cherries some officious fool
Broke in the orchard for her, the white mule
She rode with round the terrace—all and each
Would draw from her alike the approving speech,   30
Or blush, at least. She thanked men,—good! but thanked
Somehow—I know not how—as if she ranked
My gift of a nine-hundred-years-old name
With anybody's gift. Who'd stoop to blame
This sort of trifling? Even had you skill
In speech—(which I have not)—to make your will
Quite clear to such an one, and say, "Just this
Or that in you disgusts me; here you miss,

Or there exceed the mark"—and if she let
Herself be lessoned so, nor plainly set   40
Her wits to yours, forsooth, and made excuse,
—E'en then would be some stooping; and I choose
Never to stoop. Oh sir, she smiled, no doubt,
Whene'er I passed her; but who passed without
Much the same smile? This grew; I gave commands;
Then all smiles stopped together. There she stands
As if alive. Will't please you rise? We'll meet
The company below, then. I repeat,
The Count your master's known munificence
Is ample warrant that no just pretence   50
Of mine for dowry will be disallowed;
Though his fair daughter's self, as I avowed
At starting, is my object. Nay, we'll go
Together down, sir! Notice Neptune, though,
Taming a sea-horse, thought a rarity,
Which Claus of Innsbruck cast in bronze for me!

STUDY QUESTIONS

1. Experiment with locations for the duke and the envoy in relation to the portrait. Does the duke also sit? Does he move between the envoy and the portrait?

2. Note all the times in the poem when the envoy seems to be responding. You might work on this poem by acting out a monodrama, in which you play the role of the envoy listening and responding to the duke. Take careful note of your task as envoy: You have come from a count to a higher-ranking and powerful nobleman to make financial arrangements for the latter's wedding, only to find that the duke seems to be imposing another task on you.

3. In performing the role of the duke, note carefully all the times when he seems to be aware of the realities outside himself and of those that exist in his mind. Has the envoy literally asked him a question as he views the portrait? Is there a point in the poem when the duke would draw the curtain again? Why does he say, "Notice Neptune, though . . ."?

4. Obviously, analyzing the duke's character is a central problem in interpreting this poem. For that reason and because the duke is a fascinating person, this poem has been popular with oral interpreters for almost a century. This analysis, however, asks that you take careful note of other people in the poem, too— such as the envoy and the last duchess. This final question refers back to the character of the duke: To what degree do you feel sympathy for him? And do you judge him only or the total culture that has produced him?

John Logan/The Preparation

born 1923

While the class waited
I prepared the frog:

I had to hurry the needle
Through the handy opening
Just at the back of the head;

It slipped upon the skin
As on a plastic bag
For iceboxes or as on

A rind of ripe melon,
Then under urging   10
Entered to touch parts

Never meant for metal—
Causing one eye slightly
To drop from its accustomed

Plane, a cold nearly
Muscleless leg to draw
Too far up the belly,

An almost imperceptible
Darkening of green
Along the back, in whose   20

Depression a small amount
Of blood collected, like ours
Red, and causing the mouth

White and inside moist
To stretch (but it was a rabbit
In his wire cage

Who screamed)
As the hour began.

STUDY QUESTIONS

1. Notice the movement of the images in the poem. The effect is similar to a camera moving from the class to the speaker to the frog, close, closer, only to pull back again in the last line. As you perform the poem, examine the movement suggested by the images. What is the significance of this movement?
2. Compare the preceding two poems with this one in point of view.
3. How does the persona feel about what happens in this poem? What is the function or significance of the two comparisons in the third and fourth stanzas? Why does the speaker put the reference to the rabbit in parentheses and begin it with the word "but"?

Gwendolyn Brooks/*Bronzeville Woman in a Red Hat*
hires out to Mrs. Miles

born 1917

I

They had never had one in the house before.
                The strangeness of it all.   Like unleashing
A lion, really.   Poised
To pounce.   A puma.   A panther.   A black
Bear.
There it stood in the door,
Under a red hat that was rash, but refreshing—
In a tasteless way, of course—across the dull dare,
The semi-assault of that extraordinary blackness.
The slackness   10
Of that light pink mouth told little.   The eyes told of heavy care. . . .
But that was neither here nor there,
And nothing to a wage-paying mistress as should
Be getting her due whether life had been good
For her slave, or bad.
There it stood
In the door.   They had never had
One in the house before.

But the Irishwoman had left!
A message had come.   20
Something about a murder at home.
A daughter's husband—"berserk," that was the phrase:
The dear man had "gone berserk"

And short work—
With a hammer—had been made
Of this daughter and her nights and days.
The Irishwoman (underpaid,
Mrs. Miles remembered with smiles),
Who was a perfect jewel, a red-faced trump,
A good old sort, a baker   30
Of rum cake, a maker
Of Mustard, would never return.
Mrs. Miles had begged the bewitched woman
To finish, at least, the biscuit blending,
To tarry till the curry was done,
To show some concern
For the burning soup, to attend to the tending
Of the tossed salad. "Inhuman,"
Patsy Houlihan had called Mrs. Miles.
"Inhuman." And "a fool."   40
And "a cool
One."

The Alert Agency had leafed through its files—
On short notice could offer
Only this dusky duffer
That now made its way to her kitchen and sat on her kitchen stool.

II

Her creamy child kissed by the black maid! square on the mouth!
World yelled, world writhed, world turned to light and rolled
Into her kitchen, nearly knocked her down.

Quotations, of course, from baby books were great   50
Ready armor; (but her animal distress
Wore, too and under, a subtler metal dress,
Inheritance of approximately hate.)
Say baby shrieked to see his finger bleed,
Wished human humoring—there was a kind
Of unintimate love, a love more of the mind
To order the nebulousness of that need.
—This was the way to put it, this the relief.
This sprayed a honey upon marvelous grime.
This told it possible to postpone the reef.   60
Fashioned a huggable darling out of crime.
Made monster personable in personal sight
By cracking mirrors down the personal night.

Disgust crawled through her as she chased the theme.
She, quite supposing purity despoiled,
Committed to sourness, disordered, soiled,
Went in to pry the ordure from the cream.
Cooing, "Come." (Come out of the cannibal wilderness,
Dirt, dark, into the sun and bloomful air.
Return to freshness of your right world, wear   70
Sweetness again. Be done with beast, duress.)

Child with continuing cling issued his No in final fire,
        Kissed back the colored maid,
        Not wise enough to freeze or be afraid.
        Conscious of kindness, easy creature bond.
        Love had been handy and rapid to respond.

Heat at the hairline, heat between the bowels,
Examining seeming coarse unnatural scene,
She saw all things except herself serene:
Child, big black woman, pretty kitchen towels.   80

STUDY QUESTIONS

1. Two speakers seem to be involved in presenting this poem: a third-person narrator and Mrs. Miles. Can you divide the lines in the poem between these two personae, indicating exactly who speaks where? Who, for example, thinks of the Bronzeville woman as a "dusky duffer"? Are there times when the narrator seems to be imitating Mrs. Miles for the sake of commenting on her character?
2. Suppose the poem were told simply from Mrs. Miles' point of view. What would be lost? Then suppose it were told simply by a third-person narrator. What would be lost? In short, what has the poet gained by her use of shifting points of view?
3. What sort of person is Mrs. Miles? There is an even more difficult question: What sort of person is the narrator? To whom does each speak?
4. What are the rhythmical elements in this poem? Note how the rhyme reveals itself, sometimes unannounced, in various parts of the poem.
5. Why is there such a striking change in style in part II? Does this change mark a shift in point of view?

Howard Nemerov/Santa Claus

born 1920

Somewhere on his travels the strange Child
Picked up with this overstuffed confidence man,
Affection's inverted thief, who climbs at night
Down chimneys, into dreams, with this world's goods.
Bringing all the benevolence of money,
He teaches the innocent to want, thus keeps
Our fat world rolling. His prescribed costume,
White flannel beard, red belly of cotton waste,
Conceals the thinness of essential hunger,
An appetite that feeds on satisfaction;   10
Or, pregnant with possessions, he brings forth
Vanity and the void. His name itself
Is corrupted, and even Saint Nicholas, in his turn,
Gives off a faint and reminiscent stench,
The merest soupçon, of brimstone and the pit.

Now, at the season when the Child is born
To suffer for the world, suffer the world,
His bloated Other, jovial satellite
And sycophant, makes his appearance also
In a glitter of goodies, in a rock candy glare.   20
Played at the better stores by bums, for money,
This annual savior of the economy
Speaks in the parables of the dollar sign:
Suffer the little children to come to Him.

At Easter, he's anonymous again,
Just one of the crowd lunching on Calvary.

STUDY QUESTIONS

1. Try placing a pause of varying length at the end of each line. When you do
   this, what happens to the phrasing of each line? the movement of the poem?
   its tone?
2. What are the rhythmical elements in this poem? Note the repeated or echoing
   words and images.
3. Although the poem is spoken by only one persona, subtle shifts in point of
   view are presented through varying the distance between the speaker and his

subject.   Note, for example, that in the first stanza you are given a close-up of Santa Claus, as if the speaker were standing quite close to him, examining him minutely.   What are the speaker's subject and his distance to it in the second stanza? in the third?   Why do the stanzas progressively decrease in size?

4. Try performing the poem as if the speaker were meditating.   Then, as if he were communicating directly with an audience.   Which seems to work?   Why?

5. In examining the character of the speaker, pay particular attention to his choice of words.   Examine carefully the wit involved in even so apparently an ingenuous image as "overstuffed confidence man."   Note the precision of "soupçon" and its contribution to tone.   Note the speaker's values.   Do you respond favorably to this person who speaks so cynically of one of your childhood's most treasured icons?   Why does the speaker apparently refuse to put blame on anyone for the creation of Santa Claus—by saying only vaguely that he was picked up by the "Child" "Somewhere on his travels"?

LeRoi Jones/The Turncoat

born 1934

The steel fibrous slant & ribboned glint
of water.   The Sea.   Even my secret speech is moist
with it.   When I am alone & brooding, locked in
with dull memories & self hate, & the terrible disorder
of a young man.

I move slowly.   My cape spread stiff & pressing cautiously
in the first night wind off the Hudson.   I glide down
onto my own roof, peering in at the pitiful shadow of myself.

How can it mean anything?   The stop & spout, the
wind's dumb shift.   Creak of the house & wet smells   10
coming in.   Night forms on my left.   The blind still
up to admit a sun that no longer exists.   Sea move.

I dream long bays & towers . . . & soft steps on moist sand.
I become them, sometimes.   Pure flight.   Pure fantasy.   Lean.

STUDY QUESTIONS

1. What do your attempts to perform the poem indicate concerning the poet's use of punctuation?   Why is "and" indicated only by the printer's symbol?   Is "forms" a noun or a verb?   Is "lean" a verb or an adjective or what?

2. How are the stanzas organized? What is the subject or central image of
   each? (Note that both number 1 and 2 of this exercise are directed toward
   asking questions that concern the visual appearance of the poem. The poem
   makes an original, challenging use of typography that places new importance
   upon oralizing.)
3. In considering numbers 1 and 2, concentrate on point of view. Note how the
   perspective of the persona shifts.
4. Who—or what—does the persona seem to be? Why is the poem entitled "The
   Turncoat"? What indications of the persona's identity are presented in the last
   stanza?
5. To whom does the persona seem to be speaking?

Richard Wilbur/Love Calls Us to the Things of This World

born 1921

The eyes open to a cry of pulleys,
And spirited from sleep, the astounded soul
Hangs for a moment bodiless and simple
As false dawn.
                 Outside the open window
The morning air is all awash with angels.

Some are in bed-sheets, some are in blouses,
Some are in smocks: but truly there they are.
Now they are rising together in calm swells
Of halcyon feeling, filling whatever they wear
With the deep joy of their impersonal breathing;   10

Now they are flying in place, conveying
The terrible speed of their omnipresence, moving
And staying like white water; and now of a sudden
They swoon down into so rapt a quiet
That nobody seems to be there.
                 The soul shrinks

From all that it is about to remember,
From the punctual rape of every blessèd day,
And cries,
         "Oh, let there be nothing on earth but laundry,
Nothing but rosy hands in the rising steam
And clear dances done in the sight of heaven."   20

Yet, as the sun acknowledges
With a warm look the world's hunks and colors,

The soul descends once more in bitter love
To accept the waking body, saying now
In a changed voice as the man yawns and rises,

"Bring them down from their ruddy gallows;
Let there be clean linen for the backs of thieves;
Let lovers go fresh and sweet to be undone,
And the heaviest nuns walk in a pure floating
Of dark habits,
                    keeping their difficult balance."   30

STUDY QUESTIONS

1. Note the many words that are puns or have a double meaning: "spirited," "awash," "impersonal," "blessèd," to name a few. What function is served by this ambiguity? Does it determine in any way your response to the character of the persona?
2. On the other hand, note that there are three, perhaps four, personae in the poem: the central speaker (the role one normally thinks of as *the* persona), the soul, the body, and the man. Does the body, the soul, or the man say the last speech? And why "in a changed voice"? Is the first quoted speech or the second more in the style used by the central speaker, the first persona?
3. Who is the first persona? How involved, physically, is he in the action described? Why is the action seen from three, or four, points of view?
4. What are "the things of this world"? Is there a difference between the "love" named in the title and the "bitter love" experienced by the soul?
5. The clearest concept of this poem's structure should be possible once you perceive its movement, in action and images, from the opening of the eyes to the final speech. Of course, the best way to gain that perception is to try performing the poem and to empathize with its movement. Having gained that perception, ask yourself, "What is the rhythm of this poem?"

Lawrence Durrell/Alexandria

born 1912

To the lucky now who have lovers or friends,
Who move to their sweet undiscovered ends,
Or whom the great conspiracy deceives,
I wish these whirling autumn leaves:
Promontories splashed by the salty sea,
Groaned on in darkness by the tram

To horizons of love or good luck or more love—
As for me I now move
Through many negatives to what I am.

Here at the last cold Pharos between Greece   10
And all I love, the lights confide
A deeper darkness to the rubbing tide;
Doors shut, and we the living are locked inside
Between the shadows and the thoughts of peace:
And so in furnished rooms revise
The index of our lovers and our friends
From gestures possibly forgotten, but the ends
Of longings like unconnected nerves,
And in this quiet rehearsal of their acts
We dream of them and cherish them as Facts.   20

Now when the sea grows restless as a conscript,
Excited by fresh wind, climbs the sea-wall,
I walk by it and think about you all:
B. with his respect for the Object, and D.
Searching in sex like a great pantry for jars
Marked 'Plum and apple'; and the small, fell
Figure of Dorian ringing like a muffin-bell—
All indeed whom war or time threw up
On this littoral and tides could not move
Were objects for my study and my love.   30

And then turning where the last pale
Lighthouse, like a Samson blinded, stands
And turns its huge charred orbit on the sands
I think of you—indeed mostly of you,
In whom a writer would only name and lose
The dented boy's lip and the close
Archer's shoulders; but here to rediscover
By tides and faults of weather, by the rain
Which washes everything, the critic and the lover.

At the doors of Africa so many towns founded   40
Upon a parting could become Alexandria, like
The wife of Lot—a metaphor for tears;
And the queer student in his poky hot
Tenth floor room above the harbour hears
The sirens shaking the tree of his heart,
And shuts his books, while the most

Inexpressible longings like wounds unstitched
Stir in him some girl's unquiet ghost.

So we, learning to suffer and not condemn
Can only wish you this great pure wind   50
Condemned by Greece, and turning like a helm
Inland where it smokes the fires of men,
Spins weathercocks on farms or catches
The lovers at their quarrel in the sheets;
Or like a walker in the darkness might,
Knocks and disturbs the artist at his papers
Up there alone, upon the alps of night.

STUDY QUESTIONS

1. Alexandria is both a specific place and a state of mind, or state of being. Notice carefully only the details to which the persona directs the reader's attention: What kind of psychological state does Alexandria represent? Is this also the psychological state of the persona?
2. Is the persona a native of Alexandria—*either* Alexandria? What search or tasks is he embarked on? How does he plan to accomplish these tasks—by moving through "negatives," revising "the index of our lovers" and rehearsing their "acts," or thinking about them all? What *are* the objects for his study and his love? Will he rediscover "the critic and the lover" in *himself*? What affinities does he have with the student and the artist in the last two stanzas? If he is himself a writer, why does he seem to scorn the writer's efforts in the fourth stanza?
3. In studying point of view in this poem the question to ask is, "What affinities does the persona have with the wind described in the last stanza?" Would you say finally that the persona is individualized or generalized? That is, does he seem to be any one specific person?
4. Above all, who seems to be the persona's audience? Is the "you" of the third stanza the same in the fourth and in the last?

Robert Beloof/*Visiting Home in Wichita*

born 1923

A mile from town and five or six from us
were the gravel pits my mother put out of bounds.

Hitch-hiking being what it was under that sun,
I seldom disobeyed.

Visiting now I find they are no longer
"dangerous," full of "seepage water," are lakes
surrounded by expensive homes, small docks,
a "modern shopping center" arranged at one end.

We went out to see *Romeo and Juliet* in a new
cinema built there and as the movie   10
ended and the Prince cried "all are punishéd"
the curtain covering the right wall hummed back
and revealed the moon, toward which some men
were moving at 3,000 m p h,
shining with splendor across the seepage and the red
charcoal dot where someone was cooking steak near
where once, bare-assed, I dived in forbidden depths.

STUDY QUESTIONS

1. Note that each stanza is one sentence and that the sentences increase in complexity. Does this effect underscore certain effects in the speaker's ideas?
2. Explain the use of quotation marks in the third and fourth stanzas.
3. As you consider the rhythm of this poem, note particularly the organization and repetition of images: for example, "a mile from town and five or six from us" as compared to "at 3,000 m p h"; the boyhood image of the gravel pits in the day and the return visit at night; the *old* (memories, *Romeo and Juliet*) and the *new* (space travel, new cinema); and the final "seepage" that draws all these images together.
4. What is the effect of the prince's line in stanza 4? Is it prophetic or ironic?
5. What is the effect of the persona's reference to the lake as seepage? Compare his two uses of the word. Keep in mind that "seepage" would hardly be used by the real estate developer.
6. Is this poem a meditation?

Allen Ginsberg/Song

born 1926

The weight of the world
    is love.
Under the burden
    of solitude,
under the burden
    of dissatisfaction

              the weight,
the weight we carry
          is love.

Who can deny?   10
        In dreams
it touches
          the body,
in thought
          constructs
a miracle,
          in imagination
anguishes
          till born
in human—   20

looks out of the heart
          burning with purity—
for the burden of life
          is love,

but we carry the weight
          wearily,
and so must rest
in the arms of love
          at last,
must rest in the arms   30
          of love.

No rest
          without love,
no sleep
          without dreams
of love—
          be mad or chill
obsessed with angels
          or machines,
the final wish   40
          is love
—cannot be bitter,
          cannot deny,
cannot withhold
          if denied:

the weight is too heavy

    —must give
for no return
    as thought
is given   50
    in solitude
in all the excellence
    of its excess.

The warm bodies
    shine together
in the darkness,
    the hand moves
to the center
    of the flesh,
the skin trembles
    in happiness   60
and the soul comes
    joyful to the eye—

yes, yes,
    that's what
I wanted,
    I always wanted,
I always wanted,
    to return
to the body
    where I was born.   70

STUDY QUESTIONS

1. Consider that the poet has entitled this poem "Song." What clues for oral performance are in that title?
2. Does the arrangement of the lines on the page give clues for oral performance? Does the arrangement demonstrate the songlike quality of the poem?
3. Why is this poem spoken by a generalized persona, one who has few specific dramatized qualities? Note that at the end of the poem when the persona says "I," he seems to speak for many people.
4. Yet, as this book insists, you can gather some traits of the persona's image from the words he speaks and from the attitudes he takes toward his subject. What sort of person is this persona? How might you contrast him with the persona in the preceding poem?

James Dickey/The Leap

born 1923

The only thing I have of Jane MacNaughton
Is one instant of a dancing-class dance.
She was the fastest runner in the seventh grade,
My scrapbook says, even when boys were beginning
To be as big as the girls,
But I do not have her running in my mind,
Though Frances Lane is there, Agnes Fraser,
Fat Betty Lou Black in the boys-against-girls
Relays we ran at recess: she must have run

Like the other girls, with her skirts tucked up   10
So they would be like bloomers,
But I cannot tell; that part of her is gone.
What I do have is when she came,
With the hem of her skirt where it should be
For a young lady, into the annual dance
Of the dancing class we all hated, and with a light
Grave leap, jumped up and touched the end
Of one of the paper-ring decorations

To see if she could reach it. She could,
And reached me now as well, hanging in my mind   20
From a brown chain of brittle paper, thin
And muscular, wide-mouthed, eager to prove
Whatever it proves when you leap
In a new dress, a new womanhood, among the boys
Whom you easily left in the dust
Of the passionless playground. If I said I saw
In the paper where Jane MacNaughton Hill,

Mother of four, leapt to her death from a window
Of a downtown hotel, and that her body crushed-in
The top of a parked taxi, and that I held   30
Without trembling a picture of her lying cradled
In that papery steel as though lying in the grass,
One shoe idly off, arms folded across her breast,
I would not believe myself. I would say
The convenient thing, that it was a bad dream
Of maturity, to see that eternal process

Most obsessively wrong with the world
Come out of her light, earth-spurning feet
Grown heavy: would say that in the dusty heels
Of the playground some boy who did not depend   40
On speed of foot, caught and betrayed her.
Jane, stay where you are in my first mind:
It was odd in that school, at that dance.
I and the other slow-footed yokels sat in corners
Cutting rings out of drawing paper

Before you leapt in your new dress
And touched the end of something I began,
Above the couples struggling on the floor,
New men and women clutching at each other
And prancing foolishly as bears: hold on   50
To that ring I made for you, Jane—
My feet are nailed to the ground
By dust I swallowed thirty years ago—
While I examine my hands.

STUDY QUESTIONS

1. In terms of earlier distinctions made about personae, this poem would be more
   dramatic than *lyrical.* The persona is a specific person. So is Jane MacNaughton Hill. Notice the other specific details in the poem: the girls' names, the
   precision with which the persona remembers Jane's leap in the dancing class
   and what he was doing at the time, and the details captured by the photograph
   in the newspaper. Notice the vagueness of certain details: the relationship
   between the persona and Jane or the motive for her suicide. The poet obviously sees a significance in this combination of specificity with vagueness.
   Is the persona also aware of this significance?
2. What is the significance? In answering this question, consider the ring that
   forms an important connection between Jane and the persona in the persona's
   memory. Why does the persona ask her to hold on to that ring while he ex-
   amines his hands? Why is it not possible, or likely, that the persona could
   leap? In short, consider carefully the final stanza. Note that the final stanza
   not only provides a statement of what the poem is all about, but that it also
   leads inevitably back to that first image of Jane with which the poem begins.
3. Is there a conflict in the persona's mind between the two images of Jane? Does
   the significance of the persona's utterance perhaps lie in his final act of will
   whereby he will hold on to his memory of Jane's first leap, not the newspaper
   image of her last? What sort of person is the persona? In answering that
   question, consider his statement that a certain memory is "the only thing" he

has of Jane and his statement that he could say "the convenient thing" concerning the reality of her suicide or her probable motive for it. Consider, too, the age of the persona. The poet was forty-four when this poem was published; if the persona is also in his forties, he was in his early teens "thirty years ago" when he swallowed dust that nailed his feet to the ground.

4. Would you call the organization of this poem stichic or strophic? Does it have a climax? What is gained by postponing the news of Jane's suicide until just after the midpoint of the poem? Note that the persona obviously has read the news, yet he begins by stating that the only thing he has of Jane is a teen-age image of her. Is there, then, no conflict between the two images? Has the conflict been resolved before the poem begins? Will the conflict never be resolved? Are the two images now intrinsically a part of each other, fused like the paper links in the chain at the dance?

Wilfred Owen/Arms and the Boy

born 1893

Let the boy try along this bayonet-blade
How cold steel is, and keen with hunger of blood;
Blue with all malice, like a madman's flash;
And thinly drawn with famishing for flesh.

Lend him to stroke these blind, blunt bullet-heads
Which long to nuzzle in the hearts of lads,
Or give him cartridges of fine zinc teeth,
Sharp with the sharpness of grief and death.

For his teeth seem for laughing round an apple.
There lurk no claws behind his fingers supple;   10
And God will grow no talons at his heels,
Nor antlers through the thickness of his curls.

STUDY QUESTION

1. The title of this poem could allude to the opening of Virgil's *Aeneid:* "Arms and the man I sing." Virgil's great epic is a glorification of war. Placing it in the context of Owen's poem underscores the irony of the latter. Try performing the poem with full emphasis on its irony—working out some way, through facial expression or voice, a means of stressing the disparity between what the persona literally seems to be saying and what he means.

Thom Gunn/*Rites of Passage*

born 1929

Something is taking place.
Horns bud bright in my hair.
My feet are turning hoof.
And Father, see my face
—Skin that was damp and fair
Is barklike and, feel, rough.

See Greytop how I shine.
I rear, break loose, I neigh
Snuffing the air, and harden
Toward a completion, mine.   10
And next I make my way
Adventuring through your garden.

My play is earnest now.
I canter to and fro.
My blood, it is like light.
Behind an almond bough,
Horns gaudy with its snow,
I wait live, out of sight.

All planned before my birth
For you, Old Man, no other,   20
Whom your groin's trembling warns.
I stamp upon the earth
A message to my mother.
And then I lower my horns.

STUDY QUESTIONS

1. The young man speaking this poem is compared *metaphorically* to a young deer
   and to a young tree. What is the function of these comparisons? Note the
   qualities that are or can be associated with these two *tenors*, the means they
   afford the persona in referring to his qualities marked by the terms "harden,"
   "adventuring," "light."
2. What is the effect of the progression from "Father" to "Greytop" to "Old Man"
   and of calling the father's territory "your garden"?
3. When the persona says the inevitable conflict was "all planned before my birth,"

does he mean that he and his father are merely actors in some larger scene controlled by the Fates, or other gods, or that what is about to take place is a necessary part of life? Why is the poem entitled "Rites of Passage"?

4. What, literally, is signified by the trembling of the father's groin? And what, possibly, is the "message to my mother"?

5. All of these questions are aimed at seeking to solve this problem: Is the persona a *unique* individual, a specifically dramatized person whose problems and desires differentiate him from the rest of humanity; or is he rather like a lyric character, universalized, whose rites of passage in some form or another are those of every young man?

6. In considering the dramatic implications of this poem, pay careful attention to verb tenses, the steady insistence upon "now," the stages marked by "and next . . . ," "and then . . ."

Gregory Corso/Marriage

born 1930

for Mr. and Mrs. Mike Goldberg

Should I get married? Should I be good?
Astound the girl next door
with my velvet suit and faustus hood?
Don't take her to movies but to cemeteries
tell all about werewolf bathtubs and forked clarinets
then desire her and kiss her and all the preliminaries
and she going just so far and I understanding why
not getting angry saying You must feel! It's beautiful to feel!
Instead take her in my arms
lean against an old crooked tombstone   10
and woo her the entire night the constellations in the sky—

When she introduces me to her parents
back straightened, hair finally combed, strangled by a tie,
should I sit knees together on their 3rd-degree sofa
and not ask Where's the bathroom?
How else to feel other than I am,
a young man who often thinks Flash Gordon soap—
O how terrible it must be for a young man
seated before a family and the family thinking
We never saw him before! He wants our Mary Lou!   20
After tea and homemade cookies they ask What do you do?
Should I tell them? Would they like me then?
Say All right get married, we're losing a daughter

but we're gaining a son—
And should I then ask Where's the bathroom?

O God, and the wedding! All her family and her friends
and only a handful of mine all scroungy and bearded
just waiting to get at the drinks and food—
And the priest! he looking at me as if I masturbated
asking me Do you take this woman 30
for your lawful wedded wife?
And I, trembling what to say, say Pie Glue!
I kiss the bride all those corny men slapping me on the back:
She's all yours, boy! Ha-ha-ha!
And in their eyes you could see
some obscene honeymoon going on—
Then all that absurd rice and clanky cans and shoes
Niagara Falls! Hordes of us! Husbands! Wives! Flowers!
All streaming into cozy hotels
All going to do the same thing tonight 40
The indifferent clerk he knowing what was going to happen
The lobby zombies they knowing what
The whistling elevator man he knowing
The winking bellboy knowing
Everybody knows! I'd be almost inclined not to do anything!
Stay up all night! Stare that hotel clerk in the eye!
Screaming: I deny honeymoon! I deny honeymoon!
running rampant into those almost climactic suites
yelling Radio belly! Cat shovel!
O I'd live in Niagara forever! in a dark cave beneath the Falls 50
I'd sit there the Mad Honeymooner
devising ways to break marriages, a scourge of bigamy
a saint of divorce—

But I should get married I should be good
How nice it'd be to come home to her
and sit by the fireplace and she in the kitchen
aproned young and lovely wanting my baby
and so happy about me she burns the roast beef
and comes crying to me and I get up from my big papa chair
saying Christmas teeth! Radiant brains! Apple deaf! 60
God what a husband I'd make! Yes, I should get married!
So much to do! like sneaking into Mr. Jones' house late at night
and cover his golf clubs with 1920 Norwegian books
Like hanging a picture of Rimbaud on the lawnmower
Like pasting Tannu Tuva postage stamps

all over the picket fence
Like when Mrs. Kindhead comes to collect
for the Community Chest
grab her and tell her There are unfavorable omens in the sky!
And when the mayor comes to get my vote tell him   70
When are you going to stop people killing whales!
And when the milkman comes leave him a note in the bottle
Penguin dust, bring me penguin dust, I want penguin dust—

Yet if I should get married and it's Connecticut and snow
and she gives birth to a child and I am sleepless, worn,
up for nights, head bowed against a quiet window,
the past behind me,
finding myself in the most common of situations
a trembling man
knowledged with responsibility not twig-smear   80
nor Roman coin soup—
O what would that be like!
Surely I'd give it for a nipple a rubber Tacitus
For a rattle a bag of broken Bach records
Tack Della Francesca all over its crib
Sew the Greek alphabet on its bib
And build for its playpen a roofless Parthenon—

No, I doubt I'd be that kind of father
not rural not snow no quiet window
but hot smelly tight New York City   90
seven flights up, roaches and rats in the walls
a fat Reichian wife screeching over potatoes Get a job!
And five nose-running brats in love with Batman
And the neighbors all toothless and dry haired
like those hag masses of the 18th century
all wanting to come in and watch TV
The landlord wants his rent
Grocery store Blue Cross Gas & Electric Knights of Columbus
Impossible to lie back and dream Telephone snow,
ghost parking—   100
No! I should not get married I should never get married!

But—imagine if I were married to a beautiful
sophisticated woman
tall and pale wearing an elegant black dress
and long black gloves

holding a cigarette holder in one hand
and a highball in the other
and we lived high up in a penthouse with a huge window
from which we could see all of New York
and even farther on clearer days   110
No, can't imagine myself married to that pleasant prison dream—

O but what about love? I forget love
not that I am incapable of love
it's just that I see love as odd as wearing shoes—
I never wanted to marry a girl who was like my mother
And Ingrid Bergman was always impossible
And there's maybe a girl now but she's already married
And I don't like men and—
but there's got to be somebody!
Because what if I'm 60 years old and not married,   120
all alone in a furnished room with pee stains on my underwear
and everybody else is married!   All the universe married but me!

Ah, yet well I know that were a woman possible
as I am possible
then marriage would be possible—
Like SHE in her lonely alien gaud waiting her Egyptian lover
so I wait—bereft of 2,000 years and the bath of life.

STUDY QUESTIONS

1. In this poem, as in so many you have looked at that were told from the first-person perspective, the point of view shifts subtly. This happens not, as in "My Last Duchess," because the audience that is addressed shifts, but rather because the point of view shifts as the speaker takes a different perspective of himself. Note that there are times in his imaginary scenes when the speaker dramatizes himself and looks at himself as if he were a third-person observer, for example, in the second stanza. There are other times, as in the third stanza, when he sees himself not as one individual but as "hordes." Note, too, that a general bifurcation of his being is implied in his meditative stance: He becomes a speaker addressing himself directly in the seventh stanza, even conducting a kind of dialogue with himself in the eighth stanza. How do these shifts and bifurcations serve to dramatize what he means by "possible" in the last stanza? Is the speaker in search of the possibilities of his own character?
2. Is it possible to perform this poem as if it were being addressed to an audience outside the persona? If so, what characteristics must that audience have?

3. Which performance possibility—the persona communicating with an audience outside himself or the persona meditating—serves to make probable the fear expressed at the end of the eighth stanza? Does that fear constitute a climax in the poem? Or does the poem have a climax at all?
4. How particularized does this persona seem to be?

Philip Larkin/Church Going

born 1922

Once I am sure there's nothing going on
I step inside, letting the door thud shut.
Another church: matting, seats, and stone,
And little books; sprawlings of flowers, cut
For Sunday, brownish now; some brass and stuff
Up at the holy end; the small neat organ;
And a tense, musty, unignorable silence,
Brewed God knows how long. Hatless, I take off
My cycle-clips in awkward reverence,

Move forward, run my hand around the font.   10
From where I stand, the roof looks almost new—
Cleaned or restored? Someone would know: I don't.
Mounting the lectern, I peruse a few
Hectoring large-scale verses, and pronounce
'Here endeth' much more loudly than I'd meant.
The echoes snigger briefly. Back at the door
I sign the book, donate an Irish sixpence,
Reflect the place was not worth stopping for.

Yet stop I did: in fact I often do,
And always end much at a loss like this,   20
Wondering what to look for; wondering, too,
When churches fall completely out of use
What we shall turn them into, if we shall keep
A few cathedrals chronically on show,
Their parchment, plate and pyx in locked cases,
And let the rest rent-free to rain and sheep.
Shall we avoid them as unlucky places?

Or, after dark, will dubious women come
To make their children touch a particular stone;
Pick simples for a cancer; or on some   30

Advised night see walking a dead one?
Power of some sort or other will go on
In games, in riddles, seemingly at random;
But superstition, like belief, must die,
And what remains when disbelief has gone?
Grass, weedy pavement, brambles, buttress, sky,

A shape less recognisable each week,
A purpose more obscure. I wonder who
Will be the last, the very last, to seek
This place for what it was; one of the crew   40
That tap and jot and know what rood-lofts were?
Some ruin-bibber, randy for antique,
Or Christmas-addict, counting on a whiff
Of gown-and-bands and organ-pipes and myrrh?
Or will he be my representative,

Bored, uninformed, knowing the ghostly silt
Dispersed, yet tending to this cross of ground
Through suburb scrub because it held unspilt
So long and equally what since is found
Only in separation—marriage, and birth,   50
And deaths, and thoughts of these—for whom was built
This special shell? For, though I've no idea
What this accoutred frowsty barn is worth,
It pleases me to stand in silence here;

A serious house on serious earth it is,
In whose blent air all our compulsions meet,
Are recognised, and robed as destinies.
And that much never can be obsolete,
Since someone will forever be surprising
A hunger in himself to be more serious,   60
And gravitating with it to this ground,
Which, he once heard, was proper to grow wise in,
If only that so many dead lie round.

STUDY QUESTIONS

1. Consider that there are two ways whereby the persona presents his interpretation of himself and of the church: one by the action in the poem itself, particularly
   the persona's movements through the church and then the long meditative action

that comprises more than half of the poem; and the other by the statements about the meaning of his visit to church in the last two stanzas. Consider these statements in the last two stanzas as "what the poem comes to." Is the reader prepared for the persona's conclusions about himself and the church by what comes before? Do the action and meditation in the poem contradict these statements? Or present another dimension of meaning for them?

2. Note that in this poem the poet is creating a persona—a dramatization of himself, perhaps, as a casual yet curiously compelled visitor of a church. And this persona in turn creates another persona, another dramatization of himself, his "representative." What is gained by, or what is the effect of, this dramatic progression?

3. As said before, the first persona is engaged largely in a meditative action. Try performing the poem, however, as if the persona were communicating with an audience outside himself. Which seems to work? Why?

4. Note the precise extent to which the first persona is characterized—we know that he is male, rides a bicycle, and has certain attitudes toward himself and the church. Why is he no more fully characterized than that?

5. Note the change, at the end of the second stanza, from present to past tense. What is the purpose of this change? Why are the first two stanzas in the present tense?

Gwendolyn Brooks/*A Bronzeville Mother Loiters in Mississippi.*
Meanwhile, a Mississippi Mother Burns Bacon.

born 1917

From the first it had been like a
Ballad. It had the beat inevitable. It had the blood.
A wildness cut up, and tied in little bunches,
Like the four-line stanzas of the ballads she had never quite
Understood—the ballads they had set her to, in school.

Herself: the milk-white maid, the "maid mild"
Of the ballad. Pursued
By the Dark Villain. Rescued by the Fine Prince.
The Happiness-Ever-After.
That was worth anything.   10
It was good to be a "maid mild."
That made the breath go fast.

Her bacon burned. She
Hastened to hide it in the step-on can, and
Drew more strips from the meat case. The eggs and sour-milk biscuits
Did well. She set out a jar
Of her new quince preserve.

. . . But there was a something about the matter of the Dark Villain.
He should have been older, perhaps.
The hacking down of a villain was more fun to think about   20
When his menace possessed undisputed breadth, undisputed height,
And a harsh kind of vice.
And best of all, when his history was cluttered
With the bones of many eaten knights and princesses.

The fun was disturbed, then all but nullified
When the Dark Villain was a blackish child
Of fourteen, with eyes still too young to be dirty,
And a mouth too young to have lost every reminder
Of its infant softness.

That boy must have been surprised! For   30
These were grown-ups. Grown-ups were supposed to be wise.
And the Fine Prince—and that other—so tall, so broad, so
Grown! Perhaps the boy had never guessed
That the trouble with grown-ups was that under the magnificent shell of
    adulthood, just under,
Waited the baby full of tantrums.
It occurred to her that there may have been something
Ridiculous in the picture of the Fine Prince
Rushing (rich with the breadth and height and
Mature solidness whose lack, in the Dark Villain, was impressing her,
Confronting her more and more as this first day after the trial   40
And acquittal wore on) rushing
With his heavy companion to hack down (unhorsed)
That little foe.
So much had happened, she could not remember now what that foe had
    done
Against her, or if anything had been done.
The one thing in the world that she did know and knew
With terrifying clarity was that her composition
Had disintegrated. That although the pattern prevailed,
The breaks were everywhere. That she could think
Of no thread capable of the necessary   50
Sew-work.

She made the babies sit in their places at the table.
Then, before calling Him, she hurried
To the mirror with her comb and lipstick. It was necessary
To be more beautiful than ever.
The beautiful wife.

For sometimes she fancied he looked at her as though
Measuring her. As if he considered, Had she been worth It?
Had *she* been worth the blood, the cramped cries, the little stuttering
    bravado,
The gradual dulling of those Negro eyes,   60
The sudden, overwhelming *little-boyness* in that barn?
Whatever she might feel or half-feel, the lipstick necessity was something
    apart. He must never conclude
That she had not been worth It.

He sat down, the Fine Prince, and
Began buttering a biscuit. He looked at his hands.
He twisted in his chair, he scratched his nose.
He glanced again, almost secretly, at his hands.
Most papers were in from the North, he mumbled. More meddling head-
    lines.
With their pepper-words, "bestiality," and "barbarism," and
"Shocking."   70
The half-sneers he had mastered for the trial worked across
His sweet and pretty face.

What he'd like to do, he explained, was kill them all.
The time lost. The unwanted fame.
Still, it had been fun to show those intruders
A thing or two. To show that snappy-eyed mother,
That sassy, Northern, brown-black—

Nothing could stop Mississippi.
He knew that. Big Fella
Knew that.   80
And, what was so good, Mississippi knew that.
Nothing and nothing could stop Mississippi.
They could send in their petitions, and scar
Their newspapers with bleeding headlines. Their governors
Could appeal to Washington . . .

"What I want," the older baby said, "is 'lasses on my jam."
Whereupon the younger baby
Picked up the molasses pitcher and threw
The molasses in his brother's face. Instantly
The Fine Prince leaned across the table and slapped   90
The small and smiling criminal.

She did not speak. When the Hand
Came down and away, and she could look at her child,

At her baby-child,
She could think only of blood.
Surely her baby's cheek
Had disappeared, and in its place, surely,
Hung a heaviness, a lengthening red, a red that had no end.
She shook her head. It was not true, of course.
It was not true at all. The   100
Child's face was as always, the
Color of the paste in her paste-jar.

She left the table, to the tune of the children's lamentations, which were
    shriller
Than ever. She
Looked out of a window. She said not a word. *That*
Was one of the new Somethings—
The fear,
Tying her as with iron.

Suddenly she felt his hands upon her. He had followed her
To the window. The children were whimpering now.   110
Such bits of tots. And she, their mother,
Could not protect them. She looked at her shoulders, still
Gripped in the claim of his hands. She tried, but could not resist the idea
That a red ooze was seeping, spreading darkly, thickly, slowly,
Over her white shoulders, her own shoulders,
And over all of Earth and Mars.

He whispered something to her, did the Fine Prince, something
About love, something about love and night and intention.
She heard no hoof-beat of the horse and saw no flash of the shining steel.

He pulled her face around to meet   120
His, and there it was, close close,
For the first time in all those days and nights.
His mouth, wet and red,
So very, very, very red,
Closed over hers.

Then a sickness heaved within her. The courtroom Coca-Cola,
The courtroom beer and hate and sweat and drone,
Pushed like a wall against her. She wanted to bear it.
But his mouth would not go away and neither would the
Decapitated exclamation points in that Other Woman's eyes.   130

She did not scream.
She stood there.
But a hatred for him burst into glorious flower,
And its perfume enclasped them—big,
Bigger than all magnolias.

The last bleak news of the ballad.
The rest of the rugged music.
The last quatrain.

The Last Quatrain of the Ballad of Emmett Till

> after the murder,
> after the burial

Emmett's mother is a pretty-faced thing;
            the tint of pulled taffy.
She sits in a red room,
            drinking black coffee.
She kisses her killed boy.
            And she is sorry.
Chaos in windy grays
            through a red prairie.   10

STUDY QUESTIONS

1. As you perform this poem, note particularly the arrangement of its parts: The poem begins with the white woman and her romanticizing of the murder; enter the Prince; the point of view shifts to him; then it shifts back to the "maid mild." How do these shifts prepare the reader for the last stanza of the poem and "The Last Quatrain of the Ballad of Emmett Till"? Who speaks these final parts? Does this persona speak earlier in the poem? Where?

2. What is the function of the "ballad" form? Obviously, it helps explore the turmoil of the white woman's mind and her inability to come to terms with the murder in what she considers a ballad frame. Yet, does the typical tone, or attitudes, of the ballad assist the central persona (the major speaker of the poem) to establish *his* attitude? In answering this question, consider carefully the "Last Quatrain": It has the ring of a ballad. Note its ironies: It has none of the images associated with the white woman, and none of the images she expects ballads to have. Why is there such a discrepancy between this "Last Quatrain" of the ballad and "the ballad" of the first part of the poem?

3. To return to the first question, note the ways in which your sympathy for the

two women is controlled. You are not allowed to feel merely disgust for the white woman and pity for the black woman. What, finally, are your feelings? And how has the poet managed to achieve these effects?

4. This poem is placed near the end of this chapter for at least three reasons. First, it has a particularly subtle, complicated use of point of view. Second, it is closer to the short-story type than most other poems in the book. Finally, it is also very close to the nonfictional prose in its manner of presentation. This last matter might bear close examination in the following way: Find a newspaper account of the murder of Emmett Till in Mississippi in 1955. Even better, find two newspaper accounts: one in one of the Northern newspapers so hated by the white man (perhaps in Chicago, where "Bronzeville" is located) and one in a Southern, preferably Mississippian, newspaper. Regard the poem as another account. How do they compare, what are their differences, in point of view, tone, emphasis? Though stress has been placed on the similarities between literary types, this is nonetheless a good place to raise an important question: What makes this poem a poem and not a nonfictional account? Is it because the poem is, finally, like a ballad; that is, because it is a *sung* experience? Are you aware of certain rhythmical qualities in the poem that are not present in the newspaper account(s)? Or do the differences lie somewhere else—perhaps in management of point of view or in the nature and function of the images? Or are there ultimately no functional differences between this poem and the newspaper account(s)?

Agyeya (S. Vatsyayan)/The Unmastered Lute

born 1911

Even the king rose up to make obeisance,
For surely, now that Priyamvada had arrived,
His own long-hoped-for dream would come to pass.
As the court stared at that gaunt and unkempt man
Whose home was a cave in the hills, whose robe a rug,
Bristling with hair, flung around him, the king nodded
And attendants rushed out and returned, in their serving hands
The lute that no man known had ever mastered;
They set it before the sage and the whole court stiffened,
All looks sweeping the scene, then fixing themselves   10
On Priyamvada's face.

                     "This lute was brought
Long years ago from the mountain wilderness
Of the country north where hermits in the woods
Tame their bodies. Yet this much we've heard:
The tree from which the great Vajrakirti carved it
Was the primal, strange Kiriti in whose ear

The snowpeaks whispered high secrets, on whose shoulders
Clouds came to rest, below whose branches, stout
As the trunks of elephants, whole herds could shelter
From the snow and sleet, while in his hollows bears   20
Could hibernate, on his bark lions came
To comb their manes; and—we've heard too—his roots
Reached to midearth, where on their scented coolness
Vasuki, the vast serpent rested his head
To sleep. From that tree great Vajrakirti
Fashioned it, carving all his life
To carry out his unrelenting irresistable vow
And, finishing the lute, he finished vow
and life at once."

        Sighing, the king went on:
"My famous artists—all have given up,   30
Their craft confounded and their pride put down;
That instrument has found no one to match it yet
And so is called by us The Obstinate Lute;
And yet, for all of this, we still believe
That Vajrakirti's disciplined devotion
Had a purpose and that the lute will surely speak,
Though only when that master who commands
Music like an essence takes it in his lap.
Wise Priyamvada! There's Vajrakirti's lute;
And here I am, and here the queen, the court,   40
The people waiting, taut as bow strings drawn."

Priyamvada, with all eyes gripping him,
Unwrapped his bristling mat without a word,
And spreading it on the floor set down the lute
On it; eyes closed, he took a long deep breath
And gently joined his hands; then almost unseen,
So delicate was the move, he touched the chords
And said in a slow voice: "But, Majesty,
I'm no musician, merely a supplicant,
A plodding learner of and would-be witness   50
To those truths alive beyond the grasp
Of words . . . Vajrakirti! And the ancient
Kiriti! This lute grained with a power
That's superhuman! These thoughts alone can shake
The base of being!"

        Priyamvada paused:
The court had long since forgotten how to speak.

Lifting the instrument he cradled it,
This Seeker, on his lap, then slowly bent
To it until at last his forehead rested
On the strings. The court was shocked: Priyamvada too?   60
Was he asleep, fatigued? Or had he crumpled
Like all the rest, despite that prickly rug,
That discipline? Did the lute remain
Unchanged, unmastered, still unplayable?
But in the pounding silence, Priyamvada
Was taking the lute's full measure, or truer yet,
Was going back wide-eyed into himself;
He was, concerted in this solitude,
Giving himself to that Kiriti tree;
For who was he, in fact, this Priyamvada,   70
To set himself so brazenly before
This deep-spelled instrument, wanting to play
This lute that bodied a holy, given life?
Thus on the spiky mat that was his fame
He thought no more of king and court, withdrew
Into a deep occulted round of self
In which a solitary witness stood
Before that tree on whose cool scented roots
Was pillowed the huge Serpent in his sleep,
On whose shoulders the clouds could come to rest,   80
And in whose ears the snowpeaks whispered secrets,
And Priyamvada made this wordless hymn:

O great tree!
Form sprung with a million unfolding and falling of leaves,
Blazoned in countless rains with countless fireflies,
Whose days are hummed by bees,
Nights by the cicada's
Endless benisons,
Whose limbs, morning and evening,
Have shaken to the pleasure   90
Of innumerable families of birds,
O huge figure,
Older brother to the whole wilderness,
Elder, companion, mentor, support,
All-circling sanctuary,
Embodied chorus
Of a multitude of urgent wood-sounds—
Let me just hear you,
See you, meditate on you,

Unblinking, stilled, contained, whole, and speechless:　　　　100
How shall I have power to touch you even?
This lute, hewn from your body, pierced and bound,
How can I dare
With these hands to strike,
To force from its chords
By a blow, that richness of music for making
Which how many gave their full-pulsed lives?

This lute resting on my lap—but no!—
It is I myself who am
A delighted child at play in your lap,　　　　110
O Prime Tree! Hold and steady me,
Let all my childish cries
Be stilled in an exultation
In which
I hear
And gather,
And, astonished, record in myself
Each midmost note of your being,
Sway, lost to myself, with each sway of your song:
Sing,　　　　120
And may the quick air I breathe move to the cadence of you singing,
Breathing in and out, the breathing contained or at rest in release.

Sing!
Here rests the lute, your limb, a severed member!
But you are yet whole, inviolate, self-contained,
Essentially possessed.
Sing!
In the dark of my being let the light of remembrance
Wake up, memory
Of the essential sound:　　　　130
Sing, then, oh tree, sing!

I remember now:
Bellying clouds—lightning-shot—the chatter of rain on leaves
In the pit of night the soft fall of the mahua berries;
The whimper of the startled nestling;
The soft amusement of the rippled stream
Swiftly caressing the rocks;
The holiday drum from the village on the hill,
Thumping through the valley mist.
The listless flute of a shepherd;　　　　140

The woodpecker's knick; the urgent flutter of the humming-bird;
The fall of dew so soft it ends in a rain of star-flowers;
The ponds' brimming in fall, their waves a mere rustle;
The cranes' cranking, the plovers' drawn-out cry,
The hissing rush of swans in flight, their shapes like feathered darts
In pine woods the aimless clacking of the scent-drunk beetle;
The drone of cataracts, syncopated;
In stops between the cicada, frog, cuckoo, papiha, between creek, cry,
    chirr, and click—
The hum of all, being born

Yes, I remember: 150
The plunge and rush of black clouds from distant mountains,
Like herds of bellowing elephants;
The lunge of the rising flood;
The whoosh and gurgle of sand-banks falling;
The searing snort of the cyclone,
Trees ripped and crashing down;
The stinging slap of hail;
The crackle of dry grass-blades, honed by frost;
The melt of ice-caked clay, oozing in gentle sun;
Hoar-frost swabbing the earth's cracked skin softly;   160
The rebounding boom
Of falling rock filling the valleys—
Stunning crash, dulled thud, echo softened, and sigh tapering off to
    silence.

I remember:
In the green glade, behind dwarf trees by the pond,
The sounds of many forest creatures, thirsty or sated; each at his ap-
    pointed hour:
Roar, growl, cry, bark, howl, and chattering;
The quick patter of the water-fowl's thief-step
On the spreading lotus leaves;
The splash of the frog's startled leap;   170
The quick clop of the traveller's horse;
The patient, unruffled thump of the hefty buffalo hoof.

I remember:
When daylight's first tiptoe glimpse
Glistens on the dew drop—
The sudden astonished shiver of that instant:
And by noon, when
Small blossoms in the grass open unseen

To the soft roar of uncountable drunken bees—
The indolent stillness of that long-staying moment;   180
And in the evening
When the gleaming liquescence of starshine
Rains intangibly
Like the blessings of innumerable young madonnas
Looking down with great gentle eyes—
The slow surrounding mystery of that moment.

I remember
And each recalled image
Overpowers and stuns me.
I hear   190
But every resonance sucks me out of myself;
Like some hymn-pervaded air I am carried away.
I remember
But I have forgotten myself:
I hear but that I listening is beyond me, a second self lost in the very note.

No, not I, nowhere that I!
Oh, Tree, Forest,
Oh, warp and woof of music,
Fabric of cadenced being,
Tidal sweep of identity,   200
Forgive me—pass over my trivialness—
Give me cover, shelter, sanctuary;
My Refuge,
May my dumbness lose itself in the swell of your music.
Forgetting me, come,
Light upon the chords of the lute
And sing your self
To your self:
Let the birds you shelter have a voice,
The spring of the deer that keep to your shade a cadence;   210
For the rhythms of your sunlight and shade, your wind and rain,
Your leafing and flowering;
Give shape of song to the rings of your ages,
Sing your wiseness ingrained,
Oh, sing,
Compass your self, its finding, its losing,
Its being, becoming, its ever presence,
Oh, sing!

The king's eyes widened, for as if in a trance
The musician had lifted up his arm and struck;   220

The lute, as one who stretches lazily
After a heavy sleep, awakened; notes
Like tiny seraphim flew up, their joy
Singing; for that hunter-sorcerer,
Stalking with soundless steps, drew in with sure
And careful hands his net of golden strings.

All at once, the lute's chords twanged, and a strange blaze
Flashed, cold and liquid, in the player's eyes;
And lightning shuddered through every man in court.
Something descended which, self-born in light,   230
To Brahma's massive silence endlessly
Gives shape: Light in one imperious sweep
Enveloped all those present.   Then the flood
Held each one, separate, carried him across . . .
The king in his solitude heard
Victory whose body was fame,
Whose hand held a garland,
Who sang a lucky hymn
To the beat of far-off drums
And the crown sat lightly as the siris on his head.   240
Envy, ambition, hate, and flattery
Peeled from him like rags, leaving gold alive with light,
Devoutly to be given away.

The queen heard lightning speak to her apart—
(The lightning, weaving garlands for her dusky cloud-lover's chest
Where she makes love, and wearying, finds repose
In perfect trust):
These rubies, necklaces, silks and brocades,
These brilliant bands and anklets that tinkle,
Are lumps of frosted dark!   One light only there is—   250
To love constantly!
Which unchanging light, the queen devoutly will seek after.

In their singular solitudes others heard also:
To this one, musing,
It was the smallest crumb of compassion tossed from above:
To that other
A promise of no more fear;
To him
The clang of money in the safe;
To him the incredible odor of cooking after days of hunger;   260
One heard the shy clink of the new bride's ankle-bells;

Another the joyous babble of the new-born;
To another it came as the flapping of fish in a net;
To another a bird's call, far up and free;
Another heard it as the scrambled cries of competing stalls in the market;
Another as the measured chime of the temple bells;
Another as the steady fall of the hammer on the hectic anvil;
The continual lapping of waves on a hull of a boat that chafes at anchor
    to one,
While to another it was the rough-shod foot mutely falling on the village
    road,
Or, to this one, the water sluicing through the broken dyke;   270
To that one the jingle of the dancer's ankle-bells calling;
For another battle clangour;
The clank of cow-bells at lowly twilight to him;
To him, doom striking with its sullen drums;
To another, being young the very first sigh;
To another, Time yawning with swallowing jaws.
All were swamped, sucked under, floated a while,
Bobbed up, and left subdued and muted; each.
In his separate this-ness only, woke alone,
Became explicit, merged into the whole.   280
The lute was once more still.

                "Oh, marvelous!
Marvelous!" The king stepped down, in awe,
From his high throne, the queen held out her necklace,
The seven-stringed one, the people cried with one
Charmed voice: "Oh master, master, miracle!"

And he who made that music set the lute
Gently on the mat and covered it,
Like a mother who, laying her sleeping baby down
In his bed, withdraws a little and caresses him
With blessing eyes. The master then rose up   290
And, staying the king's advance with a lifted hand,
Said: "Nothing in this is Cause for praising me,
For I myself was drowned in nothingness,
Gave myself up to the whole by playing,
So what you heard was not from me or even
From the lute itself, but rather from all things
In their being thus; all presence wholly
Here, sang of itself; the Infinite,

Of Silence in the Empty Infinite,
Not to be divided, or possessed,   300
Not to be reduced, not measurable,
Without a word or sound makes in all things
Their essential music!"

                Priyamvada then
Folded his hands and bowed to everyone,
Rolled up the bristly mat and went back to his cave.
The court rose: king, courtier, commoner
All went about their business.

                Times, too changed.
You who read me, for this sufficient reason
My own voice finds its fitting silence now.

           [Translated from the Hindi by Agyeya
           and Leonard Nathan]

STUDY QUESTIONS

1. Note that the central persona, though mainly omniscient, centers on the mind of Priyamvada. Comment on the significance of this. Does it help establish an identity for the central persona? Does it clarify or prepare for the persona's reference to himself in the first person in the final stanza? Does it help establish the persona's audience—who, again, is not referred to in any personal way until the final stanza? What significance lies in the difference between the central persona's word "unmastered" (line 64) for the lute and the court's word "obstinate" (line 33)? Does the lute *remain* unmastered?

2. The central problem in understanding the poem probably lies in understanding why the lute sang for Priyamvada. We do not know why it failed to sing for other musicians or prophets; but why does the lute sing for Priyamvada?

3. Note that when Priyamvada begins his long prayer, he "speaks" to the tree, the great Kiriti. But what shift in this discursive form occurs in line 132: "I remember now." Who speaks there? And to whom? Review carefully lines 190 to 195. Does another shift occur in line 196? If it seems difficult or irrelevant to talk about shifts in modes of address in this poem, discuss the structural and rhythmic changes in the poem and their relationship to the action.

4. What is the significance of the various different desires awakened in the people by the lute's sound (lines 230 to 280)? Explain lines 277 to 281.

5. What is fitting about the rather rapid conclusion of the poem (lines 303 to 309) and the silence of the persona? Note how this concluding silence is foreshadowed by the death of Vajrakirti (lines 25 to 29) upon completion of the

lute. Note, too, that the persona claims to be presenting Priyamvada's "word-less hymn" (line 82) and that Priyamvada himself claims that the lute did not make the music the people heard (lines 295 to 296). In accepting these claims, do we not agree that poetry itself, or music, or this poem in particular, is of a certain "essential" nature (see line 303)?

6. This poem deserves examination at much greater length than that proposed by the preceding questions. One could write a paper bringing to bear on an interpretation of this poem information from Indian mythology. If such a paper is attempted, one might also find illuminating Mircea Eliade's *Shamanism* (Princeton, N.J.: Princeton University Press, 1962) as a possible explanation of the religious significance of Kiriti, whose uppermost branches reach the clouds and whose roots touch the great serpent.

EXERCISES AND BIBLIOGRAPHY

1. In this chapter the lyric persona has been described as a generalized persona, one having few specific dramatic characteristics. But to the psychologist Carl Jung apparently all great literature speaks through a kind of lyric persona. Read Jung's essay "Psychology and Literature" in *Modern Man in Search of a Soul,* translated by W. S. Dell and Cary F. Baynes (New York: Harcourt, Brace and World, 1933), Chapter 8. Note carefully Jung's argument concerning the poet's will and the "participation mystique." Compare his ideas with those offered in the present chapter concerning the role of the poet and the variety of personae he may create.

2. Paul Fussell's *Poetic Meter and Poetic Form* (New York: Random House, 1965) is one of the best discussions of modern prosody and the traditions out of which it grew. As you read that book, ask yourself, "What kind of prosodic conventions does Fussell seem to prefer?" and "Is his work limited to the appreciation of only a certain kind of modern poetry? Are there certain kinds of modern poetry that his view excludes?" Definitions of the footnoted items in the introductory essay to this chapter may be found in Fussell's book.

3. It would be interesting to compare Fussell's arguments and preferences with those set forth in the "Statements on Poetics" appended to Donald M. Allen (ed.), *The New American Poetry* (New York: Grove Press, 1960), pp. 386–426. How convincing are these arguments that a new poetry has appeared on the scene? Olson's essay on "Projective Verse," pp. 386–397, has caused considerable comment and controversy. Does his essay clarify certain aspects of modern poetry?

4. The best modern study of personae is George T. Wright's *The Poet in the Poem* (Berkeley: University of California Press, 1962). Wright's work is explicitly directed toward the study of the personae of Eliot, Yeats, and Pound, but the work is obviously meant to have implications for the study of other poets. Note Wright's argument that it is in the *structure* of a poem that we gain the most definite sense of the poet in the poem. Note, too, the historical review he presents in his first chapter concerning the varieties of personae and their

differing relationships with the poet. How applicable are Wright's conclusions to the kinds of poetry included in the Allen book referred to in question 3?

5. Among the various topics touched upon in the work of the "prophet of the electronic age," Marshall McLuhan, are a few at least that bear directly on the matter of modern poetry. Of all McLuhan's writings, *The Gutenberg Galaxy* remains the best introduction to his ideas and perhaps the clearest statement of his teachings.

From Aristotle to Stephen Daedelus literary critics have generally assigned literary works to one of three major modes—the lyric, the epic, and the dramatic—that define the relationship between the speaker in a text and the manner of his verbal presentation. To a certain extent, one could say that the speaker in the lyric mode *tells* his story in his own person; the speaker in the dramatic mode *shows* his story through others; and the speaker in the epic mode *shows and tells* his story by speaking in his own person *and* by allowing others to speak for him. If these three modes were placed on a continuum, one would find the lyric at one end, the dramatic at the other end, and the epic somewhere in the middle. In the lyric mode, as has been demonstrated in the two preceding chapters (for most nonfictional prose is, by this definition, lyrical), the experience of the text comes to the reader almost entirely through the poet's persona. In the dramatic mode the experience is presented almost entirely through speakers other than the poet. And, as can be expected from the nature of a continuum, the experience of the epic mode comes to the reader through the poet's persona *and* through other speakers. Still considering the implications of the continuum, one can also observe that the elements of the lyric and dramatic modes, coming together as they do in the epic mode, create a particular structural tension that characterizes the epic mode—the tension between the lyric and dramatic manners of presenting experience.

Of these three major literary types, prose fiction, because of its usual narrative structure, belongs to the epic mode. Although there are certainly many poems and plays that are epic in structure, this chapter will be limited to that form of the epic mode commonly known as narrative fiction and encountered most frequently in the form of novels and short stories. Because of spatial limitations the core of this study will be the short story. It should be noted that narrative fiction, like any literary art form, has its own structural principles and defines its own world. And, because form and content must be regarded as quantitatively inseparable, it would not be wise to consider the novel as an extended short story nor the short story as a truncated novel. Nonetheless, many of the principles and concepts discussed here regarding short stories would be equally applicable to the study of novels.

The central problem in any work of narrative fiction (whether it be a novel, a novella, or a short story) is "point of view." As noted in Chapter Two, the problem of point of view is critical in the study of any literary work; but the complexities become more intense in narrative fiction because of its particular structure.

A story's point of view is the angle of vision from which the story is perceived and described. In narrative fiction this angle of vision from which the reader is presented the story belongs to the major speaker in the story—the narrator. What the narrator sees and how he interprets what he sees condition what the reader sees and how he interprets it. You may well be familiar with the traditional classifications of point of view as first person and third person, or as "protagonist," [1] "omniscient narrator," [2] and objective observer. But such classifications are not very valuable unless you begin to understand how the choice of point of view is related to, and conditions, a particular story.

When an author chooses to tell a story using a first-person narrator, that is, a narrator who refers to himself as "I," he has several advantages. The first-person narrator carries with him a great deal of "credibility" [3] because his story has the illusion of an eyewitness account. If the narrator is a major character in the story he is telling, his account carries not only the credibility of an eyewitness account, but the increased credibility of one who actually took a central role in the story's events. One would think that such advantages would make the first-person narrator an obvious choice for any writer of narrative fiction. Sometimes, however, these advantages seem almost outweighed by the narrator's great subjectivity [4] and limited, prejudicial vision. In some cases an author who wishes to capitalize on the advantages of a first-person point of view but also wants to reduce the subjectivity of the narrator's account will choose to let the story be told by a first-person narrator who is a *minor* participant in the action. Here the narrator, such as Nick Carraway in *The Great Gatsby* or Ishmael in *Moby Dick,* carries all the advantages of the eyewitness participant's account; but his view of the story is not as highly prejudiced as that of the major participant. Because he is *somewhat* more peripheral to the major action of the story, his view is *somewhat* more objective. A writer wishing to push this combination of advantages even further might even choose—as does Fielding in *Tom Jones*—to use a first-person narrator who is not a participant in the action. But here the question of how the narrator gets his information is inevitably raised. Henry James manages such a point of view quite skillfully in many of his novels and short stories. In general, he first establishes, usually rather indirectly, a situation in which his narrator is someone who is privy to the history of the major characters—someone who, while not actually a

---

[1] *Protagonist:* the central character in the action of a story.

[2] *Omniscient narrator:* a narrator who displays the power or privilege of knowing what a character thinks or feels or who appears to know about simultaneous incidents occurring in separate locations.

[3] *Credibility:* the degree of believability assigned to a narrator or character. As a rule, those narrators carrying the greatest amount of credibility are the first-person major-participant narrator and the third-person objective observer.

[4] *Subjectivity:* as used in this chapter, a quality in a narrator that qualifies the authenticity of his account of a story due to his acknowledged personal involvement in the action. Subjectivity may arise from either (1) the narrator's participation in the events of the story he is recounting or (2) his rendering of the internal, subjective states of a character or several characters.

participant in the particular action he is relating, nonetheless knows these characters quite well.

In addition to subjectivity another disadvantage of using a first-person narrator is that he is restricted to reporting only his own thoughts, feelings, and perceptions. This is fine if the reader is primarily interested in the narrator's interpretation of events rather than the events themselves as some sort of objective reality, *and* if this narrator is articulate in expressing his interpretation of events, *and* if his expression of his feelings is adequate for the author's purpose. But frequently an author will find it useful to tell a story in which he employs the "objectivity" [5] of a third-person account (that is, a story in which the narrator refers to everyone as "he" or "she," and never refers to himself as "I"). One reason for an author's choosing such a point of view is that he may feel it necessary to reveal to the reader, through the narrator, the thoughts and feelings of several characters in the story. Such a privileged narrator is said to have omniscience because he apparently knows and reports the inner states of persons in the story and because he can know what is happening in many places simultaneously. This kind of narrator is most advantageous if an author wants the reader to know how several characters react inwardly as well as outwardly to a situation in the story. But the great disadvantage of such a narrator is that the more omniscience he claims, the more he strains his credibility. In other words, the narrator, by virtue of using verbal language, has acknowledged that he is a human being with human limitations. By claiming omniscience, which is clearly not a human attribute, he jeopardizes his humanity and consequently his credibility.

Henry James was probably the first author seriously to take advantage of the technique of omniscience without straining the narrator's credibility through the use of what he called the "central intelligence." Essentially, this point of view is a kind of limited omniscience wherein the narrator claims the privilege of knowing what only one or two major characters think and feel. Here the advantages of using an omniscient narrator are not so easily outweighed by the usual accompanying disadvantages. Such a point of view is particularly useful in a story where the major character is incapable of expressing his emotions but where the reader's knowledge of his emotions and perceptions is essential to the understanding of the story. This point of view is also advantageous in a narrative in which it is necessary that the reader understand the conflict between what a character says and does socially and what he thinks and

---

[5] *Objectivity:* as used in this chapter, a quality in a narrator that tends to substantiate his account of a story by apparently minimizing his judgments and prejudices. Objectivity may be achieved by the narrator's lack of participation in the story he is telling or by his reluctance to make overt value judgments about characters or incidents.

feels privately. In a story using a limited omniscient point of view it is also possible to create the distinct impression that the story is being told by the major character who has managed to achieve enough distance from his experience so that, in effect, he objectifies himself as he tells his own story by speaking of himself in the third person. A number of narratives in this chapter, such as "Flowering Judas," "A Country Love Story," "Everything That Rises Must Converge," provide illustrations of the varieties of ways in which the limited omniscient point of view can function.

The final point of view to be considered is that of an objective observer. This narrator speaks in the third person, claims no powers of omniscience, and presents an apparently factual account of the happenings in the story. He, like the first-person major-character narrator, carries a great deal of credibility—in this case because he seems to be presenting an unbiased account of "what really happened." Such a narrator is particularly useful if an author wishes to concentrate on plot and action, rather than on the narrator himself and his perceptions or on the perceptions and internal responses of participants in the action. However, it should be pointed out that this narrator, like every narrator, is presenting a *biased* account—because it is *his* version of what happened. An unprejudiced, unlimited report of any happening is humanly impossible, and although the report of a third-person objective-observer narrator may appear to be "the true story," it should be remembered that such a report is, after all, simply *his* view through one window of the house of fiction.

Perhaps the following point-of-view chart will help to summarize. If you consider the horizontal lines as continua, you can see that the first-person major-character narrator presents the most subjective account, the first-person minor-character narrator presents a less subjective account, the third-person omniscient narrator a somewhat subjective account (he speaks in the third-person, but he is dealing with subjective states), and the third-person observer the most objective account. You can also see that the movement along the continuum from first person to third person is also a movement from a narrator who is central to, and most inside, the story to narrators less central to, and less inside, the story, to narrators who are peripheral and outside the story entirely. You also move from stories in which the narrator's *interpretation* of what happened is most important to stories in which what *did* happen is most important. Finally, you can see that, as you move from first-person to third-person narrators, authors tend to dramatize these narrators less and less fully. It should be remembered, however, that, while the third-person objective-observer narrator may seem to be somewhat "characterless" and undramatized, even *he* reveals his character and attitudes (and often something of his social behavior, as does the narrator in "The Third

POINT OF VIEW

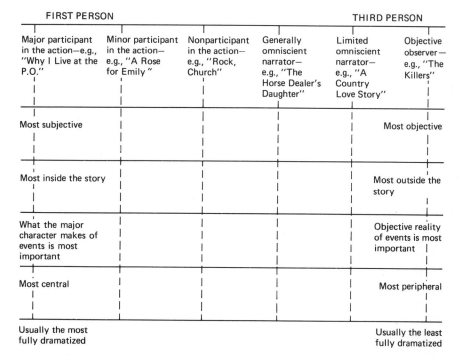

FIRST PERSON					THIRD PERSON
Major participant in the action—e.g., "Why I Live at the P.O."	Minor participant in the action—e.g., "A Rose for Emily"	Nonparticipant in the action—e.g., "Rock, Church"	Generally omniscient narrator—e.g., "The Horse Dealer's Daughter"	Limited omniscient narrator—e.g., "A Country Love Story"	Objective observer—e.g., "The Killers"
Most subjective					Most objective
Most inside the story					Most outside the story
What the major character makes of events is most important					Objective reality of events is most important
Most central					Most peripheral
Usually the most fully dramatized					Usually the least fully dramatized

Prize") through his diction, his tone, his choice of scenes, his description of characters, and so forth.

No matter what kind of narrator an author chooses to use, it is essential to remember that any study of narrative literature must begin with the narrator because he is the person who conditions everything in the story. Nothing in the story has any reality apart from his report of it. Consequently it is to him that you must always first direct your attention. All questions concerning theme, characterization, style, and the like must be considered in terms of the narrator's point of view. And, although there may be a multiplicity of speakers, attitudes, and characters, there is always a central storyteller who is responsible for the characterizations of other speakers within the story and who governs audience response in the story. Furthermore, point of view clarifies and defines the interpreter's relationship to his story and to his audience, for the interpreter, in order to explore and demonstrate a story, must first concentrate on embodying the character of the narrator as the major speaker in the work.

In Chapter Two some attention was given to dramatic analysis as a method for discovering many of the essential qualities of literary speakers. In nonfictional prose and poetry this method of analysis is fairly simple because the lyric mode by its very nature concentrates on the activities of a single speaker. But narrative literature, because of its multiplicity of speakers, is somewhat more complex in terms of its speakers' activities. Consequently, if you use the dramatic method to explore literary speakers and their activities in the epic mode, your analysis will necessarily become more complex.

From earlier remarks in this book about lyric, epic, and dramatic modes of literature you will remember that the epic mode actually combines the lyric and the dramatic. To put it another way, the narrator in a short story represents the lyric or "telling" element in the work, and his story with its characters and action is the dramatic or "showing" element in the work. When analyzing a lyric poem or a play, you pose the dramatic questions of who? what? where? when? why? how? and to whom? in reference to one person or situation. But in order to analyze the structure of narrative fiction adequately, you must really conduct what shall be called a double dramatic analysis. If you refer to the following chart (p. 240), it can be seen that you begin by asking the dramatic questions about the narrator —who is he? what is his "epic situation"?[6] who is his audience? and so on. The "what" in this set of questions is, of course, the story the narrator tells. You must then pose the dramatic questions again, this time with reference to the story itself. This kind of double dramatic analysis is absolutely necessary, not only if you are to understand the individual dramatic situations inherent in the narrator's situation and the situation of the story, but also, and more importantly, if you are to understand the tensive relationship between the narrator and his story. As can be observed from the dramatic analysis chart, because the questions are actually directed toward two different sources—the narrator and his story —the answers to the standard dramatic questions are frequently quite different. For example, the questions of "where" and "when," if directed toward a story like "Why I Live at the P.O.," will yield rather different answers depending upon whether you are asking where and when the narrator is telling her story or where and when her story took place. This narrator's telling of her story takes place in the post office of China Grove, Mississippi, on July 10; but the action of the story itself apparently took place in her home on July 4 and 5. Furthermore, much of the structural tension in this particular story derives from the very juxtaposition of these two sets of time and place as well as the juxtaposition of conflicting attitudes, actions, audiences, and so forth. The point is that the double dramatic analysis does not simply reveal the fact that there may be two sets of speakers, actions, times, places, audiences, styles, and motivations. More importantly, such a method of analysis should provide you

---

[6] *Epic situation:* the temporal and spatial location of the narrator while he is engaged in telling his story.

with basic evidence from the text with which to explore and understand some of the complexities of tensions existing between the narrator and his story, between the lyric and dramatic modes that characterize the structure of narrative fiction.

As stated before, a central problem in the study of narrative fiction is the problem of point of view. In addition to this problem one encounters the problem of "viewpoint" [7] as the other central issue in the study of narrative fiction. This problem is similar to that discussed in Chapter Two. In narrative fiction, just as in nonfictional prose, one is confronted with the problem of "ethos" in terms of the speaker in the work and the speaker of the work. But the problems of ethos appear in a more complex form in narrative literature because of its more complex structure of literary speakers. Usually any time one analyzes the relationship between viewpoint and point of view, that is, the relationship between the "implied author" [8] and his narrator, he is embarking on the rhetorical analysis. This analysis, as implied in the preceding chapters, would see the narrator as a device created by the author to place certain controls on the responses of his (the author's) audience. Furthermore, for some stories, particularly those structured by argument (such as "The Horse Dealer's Daughter" or "Everything That Rises Must Converge"), the rhetorical analysis may be crucial for the interpreter's understanding of the story.

In *all* stories, whether structured by argument or by some other principle, it is necessary to understand the relationship between the narrator and his story on the one hand and the narrator and the implied author on the other. In short, it is necessary in interpreting any story to make some use of the rhetorical analysis. The question of a narrator's "reliability" [9] is particularly crucial, not only in determining the value relationship between the narrator and the implied author, but also in understanding the nature of the tension created by the juxtaposition of the speaker in the work and the speaker of the work.

The problems of structural tension—of showing and telling and of point of view and viewpoint—find particular relevance in the interpreter's approach to the study of prose fiction. The interpreter, because of his special approach to the study of literature, recognizes the tension involved in the simultaneity of showing and telling as well as the spatial and temporal tensions inherent in the epic mode. In addition to these basic

---

[7] *Viewpoint:* the psychological and aesthetic position, the sets of norms and values from which the implied author constructs his story.

[8] *Implied author:* the image of the author of a work that is inferred from the work's structure, from the norms and values supported in the work, and from other works by the same writer. See Wayne C. Booth's *The Rhetoric of Fiction* (Chicago: University of Chicago Press, 1962) for a full discussion of this concept.

[9] *Reliability:* the degree to which a narrator reflects or embodies the norms and values of the implied author. See Booth (*ibid.*) for an elaboration of this idea.

DOUBLE DRAMATIC ANALYSIS

EPIC

(THE NARRATOR AND HIS STORY)

DRAMATIC
(THE STORY)

1. Who performs the major action in the story?
   a. Does the protagonist perform the action alone?
   b. What is revealed about him?

2. Where does the action take place?
   a. Is the locale permanent, or does the setting shift?

3. When does the action take place?
   a. Does the movement of the action through time run parallel or contrary to "actual time"?

4. Why does the action take place?
   a. What motivations are assigned to the participants?
   b. What motivations are implicit in the actions of the participants?

5. With whom or toward whom is the action directed?

6. How does the action develop?

7. What is the major action in the story?

LYRIC
(THE NARRATOR)

1. Who is the narrator?
   a. What does he reveal about himself?
   b. What is learned indirectly?

2. Where is the narrator as he tells his story?

3. When is the narrator telling this story?

4. Why is the narrator telling the story?
   a. Does he specifically voice his motivations?
   b. Are his intentions implicit in his manner of storytelling?

5. To whom is the narrator telling this story?

6. How does the narrator tell his story?
   a. What narrative techniques does he employ?
   b. How would you characterize his diction and style or manner of storytelling?
   c. How does he combine showing and telling?

7. What is the story the narrator is telling?

structural tensions the interpreter must also be aware of the tensions involved in the many speaker-audience-situation levels of a given story. Probably the major source of structural tension in narrative fiction is to be found in the juxtaposition of the tensive relationship between the narrator and his story and the equally tensive relationship between the narrator and the implied author. The interpreter's task is to translate these textual problems into the reality of his own relationship with his audience. In interpreting a scene from "Why I Live at the P.O.," for example, in addition to many of the tensive relationships mentioned earlier, the interpreter would have to be aware of at least the following speaker-audience-situation relationships: (1) Mama, as a character within Sister's story, exists within the fiction, and Sister (or Stella-Rondo or some family member) is her audience; (2) Sister is the narrator whose audience is some hapless soul who wandered into the China Grove post office; (3) Eudora Welty, as implied author, exists outside the story and has a rather generalized audience for whom she is demonstrating the character problems of a woman with an acute persecution complex; and (4) the interpreter has his own situation and his own audience—either himself alone or a group of persons—which is none of the above-mentioned audiences and all of the above simultaneously. In such a scene, here or in any other story, the interpreter's job becomes one of assuming his roles as narrator and the narrator's characters as well as his role as implied author, relating his roles as speaker in the work, speakers within the work, and speaker of the work to audiences in, within, and of the work, and translating these levels of roles and relationships into his situation as an interpreter with his own real, live audience.

The responsibilities of the interpreter in his special approach to narrative fiction are manifold and the problems of characterizing literary speakers complex. Yet, it is hoped, his awareness of the operations of structural tensions in a story will lead him to explore more adequately the levels of speakers, audiences, and situations in his interpretation of prose fiction.

In summary, then, the interpreter of prose fiction uses a dramatic analysis to understand (1) the relationship of the narrator to the story (point of view) and to his audience and (2) the nature of the action in the story. This is known as the double dramatic analysis because the first part explores the lyrical, the second part the dramatic elements in this epic mode. Or he uses the rhetorical analysis to understand (3) the relationship between the narrator and the implied author, that is, between point of view and viewpoint, for without understanding this the narrator's reliability cannot be known.

This discussion is obviously not exhaustive. Indeed, many elements of narrative structure (such as problems of characterization, the management of tone, the handling of time, and treatment of theme, to name only a few) have not been discussed at all in detail. These introductory remarks are intended, however, to provide you with a starting point, a basis for your exploration of the particular stories that follow. And, as in Chapters Two and Three, a set of study questions is suggested for each story. It is hoped that these questions will lead you to an exploration of the *particular* qualities characteristic of the individual stories. These questions, too, are not exhaustive. You will no doubt discover many other questions of equal importance to your understanding of a given story. But, as emphasized throughout this book, the best exploration will come through your own embodiment of each of these short stories.

Finally, it should be noted that there are some suggested exercises at the end of the chapter for those of you who wish to explore in more detail some of the problems raised in the study of narrative fiction.

Sherwood Anderson/I Want to Know Why

born 1876

We got up at four in the morning, that first day in the east. On the evening before we had climbed off a freight train at the edge of town, and with the true instinct of Kentucky boys had found our way across town and to the racetrack and the stables at once. Then we knew we were all right. Hanley Turner right away found a nigger we knew. It was Bildad Johnson who in the winter works at Ed Becker's livery barn in our home town, Beckersville. Bildad is a good cook as almost all our niggers are and of course he, like everyone in our part of Kentucky who is anyone at all, likes the horses. In the spring Bildad begins to scratch around. A nigger from our country can flatter and wheedle anyone into letting him do most anything he wants. Bildad wheedles the stable men and the trainers from the horse farms in our country around Lexington. The trainers come into town in the evening to stand around and talk and maybe get into a poker game. Bildad gets in with them. He is always doing little favors and telling about things to eat, chicken browned in a pan, and how is the best way to cook sweet potatoes and corn bread. It makes your mouth water to hear him.

When the racing season comes on and the horses go to the races and there is all the talk on the streets in the evenings about the new colts, and everyone says when they are going over to Lexington or to the spring meeting at Churchill Downs or to Latonia, and the horsemen that have been down to New Orleans or maybe at the winter meeting at Havana in Cuba come home to spend a week before they start out again, at such a time when everything talked about in Beckersville is just horses and nothing else and the outfits start out and horse racing is in every breath of air you breathe, Bildad shows up with a job as cook for some outfit.

Often when I think about it, his always going all season to the races and working in the livery barn in the winter where horses are and where men like to come and talk about horses, I wish I was a nigger. It's a foolish thing to say, but that's the way I am about being around horses, just crazy. I can't help it.

Well, I must tell you about what we did and let you in on what I'm talking about. Four of us boys from Beckersville, all whites and sons of men who live in Beckersville regular, made up our minds we were going to the races, not just to Lexington or Louisville, I don't mean, but to the big eastern track we were always hearing our Beckersville men talk about, to Saratoga. We were all pretty young then. I was just turned fifteen and I was the oldest of the four. It was my scheme. I admit that and I talked the others into trying it. There was Hanley Turner and Henry Rieback and Tom Tumberton and myself. I had thirty-seven dollars I had earned during the winter working nights and Saturdays in Enoch Myer's grocery. Henry Rieback had eleven dollars and the others, Hanley and Tom, had only a dollar or two each. We fixed it all up and laid low until the Kentucky spring meetings were over and some of our men, the sportiest ones, the ones we envied the most, had cut out—then we cut out too.

I won't tell you the trouble we had beating our way on freights and all. We went through Cleveland and Buffalo and other cities and saw Niagara Falls. We bought things there, souvenirs and spoons and cards and shells with pictures of the Falls on them for our sisters and mothers, but thought we had better not send any of the things home. We didn't want to put the folks on our trail and maybe be nabbed.

We got into Saratoga as I said at night and went to the track. Bildad fed us up. He showed us a place to sleep in hay over a shed and promised to keep still. Niggers are all right about things like that. They won't squeal on you. Often a white man you might meet, when you had run away from home like that, might appear to be all right and give you a quarter or a half dollar or something, and then go right and give you away. White men will do that, but not a nigger. You can trust them. They are squarer with kids. I don't know why.

At the Saratoga meeting that year there were a lot of men from home. Dave Williams and Arthur Mulford and Jerry Myers and others. Then there was a lot from Louisville and Lexington Henry Rieback knew but I didn't. They were professional gamblers and Henry Rieback's father is one too. He is what is called a sheet writer and goes away most of the year to tracks. In the winter when he is home in Beckersville he don't stay there much but goes away to cities and deals faro. He is a nice man and generous, is always sending Henry presents, a bicycle and a gold watch and a boy scout suit of clothes and things like that.

My own father is a lawyer. He's all right, but don't make much money and can't buy me things and anyway I'm getting so old now I don't expect it. He never said nothing to me against Henry, but Hanley Turner and Tom Tumberton's fathers did. They said to their boys that money so come by is no good and they didn't want their boys brought up to hear gamblers' talk and be thinking about such things and maybe embrace them.

That's all right and I guess the men know what they are talking about, but I don't see what it's got to do with Henry or horses either. That's what I'm writing this story about. I'm puzzled. I'm getting to be a man and want to think straight and be O.K., and there's something I saw at the race meeting at the eastern track I can't figure out.

I can't help it, I'm crazy about thoroughbred horses. I've always been that way. When I was ten years old and saw I was growing to be big and couldn't be a rider I was so sorry I nearly died. Harry Hellinfinger in Beckersville, whose father is Postmaster, is grown up and too lazy to work, but likes to stand around in the street and get up jokes on boys like sending them to a hardware store for a gimlet to bore square holes and other jokes like that. He played one on me. He told me that if I would eat half a cigar I would be stunted and not grow any more and maybe could be a rider. I did it. When father wasn't looking I took a cigar out of his pocket and gagged it down some way. It made me awful sick and the doctor had to be sent for, and then it did no good. I kept right on growing. It was a joke. When I told what I had done and why most fathers would have whipped me but mine didn't.

Well, I didn't get stunted and didn't die. It serves Harry Hellinfinger right. Then I made up my mind I would like to be a stable boy, but had to give that up too. Mostly niggers do that work and I knew father wouldn't let me go into it. No use to ask him.

If you've never been crazy about thoroughbreds it's because you've never been around where they are much and don't know any better. They're beautiful. There isn't anything so lovely and clean and full of spunk and honest and everything as some race horses. On the big horse farms that are all around our town Beckersville there are tracks and the horses run in the early morning. More than a thousand times I've got out of bed before daylight and walked two or three miles to the tracks. Mother wouldn't of let me go but father always says, "Let him alone." So I got some bread out of the bread box and some butter and jam, gobbled it and lit out.

At the tracks you sit on the fence with men, whites and niggers, and they chew tobacco and talk, and then the colts are brought out. It's early and the grass is covered with shiny dew and in another field a man is plowing and they are frying things in a shed where the track niggers sleep, and you know how a nigger can giggle and laugh and say things that make you laugh. A white man can't do it and some niggers can't but a track nigger can every time.

And so the colts are brought out and some are just galloped by stable boys, but almost every morning on a big track owned by a rich man who lives maybe in New York, there are always, nearly every morning, a few colts and some of the old race horses and geldings and mares that are cut loose.

It brings a lump up into my throat when a horse runs. I don't mean all horses but some. I can pick them nearly every time. It's in my blood like in the blood of race-track niggers and trainers. Even when they just go slop-jogging along with a little nigger on their backs I can tell a winner. If my throat hurts and it's hard for me to swallow, that's him. He'll run like Sam Hill when you let him out. If he don't win every time it'll be a wonder and because they've got him in a pocket behind another or he was pulled or got off bad at the post or something. If I wanted to be a gambler like Henry Rieback's father I could get rich. I know I could and Henry says so too. All I would have to do is to wait 'til that hurt comes when I see a horse and then bet every cent. That's what I would do if I wanted to be a gambler, but I don't.

When you're at the tracks in the morning—not the race tracks but the training tracks around Beckersville—you don't see a horse, the kind I've been talking about, very often, but it's nice anyway. Any thoroughbred, that is sired right and out of a good mare and trained by a man that knows how, can run. If he couldn't what would he be there for and not pulling a plow?

Well, out of the stables they come and the boys are on their backs and it's lovely to be there. You hunch down on top of the fence and itch inside you. Over in the sheds the niggers giggle and sing. Bacon is being fried and coffee made. Everything smells lovely. Nothing smells better than coffee and manure and horses and niggers and bacon frying and pipes being smoked out of doors on a morning like that. It just gets you, that's what it does.

But about Saratoga. We was there six days and not a soul from home seen us and everything came off just as we wanted it to, fine weather and horses and races and all. We beat our way home and Bildad gave us a basket with fried chicken and bread and other eatables in, and I had eighteen dollars when we got back to Beckersville. Mother jawed and cried but Pop didn't say much. I told everything we done except one thing. I did and saw that alone. That's what I'm writing about. It got me upset. I think about it at night. Here it is.

At Saratoga we laid up nights in the hay in the shed Bildad had showed us and ate with the niggers early and at night when the race people had all gone away. The men from home stayed mostly in the grandstand and betting field, and didn't come out around the places where the horses are kept except to the paddocks just before a race when the horses are saddled. At Saratoga they don't have paddocks under an open shed as at

Lexington and Churchill Downs and other tracks down in our country, but saddle the horses right out in an open place under trees on a lawn as smooth and nice as Banker Bohon's front yard here in Beckersville. It's lovely. The horses are sweaty and nervous and shine and the men come out and smoke cigars and look at them and the trainers are there and the owners, and your heart thumps so you can hardly breathe.

Then the bugle blows for post and the boys that ride come running out with their silk clothes on and you run to get a place by the fence with the niggers.

I always am wanting to be a trainer or owner, and at the risk of being seen and caught and sent home I went to the paddocks before every race. The other boys didn't but I did.

We got to Saratoga on a Friday and on Wednesday the next week the big Mullford Handicap was to be run. Middlestride was in it and Sunstreak. The weather was fine and the track fast. I couldn't sleep the night before.

What had happened was that both these horses are the kind it makes my throat hurt to see. Middlestride is long and looks awkward and is a gelding. He belongs to Joe Thompson, a little owner from home who only has a half-dozen horses. The Mullford Handicap is for a mile and Middlestride can't untrack fast. He goes away slow and is always way back at the half, then he begins to run and if the race is a mile and a quarter he'll just eat up everything and get there.

Sunstreak is different. He is a stallion and nervous and belongs on the biggest farm we've got in our country, the Van Riddle place that belongs to Mr. Van Riddle of New York. Sunstreak is like a girl you think about sometimes but never see. He is hard all over and lovely too. When you look at his head you want to kiss him. He is trained by Jerry Tillford who knows me and has been good to me lots of times, lets me walk into a horse's stall to look at him close and other things. There isn't anything as sweet as that horse. He stands at the post quiet and not letting on, but he is just burning up inside. Then when the barrier goes up he is off like his name, Sunstreak. It makes you ache to see him. It hurts you. He just lays down and runs like a bird dog. There can't anything I ever see run like him except Middlestride when he gets untracked and stretches himself.

Gee! I ached to see that race and those two horses run, ached and dreaded it too. I didn't want to see either of our horses beaten. We had never sent a pair like that to the races before. Old men in Beckersville said so and the niggers said so. It was a fact.

Before the race I went over to the paddocks to see. I looked a last look at Middlestride, who isn't such a much standing in a paddock that way, then I went to see Sunstreak.

It was his day. I knew when I seen him. I forgot all about being seen myself and walked right up. All the men from Beckersville were there and no one noticed me except Jerry Tillford. He saw me and something happened. I'll tell you about that.

I was standing looking at that horse and aching. In some way, I can't tell how, I knew just how Sunstreak felt inside. He was quiet and letting the niggers rub his legs and Mr. Van Riddle himself put the saddle on, but he was just a raging torrent inside. He was like the water in the river at Niagara Falls just before it goes plunk down. That horse wasn't thinking about running. He don't have to think about that. He was just thinking about holding himself back 'til the time for the running came. I knew that. I could just in a way see right inside him. He was going to do some awful running and I knew it. He wasn't bragging or letting on much or prancing or making a fuss, but just waiting. I knew it and Jerry Tillford his trainer knew. I looked up and then that man and I looked into each other's eyes. Something happened to me. I guess I loved the man as much as I did the horse because he knew what I knew. Seemed to me there wasn't anything in the world but that man and the horse and me. I cried and Jerry Tillford had a shine in his eyes. Then I came away to the fence to wait for the race. The horse was better than me, more steadier, and now I know better than Jerry. He was the quietest and he had to do the running.

Sunstreak ran first of course and he busted the world's record for a mile. I've seen that if I never see anything more. Everything came out just as I expected. Middlestride got left at the post and was way back and closed up to be second, just as I knew he would. He'll get a world's record too some day. They can't skin the Beckersville country on horses.

I watched the race calm because I knew what would happen. I was sure. Hanley Turner and Henry Rieback and Tom Tumberton were all more excited than me.

A funny thing happened to me. I was thinking about Jerry Tillford the trainer and how happy he was all through the race. I liked him that afternoon even more than I ever liked my own father. I almost forgot the horses thinking that way about him. It was because of what I had seen in his eyes as he stood in the paddocks beside Sunstreak before the race started. I knew he had been watching and working with Sunstreak since the horse was a baby colt, had taught him to run and be patient and when to let himself out and not to quit, never. I knew that for him it was like a mother seeing her child do something brave or wonderful. It was the first time I ever felt for a man like that.

After the race that night I cut out from Tom and Hanley and Henry. I wanted to be by myself and I wanted to be near Jerry Tillford if I could work it. Here is what happened.

The track in Saratoga is near the edge of town. It is all polished up and trees around, the evergreen kind, and grass and everything painted and nice. If you go past the track you get to a hard road made of asphalt for automobiles, and if you go along this for a few miles there is a road turns off to a little rummy-looking farmhouse set in a yard.

That night after the race I went along that road because I had seen Jerry and some other men go that way in an automobile. I didn't expect to find them. I walked for a ways and then sat down by a fence to think. It was the direction they went in. I wanted to be as near Jerry as I could. I felt close to him. Pretty soon I went up the side road—I don't know why —and came to the rummy farmhouse. I was just lonesome to see Jerry, like wanting to see your father at night when you are a young kid. Just then an automobile came along and turned in. Jerry was in it and Henry Rieback's father, and Arthur Bedford from home, and Dave Williams and two other men I didn't know. They got out of the car and went into the house, all but Henry Rieback's father who quarreled with them and said he wouldn't go. It was only about nine o'clock, but they were all drunk and the rummy-looking farmhouse was a place for bad women to stay in. That's what it was. I crept up along a fence and looked through a window and saw.

It's what give me the fantods. I can't make it out. The women in the house were all ugly mean-looking women, not nice to look at or be near. They were homely too, except one who was tall and looked a little like the gelding Middlestride, but not clean like him, but with a hard ugly mouth. She had red hair. I saw everything plain. I got up by an old rosebush by an open window and looked. The women had on loose dresses and sat around in chairs. The men came in and some sat on the women's laps. The place smelled rotten and there was rotten talk, the kind a kid hears around a livery stable in a town like Beckersville in the winter but don't ever expect to hear talked when there are women around. It was rotten. A nigger wouldn't go into such a place.

I looked at Jerry Tillford. I've told you how I had been feeling about him on account of his knowing what was going on inside of Sunstreak in the minute before he went to the post for the race in which he made a world's record.

Jerry bragged in that bad-woman house as I know Sunstreak wouldn't never have bragged. He said that he made that horse, that it was him that won the race and made the record. He lied and bragged like a fool. I never heard such silly talk.

And then, what do you suppose he did! He looked at the woman in there, the one that was lean and hard-mouthed and looked a little like the gelding Middlestride, but not clean like him, and his eyes began to shine just as they did when he looked at me and at Sunstreak in the pad-docks at the track in the afternoon. I stood there by the window—gee!— but I wished I hadn't gone away from the tracks, but had stayed with the boys and the niggers and the horses. The tall rotten-looking woman was between us just as Sunstreak was in the paddocks in the afternoon.

Then, all of a sudden, I began to hate that man. I wanted to scream and rush in the room and kill him. I never had such a feeling before. I was so mad clean through that I cried and my fists were doubled up so my fingernails cut my hands.

And Jerry's eyes kept shining and he waved back and forth, and then he went and kissed that woman and I crept away and went back to the tracks and to bed and didn't sleep hardly any, and then next day I got the other kids to start home with me and never told them anything I seen.

I been thinking about it ever since. I can't make it out. Spring has come again and I'm nearly sixteen and go to the tracks mornings same as always, and I see Sunstreak and Middlestride and a new colt named Strident I'll bet will lay them all out, but no one thinks so but me and two or three niggers.

But things are different. At the tracks the air don't taste as good or smell as good. It's because a man like Jerry Tillford, who knows what he does, could see a horse like Sunstreak run, and kiss a woman like that the same day. I can't make it out. Darn him, what did he want to do like that for? I keep thinking about it and it spoils looking at horses and smelling things and hearing niggers laugh and everything. Sometimes I'm so mad about it I want to fight someone. It gives me the fantods. What did he do it for? I want to know why.

STUDY QUESTIONS

1. How old is this narrator as he tells his story? How old was he when the action in the story took place? How mature is this narrator as he tells his story? Has he matured or changed in any way since his experience at Saratoga? Why does it seem important that this story be told by the young boy himself rather than by some other narrator?

2. Who is the narrator's audience? Is the narrator writing or speaking his story? As you look for answers to these questions, also notice other indications in the text as to the narrator's manner. Do his remarks *about* his style of storytelling ever seem undermined by the style itself?

3. How does this boy's attitude toward horses affect the way he sees and talks about human beings? What seems to happen inside the boy whenever he talks about horses? How could this aspect of the narrator impinge on your demonstration of him and his story?

4. As you begin performing this story, try experimenting with various autistic gestures that might characterize the narrator. Keep in mind, for instance, that he is a small-town boy and that this is apparently his first attempt at telling this story. For example, is he stationary or mobile? What kinds of physical activity might he be engaged in as he relates his story? How self-conscious is he as a storyteller? How could this self-consciousness be demonstrated? How

physically involved does he become in his story? Might he, for example, ever become so engaged in his storytelling that he might appear to be riding a horse? Might he ever even seem to move like a horse himself? How is he dressed, and how does his manner of dress affect what he does physically?

5. What is the implied author's position in this story? How is it related to the narrator's position? How would it be possible for you to clarify the implied author's understanding of the boy's situation without destroying the illusion of the narrator's *lack* of understanding?

Eudora Welty/Why I Live at the P.O.

born 1909

I was getting along fine with Mama, Papa-Daddy and Uncle Rondo until my sister Stella-Rondo just separated from her husband and came back home again. Mr. Whitaker! Of course I went with Mr. Whitaker first, when he first appeared here in China Grove, taking "Pose Yourself" photos, and Stella-Rondo broke us up. Told him I was one-sided. Bigger on one side than the other, which is a deliberate, calculated falsehood: I'm the same. Stella-Rondo is exactly twelve months to the day younger than I am and for that reason she's spoiled.

She's always had anything in the world she wanted and then she'd throw it away. Papa-Daddy gave her this gorgeous Add-a-Pearl necklace when she was eight years old and she threw it away playing baseball when she was nine, with only two pearls.

So as soon as she got married and moved away from home the first thing she did was separate! From Mr. Whitaker! This photographer with the popeyes she said she trusted. Came home from one of those towns up in Illinois and to our complete surprise brought this child of two.

Mama said she like to made her drop dead for a second. "Here you had this marvelous blonde child and never so much as wrote your mother a word about it," says Mama. "I'm thoroughly ashamed of you." But of course she wasn't.

Stella-Rondo just calmly takes off this *hat*, I wish you could see it. She says, "Why, Mama, Shirley-T.'s adopted, I can prove it."

"How?" says Mama, but all I says was, "H'm!" There I was over the hot stove, trying to stretch two chickens over five people and a completely unexpected child into the bargain, without one moment's notice.

"What do you mean—'H'm!'?" says Stella-Rondo, and Mama says, "I heard that, Sister."

I said that oh, I didn't mean a thing, only that whoever Shirley-T. was, she was the spit-image of Papa-Daddy if he'd cut off his beard, which of course he'd never do in the world. Papa-Daddy's Mama's papa and sulks.

Stella-Rondo got furious! She said, "Sister, I don't need to tell you you got a lot of nerve and always did have and I'll thank you to make no future reference to my adopted child whatsoever."

"Very well," I said. "Very well, very well. Of course I noticed at once she looks like Mr. Whitaker's side too. That frown. She looks like a cross between Mr. Whitaker and Papa-Daddy."

"Well, all I can say is she isn't."

"She looks exactly like Shirley Temple to me," says Mama, but Shirley-T. just ran away from her.

So the first thing Stella-Rondo did at the table was turn Papa-Daddy against me.

"Papa-Daddy!" she says. He was trying to cut up his meat. "Papa-Daddy!" I was taken completely by surprise. Papa-Daddy is about a million years old and's got this long-long beard. "Papa-Daddy, Sister says she fails to understand why you don't cut off your beard."

So Papa-Daddy l-a-y-s down his knife and fork! He's real rich. Mama says he is, he says he isn't. So he says, "Have I heard correctly? You don't understand why I don't cut off my beard?"

"Why," I says, "Papa-Daddy, of course I understand, I did not say any such of a thing, the idea!"

He says, "Hussy!"

I says, "Papa-Daddy, you know I wouldn't any more want you to cut off your beard than the man in the moon. It was the farthest thing from my mind! Stella-Rondo sat there and made that up while she was eating breast of chicken."

But he says, "So the postmistress fails to understand why I don't cut off my beard. Which job I got you through my influence with the government. 'Bird's nest'—is that what you call it?"

Not that it isn't the next to smallest P.O. in the entire state of Mississippi.

I says, "Oh, Papa-Daddy," I says, "I didn't say any such of a thing, I never dreamed it was a bird's nest, I have always been grateful though this is the next to smallest P.O. in the state of Mississippi, and I do not enjoy being referred to as a hussy by my own grandfather."

But Stella-Rondo says, "Yes, you did say it too. Anybody in the world could of heard you, that had ears."

"Stop right there," says Mama, looking at *me*.

So I pulled my napkin straight back through the napkin ring and left the table.

As soon as I was out of the room Mama says, "Call her back, or she'll starve to death," but Papa-Daddy says, "This is the beard I started growing on the Coast when I was fifteen years old." He would of gone on till nightfall if Shirley-T. hadn't lost the Milky Way she ate in Cairo.

So Papa-Daddy says, "I am going out and lie in the hammock, and you can all sit here and remember my words: I'll never cut off my beard as

long as I live, even one inch, and I don't appreciate it in you at all."
Passed right by me in the hall and went straight out and got in the hammock.

It would be a holiday. It wasn't five minutes before Uncle Rondo suddenly appeared in the hall in one of Stella-Rondo's flesh-colored kimonos, all cut on the bias, like something Mr. Whitaker probably thought was gorgeous.

"Uncle Rondo!" I says. "I didn't know who that was! Where are you going?"

"Sister," he says, "get out of my way, I'm poisoned."

"If you're poisoned stay away from Papa-Daddy," I says. "Keep out of the hammock. Papa-Daddy will certainly beat you on the head if you come within forty miles of him. He thinks I deliberately said he ought to cut off his beard after he got me the P.O., and I've told him and told him and told him, and he acts like he just don't hear me. Papa-Daddy must of gone stone deaf."

"He picked a fine day to do it then," says Uncle Rondo, and before you could say "Jack Robinson" flew out in the yard.

What he'd really done, he'd drunk another bottle of that prescription. He does it every single Fourth of July as sure as shooting, and it's horribly expensive. Then he falls over in the hammock and snores. So he insisted on zigzagging right on out to the hammock, looking like a half-wit.

Papa-Daddy woke up with this horrible yell and right there without moving an inch he tried to turn Uncle Rondo against me. I heard every word he said. Oh, he told Uncle Rondo I didn't learn to read till I was eight years old and he didn't see how in the world I ever got the mail put up at the P.O., much less read it all, and he said if Uncle Rondo could only fathom the lengths he had gone to to get me that job! And he said on the other hand he thought Stella-Rondo had a brilliant mind and deserved credit for getting out of town. All the time he was just lying there swinging as pretty as you please and looping out his beard, and poor Uncle Rondo was *pleading* with him to slow down the hammock, it was making him as dizzy as a witch to watch it. But that's what Papa-Daddy likes about a hammock. So Uncle Rondo was too dizzy to get turned against me for the time being. He's Mama's only brother and is a good case of a one-track mind. Ask anybody. A certified pharmacist.

Just then I heard Stella-Rondo raising the upstairs window. While she was married she got this peculiar idea that it's cooler with the windows shut and locked. So she has to raise the window before she can make a soul hear her outdoors.

So she raises the window and says, *"Oh!"* You would have thought she was mortally wounded.

Uncle Rondo and Papa-Daddy didn't even look up, but kept right on with what they were doing. I had to laugh.

I flew up the stairs and threw the door open! I says, "What in the wide world's the matter, Stella-Rondo? You mortally wounded?"

"No," she says, "I am not mortally wounded but I wish you would do me the favor of looking out that window there and telling me what you see."

So I shade my eyes and look out the window.

"I see the front yard," I says.

"Don't you see any human beings?" she says.

"I see Uncle Rondo trying to run Papa-Daddy out of the hammock," I says. "Nothing more. Naturally, it's so suffocating-hot in the house, with all the windows shut and locked, everybody who cares to stay in their right mind will have to go out and get in the hammock before the Fourth of July is over."

"Don't you notice anything different about Uncle Rondo?" asks Stella-Rondo.

"Why, no, except he's got on some terrible-looking flesh-colored contraption I wouldn't be found dead in, is all I can see," I says.

"Never mind, you won't be found dead in it, because it happens to be part of my trousseau, and Mr. Whitaker took several dozen photographs of me in it," says Stella-Rondo. "What on earth could Uncle Rondo *mean* by wearing part of my trousseau out in the broad open daylight without saying so much as 'Kiss my foot,' *knowing* I only got home this morning after my separation and hung my negligee up on the bathroom door, just as nervous as I could be?"

"I'm sure I don't know, and what do you expect me to do about it?" I says. "Jump out the window?"

"No, I expect nothing of the kind. I simply declare that Uncle Rondo looks like a fool in it, that's all," she says. "It makes me sick to my stomach."

"Well, he looks as good as he can," I says. "As good as anybody in reason could." I stood up for Uncle Rondo, please remember. And I said to Stella-Rondo, "I think I would do well not to criticize so freely if I were you and came home with a two-year-old child I had never said a word about, and no explanation whatever about my separation."

"I asked you the instant I entered this house not to refer one more time to my adopted child, and you gave me your word of honor you would not," was all Stella-Rondo would say, and started pulling out every one of her eyebrows with some cheap Kress tweezers.

So I merely slammed the door behind me and went down and made some green-tomato pickle. Somebody had to do it. Of course Mama had turned both the niggers loose; she always said no earthly power could hold one anyway on the Fourth of July, so she wouldn't even try. It turned out that Jaypan fell in the lake and came within a very narrow limit of drowning.

So Mama trots in. Lifts up the lid and says, "H'm! Not very good for your Uncle Rondo in his precarious condition, I must say. Or poor little adopted Shirley-T. Shame on you!"

That made me tired. I says, "Well, Stella-Rondo had better thank her lucky stars it was her instead of me came trotting in with that very peculiar-looking child. Now if it had been me that trotted in from Illinois and brought a peculiar-looking child of two, I shudder to think of the reception I'd of got, much less controlled the diet of an entire family."

"But you must remember, Sister, that you were never married to Mr. Whitaker in the first place and didn't go up to Illinois to live," says Mama, shaking a spoon in my face. "If you had I would of been just as over-joyed to see you and your little adopted girl as I was to see Stella-Rondo, when you wound up with your separation and came on back home."

"You would not," I says.

"Don't contradict me, I would," says Mama.

But I said she couldn't convince me though she talked till she was blue in the face. Then I said, "Besides, you know as well as I do that that child is not adopted."

"She most certainly is adopted," says Mama, stiff as a poker.

I says, "Why, Mama, Stella-Rondo had her just as sure as anything in this world, and is just too stuck up to admit it."

"Why, Sister," said Mama. "Here I thought we were going to have a pleasant Fourth of July, and you start right out not believing a word your own baby sister tells you!"

"Just like Cousin Annie Flo. Went to her grave denying the facts of life," I remind Mama.

"I told you if you ever mentioned Annie Flo's name I'd slap your face," says Mama, and slaps my face.

"All right, you wait and see," I says.

"I," says Mama, "*I* prefer to take my children's word for anything when it's humanly possible." You ought to see Mama, she weighs two hundred pounds and has real tiny feet.

Just then something perfectly horrible occurred to me.

"Mama," I says, "can that child talk?" I simply had to whisper! "Mama, I wonder if that child can be—you know—in any way? Do you realize," I says, "that she hasn't spoken one single, solitary word to a human being up to this minute? This is the way she looks," I says, and I looked like this.

Well, Mama and I just stood there and stared at each other. It was horrible!

"I remember well that Joe Whitaker frequently drank like a fish," says Mama. "I believed to my soul he drank *chemicals*." And without another word she marches to the foot of the stairs and calls Stella-Rondo.

"Stella-Rondo? O-o-o-o-o! Stella-Rondo!"

"What?" says Stella-Rondo from upstairs. Not even the grace to get up off the bed.

"Can that child of yours talk?" asks Mama.

Stella-Rondo says, "Can she what?"

"Talk! Talk!" says Mama. "Burdyburdyburdyburdy!"

So Stella-Ronda yells back, "Who says she can't talk?"

"Sister says so," says Mama.

"You didn't have to tell me, I know whose word of honor don't mean a thing in this house," says Stella-Rondo.

And in a minute the loudest Yankee voice I ever heard in my life yells out, "OE'm Pop-OE the Sailor-r-r-r Ma-a-an!" and then somebody jumps up and down in the upstairs hall. In another second the house would of fallen down.

"Not only talks, she can tap-dance!" calls Stella-Rondo. "Which is more than some people I won't name can do."

"Why, the little precious darling thing!" Mama says, so surprised. "Just as smart as she can be!" Starts talking baby talk right there. Then she turns on me. "Sister, you ought to be thoroughly ashamed! Run upstairs this instant and apologize to Stella-Rondo and Shirley-T."

"Apologize for what?" I says. "I merely wondered if the child was normal, that's all. Now that she's proved she is, why, I have nothing further to say."

But Mama just turned on her heel and flew out, furious. She ran right upstairs and hugged the baby. She believed it was adopted. Stella-Rondo hadn't done a thing but turn her against me from upstairs while I stood there helpless over the hot stove. So that made Mama, Papa-Daddy and the baby all on Stella-Rondo's side.

Next, Uncle Rondo.

I must say that Uncle Rondo has been marvelous to me at various times in the past and I was completely unprepared to be made to jump out of my skin, the way it turned out. Once Stella-Rondo did something perfectly horrible to him—broke a chain letter from Flanders Field—and he took the radio back he had given her and gave it to me. Stella-Rondo was furious! For six months we all had to call her Stella instead of Stella-Rondo, or she wouldn't answer. I always thought Uncle Rondo had all the brains of the entire family. Another time he sent me to Mammoth Cave, with all expenses paid.

But this would be the day he was drinking that prescription, the Fourth of July.

So at supper Stella-Rondo speaks up and says she thinks Uncle Rondo ought to try to eat a little something. So finally Uncle Rondo said he would try a little cold biscuits and ketchup, but that was all. So *she* brought it to him.

"Do you think it wise to disport with ketchup in Stella-Rondo's flesh-colored kimono?" I says. Trying to be considerate! If Stella-Rondo couldn't watch out for her trousseau, somebody had to.

"Any objections?" asks Uncle Rondo, just about to pour out all the ketchup.

"Don't mind what she says, Uncle Rondo," says Stella-Rondo. "Sister has been devoting this solid afternoon to sneering out my bedroom window at the way you look."

"What's that?" says Uncle Rondo. Uncle Rondo has got the most terrible temper in the world. Anything is liable to make him tear the house down if it comes at the wrong time.

So Stella-Rondo says, "Sister says, 'Uncle Rondo certainly does look like a fool in that pink kimono!' "

Do you remember who it was really said that?

Uncle Rondo spills out all the ketchup and jumps out of his chair and tears off the kimono and throws it down on the dirty floor and puts his foot on it. It had to be sent all the way to Jackson to the cleaners and re-pleated.

"So that's your opinion of your Uncle Rondo, is it?" he says. "I look like a fool, do I? Well, that's the last straw. A whole day in this house with nothing to do, and then to hear you come out with a remark like that behind my back!"

"I didn't say any such of a thing, Uncle Rondo," I says, "and I'm not saying who did, either. Why, I think you look all right. Just try to take care of yourself and not talk and eat at the same time," I says. "I think you better go lie down."

"Lie down my foot," says Uncle Rondo. I ought to of known by that he was fixing to do something perfectly horrible.

So he didn't do anything that night in the precarious state he was in—just played Casino with Mama and Stella-Rondo and Shirley-T. and gave Shirley-T. a nickel with a head on both sides. It tickled her nearly to death, and she called him "Papa." But at 6:30 a.m. the next morning, he threw a whole five-cent package of some unsold one-inch firecrackers from the store as hard as he could into my bedroom and they every one went off. Not one bad one in the string. Anybody else, there'd be one that wouldn't go off.

Well, I'm just terribly susceptible to noise of any kind, the doctor has always told me I was the most sensitive person he had ever seen in his whole life, and I was simply prostrated. I couldn't eat! People tell me they heard it as far as the cemetery, and old Aunt Jep Patterson, that had been holding her own so good, thought it was Judgment Day and she was going to meet her whole family. It's usually so quiet here.

And I'll tell you it didn't take me any longer than a minute to make up my mind what to do. There I was with the whole entire house on Stella-Rondo's side and turned against me. If I have anything at all I have pride.

So I just decided I'd go straight down to the P.O. There's plenty of room there in the back, I says to myself.

Well! I made no bones about letting the family catch on to what I was up to. I didn't try to conceal it.

The first thing they knew, I marched in where they were all playing Old Maid and pulled the electric oscillating fan out by the plug, and everything got real hot. Next I snatched the pillow I'd done the needlepoint on right off the davenport from behind Papa-Daddy. He went "Ugh!" I beat Stella-Rondo up the stairs and finally found my charm bracelet in her bureau drawer under a picture of Nelson Eddy.

"So that's the way the land lies," says Uncle Rondo. There he was, piecing on the ham. "Well, Sister, I'll be glad to donate my army cot if you got any place to set it up, providing you'll leave right this minute and let me get some peace." Uncle Rondo was in France.

"Thank you kindly for the cot and 'peace' is hardly the word I would select if I had to resort to firecrackers at 6:30 a.m. in a young girl's bedroom," I says back to him. "And as to where I intend to go, you seem to forget my position as postmistress of China Grove, Mississippi," I says. "I've always got the P.O."

Well, that made them all sit up and take notice.

I went out front and started digging up some four-o'clocks to plant around the P.O.

"Ah-ah-ah!" says Mama, raising the window. "Those happen to be my four-o'clocks. Everything planted in that star is mine. I've never known you to make anything grow in your life."

"Very well," I says. "But I take the fern. Even you, Mama, can't stand there and deny that I'm the one watered that fern. And I happen to know where I can send in a box top and get a packet of one thousand mixed seeds, no two the same kind, free."

"Oh, where?" Mama wants to know.

But I says, "Too late. You 'tend to your house, and I'll 'tend to mine. You hear things like that all the time if you know how to listen to the radio. Perfectly marvelous offers. Get anything you want free."

So I hope to tell you I marched in and got that radio, and they could of all bit a nail in two, especially Stella-Rondo, that it used to belong to, and she well knew she couldn't get it back, I'd sue for it like a shot. And I very politely took the sewing-machine motor I helped pay the most on to give Mama for Christmas back in 1929, and a good big calendar, with the first-aid remedies on it. The thermometer and the Hawaiian ukulele certainly were rightfully mine, and I stood on the step-ladder and got all my watermelon-rind preserves and every fruit and vegetable I'd put up, every jar.

Then I began to pull the tacks out of the bluebird wall vases on the archway to the dining room.

"Who told you you could have those, Miss Priss?" says Mama, fanning as hard as she could.

"I bought 'em and I'll keep track of 'em," I says. "I'll tack 'em up one on each side the post-office window, and you can see 'em when you come to ask me for your mail, if you're so dead to see 'em."

"Not I! I'll never darken the door to that post office again if I live to be a hundred," Mama says. "Ungrateful child! After all the money we spent on you at the Normal."

"Me either," says Stella-Rondo. "You can just let my mail lie there and *rot,* for all I care. I'll never come and relieve you of a single, solitary piece."

"I should worry," I says. "And who you think's going to sit down and write you all those big fat letters and postcards, by the way? Mr. Whitaker? Just because he was the only man ever dropped down in China Grove and you got him—unfairly—is he going to sit down and write you a lengthy correspondence after you come home giving no rhyme nor reason whatsoever for your separation and no explanation for the presence of that child? I may not have your brilliant mind, but I fail to see it."

So Mama says, "Sister, I've told you a thousand times that Stella-Rondo simply got homesick, and this child is far too big to be hers," and she says, "Now, why don't you all just sit down and play Casino?"

Then Shirley-T. sticks out her tongue at me in this perfectly horrible way. She has no more manners than the man in the moon. I told her she was going to cross her eyes like that some day and they'd stick.

"It's too late to stop me now," I says. "You should have tried that yesterday. I'm going to the P.O. and the only way you can possibly see me is to visit me there."

So Papa-Daddy says, "You'll never catch me setting foot in that post office, even if I should take a notion into my head to write a letter some place." He says, "I won't have you reachin' out of that little old window with a pair of shears and cuttin' off any beard of mine. I'm too smart for you!"

"We all are," says Stella-Rondo.

But I said, "If you're so smart, where's Mr. Whitaker?"

So then Uncle Rondo says, "I'll thank you from now on to stop reading all the orders I get on postcards and telling everybody in China Grove what you think is the matter with them," but I says, "I draw my own conclusions and will continue in the future to draw them." I says, "If people want to write their inmost secrets on penny postcards, there's nothing in the wide world you can do about it, Uncle Rondo."

"And if you think we'll ever *write* another postcard you're sadly mistaken," says Mama.

"Cutting off your nose to spite your face then," I says. "But if you're all determined to have no more to do with the U.S. mail, think of this: What will Stella-Rondo do now, if she wants to tell Mr. Whitaker to come after her?"

"Wah!" says Stella-Rondo. I knew she'd cry. She had a conniption fit right there in the kitchen.

"It will be interesting to see how long she holds out," I says. "And now —I am leaving."

"Good-bye," says Uncle Rondo.

"Oh, I declare," says Mama, "to think that a family of mine should quarrel on the Fourth of July, or the day after, over Stella-Rondo leaving old Mr. Whitaker and having the sweetest little adopted child! It looks like we'd all be glad!"

"Wah!" says Stella-Rondo, and has a fresh conniption fit.

"He left *her*—you mark my words," I says. "That's Mr. Whitaker. I know Mr. Whitaker. After all, I knew him first. I said from the beginning he'd up and leave her. I foretold every single thing that's happened."

"Where did he go?" asks Mama.

"Probably to the North Pole, if he knows what's good for him," I says.

But Stella-Rondo just bawled and wouldn't say another word. She flew to her room and slammed the door.

"Now look what you've gone and done, Sister," says Mama. "You go apologize."

"I haven't got time, I'm leaving," I says.

"Well, what are you waiting around for?" asks Uncle Rondo.

So I just picked up the kitchen clock and marched off, without saying "Kiss my foot" or anything, and never did tell Stella-Rondo good-bye.

There was a nigger girl going along on a little wagon right in front.

"Nigger girl," I says, "come help me haul these things down the hill, I'm going to live in the post office."

Took her nine trips in her express wagon. Uncle Rondo came out on the porch and threw her a nickel.

And that's the last I've laid eyes on any of my family or my family laid eyes on me for five solid days and nights. Stella-Rondo may be telling the most horrible tales in the world about Mr. Whitaker, but I haven't heard them. As I tell everybody, I draw my own conclusions.

But oh, I like it here. It's ideal, as I've been saying. You see, I've got everything cater-cornered, the way I like it. Hear the radio? All the war news. Radio, sewing machine, book ends, ironing board and that great big piano lamp—peace, that's what I like. Butter-bean vines planted all along the front where the strings are.

Of course, there's not much mail. My family are naturally the main people in China Grove, and if they prefer to vanish from the face of the earth, for all the mail they get or the mail they write, why, I'm not going to open my mouth. Some of the folks here in town are taking up for me and some turned against me. I know which is which. There are always people who will quit buying stamps just to get on the right side of Papa-Daddy.

But here I am, and here I'll stay. I want the world to know I'm happy.

And if Stella-Rondo should come to me this minute, on bended knees, and *attempt* to explain the incidents of her life with Mr. Whitaker, I'd simply put my fingers in both my ears and refuse to listen.

STUDY QUESTIONS

1. How much do you know about the narrator of this story? Be specific. Although the narrator tells the reader a great deal about herself, how credible is she? What do you know about the narrator that she does not know about herself? How do you come by such information if Sister does not tell you directly? How does the narrator feel about each member of her family? Does she ever have conflicting feelings about any of the family members? How do her attitudes affect the way in which she dramatizes and allows her audience to see the characters in her story? What are the implications of all of these questions for the interpreter?

2. How important is the use of a Southern Mississippi dialect in demonstrating this story? How would the use of a standard general American dialect, or some other regional dialect, tend to distort the character of the narrator?

3. While it is clear that Sister is *telling* this entire story, it is also obvious that she is the kind of storyteller who likes to dramatize and *show* her story as much as possible. Try performing the story as if you were telling it entirely; then try showing the entire story. How does each method supply you with rather different insights into Sister's character? Consider the possibility that you could demonstrate the story even more clearly by using two persons to portray Sister—Sister as you see her and Sister as she sees herself. What kinds of insights could such a demonstration provide? Can you think of any other ways of demonstrating this story in order to shed additional light on other aspects of this narrator and her situation?

4. Notice the narrator's unconventional use of verb tenses. How does this provide a clue to her condition?

5. What sorts of nonverbal behavior could be used to demonstrate gestural parallels to Sister's inner state and her verbal behavior?

6. Why is Sister's line, "Oh, but I like it here. It's ideal, as I've been saying," ironic? Where is "here"? Find all of the instances in her story *up to this point* where she has pointed out the "ideal" in her present situation.

William Carlos Williams/The Use of Force

born 1883

They were new patients to me, all I had was the name, Olson. Please come down as soon as you can, my daughter is very sick.

When I arrived I was met by the mother, a big startled looking woman, very clean and apologetic who merely said, Is this the doctor? and let me in. In the back, she added, You must excuse us, doctor, we have her in the kitchen where it is warm. It is very damp here sometimes. The child was fully dressed and sitting on her father's lap near the kitchen table. He tried to get up, but I motioned for him not to bother, took off my overcoat and started to look things over. I could see that they were all very nervous, eyeing me up and down distrustfully. As often, in such cases, they weren't telling me more than they had to, it was up to me to tell them; that's why they were spending three dollars on me.

The child was fairly eating me up with her cold, steady eyes, and no expression to her face whatever. She did not move and seemed, inwardly, quiet; an unusually attractive little thing, and as strong as a heifer in appearance. But her face was flushed, she was breathing rapidly, and I realized that she had a high fever. She had magnificent blonde hair, in profusion. One of those picture children often reproduced in advertising leaflets and the photogravure sections of the Sunday papers.

She's had a fever for three days, began the father and we don't know what it comes from. My wife has given her things, you know, like people do, but it don't do no good. And there's been a lot of sickness around. So we tho't you'd better look her over and tell us what is the matter.

As doctors often do I took a trial shot at it as a point of departure. Had she had a sore throat?

Both parents answered me together, No . . . No, she says her throat don't hurt her.

Does your throat hurt you? added the mother to the child. But the little girl's expression didn't change nor did she move her eyes from my face.

Have you looked?

I tried to, said the mother, but I couldn't see.

As it happens we had been having a number of cases of diphtheria in the school to which this child went during that month and we were all, quite apparently, thinking of that, though no one had as yet spoken of the thing.

Well, I said, suppose we take a look at the throat first. I smiled in my best professional manner and asking for the child's first name I said, come on, Mathilda, open your mouth and let's take a look at your throat.

Nothing doing.

Aw, come on, I coaxed, just open your mouth wide and let me take a look. Look, I said opening both hands wide, I haven't anything in my hands. Just open up and let me see.

Such a nice man, put in the mother. Look how kind he is to you. Come on, do what he tells you to. He won't hurt you.

At that I ground my teeth in disgust. If only they wouldn't use the word "hurt" I might be able to get somewhere. But I did not allow myself to be hurried or disturbed but speaking quietly and slowly I approached the child again.

As I moved my chair a little nearer suddenly with one catlike movement both her hands clawed instinctively for my eyes and she almost reached them too. In fact she knocked my glasses flying and they fell, though unbroken, several feet away from me on the kitchen floor.

Both the mother and father almost turned themselves inside out in embarrassment and apology. You bad girl, said the mother, taking her and shaking her by one arm. Look what you've done. The nice man . . .

For heaven's sake, I broke in. Don't call me a nice man to her. I'm here to look at her throat on the chance that she might have diphtheria and possibly die of it. But that's nothing to her. Look here, I said to the child, we're going to look at your throat. You're old enough to understand what I'm saying. Will you open it now by yourself or shall we have to open it for you?

Not a move. Even her expression hadn't changed. Her breaths however were coming faster and faster. Then the battle began. I had to do it. I had to have a throat culture for her own protection. But first I told the parents that it was entirely up to them. I explained the danger but said that I would not insist on a throat examination so long as they would take the responsibility.

If you don't do what the doctor says you'll have to go to the hospital, the mother admonished her severely.

Oh yeah? I had to smile to myself. After all, I had already fallen in love with the savage brat, the parents were contemptible to me. In the ensuing struggle they grew more and more abject, crushed, exhausted while she surely rose to magnificent heights of insane fury of effort bred of her terror of me.

The father tried his best, and he was a big man but the fact that she was his daughter, his shame at her behavior and his dread of hurting her made him release her just at the critical times when I had almost achieved success, till I wanted to kill him. But his dread also that she might have diphtheria made him tell me to go on, go on though he himself was almost fainting, while the mother moved back and forth behind us raising and lowering her hands in an agony of apprehension.

Put her in front of you on your lap, I ordered, and hold both her wrists.

But as soon as he did the child let out a scream. Don't, you're hurting

me. Let go of my hands. Let them go I tell you. Then she shrieked ter-
rifyingly, hysterically. Stop it! Stop it! You're killing me!

Do you think she can stand it, doctor! said the mother.

You get out, said the husband to his wife. Do you want her to die of
diphtheria?

Come on now, hold her, I said.

Then I grasped the child's head with my left hand and tried to get the
wooden tongue depressor between her teeth. She fought, with clenched
teeth, desperately! But now I also had grown furious—at a child. I tried
to hold myself down but I couldn't. I know how to expose a throat for
inspection. And I did my best. When finally I got the wooden spatula
behind the last teeth and just the point of it into the mouth cavity, she
opened up for an instant but before I could see anything she came down
again and gripping the wooden blade between her molars she reduced it
to splinters before I could get it out again.

Aren't you ashamed, the mother yelled at her. Aren't you ashamed to
act like that in front of the doctor?

Get me a smooth-handled spoon of some sort, I told the mother. We're
going through with this. The child's mouth was already bleeding. Her
tongue was cut and she was screaming in wild hysterical shrieks. Perhaps
I should have desisted and come back in an hour or more. No doubt it
would have been better. But I have seen at least two children lying dead
in bed of neglect in such cases, and feeling that I must get a diagnosis
now or never I went at it again. But the worst of it was that I too had got
beyond reason. I could have torn the child apart in my own fury and
enjoyed it. It was a pleasure to attack her. My face was burning with it.

The damned little brat must be protected against her own idiocy, one
says to one's self at such times. Others must be protected against her.
It is a social necessity. And all these things are true. But a blind fury,
a feeling of adult shame, bred of a longing for muscular release are the
operatives. One goes on to the end.

In a final unreasoning assault I overpowered the child's neck and jaws.
I forced the heavy silver spoon back of her teeth and down her throat till
she gagged. And there it was—both tonsils covered with membrane.
She had fought valiantly to keep me from knowing her secret. She had
been hiding that sore throat for three days at least and lying to her parents
in order to escape just such an outcome as this.

Now truly she was furious. She had been on the defensive before but
now she attacked. Tried to get off her father's lap and fly at me while
tears of defeat blinded her eyes.

STUDY QUESTIONS

1. This story, like "Why I Live at the P.O.," is told by a first-person narrator who is a major participant in the action. What comparisons can be drawn between the two narrators regarding (a) their relative distance (emotionally, psychologically, physically) from the story each is telling; (b) their credibility; (c) their reliability (that is, the degree to which they reflect the values of the implied author); (d) their awareness of their individual problems?

2. Notice that the narrator never uses quotation marks to set off direct discourse and that he frequently reports dialogue through indirect discourse. What does this suggest to you about the narrator? How does this technique create ambiguity in certain lines of the story? How can you demonstrate or resolve the ambiguity of speakers in such lines as "Oh yeah?"

3. The doctor who is telling this story, like Sister in "Why I Live at the P.O.," frequently engages in a technique of "bifurcating" himself. Although this technique of objectifying himself tends to be grammatically obscured in such phrases as "I had to smile to myself" and "I tried to hold myself down," what do these phrases imply about the narrator's relationship to himself? How could this technique provide indications of the kinds of tensions within the doctor who tells the story, the doctor who participated in the incident, and the two juxtaposed doctors?

4. Notice the narrator's use of verb tenses. Try to account for the relationship between the narrator's choice of verb tenses in a given phrase and his emotional involvement in the particular section he is relating. Although the narrator is telling this story *after* it occurred, what evidence is there that he has not become completely detached emotionally from the experience? What evidence is there that the narrator *has* achieved some kind of detachment? Do these sets of evidence ever conflict?

5. Who is the narrator's audience? Is it the same as, or different from, the implied author's audience?

6. Explore the sexual implications in this story. Is the narrator aware of them? Is the implied author aware of them? How do the answers to these questions lead you to considerations regarding the tension between the narrator's awareness and the implied author's awareness? Are these considerations made even more complex when you realize that Williams the author was also a doctor?

Ernest Hemingway/The Killers

born 1899

The door of Henry's lunchroom opened and two men came in. They sat down at the counter.

"What's yours?" George asked them.

"I don't know," one of the men said. "What do you want to eat, Al?"

"I don't know," said Al. "I don't know what I want to eat."

Outside it was getting dark. The street light came on outside the window. The two men at the counter read the menu. From the other end of the counter Nick Adams watched them. He had been talking to George when they came in.

"I'll have a roast pork tenderloin with apple sauce and mashed potatoes," the first man said.

"It isn't ready yet."

"What the hell do you put it on the card for?"

"That's the dinner," George explained. "You can get that at six o'clock."

George looked at the clock on the wall behind the counter.

"It's five o'clock."

"The clock says twenty minutes past five," the second man said.

"It's twenty minutes fast."

"Oh, to hell with the clock," the first man said. "What have you got to eat?"

"I can give you any kind of sandwiches," George said. "You can have ham and eggs, bacon and eggs, liver and bacon, or a steak."

"Give me chicken croquettes with green peas and cream sauce and mashed potatoes."

"That's the dinner."

"Everything we want's the dinner, eh? That's the way you work it."

"I can give you ham and eggs, bacon and eggs, liver—"

"I'll take ham and eggs," the man called Al said. He wore a derby hat and a black overcoat buttoned across the chest. His face was small and white and he had tight lips. He wore a silk muffler and gloves.

"Give me bacon and eggs," said the other man. He was about the same size as Al. Their faces were different, but they were dressed like twins. Both wore overcoats too tight for them. They sat leaning forward, their elbows on the counter.

"Got anything to drink?" Al asked.

"Silver beer, bevo, ginger ale," George said.

"I mean you got anything to *drink?*"

"Just those I said."

"This is a hot town," said the other. "What do they call it?"

"Summit."

"Ever hear of it?" Al asked his friend.

"No," said the friend.

"What do you do here nights?" Al asked.

"They eat the dinner," his friend said. "They all come here and eat the big dinner."

"That's right," George said.

"So you think that's right?" Al asked George.

"Sure."

"You're a pretty bright boy, aren't you?"

"Sure," said George.

"Well, you're not," said the other little man. "Is he, Al?"

"He's dumb," said Al. He turned to Nick. "What's your name?"

"Adams."

"Another bright boy," Al said. "Ain't he a bright boy, Max?"

"The town's full of bright boys," Max said.

George put the two platters, one of ham and eggs, the other of bacon and eggs, on the counter. He set down two side dishes of fried potatoes and closed the wicket into the kitchen.

"Which is yours?" he asked Al.

"Don't you remember?"

"Ham and eggs."

"Just a bright boy," Max said. He leaned forward and took the ham and eggs. Both men ate with their gloves on. George watched them eat.

"What are *you* looking at?" Max looked at George.

"Nothing."

"The hell you were. You were looking at me."

"Maybe the boy meant it for a joke, Max," Al said.

George laughed.

"You don't have to laugh," Max said to him. *"You* don't have to laugh at all, see?"

"All right," said George.

"So he thinks it's all right." Max turned to Al. "He thinks it's all right. That's a good one."

"Oh, he's a thinker," Al said. They went on eating.

"What's the bright boy's name down the counter?" Al asked Max.

"Hey, bright boy," Max said to Nick. "You go around on the other side of the counter with your boy friend."

"What's the idea?" Nick asked.

"There isn't any idea."

"You better go around, bright boy," Al said. Nick went around behind the counter.

"What's the idea?" George asked.

"None of your damn business," Al said. "Who's out in the kitchen?"

"The nigger."

"What do you mean the nigger?"

"The nigger that cooks."

"Tell him to come in."

"What's the idea?"

"Tell him to come in."

"Where do you think you are?"

"We know damn well where we are," the man called Max said, "Do we look silly?"

"You talk silly," Al said to him. "What the hell do you argue with this kid for? Listen," he said to George, "tell the nigger to come out here."

"What are you going to do to him?"

"Nothing. Use your head, bright boy. What would we do to a nigger?"

George opened the slit that opened back into the kitchen. "Sam," he called. "Come in here a minute."

The door to the kitchen opened and the nigger came in. "What was it?" he asked. The two men at the counter took a look at him.

"All right, nigger. You stand right there," Al said.

Sam, the nigger, standing in his apron, looked at the two men sitting at the counter. "Yes, sir," he said. Al got down from his stool.

"I'm going back to the kitchen with the nigger and bright boy," he said. "Go on back to the kitchen, nigger. You go with him, bright boy." The little man walked after Nick and Sam, the cook, back into the kitchen. The door shut after them. The man called Max sat at the counter opposite George. He didn't look at George but looked in the mirror that ran along back of the counter. Henry's had been made over from a saloon into a lunch counter.

"Well, bright boy," Max said, looking into the mirror, "why don't you say something?"

"What's it all about?"

"Hey, Al," Max called, "bright boy wants to know what it's all about."

"Why don't you tell him?" Al's voice came from the kitchen.

"What do you think it's all about?"

"I don't know."

"What do you think?"

Max looked into the mirror all the time he was talking.

"I wouldn't say."

"Hey, Al, bright boy says he wouldn't say what he thinks it's all about."

"I can hear you, all right," Al said from the kitchen. He had propped open the slit that dishes passed through into the kitchen with a catsup bottle. "Listen, bright boy," he said from the kitchen to George. "Stand a little further along the bar. You move a little to the left, Max." He was like a photographer arranging for a group picture.

"Talk to me, bright boy," Max said. "What do you think's going to happen?"

George did not say anything.

"I'll tell you," Max said. "We're going to kill a Swede. Do you know a big Swede named Ole Andreson?"

"Yes."

"He comes here to eat every night, don't he?"

"Sometimes he comes here."

"He comes here at six o'clock, don't he?"

"If he comes."

"We know all that, bright boy," Max said. "Talk about something else. Ever go to the movies?"

"Once in a while."

"You ought to go to the movies more. The movies are fine for a bright boy like you."

"What are you going to kill Ole Andreson for? What did he ever do to you?"

"He never had a chance to do anything to us. He never even seen us."

"And he's only going to see us once," Al said from the kitchen.

"What are you going to kill him for, then?" George asked.

"We're killing him for a friend. Just to oblige a friend, bright boy."

"Shut up," said Al from the kitchen. "You talk too goddamn much."

"Well, I got to keep bright boy amused. Don't I, bright boy?"

"You talk too damn much," Al said. "The nigger and my bright boy are amused by themselves. I got them tied up like a couple of girl friends in a convent."

"I suppose you were in a convent."

"You never know."

"You were in a kosher convent. That's where you were."

George looked up at the clock.

"If anybody comes in you tell them the cook is off, and if they keep after it, you tell them you'll go back and cook yourself. Do you get that, bright boy?"

"All right," George said. "What you going to do with us afterward?"

"That'll depend," Max said. "That's one of those things you never know at the time."

George looked up at the clock. It was a quarter past six. The door from the street opened. A street-car motorman came in.

"Hello, George," he said. "Can I get supper?"

"Sam's gone out," George said. "He'll be back in about half an hour."

"I'd better go up the street," the motorman said. George looked at the clock. It was twenty minutes past six.

"That was nice, bright boy," Max said. "You're a regular little gentleman."

"He knew I'd blow his head off," Al said from the kitchen.

"No," said Max. "It ain't that. Bright boy is nice. He's a nice boy. I like him."

At six-fifty-five George said: "He's not coming."

Two other people had been in the lunchroom. Once George had gone out to the kitchen and made a ham-and-egg sandwich "to go" that a man wanted to take with him. Inside the kitchen he saw Al, his derby hat tipped back, sitting on a stool beside the wicket with the muzzle of a sawed-off shotgun resting on the ledge. Nick and the cook were back to back in the corner, a towel tied in each of their mouths. George had cooked the sandwich, wrapped it up in oiled paper, put it in a bag, brought it in, and the man had paid for it and gone out.

"Bright boy can do everything," Max said. "He can cook and everything. You'd make some girl a nice wife, bright boy."

"Yes?" George said. "Your friend, Ole Andreson, isn't going to come."

"We'll give him ten minutes," Max said.

Max watched the mirror and the clock. The hands of the clock marked seven o'clock, and then five minutes past seven.

"Come on, Al," said Max. "We better go. He's not coming."

"Better give him five minutes," Al said from the kitchen.

In the five minutes a man came in, and George explained that the cook was sick.

"Why the hell don't you get another cook?" the man asked. "Aren't you running a lunch counter?" He went out.

"Come on, Al," Max said.

"What about the two bright boys and the nigger?"

"They're all right."

"You think so?"

"Sure. We're through with it."

"I don't like it," said Al. "It's sloppy. You talk too much."

"Oh, what the hell," said Max. "We got to keep amused, haven't we?"

"You talk too much, all the same," Al said. He came out from the kitchen. The cut-off barrels of the shotgun made a slight bulge under the waist of his too tight-fitting overcoat. He straightened his coat with his gloved hands.

"So long, bright boy," he said to George. "You got a lot of luck."

"That's the truth," Max said. "You ought to play the races, bright boy."

The two of them went out the door. George watched them, through the window, pass under the arc light and cross the street. In their tight overcoats and derby hats they looked like a vaudeville team. George went back through the swinging door into the kitchen and untied Nick and the cook.

"I don't want any more of that," said Sam, the cook. "I don't want any more of that."

Nick stood up. He had never had a towel in his mouth before.

"Say," he said. "What the hell?" He was trying to swagger it off.

"They were going to kill Ole Andreson," George said. "They were going to shoot him when he came in to eat."

"Ole Andreson?"

"Sure."

The cook felt the corners of his mouth with his thumbs.

"They all gone?" he asked.

"Yeah," said George. "They're gone now."

"I don't like it," said the cook. "I don't like any of it at all."

"Listen," George said to Nick. "You better go see Ole Andreson."

"All right."

"You better not have anything to do with it at all," Sam, the cook, said. "You better stay way out of it."

"Don't go if you don't want to," George said.

"Mixing up in this ain't going to get you anywhere," the cook said. "You stay out of it."

"I'll go see him," Nick said to George. "Where does he live?"

The cook turned away.

"Little boys always know what they want to do," he said.

"He lives up at Hirsch's rooming house," George said to Nick.

"I'll go up there."

Outside the arc light shone through the bare branches of a tree. Nick walked up the street beside the car tracks and turned at the next arc light down a side street. Three houses up the street was Hirsch's rooming house. Nick walked up the two steps and pushed the bell. A woman came to the door.

"Is Ole Andreson here?"

"Do you want to see him?"

"Yes, if he's in."

Nick followed the woman up a flight of stairs and back to the end of a corridor. She knocked on the door.

"Who is it?"

"It's somebody to see you, Mr. Andreson," the woman said.

"It's Nick Adams."

"Come in."

Nick opened the door and went into the room. Ole Andreson was lying on the bed with all his clothes on. He had been a heavyweight prize-fighter and he was too long for the bed. He lay with his head on two pillows. He did not look at Nick.

"What was it?" he asked.

"I was up at Henry's," Nick said, "and two fellows came in and tied up me and the cook, and they said they were going to kill you."

It sounded silly when he said it. Ole Andreson said nothing.

"They put us out in the kitchen," Nick went on. "They were going to shoot you when you came in to supper."

Ole Andreson looked at the wall and did not say anything.

"George thought I better come and tell you about it."

"There isn't anything I can do about it," Ole Andreson said.

"I'll tell you what they were like."

"I don't want to know what they were like," Ole Andreson said. He looked at the wall. "Thanks for coming to tell me about it."

"That's all right."

Nick looked at the big man lying on the bed.

"Don't you want me to go and see the police?"

"No," Ole Andreson said. "That wouldn't do any good."

"Isn't there something I could do?"

"No. There ain't anything to do."

"Maybe it was just a bluff."

"No. It ain't just a bluff."

Ole Andreson rolled over toward the wall.

"The only thing is," he said, talking toward the wall, "I just can't make up my mind to go out. I been in here all day."

"Couldn't you get out of town?"

"No," Ole Andreson said. "I'm through with all that running around."

He looked at the wall.

"There ain't anything to do now."

"Couldn't you fix it up some way?"

"No. I got in wrong." He talked in the same flat voice. "There ain't anything to do. After a while I'll make up my mind to go out."

"I better go back and see George," Nick said.

"So long," said Ole Andreson. He did not look toward Nick. "Thanks for coming around."

Nick went out. As he shut the door he saw Ole Andreson with all his clothes on, lying on the bed looking at the wall.

"He's been in his room all day," the landlady said downstairs. "I guess he don't feel well. I said to him: 'Mr. Andreson, you ought to go out and take a walk on a nice fall day like this,' but he didn't feel like it."

"He doesn't want to go out."

"I'm sorry he don't feel well," the woman said. "He's an awfully nice man. He was in the ring, you know."

"I know it."

"You'd never know it except from the way his face is," the woman said. They stood talking just inside the street door. "He's just as gentle."

"Well, good-night, Mrs. Hirsch," Nick said.

"I'm not Mrs. Hirsch," the woman said. "She owns the place. I just look after it for her. I'm Mrs. Bell."

"Well, good-night, Mrs. Bell," Nick said.

"Good-night," the woman said.

Nick walked up the dark street to the corner under the arc light, and then along the car tracks to Henry's eating house. George was inside, back of the counter.

"Did you see Ole?"

"Yes," said Nick. "He's in his room and he won't go out."

The cook opened the door from the kitchen when he heard Nick's voice.

"I don't even listen to it," he said and shut the door.

"Did you tell him about it?" George asked.

"Sure. I told him but he knows what it's all about."

"What's he going to do?"

"Nothing."

"They'll kill him."

"I guess they will."

"He must have got mixed up in something in Chicago."

"I guess so," said Nick.

"It's a hell of a thing."

"It's an awful thing," Nick said.

They did not say anything. George reached down for a towel and wiped the counter.

"I wonder what he did?" Nick said.

"Double-crossed somebody. That's what they kill them for."

"I'm going to get out of this town," Nick said.

"Yes," said George. "That's a good thing to do."

"I can't stand to think about him waiting in the room and knowing he's going to get it. It's too damned awful."

"Well," said George, "you better not think about it."

STUDY QUESTIONS

1. This story is frequently used as a classic illustration of third-person objective narration. Indeed, many critics have cited this story as one whose method Is "thoroughly objective," with "no narrative intrusions." On the other hand, having finished reading the story, one has the distinct impression that the story is about Nick Adams, that it is being told from Nick's point of view, even though the narrator is neither admittedly Nick nor omniscient about Nick. With this in mind, look, for example, at the way in which this supposedly objective narrator introduces the reader to the characters: He begins by introducing two characters, George and Nick Adams. He then tells us of "two men" who enter Henry's lunchroom. One man calls the other "Al"; and the narrator then proceeds to refer to the man as "Al." However, although this narrator is obviously telling the story after it occurred, he does not identify the other man by name until after "the man called Al" has called him "Max." In other words, we learn the identities of persons in the story *as Nick learns them*. What other evidence can you find in the story's structure that would account for your impression about the narrator's closeness to Nick?

2. If this narrator is simply interested in reporting "action" and "plot," why do you suppose he introduces such remarks as "Henry's lunchroom had been made over from a saloon into a lunch counter" and "[Nick] had never had a towel in his mouth before"? What necessary conditions would have to be present in order for this narrator to have such information?

3. The tensions in this story are created primarily through character and action. Yet, apparently either some time passes that is not accounted for, or there are lengthy periods of silence that the narrator does not report, or else the killers

take a considerable amount of time to eat their meal because they order their food at 5:20 and give George his instructions at 6:20 (according to the lunchroom clock). Does this pose any particular problem for the interpreter? What does this handling of time in the story do to underscore the tension in the action? How could you support or extend this tension in a demonstration? How are these problems made more complex by the narrator's remark, three lines after the reference to the time as 6:20, that "At six-fifty-five, George said: 'He's not coming.' "?

4. What is this story about? More specifically, is it about a contract killing or Is it about Nick Adams? The structure of the story would seem to Indicate the latter, for if the story is simply concerned with a pair of hired killers, then what is the point of the final scene in Henry's lunchroom between Nick and George? If the narrator is indeed interested primarily in focusing on Nick, then what is it about Nick and his situation that the narrator is concerned with? What Is it that happens to Nick to make the final scene necessary to the story?

A. E. Coppard/The Third Prize

born 1878

Naboth Bird and George Robins were very fond of footracing. Neither of them was a champion runner, but each loved to train and to race; that was their pastime, their passion, their principal absorption and topic of conversation; occasionally it brought one or the other of them some sort of trophy.

One August bank holiday in the late nineties they travelled fifty miles to compete in a town where prizes of solid cash were to be given instead of the usual objects of glittering inutility. The town was a big town with a garrison and a dockyard. It ought to have been a city, and it would have been a city had not the only available cathedral been just inside an annoying little snob of a borough that kept itself (and its cathedral: admission sixpence) to itself just outside the boundaries of the real and proper town. On their arrival they found almost the entire populace wending to the carnival of games in a long stream of soldiers, sailors, and quite ordinary people, harried by pertinacious and vociferous little boys who yelled: "Program?" and blind beggars who just stood in the way and said nothing. Out of this crowd two jolly girls, Margery and Minnie, by some pleasant alchemy soon attached themselves to our two runners. Margery and Minnie were very different from each other. Why young maidens who hunt in couples and invariably dress alike should differ as much in character and temperament as Boadicea and Mrs. Hemans affords a speculation as fantastic as it is futile. They were different from each other, as different as a sherry cobbler and pineapple syrup, but they were not more different than were the two lads. The short snub one was Nab Bird; a mechanic by trade, with the ambition of a bus-conductor, he sold bicycle tires and did odd things to perambulators in a shed at the corner of a street; the demure Minnie became his friend. George Robins, a cute good-looking clerk, devoted his gifts of gallantry to Margery, and none the less readily because she displayed some qualities not commonly associated with demureness.

"From London you come!" exclaimed George. "How'd you get here?"

The young lady crisply testified that she came in a train—did the fathead think she had swum? They were jolly glad when they got here, too and all. Carriage full, and ructions all the way.

"Ructions! What ructions?"

"Boozy men! Half of 'em trying to cuddle you."

Mr. Robins intimated that he could well understand such desires. Miss Margery retorted that then he was understanding much more than was good for him. Mr. Robins thought not, he hoped not. Miss Margery indicated that he could hope for much more than he was likely to get. Mr. Robins replied that, he would do that, and then double it. And he asserted, with all respect, that had he but happily been in that train he too might have, etc. and so on. Whereupon Miss Margery snapped, Would he? and Mr. Robins felt bound to say Sure!

"Would you—well, I'll tell you what I did to one of them." And she told him. It was quite unpleasant.

"Lady!" cried George sternly, "I hope you won't serve me like that."

" 'Pends on how you behave."

"How do you want me to behave?"

"Well, how *should* you behave to a lady?"

" 'Pends on what's expected of me." George delivered it with a flash of satisfaction.

"Oh, go on," she retorted, "you're as bad as the rest of 'em. It depends really on what is expected of me, don't it?"

"Oh, you're all right," he replied, "you're as good as they make 'em."

"How do you know?"

"Well, ain't you?"

"I'm as good as I *can* be. Is that good enough for you?"

" 'Pends on how good that is."

Margery declared her unqualified abhorrence of this sort of goodness.

"I'm all right when I *am* all right," George assured her.

"I know all about you!" There was a twinkle in her eyes.

"Do you!" interjected Nab; "then you know more than he'd like his mother to know."

They arrived at the sports field. Already there were ten thousand people there, and the bookmakers, having assembled their easels, cards, and boxes, were surrounded by betting men. The space adjacent to the arena was occupied by a gala fair with roundabouts, shies, booths, swings, and other uproarious seductions. The track was encircled by a wedge of on-lookers ironic or enthusiastic, the sports began, runners came and went, the bookmakers stayed and roared, the hurdy gurdies lamented or re-joiced, the vanquished explained their defeats in terms that brought grins of commiseration to the faces of the victors, who explained their successes in terms that brought gleams of pride and triumph into the eyes of all who attended them. Very beautiful and bright the day was; the air smelt of grass, fusees, and cokernuts. Amongst those scantily garbed figures on the track Margery and Minnie scarcely recognized the young men they had accompanied, and for a long time they were unaware that George had won the third prize in a mile race.

Like all the other prize-winners he was subjected to the extravagant cajoleries of Jerry Chambers, a cockney ruffian living by his wits, a calling that afforded him no very great margin of security. He had lost his money, he was without a penny, and in the dressing-room he fastened himself upon Robins and Bird in an effort to obtain something or other, little or much, from each or either.

"I tell you," he darkly whispered, "the winner of the mile is a stiff un."

"What's a stiff un?" inquired Nab Bird.

"A stiff un! What a stiff un is!" Chambers's amusement at this youth's boundless ignorance was shrill and genuine. "Why, he's run under an assumed name and got about sixty yards the best of the handicap. You was third in that race, Robins, and the winner was a stiff un. Make it worth my while and I'll get him pinched for impersonation. Know him!—I knew his father! I'll tell you what I'll do, I'll get the second man disqualified as well—how will that stand you? Give me a dollar now so I can lodge the objection at once and the first prize must be awarded to you, it must. A five-pound note ain't it? I backed you to win myself and I don't like losing my money to a stiff un—I took ten pound to two about you. Now half a dollar won't hurt you. You won't! Well, good God Almighty!"—Chambers tilted his hat over one eye and scratched his neck—"don't let me try to persuade you. Lend us a tanner."

"To hell with you!"

"Make it eighteen pence, then."

They did not. At the distribution of the prize money, there was much ringing of a bell, shouting of names, and some factitious applause as a pert and portly lady of title appeared at a table in front of the pavilion to perform the ceremony. It was the only titled person our friends had ever seen, and the announcement of her grand name and the sound of her voice despite her appearance—for though she was a countess she had a stom-ach like a publican's wife—affected them occultly. A very gentlemanly steward, in private life a vendor of fish, bawled out the names of the prize-winners, and when it came to the turn of George Robins he was surprised to hear:

"Third prize in the mile race: W. Ballantyne."

He hesitated.

"It's wrong, O George!" gasped Nab Bird, "it's a mistake."

Nobody responding to the call for W. Ballantyne, George suddenly exchanged hats with his friend. Giving Nab his tweed cap he seized Nab's bowler hat and, although it was far too small, put it on his own head, where it looked much as it would have done on the bust of Homer.

"What—George, what?" asked his bewildered friend amid the chuckles of the two girls, but without stopping to explain, George Robins pushed his way through the crowd, advanced to the table, and received in the name of W. Ballantyne his own prize of a sovereign, which he acknowledged by just raising his terrible headgear and blowing his nose with a large handkerchief.

"Thanks, Nab," said he, returning to his friends. "I'll have my cap again."

The presentation concluded, the lady of title shook hands with the gentleman fishmonger and they went, presumably, their separate ways, while part of the crowd drifted gaily over to the fair booths and the rest went home to tea. With a mysterious preoccupied air George directed Nab to take the girls into a tent for tea and await him there.

"We'll look after him," declared Minnie, linking her arm with Nab's.

"But where you going, O George?" exclaimed the puzzled one, as Margery, too, linked an arm in his.

"See you later, five minutes, only five minutes. Take him away," shouted the departing George to the girls, "give him a bun and don't let him make his face jammy."

So Nab went to tea with the girls, and says he:

"I wonder what he's up to."

"Didn't he run well?" said Minnie.

"Beautiful," agreed Margery.

"I don't want no tea," declared Nab, "I'm 'ot, but I'll have a couple of them saveloys, and then for a glass of ice cream-o. But you have just what you like, Minnie and Margery."

They had what they could get, and then, as Nab for the twentieth time was audibly wondering what George was "up to" and Margery for the dozenth time was realizing how splendidly he had run, George himself reappeared beaming with satisfaction.

"Where you been to, O George?"

"Been to get my prize."

"What prize?"

"In the mile."

"Third prize?"

"Didn't I win it?"

"But you got that before, didn't you?"

"Did I?"

"Well, 'aven't you?"

"Have I?"

Nab was mystified, George was triumphant: "I'll explain it to you. Listen, O Little Naboth. That third prize was awarded by some mischance to a chap the name of Ballantyne. Well, there wasn't any Ballantyne won that prize. That winner was G. Robins, that's me."

"Yes."

"So I go to the secretary of the sports and I say to him: 'Excuse me, sir, I'm George Robins, I won third prize in the mile, but there has been a mistake, and the prize has been given to someone called Ballantyne. What am I to do? Well, there was a lot of palavering and running about and seeing stewards, but at last they found out that what I said was absolutely true and so they gave me another sovereign."

"Two lots of prize money you got, then!" ejaculated Nab, "two quid!"

George nodded modestly. "And they apologized for the mistake!"

"My goodness, isn't he—!" remarked Margery admiringly to Minnie, and Minnie too appeared to think he was—! But Nab was perturbed. Margery's observation—"All's fair in love and war!"—did not seem very pertinent to Nab and he corrected her:

"Love and war's one thing, sport's another."

"Sport!" exclaimed George. "But you know what these professionals are, you daren't trust 'em. Jerry Chambers, now, how about him if you met him on a dark night, eh? Any of these professionals would cut your throat for fivepence. They'd bag your boots and bone your bag and your skin too if you wasn't chained up inside it."

"Yes, O George, I know, but it wasn't them you done it to, it's the committee."

"Their look-out, ain't it? Their own mistake, not mine! It wasn't my mistake, now was it?"

"Well, no, but it's a bit like what Jerry Chambers might have done himself."

Margery interposed: "I think it was jolly smart, but you were a confederate—you lent him your hat."

"Of course! I borrowed that for disguise, see! But you shall share the swag, little Naboth, so don't keep grumbling and grumbling. Here's your half-a-james." Saying which, George stretched out a hand to his friend, who saw lying upon his palm a glittering sovereign. "Give me change for half of that!"

The girls sparklingly approved this offer of the magnanimous one, but Nab, a little confused, turned away saying:

"No, thanks, George O man, no, thanks."

Although they all surrounded Nab and tried to cajole him into acceptance, the little man was adamant—very kind of George, but he'd rather not. However, they all went away very amiably together, and it was apparent to Naboth Bird that his friend's questionable manoeuvre was acclaimed by the girls as an admirable exploit, while his own qualms were regarded as an indecent exhibition of an honesty no less questionable.

Moving idly down a hill amongst the stream of people, they were brought to a standstill at the edge of a crowd surrounding an old blind beggar and his wife. The man was playing a hymn tune on a tin pipe. Tall and ragged, with white thin beard and clerical hat, there was the strange dignity inseparable from blindness in his erect figure, but his shuffling wife, older, and very feeble, held his arm with one hand and outstretched the other for the few pitying pence that came to them. George and his friends were astonished to perceive the ruffian Jerry Chambers standing mockingly in front of the beggars. His arms were spread out to the halting people, his hat had been flung upon the ground before him, he was making excruciating gestures and noises with his hands and mouth, yodelling like a costermonger and performing ridiculous antics to gain their attention. He was entirely successful; the good-natured holiday folk assembled and stretched across the road in a great crowd. With an ironical gesture of the hand Chambers directed the attention of the onlookers to the forlorn couple behind him.

"Look at 'em," he yelled, "look at 'em—roll, bowl, or pitch—but look at 'em! Did ever you see such a thing in your lives?"

He paused for a moment and then recommenced very gently: "People, men of my own fraternity! I ain't doing this bit of a job for myself—nor for no barney—nor for no bank-holiday rag. I'm a-doing this—just five minutes—for my compatriarch and his noble consort. Look at 'em, I say. I bin a-looking at 'em—I 'ad to—and it just breaks my heart. Well, you're not a brass-bellied lot—you don't look it—*your* hearts ain't made of tripe. So that's where I've pushed in."

The old man had forborne his solemn piping; he blinked the sightless eyes unobjectively upon the people, while his partner clung to him with both arms, bewildered and a little terrified.

"I am going," Chambers began to roar again, "to sing you a comical song. Shall then, if my old compatriarch will oblige with a tootle on his bangalorum, shall then dance you a jig. Shall then crawl upon my hands and knees, barking like a tiger, with my cady in me mouth to collect bullion for this suffering fambly. Look at 'em, lord alive, look at 'em!"

After singing so raucous and ridiculous a song that his kindly intentions were nearly defeated Chambers poised himself for the jig:

"Righto, play up, uncle!"

But the old beggar could only repeat the one tune, his hymn called *Marching to Zion.*

"God A'mighty! 'ark at 'im!" cried the baffled Chambers. "Well, you people, men of my own fraternity, it's no go; 'ere's my cadging 'at—give us a good whip round for those two old bits of mutton!"

So the old man piped his hymn while the cockney ruffian begged and bullied a handful of money for them. Chaffing and scolding, he approached George; Margery was searching for a coin.

"It's all right," whispered George to her, "it's all right." He showed her the coin already in his fingers, the glittering questionable sovereign. She clutched his arm to prevent such a sacrifice, but she was too late, George dropped the coin into Chambers's hat and then, curiously shamefaced, at once walked away in a little drift of pleased excitement.

"Min, Min, d'you know what he's done!" cried Margery to the friends as they all followed after him, "he's given 'em that sovereign."

In the eyes of the dazzled girls the gesture crowned George with the last uttermost grace, and even Nab was mute before its sublimity. They hurried away as if the devil himself might be coming to thrust the sovereign back upon them.

And Chambers? His triumph, too, was great, the well-used occasion had won its well-devised reward, and his pleasure, though modestly expressed, was sincere.

"Ladies and gennermen," cried the jolly ruffian a few minutes later as he counted up the coin. "I thank you one and all for your kindness to this old couple and the very handsome collection (here y'are, uncle," he whispered, "it's splendid, eight shillings and fo'pence). All correct, thank you, ladies and gennermen. God bless the lot of yer," and then, leaving the delighted beggars to their gains, and murmuring to himself "Beau-tiful beautiful Zi-on!" he hurried rapidly away.

STUDY QUESTIONS

1. Although the narrator of this story, like the one in "The Killers," speaks In the third person and is an objective observer of the action, he nonetheless has a very distinct personality, which is quite different from the personalities of the characters in the story. How do you know this? What does the narrator's diction reveal about his attitudes? How does the narrator's diction function in contrast to the diction of the other characters in the story? What kind of social character do you envision for this narrator on the evidence of his verbal behavior in the text?
2. Try to determine, from the evidence in the text, this narrator's audience and his epic situation. How could you supply social parallels to these implicit observations in a demonstration?

3. Notice the narrator's use of "direct and indirect discourse," [10] particularly in the beginning paragraphs of the story. What does his manner of reporting dialogue here suggest to you about his relationship and attitudes toward the four major characters? Exactly how does this narrator split the responsibility for dialogue when he reports conversations in indirect discourse? How could you demonstrate this?

4. What has happened at the end of this story? How much of your understanding of what has happened depends upon your understanding of the British monetary system? What are the relative values of a sovereign, two quid, a dollar, a five-pound note, and eight shillings?

5. How is a comic effect created in this story through a juxtaposition of contrasting dialects—between the narrator and the characters on the one hand and among the various characters on the other? How could you demonstrate the ways in which this comedy operates in the story?

Irwin Shaw/The Girls in Their Summer Dresses

born 1913

Fifth Avenue was shining in the sun when they left the Brevoort and started walking toward Washington Square. The sun was warm, even though it was November and everything looked like Sunday morning— the buses, and the well-dressed people walking slowly in couples and the quiet buildings with the windows closed.

Michael held Frances' arm tightly as they walked downtown in the sunlight. They walked lightly, almost smiling, because they had slept late and had a good breakfast and it was Sunday. Michael unbuttoned his coat and let it flap around him in the mild wind. They walked, without saying anything, among the young and pleasant-looking people who somehow seem to make up most of the population of that section of New York City.

---

[10] *Direct and indirect discourse:* terms referring to the manner in which the speech of a character is reported. When a writer uses direct discourse in a story, he renders a character's speech exactly as it was spoken, usually setting off the speech with quotation marks. The effect of this technique is to encourage the reader to feel as if he were hearing the character speak directly to him, as when the narrator in "Everything That Rises Must Converge" reports: " 'Let's skip it,' Julian said." Indirect discourse refers to the rendering of a character's speech or thoughts, not directly by the character, but through the narrator. Indirect discourse is sometimes signaled by the word *that* and usually involves a change in personal pronoun and verb tense, as in this dialogue report in "The Third Prize": "The young lady crisply testified that she came in a train—did the fathead think she had swum?" The use of indirect discourse allows a writer to feature the narrator and the character simultaneously during dialogue.

"Look out," Frances said, as they crossed Eighth Street. "You'll break your neck."

Michael laughed and Frances laughed with him.

"She's not so pretty, anyway," Frances said. "Anyway, not pretty enough to take a chance breaking your neck looking at her."

Michael laughed again. He laughed louder this time, but not as solidly. "She wasn't a bad-looking girl. She had a nice complexion. Country-girl complexion. How did you know I was looking at her?"

Frances cocked her head to one side and smiled at her husband under the tip-tilted brim of her hat. "Mike, darling . . ." she said.

Michael laughed, just a little laugh this time. "O.K.," he said. "The evidence is in. Excuse me. It was the complexion. It's not the sort of complexion you see much in New York. Excuse me."

Frances patted his arm lightly and pulled him along a little faster toward Washington Square.

"This is a nice morning," she said. "This is a wonderful morning. When I have breakfast with you it makes me feel good all day."

"Tonic," Michael said. "Morning pick-up. Rolls and coffee with Mike and you're on the alkali side, guaranteed."

"That's the story. Also, I slept all night, wound around you like a rope."

"Saturday night," he said. "I permit such liberties only when the week's work is done."

"You're getting fat," she said.

"Isn't it the truth? The lean man from Ohio."

"I love it," she said, "an extra five pounds of husband."

"I love it, too," Michael said gravely.

"I have an idea," Frances said.

"My wife has an idea. That pretty girl."

"Let's not see anybody all day," Frances said. "Let's just hang around with each other. You and me. We're always up to our neck in people, drinking their Scotch, or drinking our Scotch, we only see each other in bed . . ."

"The Great Meeting Place," Michael said. "Stay in bed long enough and everybody you ever knew will show up there."

"Wise guy," Frances said. "I'm talking serious."

"O.K., I'm listening serious."

"I want to go out with my husband all day long. I want him to talk only to me and listen only to me."

"What's to stop us?" Michael asked. "What party intends to prevent me from seeing my wife alone on Sunday? What party?"

"The Stevensons. They want us to drop by around one o'clock and they'll drive us into the country."

"The lousy Stevensons," Mike said. "Transparent. They can whistle.

They can go driving in the country by themselves. My wife and I have to stay in New York and bore each other tête-à-tête."

"Is it a date?"

"It's a date."

Frances leaned over and kissed him on the tip of the ear.

"Darling," Michael said. "This is Fifth Avenue."

"Let me arrange a program," Frances said. "A planned Sunday in New York for a young couple with money to throw away."

"Go easy."

"First let's go see a football game. A professional football game," Frances said, because she knew Michael loved to watch them. "The Giants are playing. And it'll be nice to be outside all day today and get hungry and later we'll go down to Cavanagh's and get a steak as big as a blacksmith's apron, with a bottle of wine, and after that, there's a new French picture at the Filmarte that everybody says . . . Say, are you listening to me?"

"Sure," he said. He took his eyes off the hatless girl with the dark hair, cut dancer-style, like a helmet, who was walking past him with the self-conscious strength and grace dancers have. She was walking without a coat and she looked very solid and strong and her belly was flat, like a boy's, under her skirt, and her hips swung boldly because she was a dancer and also because she knew Michael was looking at her. She smiled a little to herself as she went past and Michael noticed all these things before he looked back at his wife. "Sure," he said, "we're going to watch the Giants and we're going to eat steak and we're going to see a French picture. How do you like that?"

"That's it," Frances said flatly. "That's the program for the day. Or maybe you'd just rather walk up and down Fifth Avenue."

"No," Michael said carefully. "Not at all."

"You always look at other women," Frances said. "At every damn woman in the City of New York."

"Oh, come now," Michael said, pretending to joke. "Only pretty ones. And, after all, how many pretty women *are* there in New York? Seventeen?"

"More. At least you seem to think so. Wherever you go."

"Not the truth. Occasionally, maybe, I look at a woman as she passes. In the street. I admit, perhaps in the street I look at a woman once in a while . . ."

"Everywhere," Frances said. "Every damned place we go. Restaurants, subways, theaters, lectures, concerts."

"Now, darling," Michael said, "I look at everything. God gave me eyes and I look at women and men and subway excavations and moving pictures and the little flowers of the field. I casually inspect the universe."

"You ought to see the look in your eye," Frances said, "as you casually inspect the universe on Fifth Avenue."

"I'm a happily married man." Michael pressed her elbow tenderly, knowing what he was doing. "Example for the whole twentieth century, Mr. and Mrs. Mike Loomis."

"You mean it?"

"Frances, baby . . ."

"Are you *really* happily married?"

"Sure," Michael said, feeling the whole Sunday morning sinking like lead inside him. "Now what the hell is the sense in talking like that?"

"I would like to know." Frances walked faster now, looking straight ahead, her face showing nothing, which was the way she always managed it when she was arguing or feeling bad.

"I'm wonderfully happily married," Michael said patiently. "I am the envy of all men between the ages of fifteen and sixty in the State of New York."

"Stop kidding," Frances said.

"I have a fine home," Michael said. "I got nice books and a phonograph and nice friends. I live in a town I like the way I like and I do the work I like and I live with the woman I like. Whenever something good happens, don't I run to you? When something bad happens, don't I cry on your shoulder?"

"Yes," Frances said. "You look at every woman that passes."

"That's an exaggeration."

"Every woman." Frances took her hand off Michael's arm. "If she's not pretty you turn away fairly quickly. If she's halfway pretty you watch her for about seven steps . . ."

"My lord, Frances!"

"If she's pretty you practically break your neck . . ."

"Hey, let's have a drink," Michael said, stopping.

"We just had breakfast."

"Now, listen, darling," Mike said, choosing his words with care, "it's a nice day and we both feel good and there's no reason why we have to break it up. Let's have a nice Sunday."

"I could have a fine Sunday if you didn't look as though you were dying to run after every skirt on Fifth Avenue."

"Let's have a drink," Michael said.

"I don't want a drink."

"What do you want, a fight?"

"No," Frances said so unhappily that Michael felt terribly sorry for her. "I don't want a fight. I don't know why I started this. All right, let's drop it. Let's have a good time."

They joined hands consciously and walked without talking among the baby carriages and the old Italian men in their Sunday clothes and the young women with Scotties in Washington Square Park.

"I hope it's a good game today," Frances said after a while, her tone a good imitation of the tone she had used at breakfast and at the beginning of their walk. "I like professional football games. They hit each other as though they're made out of concrete. When they tackle each other," she said, trying to make Michael laugh, "they make divots. It's very exciting."

"I want to tell you something," Michael said very seriously. "I have not touched another woman. Not once. In all the five years."

"All right," Frances said.

"You believe that, don't you?"

"All right."

They walked between the crowded benches, under the scrubby city park trees.

"I try not to notice it," Frances said, as though she were talking to herself. "I try to make believe it doesn't mean anything. Some men're like that, I tell myself, they have to see what they're missing."

"Some women're like that, too," Michael said. "In my time I've seen a couple of ladies."

"I haven't even looked at another man," Frances said, walking straight ahead, "since the second time I went out with you."

"There's no law," Michael said.

"I feel rotten inside, in my stomach, when we pass a woman and you look at her and I see that look in your eye and that's the way you looked at me the first time, in Alice Maxwell's house. Standing there in the living room, next to the radio, with a green hat on and all those people."

"I remember the hat," Michael said.

"The same look," Frances said. "And it makes me feel bad. It makes me feel terrible."

"Sssh, please, darling, sssh . . ."

"I think I would like a drink now," Frances said.

They walked over to a bar on Eighth Street, not saying anything, Michael automatically helping her over curbstones, and guiding her past automobiles. He walked, buttoning his coat, looking thoughtfully at his neatly shined heavy brown shoes as they made the steps toward the bar. They sat near a window in the bar and the sun streamed in, and there was a small cheerful fire in the fireplace. A little Japanese waiter came over and put down some pretzels and smiled happily at them.

"What do you order after breakfast?" Michael asked.

"Brandy, I suppose," Frances said.

"Courvoisier," Michael told the waiter. "Two Courvoisier."

The waiter came with the glasses and they sat drinking the brandy, in the sunlight. Michael finished half his and drank a little water.

"I look at women," he said. "Correct. I don't say it's wrong or right, I look at them. If I pass them on the street and I don't look at them, I'm fooling you, I'm fooling myself."

"You look at them as though you want them," Frances said, playing with her brandy glass. "Every one of them."

"In a way," Michael said, speaking softly and not to his wife, "in a way that's true. I don't do anything about it, but it's true."

"I know it. That's why I feel bad."

"Another brandy," Michael called. "Waiter, two more brandies."

"Why do you hurt me?" Frances asked. "What're you doing?"

Michael sighed and closed his eyes and rubbed them gently with his fingertips. "I love the way women look. One of the things I like best about New York is the battalions of women. When I first came to New York from Ohio that was the first thing I noticed, the million wonderful women, all over the city. I walked around with my heart in my throat."

"A kid," Frances said. "That's a kid's feeling."

"Guess again," Michael said. "Guess again. I'm older now, I'm a man getting near middle age, putting on a little fat and I still love to walk along Fifth Avenue at three o'clock on the east side of the street between Fiftieth and Fifty-seventh Streets, they're all out then, making believe they're shopping, in their furs and their crazy hats, everything all concentrated from all over the world into eight blocks, the best furs, the best clothes, the handsomest women, out to spend money and feeling good about it, looking coldly at you, making believe they're not looking at you as you go past."

The Japanese waiter put the two drinks down, smiling with great happiness.

"Everything is all right?" he asked.

"Everything is wonderful," Michael said.

"If it's just a couple of fur coats," Frances said, "and forty-five-dollar hats . . ."

"It's not the fur coats. Or the hats. That's just the scenery for that particular kind of woman. Understand," he said, "you don't have to listen to this."

"I want to listen."

"I like the girls in the offices. Neat, with their eyeglasses, smart, chipper, knowing what everything is about, taking care of themselves all the time." He kept his eye on the people going slowly past outside the window. "I like the girls on Forty-fourth Street at lunch time, the actresses, all dressed up on nothing a week, talking to the good-looking boys, wearing themselves out being young and vivacious outside Sardi's, waiting for producers to look at them. I like the salesgirls in Macy's, paying attention to you first because you're a man, leaving lady customers waiting, flirting with you over socks and books and phonograph needles. I got all this stuff accumulated in me because I've been thinking about it for ten years and now you've asked for it and here it is."

"Go ahead," Frances said.

"When I think of New York City, I think of all the girls, the Jewish girls, the Italian girls, the Irish, Polack, Chinese, German, Negro, Spanish, Russian girls, all on parade in the city. I don't know whether it's something special with me or whether every man in the city walks around with the same feeling inside him, but I feel as though I'm at a picnic in this city. I like to sit near the women in the theaters, the famous beauties who've taken six hours to get ready and look it. And the young girls at the football games, with the red cheeks, and when the warm weather comes, the girls in their summer dresses . . ." He finished his drink. "That's the story. You asked for it, remember. I can't help but look at them. I can't help but want them."

"You want them," Frances repeated without expression. "You said that."

"Right," Michael said, being cruel now and not caring, because she had made him expose himself. "You brought this subject up for discussion, we will discuss it fully."

Frances finished her drink and swallowed two or three times extra. "You say you love me?"

"I love you, but I also want them. O.K."

"I'm pretty, too," Frances said. "As pretty as any of them."

"You're beautiful," Michael said, meaning it.

"I'm good for you," Frances said, pleading. "I've made a good wife, a good housekeeper, a good friend. I'd do any damn thing for you."

"I know," Michael said. He put his hand out and grasped hers.

"You'd like to be free to . . ." Frances said.

"Sssh."

"Tell the truth." She took her hand away from under his.

Michael flicked the edge of his glass with his finger. "O.K.," he said gently. "Sometimes I feel I would like to be free."

"Well," Frances said defiantly, drumming on the table, "anytime you say . . ."

"Don't be foolish." Michael swung his chair around to her side of the table and patted her thigh.

She began to cry, silently, into her handkerchief, bent over just enough so that nobody else in the bar would notice. "Some day," she said, crying, "you're going to make a move . . ."

Michael didn't say anything. He sat watching the bartender slowly peel a lemon.

"Aren't you?" Frances asked harshly. "Come on, tell me. Talk. Aren't you?"

"Maybe," Michael said. He moved his chair back again. "How the hell do I know?"

"You know," Frances persisted. "Don't you know?"

"Yes," Michael said after a while, "I know."

Frances stopped crying then. Two or three snuffles into the handkerchief and she put it away and her face didn't tell anything to anybody. "At least do me one favor," she said.

"Sure."

"Stop talking about how pretty this woman is, or that one. Nice eyes, nice breasts, a pretty figure, good voice," she mimicked his voice. "Keep it to yourself. I'm not interested."

"Excuse me." Michael waved to the waiter. "I'll keep it to myself."

Frances flicked the corner of her eyes. "Another brandy," she told the waiter.

"Two," Michael said.

"Yes, ma'am, yes, sir," said the waiter, backing away.

Frances regarded him coolly across the table. "Do you want me to call the Stevensons?" she asked. "It'll be nice in the country."

"Sure," Michael said. "Call them up."

She got up from the table and walked across the room toward the telephone. Michael watched her walk, thinking, what a pretty girl, what nice legs.

STUDY QUESTIONS

1. Prepare a double dramatic analysis of this story. You will no doubt find that a dramatic analysis of the story itself is relatively easy because of the story's rather simple plot construction and characterizations. On the other hand, a dramatic analysis of the narrator and his situation is more difficult. For example, how does this seemingly objective narrator come by his information of certain details in the activities of Frances and Michael, which would be unknown to any ordinary observer? What happens to the narrator's objectivity in the last paragraph? Has the reader been adequately prepared for such an abrupt shift in point of view?

2. Much of the drama of this story relies on the building tension between Michael and Frances and the rising tension within each of them. Look carefully at each scene in the story where there is a reference to Michael's girl-watching. Precisely how does this tension build from scene to scene?

3. Try to define as fully and clearly as you can, from the evidence in the story, exactly what Michael and Frances mean to each other. If something is amiss in their relationship, what is its source? Is it the same for Frances as for Michael?

4. What happens at the end of the story? What are the implications of the narrator's final remarks?

D. H. Lawrence/The Horse Dealer's Daughter

born 1885

"Well, Mabel, and what are you going to do with yourself?" asked Joe, with foolish flippancy. He felt quite safe himself. Without listening for an answer, he turned aside, worked a grain of tobacco to the tip of his tongue, and spat it out. He did not care about anything, since he felt safe himself.

The three brothers and the sister sat round the desolate breakfast table, attempting some sort of desultory consultation. The morning's post had given the final tap to the family fortune, and all was over. The dreary dining-room itself, with its heavy mahogany furniture, looked as if it were waiting to be done away with.

But the consultation amounted to nothing. There was a strange air of ineffectuality about the three men, as they sprawled at table, smoking and reflecting vaguely on their own condition. The girl was alone, a rather short, sullen-looking young woman of twenty-seven. She did not share the same life as her brothers. She would have been good-looking, save for the impassive fixity of her face, "bulldog," as her brothers called it.

There was a confused tramping of horses' feet outside. The three men all sprawled round in their chairs to watch. Beyond the dark holly-bushes that separated the strip of lawn from the highroad, they could see a cavalcade of shire horses swinging out of their own yard, being taken for exercise. This was the last time. These were the last horses that would go through their hands. The young men watched with critical, callous look. They were all frightened at the collapse of their lives, and the sense of disaster in which they were involved left them no inner freedom.

Yet they were three fine, well-set fellows enough. Joe, the eldest, was a man of thirty-three, broad and handsome in a hot, flushed way. His face was red, he twisted his black moustache over a thick finger, his eyes were shallow and restless. He had a sensual way of uncovering his teeth when he laughed, and his bearing was stupid. Now he watched the horses with a glazed look of helplessness in his eyes, a certain stupor of downfall.

The great draught-horses swung past. They were tied head to tail, four of them, and they heaved along to where a lane branched off from the highroad, planting their great hoofs floutingly in the fine black mud, swinging their great rounded haunches sumptuously, and trotting a few sudden steps as they were led into the lane, round the corner. Every movement showed a massive, slumbrous strength, and a stupidity which held them in subjection. The groom at the head looked back, jerking the leading rope. And the cavalcade moved out of sight up the lane, the tail of the last horse, bobbed up tight and stiff, held out taut from the swinging great haunches as they rocked behind the hedges in a motion like sleep.

Joe watched with glazed hopeless eyes. The horses were almost like his own body to him. He felt he was done for now. Luckily he was engaged to a woman as old as himself, and therefore her father, who was steward of a neighbouring estate, would provide him with a job. He would marry and go into harness. His life was over, he would be a subject animal now.

He turned uneasily aside, the retreating steps of the horses echoing in his ears. Then, with foolish restlessness, he reached for the scraps of bacon-rind from the plates, and making a faint whistling sound, flung them to the terrier that lay against the fender. He watched the dog swallow them, and waited till the creature looked into his eyes. Then a faint grin came on his face, and in a high, foolish voice he said:

"You won't get much more bacon, shall you, you little bitch?"

The dog faintly and dismally wagged its tail, then lowered its haunches, circled round, and lay down again.

There was another helpless silence at the table. Joe sprawled uneasily in his seat, not willing to go till the family conclave was dissolved. Fred Henry, the second brother, was erect, clean-limbed, alert. He had watched the passing of the horses with more sang-froid. If he was an animal, like Joe, he was an animal which controls, not one which is controlled. He was master of any horse, and he carried himself with a well-tempered air of mastery. But he was not master of the situations of life. He pushed his coarse brown moustache upwards, off his lip, and glanced irritably at his sister, who sat impassive and inscrutable.

"You'll go and stop with Lucy for a bit, shan't you?" he asked. The girl did not answer.

"I don't see what else you can do," persisted Fred Henry.

"Go as a skivvy," Joe interpolated laconically.

The girl did not move a muscle.

"If I was her, I should go in for training for a nurse," said Malcolm, the youngest of them all. He was the baby of the family, a young man of twenty-two, with a fresh, jaunty *museau*.

But Mabel did not take any notice of him. They had talked at her and round her for so many years, that she hardly heard them at all.

The marble clock on the mantelpiece softly chimed the half-hour, the dog rose uneasily from the hearthrug and looked at the party at the breakfast table. But still they sat on in ineffectual conclave.

"Oh, all right," said Joe suddenly, apropos of nothing. "I'll get a move on."

He pushed back his chair, straddled his knees with a downward jerk, to get them free, in horsey fashion, and went to the fire. Still he did not go out of the room; he was curious to know what the others would do or say. He began to charge his pipe, looking down at the dog and saying, in a high, affected voice:

"Going wi' me? Goin wi' me are ter? Tha'rt goin' further than tha counts on just now, dost hear?"

The dog faintly wagged its tail, the man stuck out his jaw and covered his pipe with his hands, and puffed intently, losing himself in the tobacco, looking down all the while at the dog with an absent brown eye. The dog looked up at him in mournful distrust. Joe stood with his knees stuck out, in real horsey fashion.

"Have you had a letter from Lucy?" Fred Henry asked of his sister.

"Last week," came the neutral reply.

"And what does she say?"

There was no answer.

"Does she *ask* you to go and stop there?" persisted Fred Henry.

"She says I can if I like."

"Well, then, you'd better. Tell her you'll come on Monday."

This was received in silence.

"That's what you'll do then, is it?" said Fred Henry, in some exasperation.

But she made no answer. There was a silence of futility and irritation in the room. Malcolm grinned fatuously.

"You'll have to make up your mind between now and next Wednesday," said Joe loudly, "or else find yourself lodgings on the kerbstone."

The face of the young woman darkened, but she sat on immutable.

"Here's Jack Fergusson!" exclaimed Malcolm, who was looking aimlessly out of the window.

"Where?" exclaimed Joe, loudly.

"Just gone past."

"Coming in?"

Malcolm craned his neck to see the gate.

"Yes," he said.

There was a silence. Mabel sat on like one condemned, at the head of the table. Then a whistle was heard from the kitchen. The dog got up and barked sharply. Joe opened the door and shouted:

"Come on."

After a moment a young man entered. He was muffled up in overcoat and a purple woollen scarf, and his tweed cap, which he did not remove, was pulled down on his head. He was of medium height, his face was rather long and pale, his eyes looked tired.

"Hello, Jack! Well, Jack!" exclaimed Malcolm and Joe. Fred Henry merely said, "Jack."

"What's doing?" asked the newcomer, evidently addressing Fred Henry.

"Same. We've got to be out by Wednesday. Got a cold?"

"I have—got it bad, too."

"Why don't you stop in?"

"*Me* stop in? When I can't stand on my legs, perhaps I shall have a chance." The young man spoke huskily. He had a slight Scotch accent.

"It's a knock-out, isn't it," said Joe, boisterously, "if a doctor goes round croaking with a cold. Looks bad for the patients, doesn't it?"

The young doctor looked at him slowly.

"Anything the matter with *you*, then?" he asked sarcastically.

"Not as I know of. Damn your eyes, I hope not. Why?"

"I thought you were very concerned about the patients, wondered if you might be one yourself."

"Damn it, no, I've never been patient to no flaming doctor, and hope I never shall be," returned Joe.

At this point Mabel rose from the table, and they all seemed to become aware of her existence. She began putting the dishes together. The young doctor looked at her, but did not address her. He had not greeted her. She went out of the room with the tray, her face impassive and unchanged.

"When are you off then, all of you?" asked the doctor.

"I'm catching the eleven-forty," replied Malcolm. "Are you goin' down wi' th' trap, Joe?"

"Yes, I've told you I'm going down wi' th' trap, haven't I?"

"We'd better be getting her in then. So long, Jack, if I don't see you before I go," said Malcolm, shaking hands.

He went out, followed by Joe, who seemed to have his tail between his legs.

"Well, this is the devil's own," exclaimed the doctor, when he was left alone with Fred Henry. "Going before Wednesday, are you?"

"That's the orders," replied the other.

"Where, to Northampton?"

"That's it."

"The devil!" exclaimed Fergusson, with quiet chagrin.

And there was silence between the two.

"All settled up, are you?" asked Fergusson.

"About."

There was another pause.

"Well, I shall miss yer, Freddy, boy," said the young doctor.

"And I shall miss thee, Jack," returned the other.

"Miss you like hell," mused the doctor.

Fred Henry turned aside. There was nothing to say. Mabel came in again, to finish clearing the table.

"What are *you* going to do, then, Miss Pervin?" asked Fergusson. "Going to your sister's, are you?"

Mabel looked at him with her steady, dangerous eyes, that always made him uncomfortable, unsettling his superficial ease.

"No," she said.

"Well, what in the name of fortune *are* you going to do? Say what you mean to do," cried Fred Henry, with futile intensity.

But she only averted her head, and continued her work. She folded the white table-cloth, and put on the chenille cloth.

"The sulkiest bitch that ever trod!" muttered her brother.

But she finished her task with perfectly impassive face, the young doctor watching her interestedly all the while. Then she went out.

Fred Henry stared after her, clenching his lips, his blue eyes fixing in sharp antagonism, as he made a grimace of sour exasperation.

"You could bray her into bits, and that's all you'd get out of her," he said in a small, narrowed tone.

The doctor smiled faintly.

"What's she *going* to do, then?" he asked.

"Strike me if *I* know!" returned the other.

There was a pause. Then the doctor stirred.

"I'll be seeing you to-night, shall I?" he said to his friend.

"Ay—where's it to be? Are we going over to Jessdale?"

"I don't know. I've got a cold on me. I'll come round to the Moon and Stars, anyway."

"Let Lizzie and May miss their night for once, eh?"

"That's it—if I feel as I do now."

"All's one—"

The two young men went through the passage and down to the back door together. The house was large, but it was servantless now, and desolate. At the back was a small bricked house-yard, and beyond that a big square, gravelled fine and red, and having stables on two sides. Sloping, dank, winter-dark fields stretched away on the open sides.

But the stables were empty. Joseph Pervin, the father of the family, had been a man of no education, who had become a fairly large horse dealer. The stables had been full of horses, there was a great turmoil and come-and-go of horses and of dealers and grooms. Then the kitchen was full of servants. But of late things had declined. The old man had married a second time, to retrieve his fortunes. Now he was dead and everything was gone to the dogs, there was nothing but debt and threatening.

For months, Mabel had been servantless in the big house, keeping the home together in penury for her ineffectual brothers. She had kept house for ten years. But previously it was with unstinted means. Then, however brutal and coarse everything was, the sense of money had kept her proud, confident. The men might be foul-mouthed, the women in the kitchen might have bad reputations, her brothers might have illegitimate children. But so long as there was money, the girl felt herself established, and brutally proud, reserved.

No company came to the house, save dealers and coarse men. Mabel had no associates of her own sex, after her sister went away. But she did not mind. She went regularly to church, she attended to her father. And she lived in the memory of her mother, who had died when she was fourteen, and whom she had loved. She had loved her father, too, in a different way, depending upon him, and feeling secure in him, until at the age of fifty-four he married again. And then she had set hard against him. Now he had died and left them all hopelessly in debt.

She had suffered badly during the period of poverty. Nothing, however, could shake the curious sullen, animal pride that dominated each member of the family. Now, for Mabel, the end had come. Still she would not cast about her. She would follow her own way just the same. She would always hold the keys of her own situation. Mindless and persistent, she endured from day to day. Why should she think? Why should she answer anybody? It was enough that this was the end, and there was no way out. She need not pass any more darkly along the main street of the small town, avoiding every eye. She need not demean herself any more, going into the shops and buying the cheapest food. This was at an end. She thought of nobody, not even of herself. Mindless and persistent, she seemed in a sort of ecstasy to be coming nearer to her fulfilment, her own glorification, approaching her dead mother, who was glorified.

In the afternoon she took a little bag, with shears and sponge and a small scrubbing brush, and went out. It was a grey, wintry day, with saddened, dark green fields and an atmosphere blackened by the smoke of foundries not far off. She went quickly, darkly along the causeway, heeding nobody, through the town to the churchyard.

There she always felt secure, as if no one could see her, although as a matter of fact she was exposed to the stare of every one who passed along under the churchyard wall. Nevertheless, once under the shadow of the great looming church, among the graves, she felt immune from the world, reserved within the thick churchyard wall as in another country.

Carefully she clipped the grass from the grave, and arranged the pinky white, small chrysanthemums in the tin cross. When this was done, she took an empty jar from a neighbouring grave, brought water, and carefully, most scrupulously sponged the marble headstone and the copping-stone.

It gave her sincere satisfaction to do this. She felt in immediate contact with the world of her mother. She took minute pains, went through the park in a state bordering on pure happiness, as if in performing this task she came into a subtle, intimate connection with her mother. For the life she followed here in the world was far less real than the world of death she inherited from her mother.

The doctor's house was just by the church. Fergusson, being a mere hired assistant, was slave to the country-side. As he hurried now to attend to the outpatients in the surgery, glancing across the graveyard with his quick eye, he saw the girl at her task at the grave. She seemed so intent and remote, it was like looking into another world. Some mystical element was touched in him. He slowed down as he walked, watching her as if spell-bound.

She lifted her eyes, feeling him looking. Their eyes met. And each looked away again at once, each feeling, in some way, found out by the other. He lifted his cap and passed on down the road. There remained distinct in his consciousness, like a vision, the memory of her face, lifted from the tombstone in the churchyard, and looking at him with slow, large, portentous eyes. It *was* portentous, her face. It seemed to mesmerize him. There was a heavy power in her eyes which laid hold of his whole being, as if he had drunk some powerful drug. He had been feeling weak and done before. Now the life came back into him, he felt delivered from his own fretted, daily self.

He finished his duties at the surgery as quickly as might be, hastily filling up the bottle of the waiting people with cheap drugs. Then, in perpetual haste, he set off again to visit several cases in another part of his round, before teatime. At all times he preferred to walk if he could, but particulary when he was not well. He fancied the motion restored him.

The afternoon was falling. It was grey, deadened, and wintry, with a slow, moist, heavy coldness sinking in and deadening all the faculties. But why should he think or notice? He hastily climbed the hill and turned across the dark green fields, following the black cinder-track. In the distance, across a shallow dip in the country, the small town was clustered like smouldering ash, a tower, a spire, a heap of low, raw, extinct houses. And on the nearest fringe of the town, sloping into the dip, was Oldmeadow, the Pervins' house. He could see the stables and the outbuildings distinctly, as they lay towards him on the slope. Well, he would not go there many more times! Another resource would be lost to him, another place gone: the only company he cared for in the alien, ugly little town he was losing. Nothing but work, drudgery, constant hastening from dwelling to dwelling among the colliers and iron-workers. It wore him out, but at the same time he had a craving for it. It was a stimulant to him to be in the homes of the working people, moving as it were through the innermost body of their life. His nerves were excited and gratified. He could come so near, into the very lives of the rough, inarticulate, powerfully emotional men and women. He grumbled, he said he hated the hellish hole. But as a matter of fact it excited him, the contact with the rough, strongly-feeling people was a stimulant applied direct to his nerves.

Below Oldmeadow, in the green, shallow, soddened hollow of fields, lay a square, deep pond. Roving across the landscape, the doctor's quick eye detected a figure in black passing through the gate of the field, down towards the pond. He looked again. It would be Mabel Pervin. His mind suddenly became alive and attentive.

Why was she going down there? He pulled up on the path on the slope above, and stood staring. He could just make sure of the small black figure moving in the hollow of the failing day. He seemed to see her in the midst of such obscurity, that he was like a clairvoyant, seeing rather with the mind's eye than with ordinary sight. Yet he could see her positively enough, whilst he kept his eye attentive. He felt, if he looked away from her, in the thick, ugly falling dusk, he would lose her altogether.

He followed her minutely as she moved, direct and intent, like something transmitted rather than stirring in voluntary activity, straight down the field towards the pond. There she stood on the bank for a moment. She never raised her head. Then she waded slowly into the water.

He stood motionless as the small black figure walked slowly and deliberately towards the centre of the pond, very slowly, gradually moving deeper into the motionless water, and still moving forward as the water got up to her breast. Then he could see her no more in the dusk of the dead afternoon.

"There!" he exclaimed. "Would you believe it?"

And he hastened straight down, running over the wet, soddened fields, pushing through the hedges, down into the depression of callous wintry obscurity. It took him several minutes to come to the pond. He stood on the bank, breathing heavily. He could see nothing. His eyes seemed to penetrate the dead water. Yes, perhaps that was the dark shadow of her black clothing beneath the surface of the water.

He slowly ventured into the pond. The bottom was deep, soft clay, he sank in, and the water clasped dead cold round his legs. As he stirred he could smell the cold, rotten clay that fouled up into the water. It was objectionable in his lungs. Still, repelled and yet not heeding, he moved deeper into the pond. The cold water rose over his thighs, over his loins, upon his abdomen. The lower part of his body was all sunk in the hideous cold element. And the bottom was so deeply soft and uncertain he was afraid of pitching with his mouth underneath. He could not swim, and was afraid.

He crouched a little, spreading his hands under the water and moving them round, trying to feel for her. The dead cold pond swayed upon his chest. He moved again, a little deeper, and again, with his hands underneath, he felt all around under the water. And he touched her clothing. But it evaded his fingers. He made a desperate effort to grasp it.

And so doing he lost his balance and went under, horribly, suffocating in the foul earthy water, struggling madly for a few moments. At last, after what seemed an eternity, he got his footing, rose again into the air and looked around. He gasped, and knew he was in the world. Then he looked at the water. She had risen near him. He grasped her clothing, and drawing her nearer, turned to take his way to land again.

He went very slowly, carefully, absorbed in the slow progress. He rose higher, climbing out of the pond. The water was now only about his legs; he was thankful, full of relief to be out of the clutches of the pond. He lifted her and staggered on to the bank, out of the horror of wet, grey clay.

He laid her down on the bank. She was quite unconscious and running with water. He made the water come from her mouth, he worked to restore her. He did not have to work very long before he could feel the breathing begin again in her; she was breathing naturally. He worked a little longer. He could feel her live beneath his hands; she was coming back. He wiped her face, wrapped her in his overcoat, looked round into the dim, dark grey world, then lifted her and staggered down the bank and across the fields.

It seemed an unthinkably long way, and his burden so heavy he felt he would never get to the house. But at last he was in the stable-yard, and then in the house-yard. He opened the door and went into the house. In the kitchen he laid her down on the hearthrug, and called. The house was empty. But the fire was burning in the grate.

Then again he kneeled to attend to her. She was breathing regularly, her eyes were wide open and as if conscious, but there seemed something missing in her look. She was conscious in herself, but unconscious of her surroundings.

He ran upstairs, took blankets from a bed, and put them before the fire to warm. Then he removed her saturated, earthy-smelling clothing, rubbed her dry with a towel, and wrapped her naked in the blankets. Then he went into the dining-room, to look for spirits. There was a little whisky. He drank a gulp himself, and put some into her mouth.

The effect was instantaneous. She looked full into his face, as if she had been seeing him for some time, and yet had only just become conscious of him.

"Dr. Fergusson?" she said.

"What?" he answered.

He was divesting himself of his coat, intending to find some dry clothing upstairs. He could not bear the smell of the dead, clayey water, and he was mortally afraid for his own health.

"What did I do?" she asked.

"Walked into the pond," he replied. He had begun to shudder like one sick, and could hardly attend to her. Her eyes remained full on him, he seemed to be going dark in his mind, looking back at her helplessly. The shuddering became quieter in him, his life came back in him, dark and unknowing, but strong again.

"Was I out of my mind?" she asked, while her eyes were fixed on him all the time.

"Maybe, for the moment," he replied. He felt quiet, because his strength had come back. The strange fretful strain had left him.

"Am I out of my mind now?" she asked.

"Are you?" he reflected a moment. "No," he answered truthfully, "I don't see that you are." He turned his face aside. He was afraid now, because he felt dazed, and felt dimly that her power was stronger than his, in this issue. And she continued to look at him fixedly all the time. "Can you tell me where I shall find some dry things to put on?" he asked.

"Did you dive into the pond for me?" she asked.

"No," he answered. "I walked in. But I went in overhead as well."

There was silence for a moment. He hesitated. He very much wanted to go upstairs to get into dry clothing. But there was another desire in him. And she seemed to hold him. His will seemed to have gone to sleep, and left him, standing there slack before her. But he felt warm inside himself. He did not shudder at all, though his clothes were sodden on him.

"Why did you?" she asked.

"Because I didn't want you to do such a foolish thing," he said.

"It wasn't foolish," she said, still gazing at him as she lay on the floor, with a soft cushion under her head. "It was the right thing to do. I knew best, then."

"I'll go and shift these wet things," he said. But still he had not the power to move out of her presence, until she sent him. It was as if she had the life of his body in her hands, and he could not extricate himself. Or perhaps he did not want to.

Suddenly she sat up. Then she became aware of her own immediate condition. She felt the blankets about her, she knew her own limbs. For a moment it seemed as if her reason were going. She looked round, with wild eye, as if seeking something. He stood still with fear. She saw her clothing lying scattered.

"Who undressed me?" she asked, her eyes resting full and inevitable on his face.

"I did," he replied, "to bring you round."

For some moments she sat and gazed at him awfully, her lips parted.

"Do you love me, then?" she asked.

He only stood and stared at her, fascinated. His soul seemed to melt.

She shuffled forward on her knees, and put her arms round him, round his legs, as he stood there, pressing her breasts against his knees and thighs, clutching him with strange, convulsive certainty, pressing his thighs against her, drawing him to her face, her throat, as she looked up at him with flaring, humble eyes of transfiguration, triumphant in first possession.

"You love me," she murmured, in strange transport, yearning and triumphant and confident. "You love me. I know you love me, I know."

And she was passionately kissing his knees, through the wet clothing, passionately and indiscriminately kissing his knees, his legs, as if unaware of everything.

He looked down at the tangled wet hair, the wild, bare, animal shoulders. He was amazed, bewildered, and afraid. He had never thought of loving her. He had never wanted to love her. When he rescued her and restored her, he was a doctor, and she was a patient. He had had no single personal thought of her. Nay, this introduction of the personal element was very distasteful to him, a violation of his professional honour. It was horrible to have her there embracing his knees. It was horrible. He revolted from it, violently. And yet—and yet—he had not the power to break away.

She looked at him again, with the same supplication of powerful love, and that same transcendent, frightening light of triumph. In view of the delicate flame which seemed to come from her face like a light, he was powerless. And yet he had never intended to love her. He had never intended. And something stubborn in him could not give way.

"You love me," she repeated, in a murmur of deep, rhapsodic assurance. "You love me."

Her hands were drawing him, drawing him down to her. He was afraid, even a little horrified. For he had, really, no intention of loving her. Yet her hands were drawing him towards her. He put out his hand quickly to steady himself, and grasped her bare shoulder. A flame seemed to burn the hand that grasped her soft shoulder. He had no intention of loving her: his whole will was against his yielding. It was horrible. And yet wonderful was the touch of her shoulders, beautiful the shining of her face. Was she perhaps mad? He had a horror of yielding to her. Yet something in him ached also.

He had been staring away at the door, away from her. But his hand remained on her shoulder. She had gone suddenly very still. He looked down at her. Her eyes were now wide with fear, with doubt, the light was dying from her face, a shadow of terrible greyness was returning. He could not bear the touch of her eyes' question upon him, and the look of death behind the question.

With an inward groan he gave way, and let his heart yield towards her. A sudden gentle smile came on his face. And her eyes, which never left his face, slowly, slowly filled with tears. He watched the strange water rise in her eyes, like some slow fountain coming up. And his heart seemed to burn and melt away in his breast.

He could not bear to look at her any more. He dropped on his knees and caught her head with his arms and pressed her face against his throat. She was very still. His heart, which seemed to have broken, was burning with a kind of agony in his breast. And he felt her slow, hot tears wetting his throat. But he could not move.

He felt the hot tears wet his neck and the hollows of his neck, and he remained motionless, suspended through one of man's eternities. Only now it had become indispensable to him to have her face pressed close to him; he could never let her go again. He could never let her head go away from the close clutch of his arm. He wanted to remain like that for ever, with his heart hurting him in a pain that was also life to him. Without knowing, he was looking down on her damp, soft brown hair.

Then, as it were suddenly, he smelt the horrid stagnant smell of that water. And at the same moment she drew away from him and looked at him. Her eyes were wistful and unfathomable. He was afraid of them, and he fell to kissing her, not knowing what he was doing. He wanted her eyes not to have that terrible, wistful, unfathomable look.

When she turned her face to him again, a faint delicate flush was glowing, and there was again dawning that terrible shining of joy in her eyes, which really terrified him, and yet which he now wanted to see, because he feared the look of doubt still more.

"You love me?" she said, rather faltering.

"Yes." The word cost him a painful effort. Not because it wasn't true. But because it was too newly true, the *saying* seemed to tear open again his newly-torn heart. And he hardly wanted it to be true, even now.

She lifted her face to him, and he bent forward and kissed her on the mouth, gently, with the one kiss that is an eternal pledge. And as he kissed her his heart strained again in his breast. He never intended to love her. But now it was over. He had crossed over the gulf to her, and all that he had left behind had shrivelled and become void.

After the kiss, her eyes again slowly filled with tears. She sat still, away from him, with her face drooped aside, and her hands folded in her lap. The tears fell very slowly. There was complete silence. He too sat there motionless and silent on the hearthrug. The strange pain of his heart that was broken seemed to consume him. That he should love her? That this was love! That he should be ripped open in this way! Him, a doctor! How they would all jeer if they knew! It was agony to him to think they might know.

In the curious naked pain of the thought he looked again to her. She was sitting there drooped into a muse. He saw a tear fall, and his heart flared hot. He saw for the first time that one of her shoulders was quite uncovered, one arm bare, he could see one of her small breasts; dimly, because it had become almost dark in the room.

"Why are you crying?" he asked, in an altered voice.

She looked up at him, and behind her tears the consciousness of her situation for the first time brought a dark look of shame to her eyes.

"I'm not crying really," she said, watching him half frightened.

He reached his hand, and softly closed it on her bare arm.

"I love you! I love you!" he said in a soft, low vibrating voice, unlike himself.

She shrank, and dropped her head. The soft, penetrating grip of his hand on her arm distressed her. She looked up at him.

"I want to go," she said. "I want to go and get you some dry things."

"Why?" he said. "I'm all right."

"But I want to go," she said. "And I want you to change your things."

He released her arm, and she wrapped herself in the blanket, looking at him rather frightened. And still she did not rise.

"Kiss me," she said wistfully.

He kissed her, but briefly, half in anger.

Then, after a second, she rose nervously, all mixed up in the blanket. He watched her in her confusion, as she tried to extricate herself and wrap herself up so that she could walk. He watched her relentlessly, as she knew. And as she went, the blanket trailing, and as he saw a glimpse of her feet and her white leg, he tried to remember her as she was when he had wrapped her in the blanket. But then he didn't want to remember, because she had been nothing to him then, and his nature revolted from remembering her as she was when she was nothing to him.

A tumbling, muffled noise from within the dark house startled him. Then he heard her voice:—"There are clothes." He rose and went to the foot of the stairs, and gathered up the garments she had thrown down. Then he came back to the fire, to rub himself down and dress. He grinned at his own appearance when he had finished.

The fire was sinking, so he put on coal. The house was now quite dark, save for the light of a street-lamp that shone in faintly from beyond the holly trees. He lit the gas with matches he found on the mantelpiece. Then he emptied the pockets of his own clothes, and threw all his wet things in a heap into the scullery. After which he gathered up her sodden clothes, gently, and put them in a separate heap on the copper-top in the scullery.

It was six o'clock on the clock. His own watch had stopped. He ought to go back to the surgery. He waited, and still she did not come down. So he went to the foot of the stairs and called:

"I shall have to go."

Almost immediately he heard her coming down. She had on her best dress of black voile, and her hair was tidy, but still damp. She looked at him—and in spite of herself, smiled.

"I don't like you in those clothes," she said.

"Do I look a sight?" he answered.

They were shy of one another.

"I'll make you some tea," she said.

"No, I must go."

"Must you?" And she looked at him again with the wide, strained, doubtful eyes. And again, from the pain of his breast, he knew how he loved her. He went and bent to kiss her, gently, passionately, with his heart's painful kiss.

"And my hair smells so horrible," she murmured in distraction. "And I'm so awful, I'm so awful! Oh, no, I'm too awful." And she broke into bitter, heart-broken sobbing. "You can't want to love me, I'm horrible."

"Don't be silly, don't be silly," he said, trying to comfort her, kissing her, holding her in his arms. "I want you, I want to marry you, we're going to be married, quickly, quickly—tomorrow if I can."

But she only sobbed terribly, and cried:

"I feel awful. I feel awful. I feel I'm horrible to you."

"No, I want you, I want you," was all he answered, blindly, with that terrible intonation which frightened her almost more than her horror lest he should *not* want her.

STUDY QUESTIONS

1. This story is told by what would be termed a generally omniscient narrator. But is the narrator's omniscience the same for all the characters? How is the narrator's knowledge of Mabel different in quality, in degree, from his knowledge of Jack Fergusson? What kind of intimate knowledge of Mabel does the narrator have? What kind of intimate knowledge of Jack does the narrator have?

2. Lawrence has often been cited for his "cinematic style." As you reread the story, look for illustrations of various "camera shots" such as close-ups, long shots, pans, fades, and cuts in the narrator's observations and reportings of scenes. What would these suggest to you about possible techniques for demonstrating this narrator's manner?

3. Notice the narrator's use of "scene," "summary," and "description"[11] in the story. How does the use of these techniques provide the rhythm in the story? How does it affect the focus of action in the story?

[11] *Scene, summary, and description:* terms referring to the relationship between actual time and story time, according to Phyllis Bentley in *Some Observations on the Art of the Narrative* (New York: Macmillan, 1947). "Scene" refers to a one-to-one relationship between actual time and story time; that is, the same amount of time is required for an action to occur as for that action to be related in the story. A dialogue exchange is an example of scene. "Summary" refers to a temporal relationship in which it takes less time to relate an action or set of actions than it takes for that action to occur. Time is "speeded up" in summary. A one-paragraph explanation of the twenty-five-year history of a family would provide an illustration of summary. When a writer employs "description," he either slows down or stops time in the action of the story; that is, the temporal relationship is such that story time is longer than actual time. Description would occur, for example, when a writer closes in on a setting and stops the temporal movement of the story in order to point out the particular details of the setting.

4. What is the narrator's *particular* function in the scene between Mabel and Jack in Mabel's house after the rescue from the pond? With this question in mind, notice, for example, the paragraph beginning, "He looked down at the tangled wet hair . . ." This paragraph, as well as most of the scene, is reported in the narrator's voice. Yet, you are, through the narrator, in direct contact with Fergusson's mental operations. Additionally, the paragraph seems to imply that *two* people are engaged in a verbal exchange. Otherwise, to whom and for what reason is Jack—or the narrator—obliged to reply, "Nay"? Try reading the paragraph with a questioning and answering inflection in alternate sentences. What does this suggest to you about the function of the narrator? How does it help illuminate Fergusson's dilemma?

5. How does symbolism function in this story? What is the purpose of the pond scene? Is it simply realistic, or is it a multilevel realistic and symbolic scene that serves as a key to what the story is about?

6. How would an understanding of Lawrence's ideas about the relationship between men and women help clarify and enrich your understanding of this story? Consider undertaking a project in which you explore these attitudes of Lawrence's (as evidenced in his fiction as well as in his poetry and essays) through a composite demonstration, a written analysis, or both.

7. You will notice that there are many tensions within this story. Do these tensions seem to come primarily from Mabel? from Fergusson? from the narrator? from all three? Identify the particular tensions as clearly as possible and indicate how they vary from one character to another and from one scene to another. How could you demonstrate the degrees and kinds of tensions operating in the various characters and scenes?

Flannery O'Connor/Everything That Rises Must Converge

born 1925

Her doctor had told Julian's mother that she must lose twenty pounds on account of her blood pressure, so on Wednesday nights Julian had to take her downtown on the bus for a reducing class at the Y. The reducing class was designed for working girls over fifty, who weighed from 165 to 200 pounds. His mother was one of the slimmer ones, but she said ladies did not tell their age or weight. She would not ride on the buses by herself at night since they had been integrated, and because the reducing class was one of her few pleasures, necessary for her health, and *free,* she said Julian could at least put himself out to take her, considering all she did for him. Julian did not like to consider all she did for him, but every Wednesday night he braced himself and took her.

She was almost ready to go, standing before the hall mirror, putting on her hat, while he, his hands behind him, appeared pinned to the door frame, waiting like Saint Sebastian for the arrows to begin piercing him.

The hat was new and had cost her seven dollars and a half. She kept saying, "Maybe I shouldn't have paid that for it. No, I shouldn't have. I'll take it off and return it tomorrow. I shouldn't have bought it."

Julian raised his eyes to heaven. "Yes, you should have bought it," he said. "Put it on and let's go." It was a hideous hat. A purple velvet flap came down on one side of it and stood up on the other; the rest of it was green and looked like a cushion with the stuffing out. He decided it was less comical than jaunty and pathetic. Everything that gave her pleasure was small and depressed him.

She lifted the hat one more time and set it down slowly on top of her head. Two wings of gray hair protruded on either side of her florid face, but her eyes, sky-blue, were as innocent and untouched by experience as they must have been when she was ten. Were it not that she was a widow who had struggled fiercely to feed and clothe and put him through school and who was supporting him still, "until he got on his feet," she might have been a little girl that he had to take to town.

"It's all right, it's all right," he said. "Let's go." He opened the door himself and started down the walk to get her going. The sky was a dying violet and the houses stood out darkly against it, bulbous liver-colored monstrosities of a uniform ugliness though no two were alike. Since this had been a fashionable neighborhood forty years ago, his mother persisted in thinking they did well to have an apartment in it. Each house had a narrow collar of dirt around it in which sat, usually, a grubby child. Julian walked with his hands in his pockets, his head down and thrust forward and his eyes glazed with the determination to make himself completely numb during the time he would be sacrificed to her pleasure.

The door closed and he turned to find the dumpy figure, surmounted by the atrocious hat, coming toward him. "Well," she said, "you only live once and paying a little more for it, I at least won't meet myself coming and going."

"Some day I'll start making money," Julian said gloomily—he knew he never would—"and you can have one of those jokes whenever you take the fit." But first they would move. He visualized a place where the nearest neighbors would be three miles away on either side.

"I think you're doing fine," she said, drawing on her gloves. "You've only been out of school a year. Rome wasn't built in a day."

She was one of the few members of the Y reducing class who arrived in hat and gloves and who had a son who had been to college. "It takes time," she said, "and the world is in such a mess. This hat looked better on me than any of the others, though when she brought it out I said, 'Take that thing back. I wouldn't have it on my head,' and she said, 'Now wait till you see it on,' and when she put it on me, I said, 'We-ull,' and she said, 'If you ask me, that hat does something for you and you do something for the hat, and besides,' she said, 'with that hat, you won't meet yourself coming and going.' "

Julian thought he could have stood his lot better if she had been selfish, if she had been an old hag who drank and screamed at him. He walked along, saturated in depression, as if in the midst of his martyrdom he had lost his faith. Catching sight of his long, hopeless, irritated face, she stopped suddenly with a grief-stricken look, and pulled back on his arm. "Wait on me," she said. "I'm going back to the house and take this thing off and tomorrow I'm going to return it. I was out of my head. I can pay the gas bill with that seven-fifty."

He caught her arm in a vicious grip. "You are not going to take it back," he said. "I like it."

"Well," she said, "I don't think I ought . . ."

"Shut up and enjoy it," he muttered, more depressed than ever.

"With the world in the mess it's in," she said, "it's a wonder we can enjoy anything. I tell you, the bottom rail is on the top."

Julian sighed.

"Of course," she said, "if you know who you are, you can go anywhere." She said this every time he took her to the reducing class. "Most of them in it are not our kind of people," she said, "but I can be gracious to anybody. I know who I am."

"They don't give a damn for your graciousness," Julian said savagely. "Knowing who you are is good for one generation only. You haven't the foggiest idea where you stand now or who you are."

She stopped and allowed her eyes to flash at him. "I most certainly do know who I am," she said, "and if you don't know who you are, I'm ashamed of you."

"Oh hell," Julian said.

"Your great-grandfather was a former governor of this state," she said. "Your grandfather was a prosperous landowner. Your grandmother was a Godhigh."

"Will you look around you," he said tensely, "and see where you are now?" and he swept his arm jerkily out to indicate the neighborhood, which the growing darkness at least made less dingy.

"You remain what you are," she said. "Your great-grandfather had a plantation and two hundred slaves."

"There are no more slaves," he said irritably.

"They were better off when they were," she said. He groaned to see that she was off on that topic. She rolled onto it every few days like a train on an open track. He knew every stop, every junction, every swamp along the way, and knew the exact point at which her conclusion would roll majestically into the station: "It's ridiculous. It's simply not realistic. They should rise, yes, but on their own side of the fence."

"Let's skip it," Julian said.

"The ones I feel sorry for," she said, "are the ones that are half white. They're tragic."

"Will you skip it?"

"Suppose we were half white. We would certainly have mixed feelings."

"I have mixed feelings now," he groaned.

"Well let's talk about something pleasant," she said. "I remember going to Grandpa's when I was a little girl. Then the house had double stairways that went up to what was really the second floor—all the cooking was done on the first. I used to like to stay down in the kitchen on account of the way the walls smelled. I would sit with my nose pressed against the plaster and take deep breaths. Actually the place belonged to the Godhighs but your grandfather Chestny paid the mortgage and saved it for them. They were in reduced circumstances," she said, "but reduced or not, they never forgot who they were."

"Doubtless that decayed mansion reminded them," Julian muttered. He never spoke of it without contempt or thought of it without longing. He had seen it once when he was a child before it had been sold. The double stairways had rotted and been torn down. Negroes were living in it. But it remained in his mind as his mother had known it. It appeared in his dreams regularly. He would stand on the wide porch, listening to the rustle of oak leaves, then wander through the high-ceilinged hall into the parlor that opened onto it and gaze at the worn rugs and faded draperies. It occurred to him that it was he, not she, who could have appreciated it. He preferred its threadbare elegance to anything he could name and it was because of it that all the neighborhoods they had lived in had been a torment to him—whereas she had hardly known the difference. She called her insensitivity "being adjustable."

"And I remember the old darky who was my nurse, Caroline. There was no better person in the world. I've always had a great respect for my colored friends," she said. "I'd do anything in the world for them and they'd . . ."

"Will you for God's sake get off that subject?" Julian said. When he got on a bus by himself, he made it a point to sit down beside a Negro, in reparation as it were for his mother's sins.

"You're mighty touchy tonight," she said. "Do you feel all right?"

"Yes I feel all right," he said. "Now lay off."

She pursed her lips. "Well, you certainly are in a vile humor," she observed. "I just won't speak to you at all."

They had reached the bus stop. There was no bus in sight and Julian, his hands still jammed in his pockets and his head thrust forward, scowled down the empty street. The frustration of having to wait on the bus as well as ride on it began to creep up his neck like a hot hand. The presence of his mother was borne in upon him as she gave a pained sigh. He looked at her bleakly. She was holding herself very erect under the preposterous hat, wearing it like a banner of her imaginary dignity. There was in him an evil urge to break her spirit. He suddenly unloosened his tie and pulled it off and put it in his pocket.

She stiffened. "Why must you look like *that* when you take me to town?" she said. "Why must you deliberately embarrass me?"

"If you'll never learn where you are," he said, "you can at least learn where I am."

"You look like a—thug," she said.

"Then I must be one," he murmured.

"I'll just go home," she said. "I will not bother you. If you can't do a little thing like that for me . . ."

Rolling his eyes upward, he put his tie back on. "Restored to my class," he muttered. He thrust his face toward her and hissed, "True culture is in the mind, the *mind*," he said, and tapped his head, "the mind."

"It's in the heart," she said, "and in how you do things and how you do things is because of who you *are*."

"Nobody in the damn bus cares who you are."

"I care who I am," she said icily.

The lighted bus appeared on top of the next hill and as it approached, they moved out into the street to meet it. He put his hand under her elbow and hoisted her up on the creaking step. She entered with a little smile, as if she were going into a drawing room where everyone had been waiting for her. While he put in the tokens, she sat down on one of the broad front seats for three which faced the aisle. A thin woman with protruding teeth and long yellow hair was sitting on the end of it. His mother moved up beside her and left room for Julian beside herself. He sat down and looked at the floor across the aisle where a pair of thin feet in red and white canvas sandals were planted.

His mother immediately began a general conversation meant to attract anyone who felt like talking. "Can it get any hotter?" she said and removed from her purse a folding fan, black with a Japanese scene on it, which she began to flutter before her.

"I reckon it might could," the woman with the protruding teeth said, "but I know for a fact my apartment couldn't get no hotter."

"It must get the afternoon sun," his mother said. She sat forward and looked up and down the bus. It was half filled. Everybody was white. "I see we have the bus to ourselves," she said. Julian cringed.

"For a change," said the woman across the aisle, the owner of the red and white canvas sandals. "I come on one the other day and they were thick as fleas—up front and all through."

"The world is in a mess everywhere," his mother said. "I don't know how we've let it get in this fix."

"What gets my goat is all those boys from good families stealing automobile tires," the woman with the protruding teeth said. "I told my boy, I said you may not be rich but you been raised right and if I ever catch you in any such mess, they can send you on to the reformatory. Be exactly where you belong."

"Training tells," his mother said. "Is your boy in high school?"

"Ninth grade," the woman said.

"My son just finished college last year. He wants to write but he's selling typewriters until he gets started," his mother said.

The woman leaned forward and peered at Julian. He threw her such a malevolent look that she subsided against the seat. On the floor across the aisle there was an abandoned newspaper. He got up and got it and opened it out in front of him. His mother discreetly continued the conversation in a lower tone but the woman across the aisle said in a loud voice, "Well that's nice. Selling typewriters is close to writing. He can go right from one to the other."

"I tell him," his mother said, "that Rome wasn't built in a day."

Behind the newspaper Julian was withdrawing into the inner compartment of his mind where he spent most of his time. This was a kind of mental bubble in which he established himself when he could not bear to be a part of what was going on around him. From it he could see out and judge but in it he was safe from any kind of penetration from without. It was the only place where he felt free of the general idiocy of his fellows. His mother had never entered it but from it he could see her with absolute clarity.

The old lady was clever enough and he thought that if she had started from any of the right premises, more might have been expected of her. She lived according to the laws of her own fantasy world, outside of which he had never seen her set foot. The law of it was to sacrifice herself for him after she had first created the necessity to do so by making a mess of things. If he had permitted her sacrifices, it was only because her lack of foresight had made them necessary. All of her life had been a struggle to act like a Chestny without the Chestny goods, and to give him everything she thought a Chestny ought to have; but since, said she, it was fun to struggle, why complain? And when you had won, as she had won, what fun to look back on the hard times! He could not forgive her that she had enjoyed the struggle and that she thought *she* had won.

What she meant when she said she had won was that she had brought him up successfully and had sent him to college and that he had turned out so well—good looking (her teeth had gone unfilled so that his could be straightened), intelligent (he realized he was too intelligent to be a success), and with a future ahead of him (there was of course no future ahead of him). She excused his gloominess on the grounds that he was still growing up and his radical ideas on his lack of practical experience.

She said he didn't yet know a thing about "life," that he hadn't even entered the real world—when already he was as disenchanted with it as a man of fifty.

The further irony of all this was that in spite of her, he had turned out so well. In spite of going to only a third-rate college, he had, on his own initiative, come out with a first-rate education; in spite of growing up dominated by a small mind, he had ended up with a large one; in spite of all her foolish views, he was free of prejudice and unafraid to face facts. Most miraculous of all, instead of being blinded by love for her as she was for him, he had cut himself emotionally free of her and could see her with complete objectivity. He was not dominated by his mother.

The bus stopped with a sudden jerk and shook him from his meditation. A woman from the back lurched forward with little steps and barely escaped falling in his newspaper as she righted herself. She got off and a large Negro got on. Julian kept his paper lowered to watch. It gave him a certain satisfaction to see injustice in daily operation. It confirmed his view that with a few exceptions there was no one worth knowing within a radius of three hundred miles. The Negro was well dressed and carried a briefcase. He looked around and then sat down on the other end of the seat where the woman with the red and white canvas sandals was sitting. He immediately unfolded a newspaper and obscured himself behind it. Julian's mother's elbow at once prodded insistently into his ribs. "Now you see why I won't ride on these buses by myself," she whispered.

The woman with the red and white canvas sandals had risen at the same time the Negro sat down and had gone further back in the bus and taken the seat of the woman who had got off. His mother leaned forward and cast her an approving look.

Julian rose, crossed the aisle, and sat down in the place of the woman with the canvas sandals. From this position, he looked serenely across at his mother. Her face had turned an angry red. He stared at her, making his eyes the eyes of a stranger. He felt his tension suddenly lift as if he had openly declared war on her.

He would have liked to get in conversation with the Negro and to talk with him about art or politics or any subject that would be above the comprehension of those around them, but the man remained entrenched behind his paper. He was either ignoring the change of seating or had never noticed it. There was no way for Julian to convey his sympathy.

His mother kept her eyes fixed reproachfully on his face. The woman with the protruding teeth was looking at him avidly as if he were a type of monster new to her.

"Do you have a light?" he asked the Negro.

Without looking away from his paper, the man reached in his pocket and handed him a packet of matches.

"Thanks," Julian said. For a moment he held the matches foolishly. A

NO SMOKING sign looked down upon him from over the door. This alone would not have deterred him; he had no cigarettes. He had quit smoking some months before because he could not afford it. "Sorry," he muttered and handed back the matches. The Negro lowered the paper and gave him an annoyed look. He took the matches and raised the paper again.

His mother continued to gaze at him but she did not take advantage of his momentary discomfort. Her eyes retained their battered look. Her face seemed to be unnaturally red, as if her blood pressure had risen. Julian allowed no glimmer of sympathy to show on his face. Having got the advantage, he wanted desperately to keep it and carry it through. He would have liked to teach her a lesson that would last her a while, but there seemed no way to continue the point. The Negro refused to come out from behind his paper.

Julian folded his arms and looked stolidly before him, facing her but as if he did not see her, as if he had ceased to recognize her existence. He visualized a scene in which, the bus having reached their stop, he would remain in his seat and when she said, "Aren't you going to get off?" he would look at her as at a stranger who had rashly addressed him. The corner they got off on was usually deserted, but it was well lighted and it would not hurt her to walk by herself the four blocks to the Y. He decided to wait until the time came and then decide whether or not he would let her get off by herself. He would have to be at the Y at ten to bring her back, but he could leave her wondering if he was going to show up. There was no reason for her to think she could always depend on him.

He retired again into the high-ceilinged room sparsely settled with large pieces of antique furniture. His soul expanded momentarily but then he became aware of his mother across from him and the vision shriveled. He studied her coldly. Her feet in little pumps dangled like a child's and did not quite reach the floor. She was training on him an exaggerated look of reproach. He felt completely detached from her. At that moment he could with pleasure have slapped her as he would have slapped a particularly obnoxious child in his charge.

He began to imagine various unlikely ways by which he could teach her a lesson. He might make friends with some distinguished Negro professor or lawyer and bring him home to spend the evening. He would be entirely justified but her blood pressure would rise to 300. He could not push her to the extent of making her have a stroke, and moreover, he had never been successful at making any Negro friends. He had tried to strike up an acquaintance on the bus with some of the better types, with ones that looked like professors or ministers or lawyers. One morning he had sat down next to a distinguished-looking dark brown man who had answered his questions with a sonorous solemnity but who had turned out to be an undertaker. Another day he had sat down beside a cigar-smoking Negro with a diamond ring on his finger, but after a few stilted pleasantries, the

Negro had rung the buzzer and risen, slipping two lottery tickets into Julian's hand as he climbed over him to leave.

He imagined his mother lying desperately ill and his being able to secure only a Negro doctor for her. He toyed with that idea for a few minutes and then dropped it for a momentary vision of himself participating as a sympathizer in a sit-in demonstration. This was possible but he did not linger with it. Instead, he approached the ultimate horror. He brought home a beautiful suspiciously Negroid woman. Prepare yourself, he said. There is nothing you can do about it. This is the woman I've chosen. She's intelligent, dignified, even good, and she's suffered and she hasn't thought it *fun*. Now persecute us, go ahead and persecute us. Drive her out of here, but remember, you're driving me too. His eyes were narrowed and through the indignation he had generated, he saw his mother across the aisle, purple-faced, shrunken to the dwarf-like proportions of her moral nature, sitting like a mummy beneath the ridiculous banner of her hat.

He was tilted out of his fantasy again as the bus stopped. The door opened with a sucking hiss and out of the dark a large, gaily dressed, sullen-looking colored woman got on with a little boy. The child, who might have been four, had on a short plaid suit and a Tyrolean hat with a blue feather in it. Julian hoped that he would sit down beside him and that the woman would push in beside his mother. He could think of no better arrangement.

As she waited for her tokens, the woman was surveying the seating possibilities—he hoped with the idea of sitting where she was least wanted. There was something familiar-looking about her but Julian could not place what it was. She was a giant of a woman. Her face was set not only to meet opposition but to seek it out. The downward tilt of her large lower lip was like a warning sign: DON'T TAMPER WITH ME. Her bulging figure was encased in a green crepe dress and her feet overflowed in red shoes. She had on a hideous hat. A purple velvet flap came down on one side of it and stood up on the other; the rest of it was green and looked like a cushion with the stuffing out. She carried a mammoth red pocketbook that bulged throughout as if it were stuffed with rocks.

To Julian's disappointment, the little boy climbed up on the empty seat beside his mother. His mother lumped all children, black and white, into the common category, "cute," and she thought little Negroes were on the whole cuter than little white children. She smiled at the little boy as he climbed on the seat.

Meanwhile the woman was bearing down upon the empty seat beside Julian. To his annoyance, she squeezed herself into it. He saw his mother's face change as the woman settled herself next to him and he realized with satisfaction that this was more objectionable to her than it was to him. Her face seemed almost gray and there was a look of dull recognition in her eyes, as if suddenly she had sickened at some awful confrontation. Julian saw that it was because she and the woman had, in a sense, swapped sons. Though his mother would not realize the symbolic significance of this, she would feel it. His amusement showed plainly on his face.

The woman next to him muttered something unintelligible to herself. He was conscious of a kind of bristling next to him, a muted growling like that of an angry cat. He could not see anything but the red pocketbook upright on the bulging green thighs. He visualized the woman as she had stood waiting for her tokens—the ponderous figure, rising from the red shoes upward over the solid hips, the mammoth bosom, the haughty face, to the green and purple hat.

His eyes widened.

The vision of the two hats, identical, broke upon him with the radiance of a brilliant sunrise. His face was suddenly lit with joy. He could not believe that Fate had thrust upon his mother such a lesson. He gave a loud chuckle so that she would look at him and see that he saw. She turned her eyes on him slowly. The blue in them seemed to have turned a bruised purple. For a moment he had an uncomfortable sense of her innocence, but it lasted only a second before principle rescued him. Justice entitled him to laugh. His grin hardened until it said to her as plainly as if he were saying aloud: Your punishment exactly fits your pettiness. This should teach you a permanent lesson.

Her eyes shifted to the woman. She seemed unable to bear looking at him and to find the woman preferable. He became conscious again of the bristling presence at his side. The woman was rumbling like a volcano about to become active. His mother's mouth began to twitch slightly at one corner. With a sinking heart, he saw incipient signs of recovery on her face and realized that this was going to strike her suddenly as funny and was going to be no lesson at all. She kept her eyes on the woman and an amused smile came over her face as if the woman were a monkey that had stolen her hat. The little Negro was looking up at her with large fascinated eyes. He had been trying to attract her attention for some time.

"Carver!" the woman said suddenly. 'Come heah!"

When he saw that the spotlight was on him at last, Carver drew his feet up and turned himself toward Julian's mother and giggled.

"Carver!" the woman said. "You heah me? Come heah!"

Carver slid down from the seat but remained squatting with his back against the base of it, his head turned slyly around toward Julian's mother, who was smiling at him. The woman reached a hand across the aisle and snatched him to her. He righted himself and hung backwards on her knees, grinning at Julian's mother. "Isn't he cute?" Julian's mother said to the woman with the protruding teeth.

"I reckon he is," the woman said without conviction.

The Negress yanked him upright but he eased out of her grip and shot across the aisle and scrambled, giggling wildly, onto the seat beside his love.

"I think he likes me," Julian's mother said, and smiled at the woman. It was the smile she used when she was being particularly gracious to an inferior. Julian saw everything lost. The lesson had rolled off her like rain on a roof.

The woman stood up and yanked the little boy off the seat as if she were snatching him from contagion. Julian could feel the rage in her at having no weapon like his mother's smile. She gave the child a sharp slap across his leg. He howled once and then thrust his head into her stomach and kicked his feet against her shins. "Be-have," she said vehemently.

The bus stopped and the Negro who had been reading the newspaper got off. The woman moved over and set the little boy down with a thump between herself and Julian. She held him firmly by the knee. In a moment he put his hands in front of his face and peeped at Julian's mother through his fingers.

"I see yoooooooo!" she said and put her hand in front of her face and peeped at him.

The woman slapped his hand down. "Quit yo' foolishness," she said, "before I knock the living Jesus out of you!"

Julian was thankful that the next stop was theirs. He reached up and pulled the cord. The woman reached up and pulled it at the same time. Oh my God, he thought. He had the terrible intuition that when they got off the bus together, his mother would open her purse and give the little boy a nickel. The gesture would be as natural to her as breathing. The bus stopped and the woman got up and lunged to the front, dragging the child, who wished to stay on, after her. Julian and his mother got up and followed. As they neared the door, Julian tried to relieve her of her pocketbook.

"No," she murmured, "I want to give the little boy a nickel."

"No!" Julian hissed. "No!"

She smiled down at the child and opened her bag. The bus door opened and the woman picked him up by the arm and descended with him, hanging at her hip. Once in the street she set him down and shook him.

Julian's mother had to close her purse while she got down the bus step but as soon as her feet were on the ground, she opened it again and began to rummage inside. "I can't find but a penny," she whispered, "but it looks like a new one."

"Don't do it!" Julian said fiercely between his teeth. There was a streetlight on the corner and she hurried to get under it so that she could better see into her pocketbook. The woman was heading off rapidly down the street with the child still hanging backward on her hand.

"Oh little boy!" Julian's mother called and took a few quick steps and caught up with them just beyond the lamppost. "Here's a bright new penny for you," and she held out the coin, which shone bronze in the dim light.

The huge woman turned and for a moment stood, her shoulders lifted and her face frozen with frustrated rage, and stared at Julian's mother. Then all at once she seemed to explode like a piece of machinery that had been given one ounce of pressure too much. Julian saw the black fist swing out with the red pocketbook. He shut his eyes and cringed as he heard the woman shout, "He don't take nobody's pennies!" When he opened his eyes, the woman was disappearing down the street with the little boy staring wide-eyed over her shoulder. Julian's mother was sitting on the sidewalk.

"I told you not to do that," Julian said angrily. "I told you not to do that!"

He stood over her for a minute, gritting his teeth. Her legs were stretched out in front of her and her hat was on her lap. He squatted down and looked her in the face. It was totally expressionless. "You got exactly what you deserved," he said. "Now get up."

He picked up her pocketbook and put what had fallen out back in it. He picked the hat up off her lap. The penny caught his eye on the sidewalk and he picked that up and let it drop before her eyes into the purse. Then he stood up and leaned over and held his hand out to pull her up. She remained immobile. He sighed. Rising above them on either side were black apartment buildings, marked with irregular rectangles of light. At the end of the block a man came out of a door and walked off in the opposite direction. "All right," he said, "suppose somebody happens by and wants to know why you're sitting on the sidewalk?"

She took the hand and, breathing hard, pulled heavily up on it and then stood for a moment, swaying slightly as if the spots of light in the darkness were circling around her. Her eyes, shadowed and confused, finally settled on his face. He did not try to conceal his irritation. "I hope this teaches you a lesson," he said. She leaned forward and her eyes raked his face. She seemed trying to determine his identity. Then, as if she found nothing familiar about him, she started off with a headlong movement in the wrong direction.

"Aren't you going on to the Y?" he asked.

"Home," she muttered.

"Well, are we walking?"

For answer she kept going. Julian followed along, his hands behind him. He saw no reason to let the lesson she had had go without backing it up with an explanation of its meaning. She might as well be made to understand what had happened to her. "Don't think that was just an uppity Negro woman," he said. "That was the whole colored race which will no longer take your condescending pennies. That was your black double. She can wear the same hat as you, and to be sure," he added gratuitously (because he thought it was funny), "it looked better on her than it did on you. What all this means," he said, "is that the old world is gone. The old manners are obsolete and your graciousness is not worth a damn." He thought bitterly of the house that had been lost for him. "You aren't who you think you are," he said.

She continued to plow ahead, paying no attention to him. Her hair had come undone on one side. She dropped her pocketbook and took no notice. He stooped and picked it up and handed it to her but she did not take it.

"You needn't act as if the world has come to an end," he said, "because it hasn't. From now on you've got to live in a new world and face a few realities for a change. Buck up," he said, "it won't kill you."

She was breathing fast.

"Let's wait on the bus," he said.

"Home," she said thickly.

"I hate to see you behave like this," he said. "Just like a child. I should be able to expect more of you." He decided to stop where he was and make her stop and wait for a bus. "I'm not going any farther," he said, stopping. "We're going on the bus."

She continued to go on as if she had not heard him. He took a few steps and caught her arm and stopped her. He looked into her face and caught his breath. He was looking into a face he had never seen before. "Tell Grandpa to come get me," she said.

He stared, stricken.

"Tell Caroline to come get me," she said.

Stunned, he let her go and she lurched forward again, walking as if one leg were shorter than the other. A tide of darkness seemed to be sweeping her from him. "Mother!" he cried. "Darling, sweetheart, wait!" Crumpling, she fell to the pavement. He dashed forward and fell at her side, crying, "Mamma, Mamma!" He turned her over. Her face was fiercely distorted. One eye, large and staring, moved slightly to the left as if it had become unmoored. The other remained fixed on him, raked his face again, found nothing and closed.

"Wait here, wait here!" he cried and jumped up and began to run for help toward a cluster of lights he saw in the distance ahead of him. "Help, help!" he shouted, but his voice was thin, scarcely a thread of sound. The lights drifted farther away the faster he ran and his feet moved numbly as if they carried him nowhere. The tide of darkness seemed to sweep him back to her, postponing from moment to moment his entry into the world of guilt and sorrow.

STUDY QUESTIONS

1. This story is told by a narrator who has limited omniscience. Most of the lines of the story are delivered entirely by the narrator; yet many of the lines for which the narrator assumes responsibility represent the perceptions of one of the characters. Try reading the story as if the narrator were completely responsible for all lines of narration. What does this tell you about the narrator's attitudes toward the characters, their social situation, and their interpersonal relationships? Now try reading all of the narration as if Julian were the narrator. How does this color the attitudes voiced in the narration? Are there some lines that perhaps reflect the attitudes of Julian's mother? How do some lines reflect conflicting attitudes of Julian and the narrator (for example, the paragraph beginning, "The further irony of all this was that in spite of her, he had turned out so well"). As you read this story aloud, try experimenting with as many of these alternatives as possible. Then try to discover how they can lead you to a fuller understanding of this story's rather complex point of view.

2. This story is an excellent illustration of how a skillful author can persuade a reader to accept or reject certain values without direct argument. How has the implied author of this story managed to exert control over her audience? What particular techniques has she used? What values are at issue in this story?

3. One of the implied author's most valuable rhetorical tools is the narrator. In this story, how does the narrator serve a rhetorical purpose? Consider particularly such questions as the relationship between Julian's attitude toward his mother (and all she represents), the narrator's attitude toward Julian and his mother, and the implied author's attitudes toward the entire situation.

4. What is the meaning of this story's title? Explore all the possible implications of the title's relationship to the story.

5. How do the images of darkness and light operate in this story? On what various levels are these images functioning?

6. Consider carefully the final paragraph of the story. What is the significance of the lights which drift away from Julian? What is the significance of the "tide of darkness," which has been mentioned earlier and which now sweeps him back to his mother? What is postponing Julian's "entry into the world of guilt and sorrow"? What is this world of guilt and sorrow to which the narrator refers? Given Julian's character, what is necessary for his entrance into such a world?

Frank London Brown/McDougal

born 1927

The bass was walking. Nothing but the bass. And the rhythm section waited, counting time with the tap of a foot or the tip of a finger against the piano top. Pro had just finished his solo and the blood in his neck was pumping so hard it made his head hurt. Sweat shone upon the brown backs of his fingers and the moisture stained the bright brass of his tenor where he held it. Jake, young eyeglass-wearing boy from Dallas, had stopped playing the drums, and he too was sweating, and slight stains were beginning to appear upon his thin cotton coat, and his dark skin caught the purple haze from the overhead spotlight and the sweat that gathered on his flat cheekbones seemed purple. Percy R. Brookins bent over the piano tapping the black keys but not hard enough to make a sound.

Everybody seemed to be waiting.

And the bass was walking. Doom-de-doom-doom-doom-doom-doom!

A tall thin white man whose black hair shone with sweat stood beside the tenorman, lanky, ginger-brown Pro.

Pro had wailed—had blown choruses that dripped with the smell of cornbread and cabbage and had roared like a late "L" and had cried like a blues singer on the last night of a good gig.

Now it was the white man's turn, right after the bass solo was over . . . and he waited and Pro waited and so did Jake the drummer, and Percy R. Brookins. Little Jug was going into his eighth chorus and showed no sign of letting up.

DOOM-DE-DOOM-DOOM-DOOM-DOOM-DOOM!

Jake looked out into the audience. And the shadowy faces were hard to see behind the bright colored lights that ringed the bandstand. Yet he felt that they too waited . . . Pro had laid down some righteous sound —he had told so much truth—told it so plainly, so passionately that it had scared everybody in the place, even Pro, and now he waited for the affirming bass to finish so that he could hear what the white man had to say.

McDougal was his name. And his young face had many wrinkles and his young body slouched and his shoulders hung round and loose. He was listening to Little Jug's bass yet he also seemed to be listening to something else, almost as if he were still listening to the truth Pro had told.

And the bass walked.

Jake leaned over his drums and whispered to Percy R. Brookins.

"That cat sure looks beat don't he?"

Percy R. Brookins nodded, and then put his hand to the side of his mouth, and whispered back.

"His old lady's pregnant again."

"Again?! What's that? Number three?"

"Number four," Percy R. Brookins answered.

"Hell I'd look sad too . . . Is he still living on Forty Seventh Street?"

The drums slid in underneath the bass and the bass dropped out amid strong applause and a few "Yeahs!" And Jake, not having realized it, cut in where McDougal was to begin his solo. He smiled sheepishly at Percy R. Brookins and the piano player hunched his shoulders and smiled.

McDougal didn't look around, he didn't move from his slouched one-sided stance, he didn't stop staring beyond the audience and beyond the room itself. Yet his left foot kept time with the light bombs the drummer dropped and the husky soft scrape of the brushes.

Little Jug pulled a handkerchief from his back pocket and wiped his cheeks and around the back of his neck, then he stared at the black, glistening back of McDougal's head and then leaned down and whispered to Percy R. Brookins.

"Your boy sure could stand a haircut. He looks as bad as Ol' Theo." And they both knew how bad Ol' Theo looked and they both frowned and laughed.

Percy R. Brookins touched a chord lightly to give some color to Jake's solo and then he said.

"Man, that cat has suffered for that brownskin woman."

Little Jug added.

"And those . . . three little brownskin crumb-crushers."

Percy R. Brookins, hit another chord and then

"Do you know none of the white folks'll rent to him now?"

Little Jug laughed.

"Why hell yes . . . will they rent to me?"

"Sure they will, down on Forty Seventh Street."

Little Jug nodded at Jake and Jake made a couple of breaks that meant that he was about to give in to McDougal.

Percy R. Brookins turned to face his piano and then he got an idea and he turned to Little Jug and spoke with a serious look behind the curious smile on his face.

"You know that cat's after us? I mean he's out to blow the real thing. You know what I mean? Like he's no Harry James? Do you know that?"

Little Jug ran into some triplets and skipped a couple of beats and brought McDougal in right on time.

At the same time McDougal rode in on a long, hollow, gut bucket note that made Percy R. Brookins laugh, and caused Pro to cock his head and rub his cheek. The tall worried looking white man bent his trumpet to the floor and hunched his shoulders and closed his eyes and blew.

Little Jug answered Percy R. Brookins' question about McDougal.

"I been knowing that . . . he knows the happenings . . . I mean about where we get it, you dig? I mean like with Leola and those kids and Forty Seventh Street and those jive landlords, you dig? The man's been burnt, Percy. Listen to that somitch—listen to him!"

McDougal's eyes were closed and he did not see the dark woman with the dark cotton suit that ballooned away from the great bulge of her stomach. He didn't see her ease into a chair at the back of the dark smoky room. He didn't see the smile on her face or the sweat upon her flat nose.

Frank London Brown/Singing Dinah's Song

born 1927

A Gypsy woman once told me. She said: "Son, beware of the song that will not leave you."

But then I've never liked Gypsy women no way, which is why I was so shook when my buddy Daddy-o did his number the other day. I mean his natural number.

You see, I work at Electronic Masters, Incorporated, and well, we don't make much at this joint although if you know how to talk to the man you might work up to a dollar and a half an hour.

Me, I work on a punch press. This thing cuts steel sheets and molds them into shells for radio and television speakers. Sometimes when I'm in some juice joint listening to Dinah Washington and trying to get myself together, I get to thinking about all that noise that that big ugly punch press makes, and me sweating and scuffing, trying to make my rates, and man I get *eeevil!*

This buddy of mine though, he really went for Dinah Washington; and even though his machine would bang and scream all over the place and all those high-speed drills would whine and cry like a bunch of sanctified soprano church-singers, this fool would be in the middle of all that commotion just singing Dinah Washington's songs to beat the band. One day I went up and asked this fool what in the world was he singing about; and he looked at me and tucked his thumbs behind his shirt collar and said: "Baby, I'm singing Dinah's songs. Ain't that broad mellow?"

Well, I. Really, all I could say was: "Uh, why yes."

And *I* went back to *my* machine.

It was one of those real hot days when it happened: about ten-thirty in the morning. I was sweating already. Me and that big ugly scoundrel punch press. Tussling. Lord, I was *so* beat. I felt like singing Dinah's songs myself. I had even started thinking in rhythm with those presses banging down on that steel: sh-bang boom bop! Sh, bang boom bop, sh'bang boom bop. Then all of a sudden:

In walks Daddy-o!

My good buddy. Sharp? You'd better believe it: dark blue single breast, a white on white shirt, and a black and yellow rep tie! Shoes shining like new money. And that pearl gray hat kinda pulled down over one eye. I mean to tell you, that Negro was sharp.

I was way behind on my quota because, you see, fooling around with those machines is *not* no play thing. You just get tired sometimes and fall behind. But I just *had* to slow down to look at my boy.

James, that was his real name. We call him Daddy-o because he's so.

I don't know; there just ain't no other name would fit him. Daddy-o's a long, tall, dark cat with hard eyes and a chin that looks like the back end of a brick. Got great big arms and a voice like ten lions. Actually, sometimes Daddy-o scares you.

He walked straight to his machine. Didn't punch his time card or nothing. I called him: "Hey, Daddy-o, you must have had a good one last night. What's happening?"

Do you know that Negro didn't open his mouth?

"Hey, Daddy-o, how come you come strolling in here at ten-thirty? We start at seven-thirty around this place!"

Still no answer.

So this cat walks over to his machine and looks it up and down and turns around and heads straight for the big boss's office. Well, naturally I think Daddy-o's getting ready to quit, so I kind of peeps around my machine so that I can see him better.

He walked to the big boss's office and stopped in front of the door and lit a cigarette smack-dab underneath the "No Smoking" sign. Then he turned around like he had changed his mind about quitting and headed back to his machine. Well, I just started back to work. After all it's none of my business if a man wants to work in his dark blue suit and a white on white shirt with his hat on.

By this time Charlie walked up just as Daddy-o started to stick his hand into the back of the machine.

Charlie liked to busted a blood vessel. "Hey, what the hell are you doing? You want to 'lectrocute yourself?"

Now I don't blame Charlie for hollering. Daddy-o knows that you can get killed sticking your hand in the back of a machine. Everybody in the plant knows that.

Daddy-o acted like he didn't hear Charlie, and he kept right on reaching into the hole. Charlie ran up and snatched Daddy-o's hand back. Daddy-o straightened up, reared back and filled his chest with a thousand pounds of air: one foot behind him and both of those oversized fists doubled up. Charlie cleared his throat and started feeling around in his smock like he was looking for something, which I don't think he was.

Pretty soon Mr. Grobber, the big boss, walked up. One of the other foremen came up and then a couple of set-up men from another department. They all stood around Daddy-o and he just stood there cool, smoking one of those long filter-tips. He started to smile, like he was bashful. But whenever anyone went near the machine, he filled up with more air and got those big ham-fists ready.

Well after all, Daddy-o was my buddy and I couldn't just let all those folk surround him without doing *some*thing, so I turned my machine off and walked over to where they were crowding around him.

"Daddy-o, what's the matter, huh? You mad at somebody, Daddy-o?"

Mr. Grobber said: "James, if you don't feel well, why don't you just go home and come in tomorrow?"

All Daddy-o did was to look slowly around the plant. He looked at each one of us. A lot of the people in the shop stopped working and were looking back at him. Others just kept on working. But he looked at them, kind of smiling, like he had a feeling for each and every one of them.

Then quick like a minute, he spread his legs out, and stretched his arms in front of the machine like it was all he had in this world.

I tried once again to talk to him.

"Aww come on, Daddy-o. Don't be that way."

That Negro's nose started twitching. Then he tried to talk but his breath was short like he had been running or something.

"Ain't nobody getting this machine. I own this machine, baby. This is mine. Ten years! On this machine. Baby, this belongs to me."

"I know it do, Daddy-o. I *know* it do."

Charlie Wicowycz got mad hearing him say that, so he said, "Damn," and started into Daddy-o. Daddy-o's eyes got big and he drew his arm back and kind of stood on his toes and let out a holler like, like I don't know what.

"Doonnnn't you *touch* this machiiinnneeeee!"

Naturally Charlie stopped, then he started to snicker and play like he was tickled except his face was as white as a fish belly. I thought I would try, so I touched Daddy-o's arm. It was hard like brick. I let his arm go.

"Daddy-o man, I know how you feel. Let me call your wife so she can come and get you. You'll be all right tomorrow. What's your phone number, Daddy-o? I'll call your wife for you, hear?"

His eyes started twitching and he started blinking like he was trying to keep from crying. Still he was smiling that little baby-faced smile.

"Daddy-o, listen to me. Man, *I* ain't trying to do nothing to you. Give me your number and your wife will know what to do."

His lips started trembling. Big grown man, standing there with his lips trembling. He opened his mouth. His whole chin started trembling as he started to speak: "Drexel."

I said: "Okay, Drexel. Now Drexel what?"

"*Drex*el."

"Drexel what else, Daddy-o?"

"Drexel seven-two-three."

"Seven-two-three. What else Daddy-o? Man, I'm trying to help you. I'm going to call your wife. She'll be here in a few minutes. Drexel seven-two-three-what else? What is the rest of your phone number. Daddy-o! I'm talkin' to you!"

"Eight-eight-eight-eight-nine."

"Drexel seven-two-three-eight-nine? That it, Daddy-o?"

Mr. Grobber started walking around scratching his stomach. He stopped in front of Charlie Wicowycz. "Call the police, Charlie."

Charles left.

The other foremen went back to their departments. The set-up men followed them. Mr. Grobber, seeing that he was being left alone with Daddy-o, went back to his office.

Daddy-o just stood there smiling.

I ran to the office and called the number he had given me. Daddy-o's wife wasn't home, but a little girl who said that she was Daddy-o's "Baby-girl" answered and said that she would tell her mother as soon as she came home from work.

When I walked out of the office, the police were there. I thought about the time I had to wait three hours for the police to get to my house the time somebody broke in and took every stitch I had. One of the cops, a big mean-looking something with ice-water eyes, moved in on Daddy-o with his club out and Daddy-o just shuffled his feet, doubled up his fists and waited for him.

I started talking up for my boy.

"Officer, please don't hurt him. He's just sick. He won't do no harm."

"Who are you? Stay outa."

I tried to explain to him. "Look, Officer, just let me talk to him. I . . . I'm his friend."

"All right. Talk to him. Tell him to get into the wagon."

I touched Daddy-o's arm again. He moved it away, still smiling. I said: "Man, Daddy-o, come on now. Come on go with me. I know how it is. I *know* how it is."

He still had that smile. I swear I could have cried.

I started walking, pulling his arm a bit.

"Come on, Daddy-o."

He came along easy, still smiling, and walking with a kind of strut. Looking at each and every one of us like we were his best friends. When we got to the door, he stopped and looked back at his machine. Still smiling. When we got outside, I led him right up to the wagon. The back door was open and it was *dark* in there. Some dusty light scooted through a little window at the back of the wagon that had a wire grating in it. It didn't look very nice in there. I turned to Daddy-o.

"Come on, Daddy-o. The man said you should get in. Ain't nothing going to git you, Daddy-o. Come on, man. Get in."

I felt like anybody's stoolie.

"Come on, get in."

He started moving with me, then he stopped and looked back at the plant. One of the officers touched his arm. And that's when he did his natural number.

He braced his arms against the door. And started to scream to bust his lungs: "That *is* my machine. I *own.* Me and *this* machine is *blood* kin. Don't *none* of you somitches touch it. You *heah?* You, you *heah?"*

The water-eyed policeman started to agree with Daddy-o.

"Sure kid. You *know* it. Lotsa machines. You got lots of 'em."

Daddy-o turned to look at him at the same time his partner gave him a shove. The water-eyed policeman shoved him too. Daddy-o swung at him and missed. When he did that, the water-eyed policeman chunked him right behind the ear and Daddy-o fell back into the wagon. Both policemen grabbed his feet and pushed him past the door and the water-eye slammed it.

They jumped in and started to drive away. Daddy-o was up again and at the window. He was hollering, and his voice got mixed up with the trucks and cars that went by. I watched the wagon huff out of sight and I went back into the plant.

Inside, I got to thinking about how sharp Daddy-o was. I was real proud of that. I caught sight of Daddy-o's machine. You know that thing didn't look right without Daddy-o working on it?

I got to thinking about my machine and how I know that big ugly thing better than I know most live people. Seemed funny to think that it wasn't really mine. It sure *seemed* like mine.

Ol' Daddy-o was sure crazy about Dinah Washington. Last few days that's all he sang: her songs. Like he was singing in place of crying; like being in the plant *made* him sing those songs and like finally the good buddy couldn't sing hard enough to keep up the dues on his machine and then . . . Really.

You know what? Looking around there thinking about Daddy-o and all, I caught myself singing a song that had been floating around in my head.

It goes: "I got bad news, baby, and you're the first to know."

That's one of Dinah Washington's songs.

STUDY QUESTIONS

1. These two stories by Frank London Brown are, on the surface, quite different in structure. How would you characterize the different structural principles that shape each story? In answering this question, consider the following questions first.
2. Consider the choice of narrators in these two stories. Why does it seem functional for Brown to use a third-person narrator in "McDougal" and a first-person narrator in "Singing Dinah's Song"? How would the stories be altered if he had reversed these two kinds of narrators?
3. Frank London Brown was not only a writer, he was also an accomplished jazz

musician who played with Thelonious Monk and whose knowledge of the world of jazz is apparent in all of his writings. How does the jazz world function in each of these stories? And, how critical is an understanding of this world in interpreting these stories?

4. How do the punctuation and sentence structure in these two stories provide clues for oral performance? Do punctuation and sentence structure simply suggest an oral style in the speech of the narrators and the characters, or is some other rhythmic effect operating in the styles?

5. What kinds of audiences are assumed by each of the narrators? Does each narrator's diction provide any particular clues about the assumed backgrounds of the audiences? (Consider, for example, the jazz terms used in "McDougal" or some of the slang expressions in "Singing Dinah's Song." How widespread are these terms in their usage and understanding?)

6. What image of the implied author emerges from these two stories? As a project for a paper you might read Brown's novel *Trumbull Park* and see how your original image is altered, enlarged, or enriched by his longer work.

Jean Stafford/A Country Love Story

born 1915

An antique sleigh stood in the yard, snow after snow banked up against its eroded runners. Here and there upon the bleached and splintery seat were wisps of horsehair and scraps of the black leather that had once upholstered it. It bore, with all its jovial curves, an air not so much of desuetude as of slowed-down dash, as if weary horses, unable to go another step, had at last stopped here. The sleigh had come with the house. The former owner, a gifted businesswoman from Castine who bought old houses and sold them again with all their pitfalls still intact, had said when she was showing them the place, "A picturesque detail, I think," and, waving it away, had turned to the well, which, with enthusiasm and at considerable length, she said had never gone dry. Actually, May and Daniel had found the detail more distracting than picturesque, so nearly kin was it to outdoors arts and crafts, and when the woman, as they departed in her car, gestured toward it again and said, "Paint that up a bit with something cheery and it will really add no end to your yard," simultaneous shudders coursed them. They had planned to remove the sleigh before they did anything else.

But partly because there were more important things to be done, and partly because they did not know where to put it (a sleigh could not, in the usual sense of the words, be thrown away), and partly because it seemed defiantly a part of the yard, as entitled to be there permanently as the trees, they did nothing about it. Throughout the summer, they saw birds briefly pause on its rakish front and saw the fresh rains wash the runners; in the autumn they watched the golden leaves fill the seat and nestle dryly down; and now, with the snow, they watched this new accumulation.

The sleigh was visible from the windows of the big, bright kitchen where they ate all their meals and, sometimes too bemused with country solitude to talk, they gazed out at it, forgetting their food in speculating on its history. It could have been driven cavalierly by the scion of some sea captain's family, or it could have been used soberly to haul the household's Unitarians to church or to take the womenfolk around the countryside on errands of good will. They did not speak of what its office might have been, and the fact of their silence was often nettlesome to May, for she felt they were silent too much of the time; a little morosely, she thought. If something as absurd and as provocative as this at which we look together—and which is, even though we didn't want it, our own property—cannot bring us to talk, what can? But she did not disturb Daniel in his private musings; she held her tongue, and out of the corner of her eye she watched him watch the winter cloak the sleigh, and, as if she were computing a difficult sum in her head, she tried to puzzle out what it was that had stilled tongues that earlier, before Daniel's illness, had found the days too short to communicate all they were eager to say.

It had been Daniel's doctor's idea, not theirs, that had brought them to the solemn hinterland to stay after all the summer gentry had departed in their beach wagons. The Northern sun, the pristine air, the rural walks and soundless nights, said Dr. Tellenbach, perhaps pining for his native Switzerland, would do more for the "Professor's" convalescent lung than all the doctors and clinics in the world. Privately he had added to May that after so long a season in the sanitarium (Daniel had been there a year), where everything was tuned to a low pitch, it would be difficult and it might be shattering for "the boy" (not now the "Professor," although Daniel, nearly fifty, was his wife's senior by twenty years and Dr. Tellenbach's by ten) to go back at once to the excitements and the intrigues of the university, to what, with finicking humor, the Doctor called "the omnium-gatherum of the school master's life." The rigors of a country winter would be as nothing, he insisted, when compared to the strain of feuds and cocktail parties. All professors wanted to write books, didn't they? Surely Daniel, a historian with all the material in the world at his fingertips, must have something up his sleeve that could be the *raison d'être* for this year away? May said she supposed he had, she was not sure. She could hear the reluctance in her voice as she escaped the Doctor's eyes and gazed through his windows at the mountains behind the sanitarium. In the dragging months Daniel had been gone, she had taken solace in imagining the time when they *would* return to just that pandemonium the Doctor so deplored, and because it had been pandemonium on the smallest and most discreet scale, she smiled through her disappointment at the little man's Swiss innocence and explained that they had always lived quietly, seldom dining out or entertaining more than twice a week.

"Twice a week!" He was appalled.

"But I'm afraid," she had protested, "that he would find a second year of inactivity intolerable. He does intend to write a book, but he means to write it in England, and we can't go to England now."

"England!" Dr. Tellenbach threw up his hands. "Good *air* is my recommendation for your husband. Good air and little talk."

She said, "It's talk he needs, I should think, after all this time of communing only with himself except when I came to visit."

He had looked at her with exaggerated patience, and then, courtly but authoritative, he said, "I hope you will not think I importune when I tell you that I am very well acquainted with your husband, and, as his physician, I order this retreat. *He* quite agrees."

Stung to see that there was a greater degree of understanding between Daniel and Dr. Tellenbach than between Daniel and herself, May had objected further, citing an occasion when her husband had put his head in his hands and mourned, "I hear talk of nothing but sputum cups and X-rays. Aren't people interested in the state of the world any more?"

But Dr. Tellenbach had been adamant, and at the end, when she had risen to go, he said, "You are bound to find him changed a little. A long illness removes a thoughtful man from his fellow-beings. It is like living with an exacting mistress who is not content with half a man's attention but must claim it all." She had thought his figure of speech absurd and disdained to ask him what he meant.

Actually, when the time came for them to move into the new house and she found no alterations in her husband but found, on the other hand, much pleasure in their country life, she began to forgive Dr. Tellenbach. In the beginning, it was like a second honeymoon, for they had moved to a part of the North where they had never been and they explored it together, sharing its charming sights and sounds. Moreover, they had never owned a house before but had always lived in city apartments, and though the house they bought was old and derelict, its lines and doors and windowlights were beautiful, and they were obsessed with it. All through the summer, they reiterated, "To think that we own all of this! That it actually belongs to us!" And they wandered from room to room marveling at their windows, from none of which was it possible to see an ugly sight. They looked to the south upon a river, to the north upon a lake; to the west of them were pine woods where the wind forever sighed, voicing a vain entreaty; and to the east a rich man's long meadow that ran down a hill to his old, magisterial house. It was true, even in those bewitched days, that there were times on the lake, when May was gathering water lilies as Daniel slowly rowed, that she had seen on his face a look of abstraction and she had known that he was worlds away, in his memories, perhaps, of his illness and the sanitarium (of which he would never speak) or in the thought of the book he was going to write as soon, he said, as the winter set in and there was nothing to do but work. Momentarily the look frightened her and she remembered the Doctor's words, but then, immediately herself again in the security of married love, she caught at another water lily and pulled at its long stem. Companionably, they gardened, taking special pride in the nicotiana that sent its nighttime fragrance into their bedroom. Together, and with fascination, they consulted carpenters, plasterers, and chimney sweeps. In the blue evenings they read at ease, hearing no sound but that of the night birds —the loons on the lake and the owls in the tops of trees. When the days began to cool and shorten, a cricket came to bless their house, nightly singing behind the kitchen stove. They got two fat and idle tabby cats, who lay insensible beside the fireplace and only stirred themselves to purr perfunctorily.

Because they had not moved in until July and by that time the workmen of the region were already engaged, most of the major repairs of the house were to be postponed until the spring, and in October, when May and Daniel had done all they could by themselves and Daniel had begun his own work, May suddenly found herself without occupation. Whole days might pass when she did nothing more than cook three meals and walk a little in the autumn mist and pet the cats and wait for Daniel to come down from his upstairs study to talk to her. She began to think with longing of the crowded days in Boston before Daniel was sick, and even in the year past, when he had been away and she had gone to concerts and recitals and had done good deeds for crippled children and had endlessly shopped for presents to lighten the tedium of her husband's unwilling exile. And, longing, she was remorseful, as if by desiring another she betrayed this life, and, remorseful, she hid away in sleep. Sometimes she slept for hours in the daytime, imitating the cats, and when at last she got up, she had to push away the dense sleep as if it were a door.

One day at lunch, she asked Daniel to take a long walk with her that afternoon to a farm where the owner smoked his own sausages.

"You never go outdoors," she said, "and Dr. Tellenbach said you must. Besides, it's a lovely day."

"I can't," he said. "I'd like to, but I can't. I'm busy. You go alone."

Overtaken by a gust of loneliness, she cried, "Oh, Daniel, I have nothing to *do!*"

A moment's silence fell, and then he said, "I'm sorry to put you through this, my dear, but you must surely admit that it's not my fault I got sick."

In her shame, her rapid, overdone apologies, her insistence that nothing mattered in the world except his health and peace of mind, she made everything worse, and at last he said shortly to her, "Stop being a child, May. Let's just leave each other alone."

This outbreak, the very first in their marriage of five years, was the beginning of a series. Hardly a day passed that they did not bicker over something; they might dispute a question of fact, argue a matter of taste, catch each other out in an inaccuracy, and every quarrel ended with Daniel's saying to her, "Why don't you leave me alone?" Once he said, "I've been sick and now I'm busy and I'm no longer young enough to shift the focus of my mind each time it suits your whim." Afterward, there were always apologies, and then Daniel went back to his study and did not open the door of it again until the next meal. Finally, it seemed to her that love, the very center of their being, was choked off, overgrown, invisible. And silent with hostility or voluble with trivial reproach, they tried to dig it out impulsively and could not—could only maul it in its unkempt grave. Daniel, in his withdrawal from her and from the house, was preoccupied with his research, of which he never spoke except to say that it would bore her, and most of the time, so it appeared to May, he did not worry over what was happening to them. She felt the cold, old house somehow enveloping her as if it were their common enemy, maliciously bent on bringing them to disaster. Sunken in faithlessness, they stared, at mealtimes, atrophied within the present hour, at the irrelevant and whimsical sleigh that stood abandoned in the mammoth winter.

May found herself thinking, If we redeemed it and painted it, our house would have something in common with Henry Ford's Wayside Inn. And I might make this very observation to him and he might greet it with disdain and we might once again communicate. Perhaps we could talk of Williamsburg and how we disapproved of it. Her mind went toiling on. Williamsburg was part of our honeymoon trip; somewhere our feet were entangled in suckers as we stood kissing under a willow tree. Soon she found that she did not care for this line of thought, nor did she care what his response to it might be. In her imagined conversations with Daniel, she never spoke of the sleigh. To the thin, ill scholar whose scholarship and illness had usurped her place, she had gradually taken a weighty but unviolent dislike.

The discovery of this came, not surprising her, on Christmas Day. The knowledge sank like a plummet, and at the same time she was thinking about the sleigh, connecting it with the smell of the barn on damp days, and she thought perhaps it had been drawn by the very animals who had been stabled there and had pervaded the timbers with their odor. There must have been much life within this house once—but long ago. The earth immediately behind the barn was said by everyone to be extremely rich because of the horses, although there had been none there for over fifty years. Thinking of this soil, which earlier she had eagerly sifted through her fingers, May now realized that she had no wish for the spring to come, no wish to plant a garden, and, branching out at random, she found she had no wish to see the sea again, or children, or favorite pictures, or even her own face on a happy day. For a minute or two, she was almost enraptured in this state of no desire, but then, purged swiftly of her cynicism, she knew it to be false, knew that actually she did have a desire—the desire for a desire. And now she felt that she was stationary in a whirlpool, and at the very moment she conceived the notion a bit of wind brought to the seat of the sleigh the final leaf from the elm tree that stood beside it. It crossed her mind that she might consider the wood of the sleigh in its juxtaposition to the living tree and to the horses, who, although they were long since dead, reminded her of their passionate, sweating, running life every time she went to the barn for firewood.

They sat this morning in the kitchen full of sun, and, speaking not to him but to the sleigh, to icicles, to the dark, motionless pine woods, she said, "I wonder if on a day like this they used to take the pastor home after lunch." Daniel gazed abstractedly at the bright-silver drifts beside the well and said nothing. Presently a wagon went past hauled by two oxen with bells on their yoke. This was the hour they always passed, taking to an unknown destination an aged man in a fur hat and an aged woman in a shawl. May and Daniel listened.

Suddenly, with impromptu anger, Daniel said, "What did you just say?"

"Nothing," she said. And then, after a pause, "It would be lovely at Jamaica Pond today."

He wheeled on her and pounded the table with his fist. "I did not ask for this!" The color rose feverishly to his thin cheeks and his breath was agitated. "You are trying to make me sick again. It was wonderful, wasn't it, for you while I was gone?"

"Oh, no, no! Oh, no, Daniel, it was hell!"

"Then, by the same token, this must be heaven." He smiled, the professor catching out a student in a fallacy.

"Heaven." She said the word bitterly.

"Then why do you stay here?" he cried.

It was a cheap impasse, desolate, true, unfair. She did not answer him.

After a while he said, "I almost believe there's something you haven't told me."

She began to cry at once, blubbering across the table at him. "You have said that before. What am I to say? What have I done?"

He looked at her, impervious to her tears, without mercy and yet without contempt. "I don't know. But you've done something."

It was as if she were looking through someone else's scrambled closets and bureau drawers for an object that had not been named to her, but nowhere could she find her gross offense.

Domestically she asked him if he would have more coffee and he peremptorily refused and demanded, "Will you tell me why it is you must badger me? Is it a compulsion? Can't you control it? Are you going mad?"

From that day onward, May felt a certain stirring of life within her solitude, and now and again, looking up from a book to see if the damper on the stove was right, to listen to a rat renovating its house-within-a-house, to watch the belled oxen pass, she nursed her wound, hugged it, repeated his awful words exactly as he had said them, reproduced the way his wasted lips had looked and his bright, farsighted eyes. She could not read for long at any time, nor could she sew. She cared little now for planning changes in her house; she had meant to sand the painted floors to uncover the wood of the wide boards and she had imagined how the long, paneled windows of the drawing room would look when yellow velvet curtains hung there in the spring. Now, schooled by silence and indifference, she was immune to disrepair and to the damage done by the wind and snow, and she looked, as Daniel did, without dislike upon the old and nasty wallpaper and upon the shabby kitchen floor. One day, she knew that the sleigh would stay where it was so long as they stayed there. From every thought, she returned to her deep, bleeding injury. He had asked her if she were going mad.

She repaid him in the dark afternoons while he was closeted away in his study, hardly making a sound save when he added wood to his fire or paced a little, deep in thought. She sat at the kitchen table looking at the sleigh, and she gave Daniel insult for his injury by imagining a lover. She did not imagine his face, but she imagined his clothing, which would be costly and in the best of taste, and his manner, which would be urbane and anticipatory of her least whim, and his clever speech, and his adept courtship that would begin the moment he looked at the sleigh and said, "I must get rid of that for you at once." She might be a widow, she might be divorced, she might be committing adultery. Certainly there was no need to specify in an affair so securely legal. There was no need, that is, up to a point, and then the point came when she took in the fact that she not only believed in this lover but loved him and depended wholly on his companionship. She complained to him of Daniel and he consoled her; she told him stories of her girlhood, when she had gaily gone to parties, squired by boys her own age; she dazzled him sometimes with the wise comments she made on the books she read. It came to be true that if she so much as looked at the sleigh, she was weakened, failing with starvation.

Often, about her daily tasks of cooking food and washing dishes and tending the fires and shopping in the general store of the village, she thought she should watch her step, that it was this sort of thing that *did* make one go mad; for a while, then, she went back to Daniel's question, sharpening its razor edge. But she could not corral her alien thoughts and she trembled as she bought split peas, fearful that the old men loafing by the stove could see the incubus of her sins beside her. She could not avert such thoughts when they rushed upon her sometimes at tea with one of the old religious ladies of the neighborhood, so that in the middle of a conversation about a deaconess in Bath, she retired from them, seeking her lover, who came, faceless, with his arms outstretched, even as she sat up straight in a Boston rocker, even as she accepted another cup of tea. She lingered over the cake plates and the simple talk, postponing her return to her own house and to Daniel, whom she continually betrayed.

It was not long after she recognized her love that she began to wake up even before the dawn and to be all day quick to everything, observant of all the signs of age and eccentricity in her husband, and she compared him in every particular—to his humiliation, in her eyes—with the man whom now it seemed to her she had always loved at fever pitch.

Once when Daniel, in a rare mood, kissed her, she drew back involuntarily and he said gently, "I wish I knew what you had done, poor dear." He looked, as if for written words, in her face.

"You said you knew," she said, terrified.

"I do."

"Then why do you wish you knew?" Her baffled voice was high and frantic. "You don't talk sense!"

"I do," he said sedately. "I talk sense always. It is you who are oblique." Her eyes stole like a sneak to the sleigh. "But I wish I knew your motive," he said impartially.

For a minute, she felt that they were two maniacs answering each other questions that had not been asked, never touching the matter at hand because they did not know what the matter was. But in the next moment, when he turned back to her spontaneously and clasped her head between his hands and said, like a tolerant father, "I forgive you, darling, because you don't know how you persecute me. No one knows except the sufferer what this sickness is," she knew again, helplessly, that they were not harmonious even in their aberrations.

These days of winter came and went, and on each of them, after breakfast and as the oxen passed, he accused her of her concealed misdeed. She could no longer truthfully deny that she was guilty, for she was in love, and she heard the subterfuge in her own voice and felt the guilty fever in her veins. Daniel knew it, too, and watched her. When she was alone, she felt her lover's presence protecting her—when she walked past the stiff spiraea, with icy cobwebs hung between its twigs, down to the lake, where the black, unmeasured water was hidden beneath a lid of ice; when she walked, instead, to the salt river to see the tar-paper shacks where the men caught smelt through the ice; when she walked in the dead dusk up the hill from the store, catching her breath the moment she saw the sleigh. But sometimes this splendid being mocked her when, freezing with fear of the consequences of her sin, she ran up the stairs to Daniel's room and burrowed her head in his shoulder and cried, "Come downstairs! I'm lonely, please come down!" But he would never come, and at last, bitterly, calmed by his calmly inquisitive regard, she went back alone and stood at the kitchen window, coyly half hidden behind the curtains.

For months she lived with her daily dishonor, rattled, ashamed, stubbornly clinging to her secret. But she grew more and more afraid when, oftener and oftener, Daniel said, "Why do you lie to me? What does this mood of yours mean?" and she could no longer sleep. In the raw nights, she lay straight beside him as he slept, and she stared at the ceiling, as bright as the snow it reflected, and tried not to think of the sleigh out there under the elm tree but could think only of it and of the man, her lover, who was connected with it somehow. She said to herself, as she listened to his breathing, "If I confessed to Daniel, he would understand that I was lonely and he would comfort me, saying, 'I am here, May. I shall never let you be lonely again.'" At these times, she was so separated from the world, so far removed from his touch and his voice, so solitary, that she would have sued a stranger for companionship. Daniel slept deeply, having no guilt to make him toss. He slept, indeed, so well that he never even heard the ditcher on snowy nights rising with a groan over the hill, flinging the snow from the road and warning of its approach by lights that first flashed red, then blue. As it passed their house, the hurled snow swashed like flames. All night she heard the squirrels adding up their nuts in the walls and heard the spirit of the house creaking and softly clicking upon the stairs and in the attics.

In early spring, when the whippoorwills begged in the cattails and the marsh reeds, and the northern lights patinated the lake and the tidal river, and the stars were large, and the huge vine of Dutchman's-pipe had started to leaf out, May went to bed late. Each night she sat on the back steps waiting, hearing the snuffling of a dog as it hightailed it for home, the single cry of a loon. Night after night, she waited for the advent of her rebirth while upstairs Daniel, who had spoken tolerantly of her vigils, slept, keeping his knowledge of her to himself. "A symptom," he had said, scowling in concentration, as he remarked upon her new habit. "Let it run its course. Perhaps when this is over, you will know the reason why you torture me with these obsessions and will stop.

You know, you may really have a slight disorder of the mind. It would be nothing to be ashamed of; you could go to a sanitarium."

One night, looking out the window, she clearly saw her lover sitting in the sleigh. His hand was over his eyes and his chin was covered by a red silk scarf. He wore no hat and his hair was fair. He was tall and his long legs stretched indolently along the floorboard. He was younger than she had imagined him to be and he seemed rather frail, for there was a delicate pallor on his high, intelligent forehead and there was an invalid's languor in his whole attitude. He wore a white blazer and gray flannels and there was a yellow rosebud in his lapel. Young as he was, he did not, even so, seem to belong to her generation; rather, he seemed to be the reincarnation of someone's uncle as he had been fifty years before. May did not move until he vanished, and then, even though she knew now that she was truly bedeviled, the only emotion she had was bashfulness, mingled with doubt; she was not sure, that is, that he loved her.

That night, she slept a while. She lay near to Daniel, who was smiling in the moonlight. She could tell that the sleep she would have tonight would be as heavy as a coma, and she was aware of the moment she was overtaken.

She was in a canoe in a meadow of water lilies and her lover was tranquilly taking the shell off a hard-boiled egg. "How intimate," he said, "to eat an egg with you." She was nervous lest the canoe tip over, but at the same time she was charmed by his wit and by the way he lightly touched her shoulder with the varnished paddle.

"May? May? I love you, May."

"Oh!" enchanted, she heard her voice replying. "Oh, I love you, too!"

"The winter is over, May. You must forgive the hallucinations of a sick man."

She woke to see Daniel's fair, pale head bending toward her. "He is old! He is ill!" she thought, but through her tears, to deceive him one last time, she cried, "Oh, thank God, Daniel!"

He was feeling cold and wakeful and he asked her to make him a cup of tea; before she left the room, he kissed her hands and arms and said, "If I am ever sick again, don't leave me, May."

Downstairs, in the kitchen, cold with shadows and with the obtrusion of dawn, she was belabored by a chill. "What time is it?" she said aloud, although she did not care. She remembered, not for any reason, a day when she and Daniel had stood in the yard last October wondering whether they should cover the chimneys that would not be used and he decided that they should not, but he had said, "I hope no birds get trapped." She had replied, "I thought they all left at about this time for the South," and he had answered, with an unintelligible reproach in his voice, "The starlings stay." And she remembered, again for no reason, a day when, in pride and excitement, she had burst into the house crying, "I saw an ermine. It was terribly poised and let me watch it quite a while." He had said categorically, "There are no ermines here."

She had not protested; she had sighed as she sighed now and turned to the window. The sleigh was livid in this light and no one was in it; nor had anyone been in it for many years. But at that moment the black-smith's cat came guardedly across the dewy field and climbed into it, as if by careful plan, and curled up on the seat. May prodded the clinkers in the stove and started to the barn for kindling. But she thought of the cold and the damp and the smell of the horses, and she did not go but stood there, holding the poker and leaning upon it as if it were an um-brella. There was no place warm to go. "What time is it?" she whim-pered, heartbroken, and moved the poker, stroking the lion foot of the fireless stove.

She knew now that no change would come, and that she would never see her lover again. Confounded utterly, like an orphan in solitary con-finement, she went outdoors and got into the sleigh. The blacksmith's imperturbable cat stretched and rearranged his position, and May sat beside him with her hands locked tightly in her lap, rapidly wondering over and over again how she would live the rest of her life.

[Study Questions for this story appear at the conclusion of the following story.]

Katherine Anne Porter/Flowering Judas

born 1894

Braggioni sits heaped upon the edge of a straight-backed chair much too small for him, and sings to Laura in a furry, mournful voice. Laura has begun to find reasons for avoiding her own house until the latest possible moment, for Braggioni is there almost every night. No matter how late she is, he will be sitting there with a surly, waiting expression, pulling at his kinky yellow hair, thumbing the strings of his guitar, snarling a tune under his breath. Lupe the Indian maid meets Laura at the door, and says with a flicker of a glance towards the upper room, "He waits."

Laura wishes to lie down, she is tired of her hairpins and the feel of her long tight sleeves, but she says to him, "Have you a new song for me this evening?" If he says yes, she asks him to sing it. If he says no, she remembers his favorite one, and asks him to sing it again. Lupe brings her a cup of chocolate and a plate of rice, and Laura eats at the small table under the lamp, first inviting Braggioni, whose answer is always the same: "I have eaten, and besides, chocolate thickens the voice."

Laura says, "Sing, then," and Braggioni heaves himself into song. He scratches the guitar familiarly as though it were a pet animal, and sings passionately off key, taking the high notes in a prolonged painful squeal. Laura, who haunts the markets listening to the ballad singers, and stops every day to hear the blind boy playing his reed-flute in Sixteenth of September Street, listens to Braggioni with pitiless courtesy, because she dares not smile at his miserable performance. Nobody dares to smile at him. Braggioni is cruel to everyone, with a kind of specialized insolence, but he is so vain of his talents, and so sensitive to slights, it would require a cruelty and vanity greater than his own to lay a finger on the vast cureless wound of his self-esteem. It would require courage, too, for it is dangerous to offend him, and nobody has this courage.

Braggioni loves himself with such tenderness and amplitude and eternal charity that his followers—for he is a leader of men, a skilled revolutionist, and his skin has been punctured in honorable warfare—warm themselves in the reflected glow, and say to each other: "He has a real nobility, a love of humanity raised above mere personal affections." The excess of this self-love has flowed out, inconveniently for her, over Laura, who, with so many others, owes her comfortable situation and her salary to him. When he is in a very good humor, he tells her, "I am tempted to forgive you for being a *gringa*. *Gringita!*" and Laura, burning, imagines herself leaning forward suddenly, and with a sound back-handed slap wiping the suety smile from his face. If he notices her eyes at these moments he gives no sign.

She knows what Braggioni would offer her, and she must resist tenaciously without appearing to resist, and if she could avoid it she would not admit even to herself the slow drift of his intention. During these long evenings which have spoiled a long month for her, she sits in her deep chair with an open book on her knees, resting her eyes on the consoling rigidity of the printed page when the sight and sound of Braggioni singing threaten to identify themselves with all her remembered afflictions and to add their weight to her uneasy premonitions of the future. The gluttonous bulk of Braggioni has become a symbol of her many disillusions, for a revolutionist should be lean, animated by heroic faith, a vessel of abstract virtues. This is nonsense, she knows it now and is ashamed of it. Revolution must have leaders, and leadership is a career for energetic men. She is, her comrades tell her, full of romantic error, for what she defines as cynicism in them is merely "a developed sense of reality." She is almost too willing to say, "I am wrong, I suppose I don't really understand the principles," and afterward she makes a secret truce with herself, determined not to surrender her will to such expedient logic. But she cannot help feeling that she has been betrayed irreparably by the disunion between her way of living and her feeling of what life should be, and at times she is almost contented to rest in this sense of grievance as a private store of consolation. Sometimes she wishes to run away, but she stays. Now she longs to fly out of this room, down the narrow stairs, and into the street where the houses lean together like conspirators under a single mottled lamp, and leave Braggioni singing to himself.

Instead she looks at Braggioni, frankly and clearly, like a good child who understands the rules of behavior. Her knees cling together under sound blue serge, and her round white collar is not purposely nun-like. She wears the uniform of an idea, and has renounced vanities. She was born Roman Catholic, and in spite of her fear of being seen by someone who might make a scandal of it, she slips now and again into some crumbling little church, kneels on the chilly stone, and says a Hail Mary on the gold rosary she bought in Tehuantepec. It is no good and she ends by examining the altar with its tinsel flowers and ragged brocades, and feels tender about the battered doll-shape of some male saint whose white, lace-trimmed drawers hang limply around his ankles below the hieratic dignity of his velvet robe. She has encased herself in a set of principles derived from her early training, leaving no detail of gesture or of personal taste untouched, and for this reason she will not wear lace made on machines. This is her private heresy, for in her special group the machine is sacred, and will be the salvation of the workers. She loves fine lace, and there is a tiny edge of fluted cobweb on this collar, which is one of twenty precisely alike, folded in blue tissue paper in the upper drawer of her clothes chest.

Braggioni catches her glance solidly as if he had been waiting for it, leans forward, balancing his paunch between his spread knees, and sings with tremendous emphasis, weighing his words. He has, the song relates, no father and no mother, nor even a friend to console him; lonely as a wave of the sea he comes and goes, lonely as a wave. His mouth opens round and yearns sideways, his balloon cheeks grow oily with the labor of song. He bulges marvelously in his expensive garments. Over his lavender collar, crushed upon a purple necktie, held by a diamond hoop: over his ammunition belt of tooled leather worked in silver, buckled cruelly around his gasping middle: over the tops of his glossy yellow shoes Braggioni swells with ominous ripeness, his mauve silk hose stretched taut, his ankles bound with the stout leather thongs of his shoes.

When he stretches his eyelids at Laura she notes again that his eyes are the true tawny yellow cat's eyes. He is rich, not in money, he tells her, but in power, and this power brings with it the blameless ownership of things, and the right to indulge his love of small luxuries. "I have a taste for the elegant refinements," he said once, flourishing a yellow silk handkerchief before her nose. "Smell that? It is Jockey Club, imported from New York." Nonetheless he is wounded by life. He will say so presently. "It is true everything turns to dust in the hand, to gall on the tongue." He sighs and his leather belt creaks like a saddle girth. "I am disappointed in everything as it comes. Everything." He shakes his head. "You, poor thing, you will be disappointed too. You are born for it. We are more alike than you realize in some things. Wait and see. Some day you will remember what I have told you, you will know that Braggioni was your friend."

Laura feels a slow chill, a purely physical sense of danger, a warning in her blood that violence, mutilation, a shocking death, wait for her with lessening patience. She has translated this fear into something homely, immediate, and sometimes hesitates before crossing the street. "My personal fate is nothing, except as the testimony of a mental attitude," she reminds herself, quoting from some forgotten philosophic primer, and is sensible enough to add, "Anyhow, I shall not be killed by an automobile if I can help it."

"It may be true I am as corrupt, in another way, as Braggioni," she thinks in spite of herself, "as callous, as incomplete," and if this is so, any kind of death seems preferable. Still she sits quietly, she does not run. Where could she go? Uninvited she has promised herself to this place; she can no longer imagine herself as living in another country, and there is no pleasure in remembering her life before she came here.

Precisely what is the nature of this devotion, its true motives, and what are its obligations? Laura cannot say. She spends part of her days in Xochimilco, near by, teaching Indian children to say in English, "The cat is on the mat." When she appears in the classroom they crowd about her with smiles on their wise, innocent, clay-colored faces, crying, "Good morning, my titcher!" in immaculate voices, and they make of her desk a fresh garden of flowers every day.

During her leisure she goes to union meetings and listens to busy important voices quarreling over tactics, methods, internal politics. She visits the prisoners of her own political faith in their cells, where they entertain themselves with counting cockroaches, repenting of their indiscretions, composing their memoirs, writing out manifestoes and plans for their comrades who are still walking about free, hands in pockets, sniffing fresh air. Laura brings them food and cigarettes and a little money, and she brings messages disguised in equivocal phrases from the men outside who dare not set foot in the prison for fear of disappearing into the cells kept empty for them. If the prisoners confuse night and day, and complain, "Dear little Laura, time doesn't pass in this infernal hole, and I won't know when it is time to sleep unless I have a reminder," she brings them their favorite narcotics, and says in a tone that does not wound them with pity, "Tonight will really be night for you," and though her Spanish amuses them, they find her comforting, useful. If they lose patience and all faith, and curse the slowness of their friends in coming to their rescue with money and influence, they trust her not to repeat everything, and if she inquires, "Where do you think we can find money, or influence?" they are certain to answer, "Well, there is Braggioni, why doesn't he do something?"

She smuggles letters from headquarters to men hiding from firing squads in back streets in mildewed houses, where they sit in tumbled beds and talk bitterly as if all Mexico were at their heels, when Laura knows positively they might appear at the band concert in the Alameda on Sunday morning, and no one would notice them. But Braggioni says, "Let them sweat a little. The next time they may be careful. It is very restful to have them out of the way for a while." She is not afraid to knock on any door in any street after midnight, and enter in the darkness, and say to one of these men who is really in danger: "They will be looking for you—seriously—tomorrow morning after six. Here is some money from Vicente. Go to Vera Cruz and wait."

She borrows money from the Roumanian agitator to give to his bitter enemy the Polish agitator. The favor of Braggioni is their disputed territory, and Braggioni holds the balance nicely, for he can use them both. The Polish agitator talks love to her over café tables, hoping to exploit what he believes is her secret sentimental preference for him, and he gives her misinformation which he begs her to repeat as the solemn truth to certain persons. The Roumanian is more adroit. He is generous with his money in all good causes, and lies to her with an air of ingenuous candor, as if he were her good friend and confidant. She never repeats anything they may say. Braggioni never asks questions. He has other ways to discover all that he wishes to know about them.

Nobody touches her, but all praise her gray eyes, and the soft, round under lip which promises gayety, yet is always grave, nearly always firmly closed: and they cannot understand why she is in Mexico. She walks back and forth on her errands, with puzzled eyebrows, carrying her little folder of drawings and music and school papers. No dancer dances more beautifully than Laura walks, and she inspires some amusing, unexpected ardors, which cause little gossip, because nothing comes of them. A young captain who had been a soldier in Zapata's army attempted, during a horseback ride near Cuernavaca, to express his desire for her with the noble simplicity befitting a rude folk-hero: but gently, because he was gentle. This gentleness was his defeat, for when he alighted, and removed her foot from the stirrup, and essayed to draw her down into his arms, her horse, ordinarily a tame one, shied fiercely, reared and plunged away. The young hero's horse careered blindly after his stable-mate, and the hero did not return to the hotel until rather late that evening. At breakfast he came to her table in full charro dress, gray buckskin jacket and trousers with strings of silver buttons down the leg, and he was in a humorous, careless mood. "May I sit with you?" and "You are a wonderful rider. I was terrified that you might be thrown and dragged. I should never have forgiven myself. But I cannot admire you enough for your riding!"

"I learned to ride in Arizona," said Laura.

"If you will ride with me again this morning, I promise you a horse that will not shy with you," he said. But Laura remembered that she must return to Mexico City at noon.

Next morning the children made a celebration and spent their playtime writing on the blackboard, "We lov ar ticher," and with tinted chalks they drew wreaths of flowers around the words. The young hero wrote her a letter: "I am a very foolish, wasteful, impulsive man. I should have first said I love you, and then you would not have run away. But you shall see me again." Laura thought, "I must send him a box of colored crayons," but she was trying to forgive herself for having spurred her horse at the wrong moment.

A brown, shock-haired youth came and stood in her patio one night and sang like a lost soul for two hours, but Laura could think of nothing to do about it. The moonlight spread a wash of gauzy silver over the clear spaces of the garden, and the shadows were cobalt blue. The scarlet blossoms of the Judas tree were dull purple, and the names of the colors repeated themselves automatically in her mind, while she watched not the boy, but his shadow, fallen like a dark garment across the fountain rim, trailing in the water. Lupe came silently and whispered expert counsel in her ear: "If you will throw him one little flower, he will sing another song or two and go away." Laura threw the flower, and he sang a last song and went away with the flower tucked in the band of his hat. Lupe said, "He is one of the organizers of the Typographers Union, and before that he sold corridos in the Merced market, and before that, he came from Guanajuato, where I was born. I would not trust any man, but I trust least those from Guanajuato."

She did not tell Laura that he would be back again the next night, and the next, nor that he would follow her at a certain fixed distance around the Merced market, through the Zócolo, up Francisco I. Madero Avenue, and so along the Paseo de la Reforma to Chapultepec Park, and into the Philosopher's Footpath, still with that flower withering in his hat, and an indivisible attention in his eyes.

Now Laura is accustomed to him, it means nothing except that he is nineteen years old and is observing a convention with all propriety, as though it were founded on a law of nature, which in the end it might well prove to be. He is beginning to write poems which he prints on a wooden press, and he leaves them stuck like handbills in her door. She is pleasantly disturbed by the abstract, unhurried watchfulness of his black eyes which will in time turn easily towards another object. She tells herself that throwing the flower was a mistake, for she is twenty-two years old and knows better; but she refuses to regret it, and persuades herself that her negation of all external events as they occur is a sign that she is gradually perfecting herself in the stoicism she strives to cultivate against that disaster she fears, though she cannot name it.

She is not at home in the world. Every day she teaches children who remain strangers to her, though she loves their tender round hands and their charming opportunist savagery. She knocks at unfamiliar doors not knowing whether a friend or a stranger shall answer, and even if a known face emerges from the sour gloom of that unknown interior, still it is the face of a stranger. No matter what this stranger says to her, nor what her message to him, the very cells of her flesh reject knowledge and kinship in one monotonous word. No. No. No. She draws her strength from this one holy talismanic word which does not suffer her to be led into evil. Denying everything, she may walk anywhere in safety, she looks at everything without amazement.

No, repeats this firm unchanging voice of her blood; and she looks at Braggioni without amazement. He is a great man, he wishes to impress this simple girl who covers her great round breasts with thick dark cloth, and who hides long, invaluably beautiful legs under a heavy skirt. She is almost thin except for the incomprehensible fullness of her breasts, like a nursing mother's, and Braggioni, who considers himself a judge of women, speculates again on the puzzle of her notorious virginity, and takes the liberty of speech which she permits without a sign of modesty, indeed, without any sort of sign, which is disconcerting.

"You think you are so cold, *gringita!* Wait and see. You will surprise yourself some day! May I be there to advise you!" He stretches his eyelids at her, and his ill-humored cat's eyes waver in a separate glance for the two points of light marking the opposite ends of a smoothly drawn path between the swollen curve of her breasts. He is not put off by that blue serge, nor by her resolutely fixed gaze. There is all the time in the world. His cheeks are bellying with the wind of song. "O girl with the dark eyes," he sings, and reconsiders. "But yours are not dark. I can change all that. O girl with the green eyes, you have stolen my heart away!" then his mind wanders to the song, and Laura feels the weight of his attention being shifted elsewhere. Singing thus, he seems harmless, he is quite harmless, there is nothing to do but sit patiently and say "No," when the moment comes. She draws a full breath, and her mind wanders also, but not far. She dares not wander too far.

Not for nothing has Braggioni taken pains to be a good revolutionist and a professional lover of humanity. He will never die of it. He has the malice, the cleverness, the wickedness, the sharpness of wit, the hardness of heart, stipulated for loving the world profitably. *He will never die of it.* He will live to see himself kicked out from his feeding trough by other hungry world-saviors. Traditionally he must sing in spite of his life which drives him to bloodshed, he tells Laura, for his father was a Tuscany peasant who drifted to Yucatan and married a Maya woman: a woman of race, an aristocrat. They gave him the love and knowledge of music, thus: and under the rip of his thumbnail, the strings of the instrument complain like exposed nerves.

Once he was called Delgadito by all the girls and married women who ran after him; he was so scrawny all his bones showed under his thin cotton clothing, and he could squeeze his emptiness to the very backbone with his two hands. He was a poet and the revolution was only a dream then; too many women loved him and sapped away his youth, and he could never find enough to eat anywhere, anywhere! Now he is a leader of men, crafty men who whisper in his ear, hungry men who wait for hours outside his office for a word with him, emaciated men with wild faces who waylay him at the street gate within a timid, "Comrade, let me tell you . . ." and they blow the foul breath from their empty stomachs in his face.

He is always sympathetic. He gives them handfuls of small coins from his own pocket, he promises them work, there will be demonstrations, they must join the unions and attend the meetings, above all they must be on the watch for spies. They are closer to him than his own brothers, without them he can do nothing—until tomorrow, comrade!

Until tomorrow. "They are stupid, they are lazy, they are treacherous, they would cut my throat for nothing," he says to Laura. He has good food and abundant drink, he hires an automobile and drives in the Paseo on Sunday mornings, and enjoys plenty of sleep in a soft bed beside a wife who dares not disturb him; and he sits pampering his bones in easy billows of fat, singing to Laura, who knows and thinks these things about him. When he was fifteen, he tried to drown himself because he loved a girl, his first love, and she laughed at him. "A thousand women have paid for that," and his tight little mouth turns down at the corners. Now he perfumes his hair with Jockey Club, and confides to Laura: "One woman is really as good as another for me, in the dark. I prefer them all."

His wife organizes unions among the girls in the cigarette factories, and walks in picket lines, and even speaks at meetings in the evening. But she cannot be brought to acknowledge the benefits of true liberty. "I tell her I must have my freedom, net. She does not understand my point of view." Laura has heard this many times. Braggioni scratches the guitar and meditates. "She is an instinctively virtuous woman, pure gold, no doubt of that. If she were not, I should lock her up, and she knows it."

His wife, who works so hard for the good of the factory girls, employs part of her leisure lying on the floor weeping because there are so many women in the world, and only one husband for her, and she never knows where nor when to look for him. He told her: "Unless you can learn to cry when I am not here, I must go away for good." That day he went away and took a room at the Hotel Madrid.

It is this month of separation for the sake of higher principles that has been spoiled not only for Mrs. Braggioni, whose sense of reality is beyond criticism, but for Laura, who feels herself bogged in a nightmare. Tonight Laura envies Mrs. Braggioni, who is alone, and free to weep as much as she pleases about a concrete wrong. Laura has just come from a visit to the prison, and she is waiting for tomorrow with a bitter anxiety as if tomorrow may not come, but time may be caught immovably in this hour, with herself transfixed, Braggioni singing on forever, and Eugenio's body not yet discovered by the guard.

Braggioni says: "Are you going to sleep?" Almost before she can shake her head, he begins telling her about the May-day disturbances coming on in Morelia, for the Catholics hold a festival in honor of the Blessed Virgin, and the Socialists celebrate their martyrs on that day. "There will be two independent processions, starting from either end of town, and they will march until they meet, and the rest depends . . ." He asks her to oil and load his pistols. Standing up, he unbuckles his ammunition belt, and spreads it laden across her knees. Laura sits with the shells slipping through the cleaning cloth dipped in oil, and he says again he cannot understand why she works so hard for the revolutionary idea unless she loves some man who is in it. "Are you not in love with someone?" "No," says Laura. "And no one is in love with you?" "No." "Then it is your own fault. No woman need go begging. Why, what is the matter with you? The legless beggar woman in the Alameda has a perfectly faithful lover. Did you know that?"

Laura peers down the pistol barrel and says nothing, but a long, slow faintness rises and subsides in her; Braggioni curves his swollen fingers around the throat of the guitar and softly smothers the music out of it, and when she hears him again he seems to have forgotten her, and is speaking in the hypnotic voice he uses when talking in small rooms to a listening, close-gathered crowd. Some day this world, now seemingly so composed and eternal, to the edges of every sea shall be merely a tangle of gaping trenches, of crashing walls and broken bodies. Everything must be torn from its accustomed place where it has rotted for centuries, hurled skyward and distributed, cast down again clean as rain, without separate identity. Nothing shall survive that the stiffened hands of poverty have created for the rich and no one shall be left alive except the elect spirits destined to procreate a new world cleansed of cruelty and injustice, ruled by benevolent anarchy: "Pistols are good, I love them, cannon are even better, but in the end I pin my faith to good dynamite," he concludes, and strokes the pistol lying in her hands. "Once I dreamed of destroying this city, in case it offered resistance to General Ortiz, but it fell into his hands like an overripe pear."

He is made restless by his own words, rises and stands waiting. Laura holds up the belt to him: "Put that on, and go kill somebody in Morelia, and you will be happier," she says softly. The presence of death in the room makes her bold. "Today, I found Eugenio going into a stupor. He refused to allow me to call the prison doctor. He had taken all the tablets I brought him yesterday. He said he took them because he was bored."

"He is a fool, and his death is his own business," says Braggioni, fastening his belt carefully.

"I told him if he had waited only a little while longer, you would have got him set free," says Laura. "He said he did not want to wait."

"He is a fool and we are well rid of him," says Braggioni, reaching for his hat.

He goes away. Laura knows his mood has changed, she will not see him any more for a while. He will send word when he needs her to go on errands into strange streets, to speak to the strange faces that will appear, like clay masks with the power of human speech, to mutter their thanks to Braggioni for his help. Now she is free, and she thinks, I must run while there is time. But she does not go.

Braggioni enters his own house where for a month his wife has spent many hours every night weeping and tangling her hair upon her pillow. She is weeping now, and she weeps more at the sight of him, the cause of all her sorrows. He looks about the room. Nothing is changed, the smells are good and familiar, he is well acquainted with the woman who comes toward him with no reproach except grief on her face. He says to her tenderly: "You are so good, please don't cry any more, you dear good creature." She says, "Are you tired, my angel? Sit here and I will wash your feet." She brings a bowl of water, and kneeling, unlaces his shoes, and when from her knees she raises her sad eyes under her blackened lids, he is sorry for everything, and bursts into tears. "Ah, yes, I am hungry, I am tired, let us eat something together," he says, between sobs. His wife leans her head on his arm and says, "Forgive me!" and this time he is refreshed by the solemn, endless rain of her tears.

Laura takes off her serge dress and puts on a white linen nightgown and goes to bed. She turns her head a little to one side, and lying still, reminds herself that it is time to sleep. Numbers tick in her brain like little clocks, soundless doors close of themselves around her. If you would sleep, you must not remember anything, the children will say tomorrow, good morning, my teacher, the poor prisoners who come every day bringing flowers to their jailor. 1–2–3–4–5—it is monstrous to confuse love with revolution, night with day, life with death—ah, Eugenio!

The tolling of the midnight bell is a signal, but what does it mean? Get up, Laura, and follow me: come out of your sleep, out of your bed, out of this strange house. What are you doing in this house? Without a word, without fear she rose and reached for Eugenio's hand, but he eluded her with a sharp, sly smile and drifted away. This is not all, you shall see—Murderer, he said, follow me, I will show you a new country, but it is far away and we must hurry. No, said Laura, not unless you take my hand, no; and she clung first to the stair rail, and then to the topmost branch of the Judas tree that bent down slowly and set her upon the earth, and then to the rocky ledge of a cliff, and then to the jagged wave of a sea that was not water but a desert of crumbling stone. Where are you taking me, she asked in wonder but without fear. To death, and it is a long way off, and we must hurry, said Eugenio. No, said Laura, not unless you take my hand. Then eat these flowers, poor prisoner, said Eugenio in a voice of pity, take and eat: and from the Judas tree he stripped the warm bleeding flowers, and held them to her lips. She saw that his hand was fleshless, a cluster of small white petrified branches, and his eye sockets were without light, but she ate the flowers greedily for they satisfied both hunger and thirst. Murderer! said Eugenio, and Cannibal! This is my body and my blood. Laura cried No! and at the sound of her own voice, she awoke trembling, and was afraid to sleep again.

STUDY QUESTIONS

1. If you were to compare these two stories, you would find that both focus primarily upon character exploration rather than on external or social action. Both stories take as their central character a young woman with a dilemma. And both stories are told by a narrator with limited omniscience—with the young woman in each story providing the central intelligence through which the story is viewed. With these things in mind explore the different techniques employed by Katherine Anne Porter and Jean Stafford in their renderings of Laura and May respectively.

2. How close is each of these narrators to the central character? What are the attitudes of each narrator toward the protagonist? What is the relationship between the implied author, the narrator, and the central character in each story? Consider the possibility that, in each story, the narrator *is* the protagonist, who has objectified herself for the purpose of telling the story. What evidence could you find in each story to support such a position? To refute such a position?

3. Define as clearly as possible the nature of Laura's central problems. How does Laura attempt to resolve her problems? What is the function of Laura's action and inaction in "Flowering Judas"?

4. Define as clearly as possible the nature of May's problems. How does May attempt to resolve her problems? What is the function of May's relationship to fantasy and actuality in the story?

5. Are the dilemmas of May and Laura the same for each at the end of their stories as they were at the beginning? If any changes have occurred for either of the young women, what is the nature of these changes? How does each narrator influence the reader's conclusions about May and Laura regarding their solutions to their problems?

6. Explore the operation of symbols in each of these stories. Take into account not only the presence of symbolism in critical scenes (for example, in May's hallucination and dream and in Laura's dream), but also the way in which the dominant symbols are developed in each story. How do objects of each woman's everyday life take on symbolic significance for each of them?

7. If you were to demonstrate each story using any number of persons to portray the narrators and central characters of each, how many Lauras and narrators would you use in "Flowering Judas"? What would each of these Lauras and narrators represent? What would these demonstrations do to clarify aspects of Laura's character and the relationship between Laura and the narrator. Consider these same questions with regard to "A Country Love Story."

8. Given the complexity of the points of view in these two stories, the reader receives somewhat unreliable pictures of the men with whom these women are involved. With this in mind consider the descriptions of Braggioni and Eugenio in "Flowering Judas." In what terms does Laura see each man? How reliable is her picture? In "A Country Love Story" notice the descriptions of May's imaginary lover and the remarks made about Daniel. Are there any overlappings or conflicts in the total descriptions of both? Does the picture of the imaginary lover provide a clearer image of him for the reader than it does for May?

John Barth/Night-Sea Journey

born 1930

"One way or another, no matter which theory of our journey is correct, it's myself I address; to whom I rehearse as to a stranger our history and condition, and will disclose my secret hope though I sink for it.

"Is the journey my invention? Do the night, the sea, exist at all, I ask myself, apart from my experience of them? Do I myself exist, or is this a dream? Sometimes I wonder. And if I am, who am I? The Heritage I supposedly transport? But how can I be both vessel and contents? Such are the questions that beset my intervals of rest.

"My trouble is, I lack conviction. Many accounts of our situation seem plausible to me—where and what we are, why we swim and whither. But implausible ones as well, perhaps especially those, I must admit as possibly correct. Even likely. If at times, in certain humors—stroking in unison, say, with my neighbors and chanting with them 'Onward! Upward!'—I have supposed that we have after all a common Maker, Whose nature and motives we may not know, but Who engendered us in some mysterious wise and launched us forth toward some end known but to Him—if (for a moodslength only) I have been able to entertain such notions, very popular in certain quarters, it is because our night-sea journey partakes of their absurdity. One might even say: I can believe them *because* they are absurd.

"Has that been said before?

"Another paradox: it appears to be these recesses from swimming that sustain me in the swim. Two measures onward and upward, flailing with the rest, then I float exhausted and dispirited, brood upon the night, the sea, the journey, while the flood bears me a measure back and down: slow progress, but I live, I live, and make my way, aye, past many a drowned comrade in the end, stronger, worthier than I, victims of their unremitting *joie de nager*. I have seen the best swimmers of my generation go under. Numberless the number of the dead! Thousands drown as I think this thought, millions as I rest before returning to the swim. And scores, hundreds of millions have expired since we surged forth, brave in our innocence, upon our dreadful way. 'Love! Love!' we sang then, a quarter-billion strong, and churned the warm sea white with joy of swimming! Now all are gone down—the buoyant, the sodden, leaders and followers, all gone under, while wretched I swim on. Yet these same reflective intervals that keep me afloat have led me into wonder, doubt, despair—strange emotions for a swimmer!—have led me, even, to suspect . . . that our night-sea journey is without meaning.

"Indeed, if I have yet to join the hosts of the suicides, it is because (fatigue apart) I find it no meaningfuller to drown myself than to go on swimming.

"I know that there are those who seem actually to enjoy the night-sea; who claim to love swimming for its own sake, or sincerely believe that 'reaching the Shore,' 'transmitting the Heritage' (*Whose* Heritage, I'd like to know? And to whom?) is worth the staggering cost. I do not. Swimming itself I find at best not actively unpleasant, more often tiresome, not infrequently a torment. Arguments from function and design don't impress me: granted that we can and do swim, that in a manner of speaking our long tails and streamlined heads are 'meant for' swimming; it by no means follows—for me, at least—that we *should* swim, or otherwise endeavor to 'fulfill our destiny.' Which is to say, Someone Else's destiny, since ours, so far as I can see, is merely to perish, one way or another, soon or late. The heartless zeal of our (departed) leaders, like the blind ambition and good cheer of my own youth, appalls me now; for the death of my comrades I am inconsolable. If the night-sea journey has justification, it is not for us swimmers ever to discover it.

"Oh, to be sure, 'Love!' one heard on every side: 'Love it is that drives and sustains us!' I translate: we don't know *what* drives and sustains us, only that we are most miserably driven and, imperfectly, sustained. *Love* is how we call our ignorance of what whips us. 'To reach the Shore,' then: but what if the Shore exists in the fancies of us swimmers merely, who dream it to account for the dreadful fact that we swim, have always and only swum, and continue swimming without respite (myself excepted) until we die? Supposing even that there *were* a Shore—that, as a cynical companion of mine once imagined, we rise from the drowned to discover all those vulgar superstitions and exalted metaphors to be literal truth: the giant Maker of us all, the Shores of Light beyond our night-sea journey!—whatever would a swimmer do there? The fact is, when we imagine the Shore, what comes to mind is just the opposite of our condition: no more night, no more sea, no more journeying. In short, the blissful estate of the drowned.

" 'Ours not to stop and think; ours but to swim and sink. . . .' Because a moment's thought reveals the pointlessness of swimming. 'No matter,' I've heard some say, even as they gulped their last: 'The night-sea journey may be absurd, but here we swim, will-we nill-we, against the flood, onward and upward, toward a Shore that may not exist and couldn't be reached if it did.' The thoughtful swimmer's choices, then, they say, are two: give over thrashing and go under for good, or embrace the absurdity; affirm in and for itself the night-sea journey; swim on with neither motive nor destination, for the sake of swimming, and compassionate moreover with your fellow swimmer, we being all at sea and equally in the dark. I find neither course acceptable. If not even the hypothetical Shore can justify a sea-full of drownèd comrades, to speak of the swim-in-itself as somehow doing so strikes me as obscene. I continue to swim —but only because blind habit, blind instinct, blind fear of drowning are still more strong than the horror of our journey. And if on occasion I have assisted a fellow-thrasher, joined in the cheers and songs, even passed along to others strokes of genius from the drownèd great, it's that I shrink by temperament from making myself conspicuous. To paddle off in one's own direction, assert one's independent right-of-way, overrun one's fellows without compunction, or dedicate oneself entirely to pleasures and diversions without regard for conscience—I can't finally condemn those who journey in this wise; in half my moods I envy them and despise the weak vitality that keeps me from following their example. But in reasonabler moments I remind myself that it's their very freedom and self-responsibility I reject, as more dramatically absurd, in our senseless circumstances, than tailing along in conventional fashion. Suicides, rebels, affirmers of the paradox—nay-sayers and yea-sayers alike to our fatal journey—I finally shake my head at them. And splash sighing past their corpses, one by one, as past a hundred sorts of others: friends, enemies, brothers; fools, sages, brutes—and nobodies, million upon million. I envy them all.

"A poor irony: that I, who find abhorrent and tautological the doctrine of survival of the fittest (*fitness* meaning, in my experience, nothing more than survival-ability, a talent whose only demonstration is the fact of survival, but whose chief ingredients seem to be strength, guile, callousness), may be the sole remaining swimmer! But the doctrine is false as well as repellent: Chance drowns the worthy with the unworthy, bears up the unfit with the fit by whatever definition, and makes the night-sea journey essentially *haphazard* as well as murderous and unjustified.

" 'You only swim once.' Why bother, then?

" 'Except ye drown, ye shall not reach the Shore of Life.' Poppycock.

"One of my late companions—that same cynic with the curious fancy, among the first to drown—entertained us with odd conjectures while we waited to begin our journey. A favorite theory of his was that the Father does exist, and did indeed make us and the sea we swim—but not a-purpose or even consciously; He made us, as it were, despite Himself, as we make waves with every tail-thrash, and may be unaware of our existence. Another was that He knows we're here but doesn't care what happens to us, inasmuch as He creates (voluntarily or not) other seas and swimmers at more or less regular intervals. In bitterer moments, such as just before he drowned, my friend even supposed that our Maker wished us unmade; there was indeed a Shore, he'd argue, which could save at least some of us from drowning and toward which it was our function to struggle—but for reasons unknowable to us He wanted desperately to prevent our reaching that happy place and fulfilling our destiny. Our 'Father,' in short, was our adversary and would-be killer! No less outrageous, and offensive to traditional opinion, were the fellow's speculations on the nature of our Maker: that He might well be no swimmer Himself at all, but some sort of monstrosity, perhaps even tailless; that He might be stupid, malicious, insensible, perverse, or asleep and dreaming; that the end for which He created and launched us forth, and which we flagellate ourselves to fathom, was perhaps immoral, even obscene. Et cetera, et cetera: there was no end to the chap's conjectures, or the impoliteness of his fancy; I have reason to suspect that his early demise, whether planned by 'our Maker' or not, was expedited by certain fellow-swimmers indignant at his blasphemies.

"In other moods, however (he was as given to moods as I), his theorizing would become half-serious, so it seemed to me, especially upon the subjects of Fate and Immortality, to which our youthful conversations often turned. Then his harangues, if no less fantastical, grew solemn and obscure, and if he was still baiting us, his passion undid the joke. His objection to popular opinions of the hereafter, he would declare, was their claim to general validity. Why need believers hold that *all* the drownèd rise to be judged at journey's end, and non-believers that drowning is final without exception? In *his* opinion (so he'd vow at least), nearly everyone's fate was permanent death; indeed he took a sour pleasure in supposing that every 'Maker' made thousands of separate seas in His creative lifetime, each populated like ours with millions of swimmers, and that in almost every instance both sea and swimmers were utterly annihilated, whether accidentally or by malevolent design. (Nothing if not pluralistical, he imagined there might be millions and billions of 'Fathers,' perhaps in some 'night-sea' of their own!) However —and here he turned infidels against him with the faithful—he professed to believe that in possibly a single night-sea per thousand, say, one of its quarter-billion swimmers (that is, one swimmer in two hundred fifty billions) achieved a qualified immortality. In some cases the rate might be slightly higher; in others it was vastly lower, for just as there are swimmers of every degree of proficiency, including some who drown before the journey starts, unable to swim at all, and others created drowned, as it were, so he imagined what can only be termed impotent Creators, Makers unable to Make, as well as uncommonly fertile ones and all grades between. And it pleased him to deny any necessary relation between a Maker's productivity and His other virtues—including, even, the quality of His creatures.

"I could go on (*he* surely did) with his elaboration of these mad notions —such as that swimmers in other night-seas needn't be of our kind; that Makers themselves might belong to different *species,* so to speak; that our particular Maker mightn't Himself be immortal, or that we might be not only His emissaries but His 'immortality,' continuing His life and our own, transmogrified, beyond our individual deaths. Even this modified immortality (meaningless to me) he conceived as relative and contingent, subject to accidental or deliberate termination: his pet hypothesis was that Makers and swimmers *each generate the other*—against all odds, their number being so great—and that any given 'immortality-chain' could terminate after any number of cycles, so that what was 'immortal' (still speaking relatively) was only the cyclic process of incarnation, which itself might have a beginning and an end. Alternatively he liked to imagine cycles within cycles, either finite or infinite: for example, the 'night-sea,' as it were, in which Makers 'swam' and created night-seas and swimmers like ourselves, might be the creation of a larger Maker, Himself one of many, Who in turn et cetera. Time itself he regarded as relative to our experience, like magnitude: who knew but what, with each thrash of our tails, minuscule seas and swimmers, whole eternities, came to pass—as ours, perhaps, and our Maker's Maker's, was elapsing between the strokes of some supertail, in a slower order of time?

"Naturally I hooted with the others at this nonsense. We were young then, and had only the dimmest notion of what lay ahead; in our ignorance we imagined night-sea journeying to be a positively heroic enterprise. Its meaning and value we never questioned; to be sure, some must go down by the way, a pity no doubt, but to win a race requires that others lose, and like all my fellows I took for granted that I would be the winner. We milled and swarmed, impatient to be off, never mind where or why, only to try our youth against the realities of night and sea; if we indulged the skeptic at all, it was as a droll, half-contemptible mascot. When he died in the initial slaughter, no one cared.

"And even now I don't subscribe to all his views—but I no longer scoff. The horror of our history has purged me of opinions, as of vanity, confidence, spirit, charity, hope, vitality, everything—except dull dread and a kind of melancholy, stunned persistence. What leads me to recall his fancies is my growing suspicion that I, of all swimmers, may be the sole survivor of this fell journey, tale-bearer of a generation. This suspicion, together with the recent sea-change, suggests to me now that nothing is impossible, not even my late companion's wildest visions, and brings me to a certain desperate resolve, the point of my chronicling.

"Very likely I have lost my senses. The carnage at our setting out; our decimation by whirlpool, poisoned cataract, sea-convulsion; the panic stampedes, mutinies, slaughters, mass suicides; the mounting evidence that none will survive the journey—add to these anguish and fatigue; it were a miracle if sanity stayed afloat. Thus I admit, with the other possibilities, that the present sweetening and calming of the sea, and what seems to be a kind of vasty presence, song, or summons from the near upstream, may be hallucinations of disordered sensibility. . . .

"Perhaps, even, I am drowned already. Surely I was never meant for the rough-and-tumble of the swim; not impossibly I perished at the outset and have only imaged the night-sea journey from some final deep. In any case, I'm no longer young, and it is we spent old swimmers, disabused of every illusion, who are most vulnerable to dreams.

"Sometimes I think I am my drownèd friend.

"Out with it: I've begun to believe, not only that *She* exists, but that She lies not far ahead, and stills the sea, and draws me Herward! Aghast, I recollect his maddest notion: that our destination (which existed, mind, in but one night-sea out of hundreds and thousands) was no Shore, as commonly conceived, but a mysterious being, indescribable except by paradox and vaguest figure: wholly different from us swimmers, yet our complement; the death of us, yet our salvation and resurrection; simultaneously our journey's end, mid-point, and commencement; not membered and thrashing like us, but a motionless or hugely gliding sphere of unimaginable dimension; self-contained, yet dependent absolutely, in some wise, upon the chance (always monstrously improbable) that one of us will survive the night-sea journey and reach . . . Her! *Her,* he called it, or *She,* which is to say, Other-than-a-he. I shake my head; the thing is too preposterous; it is myself I talk to, to keep my reason in this awful darkness. There is no She! There is no You! I rave to myself;

it's Death alone that hears and summons. To the drowned, all seas are calm. . . .

"Listen: my friend maintained that in every order of creation there are two sorts of creators, contrary yet complementary, one of which gives rise to seas and swimmers, the other to the Night-which-contains-the-sea and to What-waits-at-the-journey's-end: the former, in short, to destiny, the latter to destination (and both profligately, involuntarily, perhaps indifferently or unwittingly). The 'purpose' of the night-sea journey—but not necessarily of the journeyer or of either Maker!—my friend could describe only in abstractions: *consummation, transfiguration, union of contraries, transcension of categories.* When we laughed, he would shrug and admit that he understood the business no better than we, and thought it ridiculous, dreary, possibly obscene. 'But one of you,' he'd add with his wry smile, 'may be the Hero destined to complete the night-sea journey and be one with Her. Chances are, of course, you won't make it.' He himself, he declared, was not even going to try; the whole idea repelled him; if we chose to dismiss it as an ugly fiction, so much the better for us; thrash, splash, and be merry, we were soon enough drowned. But there it was, he could not say how he knew or why he bothered to tell us, any more than he could say what would happen after She and Hero, Shore and Swimmer, 'merged identities' to become something both and neither. He quite agreed with me that if the issue of that magical union had no memory of the night-sea journey, for example, it enjoyed a poor sort of immortality; even poorer if, as he rather imagined, a swimmer-hero plus a She equaled or became merely another Maker of future night-seas and the rest, at such incredible expense of life. This being the case—he was persuaded it was—the merciful thing to do was refuse to participate; the genuine heroes, in his opinion, were the suicides, and the hero of heroes would be the swimmer who, in the very presence of the Other, refused Her proffered 'immortality' and thus put an end to at least one cycle of catastrophes.

"How we mocked him! Our moment came, we hurtled forth, pretending to glory in the adventure, thrashing, singing, cursing, strangling, rationalizing, rescuing, killing, inventing rules and stories and relationships, giving up, struggling on, but dying all, and still in darkness, until only a battered remnant was left to croak 'Onward, upward,' like a bitter echo. Then they too fell silent—victims, I can only presume, of the last frightful wave—and the moment came when I also, utterly desolate and spent, thrashed my last and gave myself over to the current, to sink or float as might be, but swim no more. Whereupon, marvelous to tell, in an instant the sea grew still! Then warmly, gently, the great tide turned, began to bear me, as it does now, onward and upward will-I nill-I, like a flood of joy—and I recalled with dismay my dead friend's teaching.

"I am not deceived. This new emotion is Her doing; the desire that possesses me is Her bewitchment. Lucidity passes from me; in a moment I'll cry 'Love!' bury myself in Her side, and be 'transfigured.' Which is to say, I die already; this fellow transported by passion is not I; *I am he who abjures and rejects the night-sea journey!* I. . . .

"I am all love. 'Come!' She whispers, and I have no will.

"You who I may be about to become, whatever You are: with the last twitch of my real self I beg You to listen. It is *not* love that sustains me! No; though Her magic makes me burn to sing the contrary, and though I drown even now for the blasphemy, I will say truth. What has fetched me across this dreadful sea is a single hope, gift of my poor dead comrade: that You may be stronger-willed than I, and that by sheer force of concentration I may transmit to You, along with Your official Heritage, a private legacy of awful recollection and negative resolve. Mad as it may be, my dream is that some unimaginable embodiment of myself (or myself plus Her if that's how it must be) will come to find itself expressing, in however garbled or radical a translation, some reflection of these reflections. If against all odds this comes to pass, may You to whom, through whom I speak, do what I cannot: terminate this aimless, brutal business! Stop Your hearing against Her song! Hate love!

"Still alive, afloat, afire. Farewell then my penultimate hope: that one may be sunk for direst blasphemy on the very shore of the Shore. Can it be (my old friend would smile) that only utterest nay-sayers survive the night? But even that were Sense, and there is no sense, only senseless love, senseless death. Whoever echoes these reflections: be more courageous than their author! An end to night-sea journeys! Make no more! And forswear me when I shall forswear myself, deny myself, plunge into Her who summons, singing . . .

" 'Love! Love! Love!' "

STUDY QUESTIONS

1. This story is from a volume of stories by John Barth entitled *Lost in the Funhouse,* subtitled *Fiction for Print, Tape, Live Voice.* In his "Author's Note" to the volume, Barth says of this story, " 'Night-Sea Journey' was meant for either print or recorded authorial voice." What is it about this story that would probably lead Barth to such a position? What is it about the identity of the narrator that presents problems for the interpreter? How could you refute Barth's position?
2. Does the narrator's identity change within the story?
3. How would you identify the narrator's epic situation? If he is indeed telling his story as it happens, then what becomes of the narrator at the end of the story? If the narrator is not precisely "human" throughout most of the story, does the climax of the story alter his condition? How do these complexities

regarding the narrator's dramatic situation present special problems for the interpreter?

4. Although it is clear that the narrator of this story does not fully comprehend the speculations of his "friend" about the meaning and function of their night-sea journey, it is equally clear that the implied author is using the juxtaposition of the narrator's comments and his friend's speculations for ironic purposes. Precisely how does this irony operate within the story? For what rhetorical purpose is the implied author using this narrator?

5. How can the interpreter demonstrate the tension in this story created through the juxtaposition of the narrator's voice and the implied author's voice?

6. Who is the audience *in* the story? Is the swimmer speaking to fellow swimmers? If so, then what happens to his audience when he is the only swimmer left alive? The narrator would seem to be meditating; but how is this answer contradicted by evidence in his manner of storytelling?

James Purdy/Eventide

born 1923

Mahala had waited as long as she thought she could; after all, Plumy had left that morning and now here it was going on four o'clock. It was hardly fair if she was loitering, but she knew that certainly Plumy would never loiter on a day like this when Mahala wanted so to hear. It was in a way the biggest day of her whole life, bigger than any day she had ever lived through as a girl or young woman. It was the day that decided whether her son would come back to live with her or not.

And just think, a whole month had rolled past since he left home. Two months ago if anyone would have said that Teeboy would leave home, she would have stopped dead in her tracks, it would have been such a terrible thing even to say, and now here she was, talking over the telephone about how Teeboy had gone.

"My Teeboy is gone," that is what Mahala said for a long time after the departure. These words announced to her mind what had happened, and just as an announcement they gave some mild comfort, like a pain-killer with a fatal disease.

"My Teeboy," she would say, like the mother of a dead son, like the mother of a son who had died in battle, because it hurt as much to have a son missing in peacetime as to have lost him through war.

The room seemed dark even with the summer sunshine outside, and close, although the window was open. There was a darkness all over the city. The fire department had been coming and going all afternoon. There were so many fires in the neighborhood—that is what she was saying to Cora on the telephone, too many fires: the fire chief had just whizzed past again. No, she said to Cora, she didn't know if it was in the white section of town or theirs, she couldn't tell, but oh it was so hot to have a fire.

Talking about the fires seemed to help Mahala more than anything. She called several other old friends and talked about the fires and she mentioned that Teeboy had not come home. The old friends did not say much about Teeboy's not having returned, because, well, what was there to say about a boy who had been practicing to leave home for so long. Everyone had known it but her blind mother love.

"What do you suppose can be keeping my sister Plumy?" Mahala said to herself as she walked up and down the hall and looked out from behind the screen in the window. "She would have to fail me on the most important errand in the world."

Then she thought about how much Plumy hated to go into white neighborhoods, and how the day had been hot and she thought of the fires and how perhaps Plumy had fallen under a fire truck and been crushed. She thought of all the possible disasters and was not happy, and always in the background there was the fresh emotion of having lost Teeboy.

"People don't know," she said, "that I can't live without Teeboy."

She would go in the clothes closet and look at his dirty clothes just as he had left them; she would kiss them and press them to her face, smelling them; the odors were especially dear to her. She held his rayon trousers to her bosom and walked up and down the small parlor. She had not prayed; she was waiting for Plumy to come home first, then maybe they would have prayer.

"I hope I ain't done anything I'll be sorry for," she said.

It was then, though, when she felt the worst, that she heard the steps on the front porch. Yes, those were Plumy's steps, she was coming with the news. But whatever the news was, she suddenly felt, she could not accept it.

As she came up the steps, Plumy did not look at Mahala with any particular kind of meaning on her face. She walked unsteadily, as if the heat had been too much for her.

"Come on in now, Plumy, and I will get you something cool to drink."

Inside, Plumy watched Mahala as if afraid she was going to ask her to begin at once with the story, but Mahala only waited, not saying anything, sensing the seriousness of Plumy's knowledge and knowing that this knowledge could be revealed only when Plumy was ready.

While Mahala waited patiently there in the kitchen, Plumy arranged herself in the easy chair, and when she was once settled, she took up the straw fan which lay on the floor.

"Well, I seen him!" Plumy brought the words out.

This beginning quieted the old mother a little. She closed her mouth and folded her hands, moving now to the middle of the parlor, with an intentness on her face as if she was listening to something high up in the sky, like a plane which is to drop something, perhaps harmless and silver, to the ground.

"I seen him!" Plumy repeated, as if to herself. "And I seen all the white people!" she finished, anger coming into her voice.

"Oh, Plumy," Mahala whined. Then suddenly she made a gesture for her sister to be quiet because she thought she heard the fire department going again, and then when there was no sound, she waited for her to go on, but Plumy did not say anything. In the slow afternoon there was nothing, only a silence a city sometimes has within itself.

Plumy was too faint from the heat to go on at once; her head suddenly shook violently and she slumped in the chair.

"Plumy Jackson!" Mahala said, going over to her. "You didn't *walk* here from the white district! You didn't walk them forty-seven blocks in all this August heat!"

Plumy did not answer immediately. Her hand caressed the worn upholstery of the chair.

"You know how nervous white folks make me," she said at last.

Mahala made a gesture of disgust. "Lord, to think you walked it in this hot sun. Oh, I don't know why God wants to upset me like this. As if I didn't have enough to make me wild already, without havin' you come home in this condition."

Mahala watched her sister's face for a moment with the same figuring expression of the man who comes to read the water meter. She saw everything she really wanted to know there, yet she pretended she didn't know the verdict; she brought the one question out:

"You did see Teeboy, honey?" she said, her voice changed from her tears. She waited a few seconds, and then as Plumy did not answer but only sank deeper into the chair, she continued: "What word did he send?"

"It's the way I told you before," Plumy replied crossly. "Teeboy ain't coming back. I thought you knowed from the way I looked at you that he ain't coming back."

Mahala wept quietly into a small handkerchief.

"Your pain is realer to me sometimes than my own," Plumy said, watching her cry. "That's why I hate to say to you he won't never come back, but it's true as death he won't."

"When you say that to me I got a feeling inside myself like everything had been busted and taken; I got the feeling like I don't have nothing left inside of me."

"Don't I know that feeling!" Plumy said, almost angrily, resting the straw fan on the arm of the chair, and then suddenly fanning herself violently so that the strokes sounded like those of a small angry whip. "Didn't I lost George Watson of sleeping sickness and all 'cause doctor wouldn't come?"

Plumy knew that Mahala had never shown any interest in the death of her own George Watson and that it was an unwelcome subject, especially tonight, when Teeboy's never coming back had become final, yet she could not help mentioning George Watson just the same. In Mahala's eyes there really had never been any son named George Watson; there was only a son named Teeboy and Mahala was the only mother.

"It ain't like there bein' no way out to your troubles: it's the way out that kills you," Mahala said. "If it was good-bye for always like when someone dies, I think I could stand it better. But this kind of parting ain't like the Lord's way!"

Plumy continued fanning herself, just letting Mahala run on.

"So he ain't never coming back!" Mahala began beating her hands together as if she were hearing music for a dance.

Plumy looked away as the sound of the rats downstairs caught her attention; there seemed to be more than usual tonight and she wondered why they were running so much, for it was so hot everywhere.

Her attention strayed back to Mahala standing directly in front of her now, talking about her suffering: "You go through all the suffering and the heartache," she said, "and then they go away. The only time children is nice is when they're babies and you know they can't get away from you. You got them then and your love is all they crave. They don't know who you are exactly, they just know you are the one to give them your love, and they ask you for it until you're worn out giving it."

Mahala's speech set Plumy to thinking of how she had been young and how she had had George Watson, and how he had died of sleeping sickness when he was four.

"My only son died of sleeping sickness," Plumy said aloud, but not really addressing Mahala. "I never had another. My husband said it was funny. He was not a religious man, but he thought it was queer."

"Would you like a cooling drink?" Mahala said absently.

Plumy shook her head and there was a silence of a few minutes in which the full weight of the heat of evening took possession of the small room.

"I can't get used to that idea of him *never* coming back!" Mahala began again. "I ain't never been able to understand that word *never* anyhow. And now it's like to drive me wild."

There was another long silence, and then, Mahala suddenly rousing herself from drowsiness and the heat of the evening, began eagerly: "How did he look, Plumy? Tell me how he looked, and what he was doing. Just describe."

"He wasn't doin' nothin'!" Plumy said flatly. "He looked kind of older, though, like he had been thinking about new things."

"Don't keep me waiting," Mahala whined. "I been waitin' all day for the news, don't keep me no more, when I tell you I could suicide over it all. I ain't never been through such a hell day. Don't you keep me waitin'."

"Now hush," Plumy said. "Don't go frettin' like this. Your heart won't take a big grief like this if you go fret so."

"It's *so* unkind of you not to tell," she muffled her lips in her handkerchief.

Plumy said: "I told you I talked to him, but I didn't tell you where. It was in a drinking place called the Music Box. He called to me from inside. The minute I looked at him I knew there was something wrong. There was something wrong with his hair."

"With his hair!" Mahala cried.

"Then I noticed he had had it all made straight! That's right," she said looking away from Mahala's eyes. "He had had his hair straightened. 'Why ain't you got in touch with your mother,' I said. 'If you only knowed how she was carryin' on.'

"Then he told me how he had got a tenor sax and how he was playing it in the band at the Music Box and that he had begun a new life, and it was all on account of his having the tenor sax and being a musician. He said the players didn't have time to have homes. He said they were playing all the time, they never went home, and that was why he hadn't been."

Plumy stopped. She saw the tenor sax only in her imagination because he had not shown it to her, she saw it curved and golden and heard it playing far-off melodies. But the real reason she stopped was not on account of the tenor sax but because of the memory of the white woman who had come out just then. The white woman had come out and put her arm around Teeboy. It had made her get creepy all over. It was the first time that Plumy had realized that Teeboy's skin was nearly as light as the white people's.

Both Teeboy and the woman had stood there looking at Plumy, and Plumy had not known how to move away from them. The sun beat down on her in the street but she could not move. She saw the streetcars going by with all the white people pushing one another around and she looked around on the scorched pavements and everyone was white, with Teeboy looking just as white as the rest of them, looking just as white as if he had come out of Mahala's body white, and as if Mahala had been a white woman and not her sister, and as if Mahala's mother and hers had not been black.

Then slowly she had begun walking away from Teeboy and the Music Box, almost without knowing she was going herself, walking right on through the streets without knowing what was happening, through the big August heat, without an umbrella or a hat to keep off the sun; she could see no place to stop, and people could see the circles of sweat that were forming all over her dress. She was afraid to stop and she was afraid to go on walking. She felt she would fall down eventually in the afternoon sun and it would be like the time George Watson had died of sleeping sickness, nobody would help her to an easy place.

Would George Watson know her now? That is what she was thinking as she walked through the heat of that afternoon. Would he know her— because when she had been his mother she had been young and her skin, she was sure, had been lighter; and now she was older looking than she remembered her own mother ever being, and her skin was very black.

It was Mahala's outcries which brought her back to the parlor, now full of the evening twilight.

"Why can't God call me home?" Mahala was asking. "Why can't He call me to His Throne of Grace?"

Then Mahala got up and wandered off into her own part of the house. One could hear her in her room there, faintly kissing Teeboy's soiled clothes and speaking quietly to herself.

"Until you told me about his having his hair straightened, I thought maybe he would be back," Mahala was saying from the room. "But when you told me that, I knew. He won't never be back."

Plumy could hear Mahala kissing the clothes after she had said this.

"He was so dear to her," Plumy said aloud. It was necessary to speak aloud at that moment because of the terrible feeling of evening in the room. Was it the smell of the four o'clocks, which must have just opened to give out their perfume, or was it the evening itself which made her uneasy? She felt not alone, she felt someone else had come, uninvited and from far away.

Plumy had never noticed before what a strong odor the four o'clocks had, and then she saw the light in the room, growing larger, a light she had not recognized before, and then she turned and saw *him,* George Watson Jackson, standing there before her, large as life. Plumy wanted to call out, she wanted to say *No* in a great voice, she wanted to brush the sight before her all away, which was strange because she was always wanting to see her baby and here he was, although seventeen years had passed since she had laid him away.

She looked at him with unbelieving eyes because really he was the same, the same except she did notice that little boys' suits had changed fashion since his day, and how that everything about him was slightly different from the little children of the neighborhood now.

"Baby!" she said, but the word didn't come out from her mouth, it was only a great winged thought that could not be made into sound. "George Watson, honey!" she said still in her silence.

He stood there, his eyes like they had been before. Their beauty stabbed at her heart like a great knife; the hair looked so like she had just pressed the wet comb to it and perhaps put a little pomade on the sides; and the small face was clean and sad. Yet her arms somehow did not ache to hold him like her heart told her they should. Something too far away and too strong was between her and him; she only saw him as she had always seen resurrection pictures, hidden from us as in a wonderful mist that will not let us see our love complete.

There was this mist between her and George Watson like the dew that will be on the four o'clocks when you pick one of them off the plant.

It was her baby come home, and at such an hour.

Then as she came slowly to herself, she began to raise herself slightly, stretching her arms and trying to get the words to come out to him:

"George Watson, baby!"

This time the words did come out, with a terrible loudness, and as they did so the light began to go from the place where he was standing: the last thing she saw of him was his bright forehead and hair, then there was nothing at all, not even the smell of flowers.

Plumy let out a great cry and fell back in the chair. Mahala heard her and came out of her room to look at her.

"What you got?" Mahala said.

"I seen *him!* I seen *him!* Big as life!"

"Who?" Mahala said.

"George Watson, just like I laid him away seventeen years ago!"

Mahala did not know what to say. She wiped her eyes dry, for she had quit crying.

"You was exposed too long in the sun," Mahala said vaguely.

As she looked at her sister she felt for the first time the love that Plumy had borne all these years for a small son Mahala had never seen, George Watson. For the first time she dimly recognized Plumy as a mother, and she had suddenly a feeling of intimacy for her that she never had before.

She walked over to the chair where Plumy was and laid her hand on her. Somehow the idea of George Watson's being dead so long and yet still being a baby a mother could love had a kind of perfect quality that she liked. She thought then, quietly and without shame, how nice it would be if Teeboy could also be perfect in death, so that he would belong to her in the same perfect way as George Watson belonged to Plumy. There was comfort in tending the grave of a dead son, whether he was killed in war or peace, and it was so difficult to tend the memory of a son who just went away and never came back. Yet somehow she knew as she looked at Plumy, somehow she would go on with the memory of Teeboy Jordan even though he still lived in the world.

As she stood there considering the lives of the two sons Teeboy Jordan and George Watson Jackson, the evening which had for some time been moving slowly into the house entered now as if in one great wave, bringing the small parlor into the heavy summer night until you would have believed daylight would never enter there again, the night was so black and secure.

STUDY QUESTIONS

1. The diction of the narrator of this story and the knowledge that he apparently has about both characters, their customs, jargon, beliefs, and suspicions, seem to define him as someone very much like Plumy and Mahala; yet, one realizes the narrator's maturity and sophistication that go beyond either Plumy's or Mahala's. Find as many examples from the text as you can that will help formulate each of these images of the narrator. How does this evidence provide the basis for certain conclusions you could draw about the narrator's ability to relate this particular story?
2. Where does this story take place? How does the locale affect the way the characters speak? Does this in any way affect the narrator's speech? What happens to the narrator's speech when he assumes the attitudes and enters the thoughts of Plumy and Mahala?
3. In *A Portrait of the Artist as a Young Man* James Joyce describes an occurrence that appears in many of his stories and that he calls an "epiphany." An epiphany is a sudden illumination of awareness that occurs to a character. In "Eventide," is there an epiphany for either of the two central characters? For both? If so, point out where the epiphanies occur and explain them. If not, what does happen to the characters during the course of the story that causes the reader's change in attitude toward them?
4. Is this story primarily about Mahala? about Plumy? about their relationship?
5. Throughout this story you are presented with rather different pictures of each of the two women. Describe as clearly as possible the way each sister sees the other and the way each woman sees herself. How do these pictures conflict? Do these conflicting pictures provide a source of understanding about the story's central conflict?
6. How involved is the narrator in the lives of these two women? How much does the narrator create the illusion of showing the story? What kinds of demands does this place on the interpreter in demonstrating this story?
7. In the last line of the story the narrator says that evening moved in "bringing the small parlor into the heavy summer night until you would have believed daylight would never enter there again, the night was so black and secure." Is this not a contradictory statement? Does this statement make a comment on the two women and their individual perceptions of their relationship? Or is this comment made specifically from Mahala's point of view?

William Faulkner/A Rose for Emily

born 1897

When Miss Emily Grierson died, our whole town went to her funeral: the men through a sort of respectful affection for a fallen monument, the women mostly out of curiosity to see the inside of her house, which no one save an old man-servant—a combined gardener and cook—had seen in at least ten years.

It was a big, squarish frame house that had once been white, decorated with cupolas and spires and scrolled balconies in the heavily lightsome style of the seventies, set on what had once been our most select street. But garages and cotton gins had encroached and obliterated even the august names of that neighborhood; only Miss Emily's house was left, lifting its stubborn and coquettish decay above the cotton wagons and the gasoline pumps—an eyesore among eyesores. And now Miss Emily had gone to join the representatives of those august names where they lay in the cedar-bemused cemetery among the ranked and anonymous graves of Union and Confederate soldiers who fell at the battle of Jefferson.

Alive, Miss Emily had been a tradition, a duty, and a care; a sort of hereditary obligation upon the town, dating from that day in 1894 when Colonel Sartoris, the mayor—he who fathered the edict that no Negro woman should appear on the streets without an apron—remitted her taxes, the dispensation dating from the death of her father on into perpetuity. Not that Miss Emily would have accepted charity. Colonel Sartoris invented an involved tale to the effect that Miss Emily's father had loaned money to the town, which the town, as a matter of business, preferred this way of repaying. Only a man of Colonel Sartoris' generation and thought could have invented it, and only a woman could have believed it.

When the next generation, with its more modern ideas, became mayors and aldermen, this arrangement created some little dissatisfaction. On the first of the year they mailed her a tax notice. February came, and there was no reply. They wrote her a formal letter, asking her to call at the sheriff's office at her convenience. A week later the mayor wrote her himself, offering to call or to send his car for her, and received in reply a note on paper of an archaic shape, in a thin, flowing calligraphy in faded ink, to the effect that she no longer went out at all. The tax notice was also enclosed, without comment.

They called a special meeting of the Board of Aldermen. A deputation waited upon her, knocked at the door through which no visitor had passed since she ceased giving china-painting lessons eight or ten years earlier. They were admitted by the old Negro into a dim hall from which a stairway mounted into still more shadow. It smelled of dust and disuse—a close, dank smell. The Negro led them into the parlor. It was furnished in heavy, leather-covered furniture. When the Negro opened the blinds of one window, they could see that the leather was cracked; and when they sat down, a faint dust rose sluggishly about their thighs, spinning with slow motes in the single sun-ray. On a tarnished gilt easel before the fireplace stood a crayon portrait of Miss Emily's father.

They rose when she entered—a small, fat woman in black, with a thin gold chain descending to her waist and vanishing into her belt, leaning on an ebony cane with a tarnished gold head. Her skeleton was small and spare; perhaps that was why what would have been merely plumpness in another was obesity in her. She looked bloated, like a body long submerged in motionless water, and of that pallid hue. Her eyes, lost in the fatty ridges of her face, looked like two small pieces of coal pressed into a lump of dough as they moved from one face to another while the visitors stated their errand.

She did not ask them to sit. She just stood in the door and listened quietly until the spokesman came to a stumbling halt. Then they could hear the invisible watch ticking at the end of the gold chain.

Her voice was dry and cold. "I have no taxes in Jefferson. Colonel Sartoris explained it to me. Perhaps one of you can gain access to the city records and satisfy yourselves."

"But we have. We are the city authorities, Miss Emily. Didn't you get a notice from the sheriff, signed by him?"

"I received a paper, yes," Miss Emily said. "Perhaps he considers himself the sheriff . . . I have no taxes in Jefferson."

"But there is nothing on the books to show that, you see. We must go by the—"

"See Colonel Sartoris. I have no taxes in Jefferson."

"But, Miss Emily—"

"See Colonel Sartoris." (Colonel Sartoris had been dead almost ten years.) "I have no taxes in Jefferson. Tobe!" The Negro appeared. "Show these gentlemen out."

II

So she vanquished them, horse and foot, just as she had vanquished their fathers thirty years before about the smell. That was two years after her father's death and a short time after her sweetheart—the one we believed would marry her—had deserted her. After her father's death she went out very little; after her sweetheart went away, people hardly saw her at all. A few of the ladies had the temerity to call, but were not received, and the only sign of life about the place was the Negro man—a young man then—going in and out with a market basket.

"Just as if a man—any man—could keep a kitchen properly," the ladies said; so they were not surprised when the smell developed. It was another link between the gross, teeming world and the high and mighty Griersons.

A neighbor, a woman, complained to the mayor, Judge Stevens, eighty years old.

"But what will you have me do about it, madam?" he said.

"Why, send her word to stop it," the woman said. "Isn't there a law?"

"I'm sure that won't be necessary," Judge Stevens said. "It's probably just a snake or a rat that nigger of hers killed in the yard. I'll speak to him about it."

The next day he received two more complaints, one from a man who came in diffident deprecation. "We really must do something about it, Judge. I'd be the last one in the world to bother Miss Emily, but we've got to do something." That night the Board of Aldermen met—three graybeards and one younger man, a member of the rising generation.

"It's simple enough," he said. "Send her word to have her place cleaned up. Give her a certain time to do it in, and if she don't . . ."

"Dammit, sir," Judge Stevens said, "will you accuse a lady to her face of smelling bad?"

So the next night, after midnight, four men crossed Miss Emily's lawn and slunk about the house like burglars, sniffing along the base of the brickwork and at the cellar openings while one of them performed a regular sowing motion with his hand out of a sack slung from his shoulder. They broke open the cellar door and sprinkled lime there, and in all the outbuildings. As they recrossed the lawn, a window that had been dark was lighted and Miss Emily sat in it, the light behind her, and her upright torso motionless as that of an idol. They crept quietly across the lawn and into the shadow of the locusts that lined the street. After a week or two the smell went away.

That was when people had begun to feel really sorry for her. People in our town, remembering how old lady Wyatt, her great-aunt, had gone completely crazy at last, believed that the Griersons held themselves a little too high for what they really were. None of the young men were quite good enough for Miss Emily and such. We had long thought of them as a tableau, Miss Emily a slender figure in white in the background, her father a spraddled silhouette in the foreground, his back to her and clutching a horsewhip, the two of them framed by the back-flung front door. So when she got to be thirty and was still single, we were not pleased exactly, but vindicated; even with insanity in the family she wouldn't have turned down all of her chances if they had really materialized.

When her father died, it got about that the house was all that was left to her; and in a way, people were glad. At last they could pity Miss Emily. Being left alone, and a pauper, she had become humanized. Now she too would know the old thrill and the old despair of a penny more or less.

The day after his death all the ladies prepared to call at the house and offer condolence and aid, as is our custom. Miss Emily met them at the door, dressed as usual and with no trace of grief on her face. She told them that her father was not dead. She did that for three days, with the ministers calling on her, and the doctors, trying to persuade her to let them dispose of the body. Just as they were about to resort to law and force, she broke down, and they buried her father quickly.

We did not say she was crazy then. We believed she had to do that. We remembered all the young men her father had driven away, and we knew that with nothing left, she would have to cling to that which had robbed her, as people will.

III

She was sick for a long time. When we saw her again, her hair was cut short, making her look like a girl, with a vague resemblance to those angels in colored church windows—sort of tragic and serene.

The town had just let the contracts for paving the sidewalks, and in the summer after her father's death they began to work. The construction company came with niggers and mules and machinery, and a foreman named Homer Barron, a Yankee—a big, dark, ready man, with a big voice and eyes lighter than his face. The little boys would follow in groups to hear him cuss the niggers, and the niggers singing in time to the rise and fall of picks. Pretty soon he knew everybody in town. Whenever you heard a lot of laughing anywhere about the square, Homer Barron would be in the center of the group. Presently we began to see him and Miss Emily on Sunday afternoons driving in the yellow-wheeled buggy and the matched team of bays from the livery stable.

At first we were glad that Miss Emily would have an interest, because the ladies all said, "Of course a Grierson would not think seriously of a Northerner, a day laborer." But there were still others, older people, who said that even grief could not cause a real lady to forget *noblesse oblige* —without calling it *noblesse oblige.* They just said, "Poor Emily. Her kinsfolk should come to her." She had some kin in Alabama; but years ago her father had fallen out with them over the estate of old lady Wyatt, the crazy woman, and there was no communication between the two families. They had not even been represented at the funeral.

And as soon as the old people said, "Poor Emily," the whispering began. "Do you suppose it's really so?" they said to one another. "Of course it is. What else could . . ." This behind their hands; rustling of craned silk and satin behind jalousies closed upon the sun of Sunday afternoon as the thin, swift clop-clop-clop of the matched team passed: "Poor Emily."

She carried her head high enough—even when we believed that she was fallen. It was as if she demanded more than ever the recognition of her dignity as the last Grierson; as if it had wanted that touch of earthiness to reaffirm her imperviousness. Like when she bought the rat poison, the arsenic. That was over a year after they had begun to say "Poor Emily," and while the two female cousins were visiting her.

"I want some poison," she said to the druggist. She was over thirty then, still a slight woman, though thinner than usual, with cold, haughty black eyes in a face the flesh of which was strained across the temples and about the eyesockets as you imagine a lighthouse-keeper's face ought to look. "I want some poison," she said.

"Yes, Miss Emily. What kind? For rats and such? I'd recom—"

"I want the best you have. I don't care what kind."

The druggist named several. "They'll kill anything up to an elephant. But what you want is—"

"Arsenic," Miss Emily said. "Is that a good one?"

"Is . . . arsenic? Yes ma'am. But what you want—"

"I want arsenic."

The druggist looked down at her. She looked back at him, erect, her face like a strained flag. "Why, of course," the druggist said. "If that's what you want. But the law requires you to tell what you are going to use it for."

Miss Emily just stared at him, her head tilted back in order to look him eye for eye, until he looked away and went and got the arsenic and wrapped it up. The Negro delivery boy brought her the package; the druggist didn't come back. When she opened the package at home there was written on the box, under the skull and bones: "For rats."

IV

So the next day we all said, "She will kill herself"; and we said it would be the best thing. When she had first begun to be seen with Homer Barron, we had said, "She will marry him." Then we said, "She will persuade him yet," because Homer himself had remarked—he liked men, and it was known that he drank with the younger men in the Elk's Club —that he was not a marrying man. Later we said, "Poor Emily" behind the jalousies as they passed on Sunday afternoon in the glittering buggy, Miss Emily with her head high and Homer Barron with his hat cocked and a cigar in his teeth, reins and whip in a yellow glove.

Then some of the ladies began to say that it was a disgrace to the town and a bad example to the young people. The men did not want to interfere, but at last the ladies forced the Baptist minister—Miss Emily's people were Episcopal—to call upon her. He would never divulge what happened during that interview, but he refused to go back again. The next Sunday they again drove about the streets, and the following day the minister's wife wrote to Miss Emily's relations in Alabama.

So she had blood-kin under her roof again and we sat back to watch developments. At first nothing happened. Then we were sure that they were to be married. We learned that Miss Emily had been to the jeweler's and ordered a man's toilet set in silver, with the letters H. B. on each piece. Two days later we learned that she had bought a complete outfit of men's clothing, including a nightshirt, and we said, "They are married." We were really glad. We were glad because the two female cousins were even more Grierson than Miss Emily had ever been.

So we were not surprised when Homer Barron—the streets had been finished some time since—was gone. We were a little disappointed that there was not a public blowing-off, but we believed that he had gone on to prepare for Miss Emily's coming, or to give her a chance to get rid of the cousins. (By that time it was a cabal, and we were all Miss Emily's allies to help circumvent the cousins.) Sure enough, after another week they departed. And, as we had expected all along, within three days Homer Barron was back in town. A neighbor saw the Negro man admit him at the kitchen door at dusk one evening.

And that was the last we saw of Homer Barron. And of Miss Emily for some time. The Negro man went in and out with the market basket, but the front door remained closed. Now and then we would see her at a window for a moment, as the men did that night when they sprinkled the lime, but for almost six months she did not appear on the streets. Then we knew that this was to be expected too; as if that quality of her father which had thwarted her woman's life so many times had been too virulent and too furious to die.

When we next saw Miss Emily, she had grown fat and her hair was turning gray. During the next few years it grew grayer and grayer until it attained an even pepper-and-salt iron-gray, when it ceased turning. Up to the day of her death at seventy-four it was still that vigorous iron-gray, like the hair of an active man.

From that time on her front door remained closed, save for a period of six or seven years, when she was about forty, during which she gave lessons in china-painting. She fitted up a studio in one of the downstairs rooms, where the daughters and granddaughters of Colonel Sartoris' contemporaries were sent to her with the same regularity and in the same spirit that they were sent to church on Sundays with a twenty-five-cent piece for the collection plate. Meanwhile her taxes had been remitted.

Then the newer generation became the backbone and the spirit of the town, and the painting pupils grew up and fell away and did not send their children to her with boxes of color and tedious brushes and pictures cut from the ladies' magazines. The front door closed upon the last one and remained closed for good. When the town got free postal delivery, Miss Emily alone refused to let them fasten the metal numbers above her door and attach a mailbox to it. She would not listen to them.

Daily, monthly, yearly we watched the Negro grow grayer and more stooped, going in and out with the market basket. Each December we sent her a tax notice, which would be returned by the post office a week later, unclaimed. Now and then we would see her in one of the downstairs windows—she had evidently shut up the top floor of the house—like the carven torso of an idol in a niche, looking or not looking at us, we could never tell which. Thus she passed from generation to generation—dear, inescapable, impervious, tranquil, and perverse.

And so she died. Fell ill in the house filled with dust and shadows, with only a doddering Negro man to wait on her. We did not even know she was sick; we had long since given up trying to get any information from the Negro. He talked to no one, probably not even to her, for his voice had grown harsh and rusty, as if from disuse.

She died in one of the downstairs rooms, in a heavy walnut bed with a curtain, her gray head propped on a pillow yellow and moldy with age and lack of sunlight.

V

The Negro met the first of the ladies at the front door and let them in, with their hushed, sibilant voices and their quick, curious glances, and then he disappeared. He walked right through the house and out the back and was not seen again.

The two female cousins came at once. They held the funeral on the second day, with the town coming to look at Miss Emily beneath a mass of bought flowers, with the crayon face of her father musing profoundly above the bier and the ladies sibilant and macabre; and the very old men—some in their brushed Confederate uniforms—on the porch and the lawn, talking of Miss Emily as if she had been a contemporary of theirs, believing that they had danced with her and courted her perhaps, confusing time with its mathematical progression, as the old do, to whom all the past is not a diminishing road, but, instead, a huge meadow which no winter ever quite touches, divided from them now by the narrow bottle-neck of the most recent decade of years.

Already we knew that there was one room in that region above stairs which no one had seen in forty years, and which would have to be forced. They waited until Miss Emily was decently in the ground before they opened it.

The violence of breaking down the door seemed to fill this room with pervading dust. A thin, acrid pall as of the tomb seemed to lie every-where upon this room decked and furnished as for a bridal: upon the valance curtains of faded rose color, upon the rose-shaded lights, upon the dressing table, upon the delicate array of crystal and the man's toilet things backed with tarnished silver, silver so tarnished that the mono-gram was obscured. Among them lay a collar and tie, as if they had just been removed, which, lifted, left upon the surface a pale crescent in the dust. Upon a chair hung the suit, carefully folded; beneath it the two mute shoes and the discarded socks.

The man himself lay in the bed.

For a long while we just stood there, looking down at the profound and fleshless grin. The body had apparently once lain in the attitude of an embrace, but now the long sleep that outlasts love, that conquers even the grimace of love, had cuckolded him. What was left of him, rotted beneath what was left of the nightshirt, had become inextricable from the bed in which he lay; and upon him and upon the pillow beside him lay that even coating of the patient and biding dust.

Then we noticed that in the second pillow was the indentation of a head. One of us lifted something from it, and leaning forward, that faint and invisible dust dry and acrid in the nostrils, we saw a long strand of iron-gray hair.

STUDY QUESTIONS

1. As said earlier, the use of a first-person narrator who is a minor participant in the action tends to provide the advantages of an eyewitness account while managing to create more objectivity than an account by a major participant. In this story, are these the only advantages of using a minor participant in the action as the narrator? Obviously, the story would be quite different if told from Miss Emily's point of view; but is this simply the macabre story of an eccentric aging woman, or is it a story about the narrator as well?

2. What clues are provided in the text by the narrator concerning his identity? his occupation? his social relationship with Miss Emily? his age? Is the narrator a man or a woman, or is this possible to determine from the evidence in the text?

3. Try to reconstruct the temporal sequence of events in the story and the narrator's reporting of Miss Emily's age. What inconsistencies do you find in his report? What does this suggest to you about the narrator?

4. Notice the conflicting attitudes toward Miss Emily that are voiced by the narrator. Pay particular attention to the images he uses to describe her. How do these contradictory attitudes prevent you from getting a "true" picture of Miss Emily? Do these conflicts in the narrator coincide with the attitudes of most of the other townspeople? Does this suggest that Faulkner is using the narrator as an embodiment of the misguided and compassionless attitudes of the townspeople? Consider the possibility that the story is really concerned with the inability of Miss Emily and the townspeople to recognize each other as human beings. What evidence for this position can you find in the text?

5. Consider the relationship between the narrator's values and judgments and the implied author's values and judgments. What similarities do you find? What contradictions or differences do you find? Has Faulkner managed to make the reader identify with the narrator's position? If so, how? Has Faulkner allowed the narrator to undermine his own position? If so, how?

Archibald Marshall/The Ancient Roman

born 1866

Once there was an ancient Roman, and he lived in a Roman villa with a pavement and wore a toga and sandals and all those things, and he talked Latin quite easily, and he was a Senator and very important.

Well he had a wife who was a Roman matron and a very nice boy called Claudius, and one day Claudius came to him and said O pater, because he could talk Latin too, will you give me a denarius?

And his father said what for?

And he said I want to buy a catapult.

So his father gave him a denarius and he bought a catapult, and one day when he was playing with it he killed a slave by mistake.

Well killing a slave wasn't against the law so it wasn't murder or anything like that, but Claudius was very sorry all the same, and he threw away his catapult and wouldn't use it any more.

And his father bought another slave instead of that one, and he said you must be more careful because slaves are very expensive.

And he said he would.

And Claudius was very kind to that slave and never beat him as he would have been allowed to do if he had wanted, because he was very sorry that he had killed the other one by mistake.

Well the slave came from Gaul, and he was very homesick and wanted to go back there because he had a mother and a little sister and he loved them.

So one day he told Claudius that he would like to escape, and Claudius said he would help him and he did, and the slave escaped.

Well when he found out that the slave had escaped the ancient Roman was very angry and he said I can't afford to go on losing slaves like this, that's the second in a fortnight, and if I find out that anybody has helped him to escape I will put him to death.

Now Claudius had told his mother that he had helped the slave to escape, so she said to the ancient Roman you had better be careful what you say or you may be sorry, and he said what do you mean?

So she thought she had better tell him, and she said well Claudius helped the slave to escape because he was sorry for him.

So the ancient Roman hid his head in his toga or one of those things and said eheu, which is Latin for alas, I shall have to put my own son to death.

And his wife said don't be so silly, what for?

And he said because I said I would and I can't go on being an ancient Roman unless I do.

She said I call it too silly and you'll do nothing of the sort.

And he said are you a Roman matron or not?

She said yes I am, and he said well then behave like one.

Well the ancient Roman didn't put Claudius to death at once because he wanted everybody to know about it, and all their relations came to him and knelt down and asked him not to, but he said he must.

Then they put dust on their heads, but that didn't make any difference either.

So then they brought Claudius to him, and he nearly said he wouldn't, because he looked so nice and he did love him.

But Claudius was very brave, and he said what is all the fuss about O pater?

And they told him.

And he said of course you must put me to death O pater if you said you would.

And everybody said it was very wonderful, and Claudius was an ancient Roman too though he was so young. And they all cried very loud which grown-up people used to do then and tore their togas.

Well all this time the slave was hiding in Rome with some friends and he hadn't started for Gaul yet. So when he heard about Claudius he came and gave himself up, and he said if you must put somebody to death put me.

Well the ancient Roman wasn't sure whether it would count, but his wife said don't be so silly, you said you would put anybody to death who helped the slave escape, and he hasn't escaped.

So he said oh very well then I will put the slave to death, but I don't quite like it and I hope everybody will remember how it was.

Then Claudius said O pater either put me to death or don't put anybody to death and let the slave go free.

And he said why?

And he said because he has been so brave and I like him.

So the ancient Roman thought that was the best way out of it though it was very expensive, and he let the slave go free.

And the slave was so grateful that he said he would just go to Gaul to see his mother and his little sister and then come back and serve Claudius for nothing, and clean his sandals and brush his togas.

Well the slave was really a sort of Prince in his own country though he hadn't said so, and his mother was a Princess and had plenty of money. So they all came back and lived in Rome, and when Claudius grew up he married his little sister who was very beautiful.

And the ancient Roman was very pleased and he said it all comes of doing your duty.

370 / INTERPRETING PROSE FICTION

STUDY QUESTIONS

1. How would you characterize the narrator of this story? What is his attitude toward his characters? toward his audience? What kind of social behavior seems indicated for this narrator by his verbal behavior in telling his story?
2. Read this story aloud, punctuating nonverbally (that is, using pauses) *only* where commas and periods occur in the text. Does this give you any clues to the character and social manner of the narrator?
3. What is the function of the "and's" and "well's" that begin many of the narrator's sentences? What do these stylistic traits suggest to you about the narrator?
4. Would you describe the narrator's style as oral or written? What evidence can be found in the text to support your position?
5. What is the function of the opening and closing sentences of this story? What kind of frame do they provide for the story? Does the story's content support this frame? Does the story seem to contradict the implications of the frame?
6. What is the value in the fact that all of the characters in this story are flat? What would happen to the story if one or more of the characters were made three-dimensional, or round?
7. Define, as precisely as possible, how comic effect is created in this story.

Langston Hughes/Rock, Church

born 1902

Elder William Jones was one of them rock-church preachers who know how to make the spirit rise and the soul get right. Sometimes in the pulpit he used to start talking real slow, and you'd think his sermon warn't gonna be nothing, but by the time he got through, the walls of the building would be almost rent, the doors busted open, and the benches turned over from pure shouting on the part of the brothers and sisters.

He were a great preacher, was Reverend William Jones. But he warn't satisfied—he wanted to be greater than he was. He wanted to be another Billy Graham or a Aimee McPherson or a resurrected Reverend Becton. And that's what brought about his downfall—ambition!

Now, Reverend Jones had been for nearly a year the pastor of one of them little colored churches in the back alleys of St. Louis that are open every night in the week for preaching, singing, and praying, where sisters come to shake tambourines, shout, sing gospel songs, and get happy while the Reverend presents the Word.

Elder Jones always opened his part of the services with "In His Hand," his theme song, and he always closed his services with the same. Now, the rhythm of "In His Hand" was such that once it got to swinging, you couldn't help but move your arms or feet or both, and since the Reverend always took up collection at the beginning and ending of his sermons, the dancing movement of the crowd at such times was always toward the collection table—which was exactly where the Elder wanted it to be.

In His hand!
In His hand!
I'm safe and sound
I'll be bound—
Settin' in Jesus' hand!

"Come one! Come all! Come, my Lambs," Elder Jones would shout, "and put it down for Jesus!"

Poor old washerladies, big fat cooks, long lean truck drivers, and heavy-set roustabouts would come up and lay their money down, two times every evening for Elder Jones.

That minister was getting rich right there in that St. Louis alley.

In His hand!
In His hand!
I'll have you know
I'm white as snow—
Settin' in Jesus' hand!

With the piano just a-going, tambourines a-flying, and people shouting right on up to the altar.

"Rock, church, rock!" Elder Jones would cry at such intensely lucrative moments.

But he were too ambitious. He wouldn't let well enough alone. He wanted to be a big shot and panic Harlem, gas Detroit, sew up Chicago, then move on to Hollywood. He warn't satisfied with just St. Louis.

So he got to thinking now what can I do to get everybody excited, to get everybody talking about my church, to get the streets outside crowded and my name known all over, even unto the far reaches of the nation? Now, what can I do?

Billy Sunday had a sawdust trail, so he had heard. Reverend Becton had two valets in the pulpit with him as he cast off garment after garment in the heat of preaching, and used up dozens of white handkerchiefs every evening wiping his brow while calling on the Lord to come. Meanwhile, the Angel of Angelus Temple had just kept on getting married and divorced and making the front pages of everybody's newspapers.

"I got to be news, too, in my day and time," mused Elder Jones. "This town's too small for me! I want the world to hear my name!"

Now, as I've said before, Elder Jones was a good preacher—and a good-looking preacher, too. He could cry real loud and moan real deep, and he could move the sisters as no other black preacher on this side of town had ever moved them before. Besides, in his youth, as a sinner, he had done a little light hustling around Memphis and Vicksburg—so he knew just how to appeal to the feminine nature.

Since his recent sojourn in St. Louis, Elder Jones had been looking for a special female lamb to shelter in his private fold. Out of all the sisters in his church, he had finally chosen Sister Maggie Bradford. Not that Sister Maggie was pretty. No, far from it. But Sister Maggie was well fed, brownskin, good-natured, fat, and *prosperous.* She owned four two-family houses that she rented out, upstairs and down, so she made a good living. Besides, she had sweet and loving ways as well as the interest of her pastor at heart.

Elder Jones confided his personal ambitions to said Sister Bradford one morning when he woke up to find her by his side.

"I want to branch out, Maggie," he said. "I want to be a really big man! Now, what can I do to get the 'tention of the world on me? I mean in a religious way?"

They thought and they thought. Since it was a Fourth of July morning, and Sister Maggie didn't have to go collect rents, they just lay there and thought.

Finally, Sister Maggie said, "Bill Jones, you know something I ain't never forgot that I seed as a child? There was a preacher down in Mississippi named old man Eubanks who one time got himself dead and buried and then rose from the dead. Now, I ain't never forgot that. Neither has nobody else in that part of the Delta. That's something mem'rable. Why don't you do something like that?"

"How did he do it, Sister Maggie?"

"He ain't never told nobody how he do it, Brother Bill. He say it were the Grace of God, that's all."

"It might a-been," said Elder Jones. "It might a-been."

He lay there and thought awhile longer. By and by, he said, "But, honey, I'm gonna do something better'n that. I'm gonna be nailed on a cross."

"Do, Jesus!" said Sister Maggie Bradford. "Jones, you's a mess!"

Now, the Elder, in order to pull off his intended miracle, had, of necessity, to take somebody else into his confidence, so he picked out Brother Hicks, his chief deacon, one of the main pillars of the church long before Jones came as pastor.

It was too bad, though, that Jones never knew that Brother Hicks (more familiarly known as Bulldog) used to be in love with Sister Bradford. Sister Bradford neglected to tell the new Reverend about any of her former sweethearts. So how was Elder Jones to know that some of them still coveted her, and were envious of him in their hearts?

"Hicks," whispered Elder Jones in telling his chief deacon of his plan to die on the cross and then come back to life, "that miracle will make me the greatest minister in the world. No doubt about it! When I get to be world-renowned, Bulldog, and go traveling about the firmament, I'll take you with me as my chief deacon. You shall be my right hand, and Sister Maggie Bradford shall be my left. Amen!"

"I hear you," said Brother Hicks. "I hope it comes true."

But if Elder Jones had looked closely, he would have seen an evil light in his deacon's eyes.

"It will come true," said Elder Jones, "if you keep your mouth shut and follow out my instructions—exactly as I lay 'em down to you. I trust you, so listen! You know and I know that I ain't gonna *really* die. Neither is I *really* gonna be nailed. That's why I wants you to help me. I wants you to have me a great big cross made, higher than the altar—so high I has to have a stepladder to get up to it to be nailed thereon, and you to nail me. The higher the better, so's they won't see the straps—'cause I'm gonna be tied on by straps, you hear. The light'll be rose-colored so they can't see the straps. Now, here you come and do the nailin'—nobody else but you. Put them nails *between* my fingers and toes, not through 'em—*between*—and don't nail too deep. Leave the heads kinder stickin' out. You get the jibe?"

"I get the jibe," said Brother Bulldog Hicks.

"Then you and me'll stay right on there in the church all night and all day till the next night when the people come back to see me rise. Ever so often, you can let me down to rest a little bit. But as long as I'm on the cross, I play off like I'm dead, particularly when reporters come around. On Monday night—Hallelujah! I will rise, and take up collection!"

"Amen!" said Brother Hicks.

Well, you couldn't get a-near the church on the night that Reverend Jones had had it announced by press, by radio, and by word of mouth that he would be crucified *dead,* stay dead, and rise. Negroes came from all over St. Louis, East St. Louis, and mighty nigh everywhere else to be present at the witnessing of the miracle. Lots of 'em didn't believe in Reverend Jones, but lots of 'em *did.* Sometimes false prophets can bamboozle you so you can't tell yonder from hither—and that's the way Jones had the crowd.

The church was packed and jammed. Not a seat to be found and tears were flowing (from sorrowing sisters' eyes) long before the Elder even approached the cross which, made out of new lumber right straight from the sawmill, loomed up behind the pulpit. In the rose-colored lights, with big paper lilies that Sister Bradford had made decorating its head and foot, the cross looked mighty pretty.

Elder Jones preached a mighty sermon that night and, hot as it was, there was plenty of leaping and jumping and shouting in that crowded church. It looked like the walls would fall. Then when he got through preaching, Elder Jones made a solemn announcement. As he termed it, for a night and a day, his last pronouncement.

"Church! Tonight, as I have told the world, I'm gonna die. I'm gonna be nailed to this cross and let the breath pass from me. But tomorrow, Monday night, August the twenty-first, at twelve p.m., I am coming back to life. Amen! After twenty-four hours on the cross, Hallelujah! And all the city of St. Louis can be saved—if they will just come out to see me. Now, before I mounts the steps to the cross, let us sing for the last time 'In His Hand'—'cause I tell you, that's where I am! As we sing, let everybody come forward to the collection table and help this church before I go. Give largely!"

The piano tinkled, the tambourines rang, hands clapped. Elder Jones and his children sang:

In His hand!
In His hand!
You'll never stray
Down the Devil's way—
Settin' in Jesus' hand!

Oh, in His hand!
In His hand!
Though I may die
I'll mount on high—
Settin' in Jesus' hand!

"Let us pray." And while every back was bowed in prayer, the Elder went up the stepladder to the cross. Brother Hicks followed with the hammer and nails. Sister Bradford wailed at the top of her voice. Woe filled the Amen Corner. Emotion rocked the church.

Folks outside was saying all up and down the streets, "Lawd, I wish we could have got in. Listen yonder at that noise! I wonder what *is* going on!"

Elder Jones was about to make himself famous—that's what was going on. And all would have went well had it not been for Brother Hicks—a two-faced rascal. Somehow that night the devil got into Bulldog Hicks and took full possession.

The truth of the matter is that Hicks got to thinking about Sister Maggie Bradford, and how Reverend Jones had worked up to be her No. 1 man. That made him mad. The old green snake of jealousy began to coil around his heart, right there in the meeting, right there on the steps of the cross, at the very high point of the ceremonies. Lord, have Mercy!

Hicks had the hammer in one hand and his other hand was full of nails as he mounted the ladder behind his pastor. He was going up to nail Elder Jones on that sawmill cross.

"While I'm nailin', I might as well nail him right," Hicks thought. "A low-down klinker—comin' here out of Mississippi to take my woman away from me! He'll never know the pleasure of my help in none o' his schemes to out-Divine Father! No, sir!"

Elder Jones had himself all fixed up with a system of straps round his waist, round his shoulder blades, and round his wrists and ankles, hidden under his long black coat. These straps fastened in hooks on the back of the cross, out of sight of the audience, so he could just hang up there all sad and sorrowful-looking, and make out like he was being nailed. Brother Bulldog Hicks was to plant the nails *between* his fingers and toes. Hallelujah! Rock, church, rock!

Excitement was intense.

All went well, until the nailing began. Elder Jones removed his shoes and socks, in his bare black feet, bade farewell to his weeping congregation. As he leaned back against the cross and allowed Brother Hicks to compose him there, the crowd began to moan. But it was when Hicks placed the first nail between Elder Jones's toes that they become hysterical. Sister Bradford outyelled them all.

Hicks placed the first nail between the big toe and the next toe of the left foot and began to hammer. The foot was well strapped down, so the Elder couldn't move it. The closer the head of the nail got to his toes, the harder Hicks struck it. Finally the hammer collided with Elder Jones's foot, *bam* against his big toe.

"Aw-oh!" he moaned under his breath. "Go easy, man!"

"Have mercy," shouted the brothers and sisters of the church. "Have mercy on our Elder!"

Once more the hammer struck his toe. But the all too human sound of his surprised and agonized "Ouch!" was lost in the tumult of the shouting church.

"Bulldog, I say, go easy," hissed the Elder. "This *ain't* real."

Brother Hicks desisted, a grim smile on his face. Then he turned his attention to the right foot. There he placed another nail between the toes, and began to hammer. Again, as the nail went into the wood, he showed no signs of stopping when the hammer reached the foot. He just kept on landing cruel, metallic blows on the Elder's bare toenails until the preacher howled with pain, no longer able to keep back a sudden hair-raising cry. The sweat popped out on his forehead and dripped down on his shirt.

At first the Elder thought, naturally, that it was just a slip of the hammer on the deacon's part. Then he thought the man must have gone crazy—like the rest of the audience. Then it hurt him so bad he didn't know what he thought—so he just hollered, "Aw-ooo-oo-o!"

It was a good thing the church was full of noise, or they would have heard a strange dialogue.

"My God, Hicks, what are you doing?" the Elder cried, staring wildly at his deacon on the ladder.

"I'm nailin' you to the cross, Jones! And man, I'm *really* nailin'."

"Aw-oow-ow! Don't you know you're hurting me? I told you *not* to nail so hard!"

But the deacon was unruffled.

"Who'd you say's gonna be your right hand, when you get down from here and start your travelings?" Hicks asked.

"You, brother," the sweating Elder cried.

"And who'd you say was gonna be your left hand?"

"Sister Maggie Bradford," moaned Elder Jones from the cross.

"Naw, she ain't," said Brother Hicks, whereupon he struck the Reverend's toe a really righteous blow.

"Lord, help me!" cried the tortured minister. The weeping congregation echoed his cry. It was certainly real. The Elder *was* being crucified!

Brother Bulldog Hicks took two more steps up the ladder, preparing to nail the hands. With his evil face right in front of Elder Jones, he hissed: "I'll teach you nappy-headed jack-leg ministers to come to St. Louis and think you all can walk away with any woman you's a mind to. I'm gonna teach you to leave my women alone. Here—here's a nail!"

Brother Hicks placed a great big spike right in the palm of Elder Jones's left hand. He was just about to drive it in when the frightened Reverend let out a scream that could be heard two blocks away. At the same time, he began to struggle to get down. Jones tried to bust the straps, but they was too strong for him.

If he could just get one foot loose to kick Brother Bulldog Hicks!

Hicks lifted the hammer to let go when the Reverend's second yell, this time, was loud enough to be heard in East St. Louis. It burst like a bomb above the shouts of the crowd—and it had its effect. Suddenly the congregation was quiet. Everybody knew that was no way for a dying man to yell.

Sister Bradford realized that something had gone wrong, so she began to chant the song her beloved pastor had told her to chant at the propitious moment after the nailing was done. Now, even though the nailing was not done, Sister Bradford thought she had better sing:

Elder Jones will rise again,
Elder Jones will rise again,
Rise again, rise again!
Elder Jones will rise again,
Yes, my Lawd!

But nobody took up the refrain to help her carry it on. Everybody was too interested in what was happening in front of them, so Sister Bradford's voice just died out.

Meanwhile, Brother Hicks lifted the hammer again, but Elder Jones spat right in his face. He not only spat, but suddenly called his deacon a name unworthy of man or beast. Then he let out another frightful yell and, in mortal anguish, called "Sister Maggie Bradford, lemme down from here! I say, come and get . . . me . . . down . . . *from here!*"

Those in the church that had not already stopped moaning and shouting, did so at once. You could have heard a pin drop. Folks were petrified.

Brother Hicks stood on the ladder glaring with satisfaction at Reverend Jones, his hammer still raised. Under his breath, the panting Elder dared him to nail another nail, and threatened to kill him stone-dead with a forty-four if he did.

"Just lemme get loose from here, and I'll fight you like a natural man," he gasped, twisting and turning like a tree in a storm.

"Come down, then," yelled Hicks, right out loud from the ladder. "Come on down! As sure as water runs, Jones, I'll show you up for what you is—a woman-chasing, no-good, low-down faker! I'll beat you to a batter with my bare hands!"

"Lawd, have mercy!" cried the church.

Jones almost broke a blood vessel trying to get loose from his cross.

"Sister Maggie, come and lemme down," he pleaded, sweat streaming from his face.

But Sister Bradford was covered with confusion. In fact, she was petrified. What could have gone wrong for the Elder to call on her like this in public in the very midst of the thing that was to bring him famous—glory and make them all rich preaching throughout the land with her at his side? Sister Bradford's head was in a whirl, her heart was in her mouth.

"Elder Jones, you means you really wants to get down?" she asked weakly from her seat in the Amen Corner.

"Yes," said the Elder, "can't you hear? I done called on you twenty times to let me down!"

At this point, Brother Hicks gave the foot nails one more good hammering. The words that came from the cross were nobody's business.

In a twinkling, Sister Bradford was at Jones's side. Realizing at last that the devil must've done got into Hicks (like it used to sometimes in the days when she knowed him), she went to the aid of her battered Elder, grabbed the foot of the ladder, and sent Hicks sprawling across the pulpit.

"You'll never crucify my Elder," she cried, "not for real." Energetically, she began to cut the straps away that bound the Reverend. Soon poor

Jones slid to the floor, his feet too sore from the hammer's blows to even stand on them without help.

"Just lemme get at Hicks," was all Reverend Jones could gasp.

"He knowed I didn't want them nails that close." In the dead silence that took possession of the church, everybody heard him moan, "Lawd, lemme get at Hicks," as he hobbled away on the protecting arm of Sister Maggie.

"Stand back, Bulldog," Sister Maggie said to the deacon, "and let your pastor pass. Soon as he's able, he'll flatten you out like a shadder—but now, I'm in charge. Stand back, I say, and let him pass!"

Hicks stood back. The crowd murmured. The minister made his exit.

Thus ended the ambitious career of Elder William Jones. He never did pastor in St. Louis any more. Neither did he fight Hicks. He just snuck away.

STUDY QUESTIONS

1. The narrator in this story poses some interesting problems for investigation. He acknowledges himself as the teller of the story (for example, "Now, as I've said before . . ."), but he never tries to account for the source of his information. How does this narrator seem to know what happened, not only in the church, but also between Elder Jones and Sister Maggie, and between Elder Jones and Hicks? How credible does this narrator seem to be?

2. Consider the style of this narrator. Does he seem to be talking or writing his story? What clues are provided in the text? Does the narrator ever seem inconsistent in his style? If so, do these inconsistencies seem functional, or do they detract from the story?

3. Define as fully as possible the narrator's attitude toward Elder Jones. Does he see the preacher as a comic figure? a pathetic one? How does the narrator feel about Elder Jones' fate at the end of the story when he says, "He just snuck away"?

4. Does the narrator appear to be reliable, or is Hughes using him as a rhetorical device? If the latter, for what rhetorical purpose is this narrator being employed? How effective is the narrator in this sense?

5. The narrator in this story has certain structural similarities with the narrator in "A Rose for Emily," in that both narrators are ostensibly outside the major action in the story, neither narrator is the protagonist in the story being told, and both acknowledge themselves as first-person narrators. How do the functions of these two narrators differ?

Henry James/Greville Fane

born 1811

Coming in to dress for dinner I found a telegram: "Mrs. Stormer dying; can you give us half a column for tomorrow evening? Let me down easily, but not too easily." I was late; I was in a hurry; I had very little time to think; but at a venture I despatched a reply: "Will do what I can." It was not till I had dressed and was rolling away to dinner that, in the hansom, I bethought myself of the difficulty of the condition attached. The difficulty was not of course in letting her down easily but in qualifying that indulgence. "So I simply won't qualify it," I said. I didn't admire but liked her, and had known her so long that I almost felt heartless in sitting down at such an hour to a feast of indifference. I must have seemed abstracted, for the early years of my acquaintance with her came back to me. I spoke of her to the lady I had taken down, but the lady I had taken down had never heard of Greville Fane. I tried my other neighbour, who pronounced her books "too vile." I had never thought them very good, but I should let her down more easily than that.

I came away early, for the express purpose of driving to ask about her. The journey took time, for she lived in the northwest district, in the neighbourhood of Primrose Hill. My apprehension that I should be too late was justified in a fuller sense than I had attached to it—I had only feared that the house would be shut up. There were lights in the windows, and the temperate tinkle of my bell brought a servant immediately to the door; but poor Mrs. Stormer had passed into a state in which the resonance of no earthly knocker was to be feared. A lady hovering behind the servant came forward into the hall when she heard my voice. I recognised Lady Luard, but she had mistaken me for the doctor.

"Pardon my appearing at such an hour," I said; "it was the first possible moment after I heard."

"It's all over," Lady Luard replied. "Dearest mamma!"

She stood there under the lamp with her eyes on me; she was very tall, very stiff, very cold, and always looked as if these things, and some others beside, in her dress, in her manner and even in her name, were an implication that she was very admirable. I had never been able to follow the argument, but that's a detail. I expressed briefly and frankly what I felt, while the little mottled maidservant flattened herself against the wall of the narrow passage and tried to look detached without looking indifferent. It was not a moment to make a visit, and I was on the point of retreating when Lady Luard arrested me with a queer casual drawling "Would you—a—would you perhaps be *writing* something?" I felt for the instant like an infamous interviewer, which I wasn't. But I pleaded guilty to this intention, on which she returned: "I'm so very glad—but I think my brother would like to see you." I detested her brother, but it wasn't an occasion to act this out; so I suffered myself to be inducted, to my surprise, into a small back room which I immediately recognised as the scene, during the later years, of Mrs. Stormer's imperturbable industry. Her table was there, the battered and blotted accessory to innumerable literary lapses, with its contracted space for the arms (she wrote only from the elbow down) and the confusion of scrappy scribbled sheets which had already become literary remains. Leolin was also there, smoking a cigarette before the fire and looking impudent even in his grief, sincere as it well might have been.

To meet him, to greet him, I had to make a sharp effort; for the air he wore to me as he stood before me was quite that of his mother's murderer. She lay silent for ever upstairs—as dead as an unsuccessful book, and his swaggering erectness was a kind of symbol of his having killed her. I wondered if he had already, with his sister, been calculating what they could get for the poor papers on the table; but I hadn't long to wait to learn, since in reply to the few words of sympathy I addressed him he puffed out: "It's miserable, miserable, yes; but she has left three books complete." His words had the oddest effect; they converted the cramped little room into a seat of trade and made the "book" wonderfully feasible. He would certainly get all that could be got for the three. Lady Luard explained to me that her husband had been with them, but had had to go down to the House. To her brother she mentioned that I was going to write something, and to me again made it clear that she hoped I would "do mamma justice." She added that she didn't think this had ever been done. She said to her brother: "Don't you think there are some things he ought thoroughly to understand?" and on his instantly exclaiming "Oh thoroughly, thoroughly!" went on rather austerely: "I mean about mamma's birth."

"Yes and her connexions," Leolin added.

I professed every willingness, and for five minutes I listened; but it would be too much to say I clearly understood. I don't even now, but it's not important. My vision was of other matters than those they put before me, and while they desired there should be no mistake about their ancestors I became keener and keener about themselves. I got away as soon as possible and walked home through the great dusky empty London—the best of all conditions for thought. By the time I reached my door my little article was practically composed—ready to be transferred on the morrow from the polished plate of fancy. I believe it attracted some notice, was thought "graceful" and was said to be by some one else. I had to be pointed without being lively, and it took some doing. But what I said was much less interesting than what I thought—especially during the half-hour I spent in my armchair by the fire, smoking the cigar

I always light before going to bed. I went to sleep there, I believe; but I continued to moralise about Greville Fane. I'm reluctant to lose that retrospect altogether, and this is a dim little memory of it, a document not to "serve." The dear woman had written a hundred stories, but none so curious as her own.

When first I knew her she had published half a dozen fictions, and I believe I had also perpetrated a novel. She was more than a dozen years my elder, but a person who always acknowledged her comparative state. It wasn't so very long ago, but in London, amid the big waves of the present, even a near horizon gets hidden. I met her at some dinner and took her down, rather flattered at offering my arm to a celebrity. She didn't look like one, with her matronly mild inanimate face, but I supposed her greatness would come out in her conversation. I gave it all the opportunities I could, but was nevertheless not disappointed when I found her only a dull kind woman. This was why I liked her—she rested me so from literature. To myself literature was an irritation, a torment; but Greville Fane slumbered in the intellectual part of it even as a cat on a hearthrug or a Creole in a hammock. She wasn't a woman of genius, but her faculty was so special, so much a gift out of hand, that I've often wondered why she fell below that distinction. This was doubtless because the transaction, in her case, had remained incomplete; genius always pays for the gift, feels the debt, and she was placidly unconscious of a call. She could invent stories by the yard, but couldn't write a page of English. She went down to her grave without suspecting that though she had contributed volumes to the diversion of her contemporaries she hadn't contributed a sentence to the language. This hadn't prevented bushels of criticism from being heaped on her head; she was worth a couple of columns any day to the weekly papers, in which it was shown that her pictures of life were dreadful but her style superior. She asked me to come and see her and I complied. She lived then in Montpellier Square; which helped me to see how dissociated her imagination was from her character.

An industrious widow, devoted to her daily stint, to meeting the butcher and baker and making a home for her son and daughter, from the moment she took her pen in her hand she became a creature of passion. She thought the English novel deplorably wanting in that element, and the task she had cut out for herself was to supply the deficiency. Passion in high life was the general formula of this work, for her imagination was at home only in the most exalted circles. She adored in truth the aristocracy, and they constituted for her the romance of the world or what is more to the point, the prime material of fiction. Their beauty and luxury, their loves and revenges, their temptations and surrenders, their immoralities and diamonds were as familiar to her as the blots on her writing-table. She was not a belated producer of the old fashionable novel, but, with a cleverness and a modernness of her own, had freshened up the fly-blown tinsel. She turned off plots by the hundred and—so far as her flying quill could convey her—was perpetually going abroad. Her types, her illustrations, her tone were nothing if not cosmopolitan. She recognised nothing less provincial than European society, and her fine folk knew each other and made love to each other from Doncaster to Bucharest. She had an idea that she resembled Balzac, and her favourite historical characters were Lucien de Rubempré and the Vidame de Pamiers. I must add that when I once asked her who the latter personage was she was unable to tell me. She was very brave and healthy and cheerful, very abundant and innocent and wicked. She was expert and vulgar and snobbish, and never so intensely British as when she was particularly foreign.

This combination of qualities had brought her early success, and I remember having heard with wonder and envy of what she "got," in those days, for a novel. The revelation gave me a pang: it was such a proof that, practising a totally different style, I should never make my fortune. And yet when, as I knew her better she told her real tariff and I saw how rumour had quadrupled it, I liked her enough to be sorry. After a while I discovered too that if she got less it was not that *I* was to get any more. My failure never had what Mrs. Stormer would have called the banality of being relative—it was always admirably absolute. She lived at ease however in those days—ease is exactly the word, though she produced three novels a year. She scorned me when I spoke of difficulty—it was the only thing that made her angry. If I hinted at the grand licking into shape that a work of art required she thought it a pretension and a *pose.* She never recognised the "torment of form"; the furthest she went was to introduce into one of her books (in satire her hand was heavy) a young poet who was always talking about it. I couldn't quite understand her irritation on this score, for she had nothing at stake in the matter. She had a shrewd perception that form, in prose at least, never recommended any one to the public we were condemned to address; according to which she lost nothing (her private humiliation not counted) by having none to show. She made no pretence of producing works of art, but had comfortable tea-drinking hours in which she freely confessed herself a common pastrycook, dealing in such tarts and puddings as would bring customers to the shop. She put in plenty of sugar and of cochineal, or whatever it is that gives these articles a rich and attractive colour. She had a calm independence of observation and opportunity which constituted an inexpugnable strength and would enable her to go on indefinitely. It's only real success that wanes, it's only solid things that melt. Greville Fane's ignorance of life was a resource still more unfailing than the most approved receipt. On her saying once that the day would come when she should have written herself out I answered: "Ah you open straight into fairyland, and the fairies love you and *they* never change. Fairyland's always there; it always was from the beginning of time and always will be to the end. They've given you the key and you can always open the door. With me it's different; I try, in my clumsy way, to be in some direct relation to life." "Oh bother your direct relation to life!" she used to reply, for she was always annoyed by the phrase— which wouldn't in the least prevent her using it as a note of elegance. With no more prejudices than an old sausage-mill, she would give forth again with patient punctuality any poor verbal scrap that had been dropped into her. I cheered her with saying that the dark day, at the end, would be for the "likes" of *me;* since, proceeding in our small way by experience and study—priggish we!—we depended not on a revelation but on a little tiresome process. Attention depended not on occasion, and where should we be when occasion failed?

One day she told me that as the novelist's life was so delightful and, during the good years at least, such a comfortable support—she had these staggering optimisms—she meant to train up her boy to follow it. She took the ingenious view that it was a profession like another and that therefore everything was to be gained by beginning young and serving an apprenticeship. Moreover the education would be less expensive than any other special course, inasmuch as she could herself administer it. She didn't profess to keep a school, but she could at least teach her own child. It wasn't that she had such a gift, but—she confessed to me as if she were afraid I should laugh at her—that *he* had. I didn't laugh at her for that, because I thought the boy sharp—I had seen him sundry times. He was well-grown and good-looking and unabashed, and both he and his sister made me wonder about their defunct papa, concerning whom the little I knew was that he had been a country vicar and brother to a small squire. I explained them to myself by suppositions and imputations possibly unjust to the departed; so little were they—superficially at least—the children of their mother. There used to be on an easel in her drawing-room an enlarged photograph of her husband, done by some horrible posthumous "process" and draped, as to its florid frame, with a silken scarf which testified to the candour of Greville Fane's bad taste. It made him look like an unsuccessful tragedian, but it wasn't a thing to trust. He may have been a successful comedian. Of the two children the girl was the elder, and struck me in all her younger years as singularly colourless. She was only long, very long, like an undecipherable letter. It wasn't till Mrs. Stormer came back from a protracted residence abroad that Ethel (which was this young lady's name) began to produce the effect, large and stiff and afterwards eminent in her, of a certain kind of resolution, something as public and important as if a meeting and a chairman had passed it. She gave one to understand she meant to do all she could for herself. She was long-necked and nearsighted and striking, and I thought I had never seen sweet seventeen in a form so hard and high and dry. She was cold and affected and ambitious, and she carried an eyeglass with a long handle, which she put up whenever she wanted not to see. She had come out, as the phrase is, immensely; and yet I felt as if she were surrounded with a spiked iron railing. What she meant to do for herself was to marry, and it was the only thing, I think, that she meant to do for any one else; yet who would be inspired to clamber over that bristling barrier? What flower of tenderness or of intimacy would such an adventurer conceive as his reward?

This was for Sir Baldwin Luard to say; but he naturally never confided me the secret. He was a joyless jokeless young man, with the air of having other secrets as well, and a determination to get on politically that was indicated by his never having been known to commit himself—as regards any proposition whatever—beyond an unchallengeable "Oh!" His wife and he must have conversed mainly in prim ejaculations, but they understood sufficiently that they were kindred spirits. I remember being angry with Greville Fane when she announced these nuptials to me as magnificent; I remember asking her what splendour there was in the union of the daughter of a woman of genius with an irredeemable mediocrity. "Oh he has immense ability," she said; but she blushed for the maternal fib. What she meant was that though Sir Baldwin's estates were not vast—he had a dreary house in South Kensington and a still drearier "Hall" somewhere in Essex, which was let—the connexion was a "smarter" one than a child of hers could have aspired to form. In spite of the social bravery of her novels she took a very humble and dingy view of herself, so that of all her productions "my daughter Lady Luard" was quite the one she was proudest of. That personage thought our authoress vulgar and was distressed and perplexed by the frequent freedoms of her pen, but had a complicated attitude for this indirect connexion with literature. So far as it was lucrative her ladyship approved of it and could compound with the inferiority of the pursuit by practical justice to some of its advantages. I had reason to know—my reason was simply that poor Mrs. Stormer told me—how she suffered the inky fingers to press an occasional banknote into her palm. On the other hand she deplored the "peculiar style" to which Greville Fane had devoted herself, and wondered where a spectator with the advantage of so ladylike a daughter could have picked up such views about the best society. "She might know better, with Leolin and me," Lady Luard had been heard to remark; but it appeared that some of Greville Fane's superstitions were incurable. She didn't live in Lady Luard's society, and the best wasn't good enough for her—she must improve on it so prodigiously.

I could see this necessity increase in her during the years she spent abroad, when I had glimpses of her in the shifting sojourns that lay in the path of my annual ramble. She betook herself from Germany to

Switzerland and from Switzerland to Italy; she favoured cheap places and set up her desk in the smaller capitals. I took a look at her whenever I could, and I always asked how Leolin was getting on. She gave me beautiful accounts of him, and, occasion favouring, the boy was produced for my advantage. I had entered from the first into the joke of his career —I pretended to regard him as a consecrated child. It had been a joke for Mrs. Stormer at first, but the youth himself had been shrewd enough to make the matter serious. If his parent accepted the principle that the intending novelist can't begin too early to see life, Leolin wasn't interested in hanging back from the application of it. He was eager to qualify himself and took to cigarettes at ten on the highest literary grounds. His fond mother gazed at him with extravagant envy and, like Desdemona, wished heaven had made *her* such a man. She explained to me more than once that in her profession she had found her sex a dreadful drawback. She loved the story of Madame George Sand's early rebellion against this hindrance, and believed that if she had worn trousers she could have written as well as that lady. Leolin had for the career at least the qualification of trousers, and as he grew older he recognised its importance by laying in ever so many pair. He grew up thus in gorgeous apparel, which was his way of interpreting his mother's system. Whenever I met her, accordingly, I found her still under the impression that she was carrying this system out and that the sacrifices made him were bearing heavy fruit. She was giving him experience, she was giving him impressions, she was putting a *gagne-pain* into his hand. It was another name for spoiling him with the best conscience in the world. The queerest pictures come back to me of this period of the good lady's life and of the extraordinarily virtuous muddled bewildering tenor of it. She had an idea she was seeing foreign manners as well as her petticoats would allow; but in reality she wasn't seeing anything, least of all, fortunately, how much she was laughed at. She drove her whimsical pen at Dresden and at Florence—she produced in all places and at all times the same romantic and ridiculous fictions. She carried about her box of properties, tumbling out promptly the familiar tarnished old puppets. She believed in them when others couldn't, and as they were like nothing that was to be seen under the sun it was impossible to prove by comparison that they were wrong. You can't compare birds and fishes; you could only feel that, as Greville Fane's characters had the fine plumage of the former species, human beings must be of the latter.

It would have been droll if it hadn't been so exemplary to see her tracing the loves of the duchesses beside the innocent cribs of her children. The immoral and the maternal lived together, in her diligent days, on the most comfortable terms, and she stopped curling the moustaches of her Guardsmen to pat the heads of her babes. She was haunted by solemn spinsters who came to tea from Continental pensions, and by unsophisticated Americans who told her she was just loved in *their* country. "I had rather be just paid there," she usually replied; for this tribute of transatlantic opinion was the only thing that galled her. The Americans went away thinking her coarse; though as the author of so many beautiful love-stories she was disappointing to most of these pilgrims, who hadn't expected to find a shy stout ruddy lady in a cap like a crumbled pyramid. She wrote about the affections and the impossibility of controlling them, but she talked of the price of pension and the convenience of an English chemist. She devoted much thought and many thousands of francs to the education of her daughter, who spent three years at a very superior school at Dresden, receiving wonderful instruction in sciences, arts and tongues, and who, taking a different line from Leolin, was to be brought up wholly as a *femme du monde.* The girl was musical and philological; she went in for several languages and learned enough about them to be inspired with a great contempt for her mother's artless accents. Greville Fane's French and Italian were droll; the imitative faculty had been denied her, and she had an unequalled gift, especially pen in hand, of squeezing big mistakes into small opportunities. She knew it but didn't care; correctness was the virtue in the world that, like her heroes and heroines, she valued least. Ethel, who had noted in her pages some remarkable lapses, undertook at one time to revise her proofs; but I remember her telling me a year after the girl had left school that this function had been very briefly exercised. "She can't read me," said Mrs. Stormer; "I offend her taste. She tells me that at Dresden—at school—I was never allowed." The good lady seemed surprised at this, having the best conscience in the world about her lucubrations. She had never meant to fly in the face of anything, and considered that she grovelled before the Rhadamanthus of the English literary tribunal, the celebrated and awful Young Person. I assured her, as a joke, that she was frightfully indecent —she had in fact that element of truth as little as any other—my purpose being solely to prevent her guessing that her daughter had dropped her not because she was immoral but because she was vulgar. I used to figure her children closeted together and putting it to each other with a gaze of dismay: "Why should she *be* so—and so *fearfully* so—when she has the advantage of our society? Shouldn't *we* have taught her better?" Then I imagined their recognising with a blush and a shrug that she was unteachable, irreformable. Indeed she was, poor lady, but it's never fair to read by the light of taste things essentially not written in it. Greville Fane kept through all her riot of absurdity a witless confidence that should have been as safe from criticism as a stutter or a squint.

She didn't make her son ashamed of the profession to which he was destined, however; she only made him ashamed of the way she herself exercised it. But he bore his humiliation much better than his sister, being ready to assume he should one day restore the balance. A canny and far-seeing youth, with appetites and aspirations, he hadn't a scruple in his composition. His mother's theory of the happy knack he could pick up deprived him of the wholesome discipline required to prevent young idlers from becoming cads. He enjoyed on foreign soil a casual tutor and the common snatch or two of a Swiss school, but addressed himself to no consecutive study nor to any prospect of a university or a degree. It may be imagined with what zeal, as the years went on, he entered into the pleasantry of there being no manual so important to him as the massive book of life. It was an expensive volume to peruse, but Mrs. Stormer was willing to lay out a sum in what she would have called her *premiers frais*. Ethel disapproved—she found this education irregular for an English gentleman. Her voice was for Eton and Oxford or for any public school—she would have resigned herself to one of the scrubbier—with the army to follow. But Leolin never was afraid of his sister, and they visibly disliked, though they sometimes agreed to assist, each other. They could combine to work the oracle—to keep their mother at her desk.

When she reappeared in England, telling me she had "secured" all the Continent could give her, Leolin was a broad-shouldered red-faced young man with an immense wardrobe and an extraordinary assurance of manner. She was fondly, quite aggressively certain she had taken the right course with him, and addicted to boasting of all he knew and had seen. He was now quite ready to embark on the family profession, to commence author, as they used to say, and a little while later she told me he had started. He had written something tremendously clever which was coming out in the *Cheapside.* I believe it came out; I had no time to look for it; I never heard anything about it. I took for granted that if this contribution had passed through his mother's hands it would virtually rather illustrate *her* fine facility, and it was interesting to consider the poor lady's future in the light of her having to write her son's novels as well as her own. This wasn't the way she looked at it herself—she took the charming ground that he'd help her to write hers. She used to assure me he supplied passages of the greatest value to these last—all sorts of telling technical things, happy touches about hunting and yachting and cigars and wine, about City slang and the way men talk at clubs —that she couldn't be expected to get very straight. It was all so much practice for him and so much alleviation for herself. I was unable to identify such pages, for I had long since ceased to "keep up" with Greville Fane; but I could quite believe at least that the wine-question had been put by Leolin's good offices on a better footing, for the dear woman used to mix her drinks—she was perpetually serving the most splendid suppers—in the queerest fashion. I could see him quite ripe to embrace regularly that care. It occurred to me indeed, when she settled in England again, that she might by a shrewd use of both her children be able to rejuvenate her style. Ethel had come back to wreak her native, her social yearning, and if she couldn't take her mother into company would at least go into it herself. Silently, stiffly, almost grimly, this young lady reared her head, clenched her long teeth, squared her lean elbows and found her way up the staircases she had marked. The only communication she ever made, the only effusion of confidence with which she ever honoured me, was when she said "I don't want to know the people mamma knows, I mean to know others." I took due note of the remark, for I wasn't one of the "others." I couldn't trace therefore the steps and stages of her climb; I could only admire it at a distance and congratulate her mother in due course on the results. The results, the gradual, the final, the wonderful, were that Ethel went to "big" parties and got people to take her. Some of them were people she had met abroad, and others people the people she had met abroad had met. They ministered alike to Miss Ethel's convenience, and I wondered how she extracted so many favours without the expenditure of a smile. Her smile was the dimmest thing in nature, diluted, unsweetened, inexpensive lemonade, and she had arrived precociously at social wisdom, recognising that if she was neither pretty enough nor rich enough nor clever enough, she could at least, in her muscular youth, be rude enough. Therefore, so placed to give her parent tips, to let her know what really occurred in the mansions of the great, to supply her with local colour, with *data* to work from, she promoted the driving of the well-worn quill, over the brave old battered blotting book, to a still lustier measure and precisely at the moment when most was to depend on this labour. But if she became a great critic it appeared that the labourer herself was constitutionally inapt for the lesson. It was late in the day for Greville Fane to learn, and I heard nothing of her having developed a new manner. She was to have had only one manner, as Leolin would have said, from start to finish.

She was weary and spent at last, but confided to me that she couldn't afford to pause. She continued to speak of her son's work as the great hope of their future—she had saved no money—though the young man wore to my sense an air more and more professional if you like, but less and less literary. There was at the end of a couple of years something rare in the impudence of his playing of his part in the comedy. When I wondered how she could play hers it was to feel afresh the fatuity of her fondness, which was proof, I believed—I indeed saw to the end—against any interference of reason. She loved the young impostor with a simple blind benighted love, and of all the heroes of romance who had passed before her eyes he was by far the brightest. He was at any rate the most real—she could touch him, pay for him, suffer for him, worship him. He made her think of her princes and dukes, and when she wished to fix these figures in her mind's eye she thought of her boy. She had often told me she was herself carried away by her creations, and she was

certainly carried away by Leolin.   He vivified—by what romantically might
have been at least—the whole question of youth and passion.   She held,
not unjustly, that the sincere novelist should feel the whole flood of life;
she acknowledged with regret that she hadn't had time to feel it herself, and the lapse in her history was in a manner made up by the sight
of its rush through this magnificent young man.   She exhorted him, I
suppose, to encourage the rush; she wrung her own flaccid little sponge
into the torrent.   What passed between them in her pedagogic hours was
naturally a blank to me, but I gathered that she mainly impressed on
him that the great thing was to live, because that gave you material.   He
asked nothing better; he collected material, and the recipe served as a
universal pretext.   You had only to look at him to see that, with his rings
and breastpins, his crossbarred jackets, his early *embonpoint,* his eyes
that looked like imitation jewels, his various indications of a dense full-
blown temperament, his idea of life was singularly vulgar; but he was so
far auspicious as that his response to his mother's expectations was in a
high degree practical.   If she had imposed a profession on him from his
tenderest years it was exactly a profession that he followed.   The two
were not quite the same, inasmuch as the one he had adopted was simply
to live at her expense; but at least she couldn't say he hadn't taken a line.
If she insisted on believing in him he offered himself to the sacrifice.
My impression is that her secret dream was that he should have a *liaison*
with a countess, and he persuaded her without difficulty that he had one.
I don't know what countesses are capable of, but I've a clear notion of
what Leolin was.

He didn't persuade his sister, who despised him—she wished to work
her mother in her own way; so that I asked myself why the girl's judgment of him didn't make me like her better.   It was because it didn't save
her after all from the mute agreement with him to go halves.   There were
moments when I couldn't help looking hard into his atrocious young
eyes, challenging him to confess his fantastic fraud and give it up.   Not
a little tacit conversation passed between us in this way, but he had always the best of the business.   If I said: "Oh come now, with *me* you
needn't keep it up; plead guilty and I'll let you off," he wore the most
ingenuous, the most candid expression, in the depths of which I could
read: "Ah yes, I know it exasperates you—that's just why I do it."   He
took the line of earnest enquiry, talked about Balzac and Flaubert, asked
me if I thought Dickens *did* exaggerate and Thackeray *ought* to be called
a pessimist.   Once he came to see me, at his mother's suggestion he
declared, on purpose to ask me how far, in my opinion, in the English
novel, one really might venture to "go."   He wasn't resigned to the usual
pruderies, the worship of childish twaddle; he suffered already from too
much bread and butter.   He struck out the brilliant idea that nobody
knew how far we might go, since nobody had ever tried.   Did I think *he*

might safely try—would it injure his mother if he did? He would rather disgrace himself by his timidities than injure his mother, but certainly some one ought to try. Wouldn't *I* try—couldn't I be prevailed upon to look at it as a duty? Surely the ultimate point ought to be fixed—he was worried, haunted by the question. He patronised me unblushingly, made me feel a foolish amateur, a helpless novice, inquired into my habits of work and conveyed to me that I was utterly *vieux jeu* and hadn't had the advantage of an early training. I hadn't been brought up from the egg, I knew nothing of life—didn't go at it on *his* system. He had dipped into French feuilletons and picked up plenty of phrases, and he made a much better show in talk than his poor mother, who never had time to read anything and could only be showy with her pen. If I didn't kick him downstairs it was because he would have landed on her at the bottom.

When she went to live at Primrose Hill I called there and found her wasted and wan. It had visibly dropped, the elation caused the year before by Ethel's marriage; the foam on the cup had subsided and there was bitterness in the draught. She had had to take a cheaper house—and now had to work still harder to pay even for that. Sir Baldwin was obliged to be close; his charges were fearful, and the dream of her living with her daughter—a vision she had never mentioned to me—must be renounced. "I'd have helped them with things, and could have lived perfectly in one room," she said; "I'd have paid for everything, and—after all—I'm some one, ain't I? But I don't fit in, and Ethel tells me there are tiresome people she *must* receive. I can help them from here, no doubt, better than from there. She told me once, you know, what she thinks of my picture of life. 'Mamma, your picture of life's preposterous!' No doubt it is, but she's vexed with me for letting my prices go down; and I had to write three novels to pay for all her marriage cost me. I did it very well—I mean the outfit and the wedding; but that's why I'm here. At any rate she doesn't want a dingy old woman at Blicket. I should give the place an atmosphere of literary prestige, but literary prestige is only the eminence of nobodies. Besides, she knows what to think of my glory—she knows I'm glorious only at Peckham and Hackney. She doesn't want her friends to ask if I've never known nice people. She can't tell them I've never been in society. She tried to teach me better once, but I couldn't catch on. It would seem too as if Peckham and Hackney had had enough of me; for (don't tell any one) I've had to take less for my last than I ever took for anything." I asked her how little this had been, not from curiosity, but in order to upbraid her, more disinterestedly than Lady Luard had done, for such concessions. She answered "I'm ashamed to tell you" and then began to cry.

I had never seen her break down and I was proportionately moved; she sobbed like a frightened child over the extinction of her vogue and the exhaustion of her vein. Her little workroom seemed indeed a barren place to grow flowers for the market, and I wondered in the after years (for she continued to produce and publish) by what desperate and heroic process she dragged them out of the soil. I remember asking her on that occasion what had become of Leolin and how much longer she intended to allow him to amuse himself at her cost. She retorted with spirit, wiping her eyes, that he was down at Brighton hard at work—he was in the midst of a novel—and that he *felt* life so, in all its misery and mystery, that it was cruel to speak of such experiences as a pleasure. "He goes beneath the surface," she said, "and he *forces* himself to look at things from which he'd rather turn away. Do you call that amusing yourself? You should see his face sometimes! And he does it for me as much as for himself. He tells me everything—he comes home to me with his *trouvailles*. We're artists together, and to the artist all things are pure. I've often heard you say so yourself." The novel Leolin was engaged in at Brighton never saw the light, but a friend of mine and of Mrs. Stormer's who was staying there happened to mention to me later that he had seen the young apprentice to fiction driving, in a dog-cart, a young lady with a very pink face. When I suggested that she was perhaps a woman of title with whom he was conscientiously flirting my informant replied: "She is indeed, but do you know what her title is?" He pronounced it—it was familiar and descriptive—but I won't reproduce it here. I don't know whether Leolin mentioned it to his mother: she would have needed all the purity of the artist to forgive him. I hated so to come across him that in the very last years I went rarely to see her, though I knew she had come pretty well to the end of her rope. I didn't want her to tell me she had fairly to give her books away; I didn't want to see her old and abandoned and derided; I didn't want, in a word, to see her terribly cry. She still, however, kept it up amazingly, and every few months, at my club, I saw three new volumes, in green, in crimson, in blue, on the booktable that groaned with light literature. Once I met her at the Academy soirée, where you meet people you thought were dead, and she vouchsafed the information, as if she owed it to me in candour, that Leolin had been obliged to recognise the insuperable difficulties of the question of *form*—he was so fastidious; but that she had now arrived at a definite understanding with him (it was such a comfort!) that *she* would do the form if he would bring home the substance. That was now his employ—he foraged for her in the great world at a salary. "He's my 'devil,' don't you see? as if I were a great lawyer: he gets up the case and I argue it." She mentioned further that in addition to his salary he was paid by the piece: he got so much for a striking character, so much for a pretty name, so much for a plot, so much for an incident, and had so much promised him if he would invent a new crime.

"He *has* invented one," I said, "and he's paid every day of his life."

"What is it?" she asked, looking hard at the picture of the year, "Baby's Tub," near which we happened to be standing.

I hesitated a moment. "I myself will write a little story about it, and then you'll see."

But she never saw; she had never seen anything, and she passed away with her fine blindness unimpaired. Her son published every scrap of scribbled paper that could be extracted from her table-drawers, and his sister quarrelled with him mortally about the proceeds, which showed her only to have wanted a pretext, for they can't have been great. I don't know what Leolin lives on unless on a queer lady many years older than himself, whom he lately married. The last time I met him he said to me with his infuriating smile: "Don't you think we can go a little further still—just a little?" *He* really—with me at least—goes too far.

STUDY QUESTIONS

1. How does the narrator's particular kind of wit function in this story? Given the character of Greville Fane, does the narrator's style serve any specific function in terms of the story's thematic development?

2. Notice that the narrator refers to the title character at times as "Mrs. Stormer" and at other times as "Greville Fane." What seems to motivate his choice in each instance? What is revealed, through his choices, about the narrator's relationship to the title character?

3. What is the function of the narrator's enclosing certain words and phrases in quotation marks? What is revealed about the narrator by his practice of setting off such words as "process," "likes," "smarter," "peculiar style."

4. What is James' purpose in writing this story? Consider two of James' other stories that deal with problems of the artist—"The Tree of Knowledge" and "The Real Thing." Do the stories have similar rhetorical aims? If so, how are the aims variously achieved? If not, what are the different values in question in each story? Having read the three stories, what image of James emerges relevant to the role of the artist in society?

5. In the introduction to this chapter James was discussed as one of the great artists of narrative fiction, and his development of the third-person limited-omniscience point of view was pointed out. Fairly early in his career James abandoned the first-person narrative (which he uses in this early story) in favor of the third-person limited-omniscience narrative. For the purpose of comparison, rewrite this story using as the central intelligence the newspaper man who narrates James' story. Unlike James' story, however, let your account be narrated by someone other than the newspaper man. What structural changes occur? How does your view of James' narrator change? Does your view of the other characters alter? What changes occur in the implied author's argument?

EXERCISES AND BIBLIOGRAPHY

1. Phyllis Bentley, in *Some Observations on the Art of the Narrative* (New York: Macmillan, 1947), has observed that the rhythm of action in narrative writing is determined by the way in which a writer uses "scene, summary, and description." (These terms were defined in the study section following "The Horse Dealer's Daughter" in this chapter.) Read Bentley's discussion of these techniques for manipulating time and tempo of action and try to see some implications of her argument for the interpreter of fiction.

2. In this chapter certain kinds of narrators and their relative degrees of subjectivity and objectivity have been discussed. Bertil Romberg, in *Studies in the Narrative Techniques of the First-Person Novel* (Stockholm: Almquist & Wiksel, 1963), is also interested in the subjectivity and objectivity of narrators. What does Romberg mean by a subjective narrator? If his description were used in this text, why would the narrators labeled "subjective" seem to be "objective" and vice versa?

3. Jonathan Rabin, in *The Technique of Modern Fiction* (Notre Dame, Ind.: Notre Dame University Press, 1969), seems to see as basic to the understanding of modern fiction the organic relationship between point of view, characterization, setting, tone, and other traditional features labeled as "technique" in fiction. Compare Rabin's view of technique and structure with that of Mark Schorer in "Technique as Discovery" (John Aldridge, ed., *Critiques and Essays in Modern Fiction,* New York: Ronald Press, 1952). It is interesting to see another view of Schorer's regarding narrative techniques in his article "Fiction and the Analogical Matrix," which appears in the same collection of essays. Consider some of the stories in this chapter as possibly revealing analogical matrices in their structures.

4. Wayne C. Booth's *The Rhetoric of Fiction* (Chicago: University of Chicago Press, 1963) presents one of the fullest expositions of the rhetorical approach to the study of fiction. Read this book and try to determine precisely what Booth means by "rhetoric." When Booth speaks of the "reliability" of narrators, how does he propose that the reader go about discovering and testing a particular narrator's reliability? Does he seem to get into a dilemma when he discusses the morality and ethics of certain authors, such as Céline and Robbe-Grillet? How do you suppose Booth would respond to a narrator such as the one Barth uses in "Night-Sea Journey"? What about the narrator in "The Horse Dealer's Daughter"?

INDEX